Mervelous Signals

EUGENE VANCE

Mervelous Signals

Poetics and Sign Theory
in the Middle Ages

UNIVERSITY OF NEBRASKA PRESS

LINCOLN AND LONDON

Acknowledgments for the
use of copyrighted material
appear on page xviii.

The paper in this book meets
the guidelines for
permanence and durability
of the Committee on
Production Guidelines for
Book Longevity of the
Council on Library Resources.

Library of Congress
Cataloging-in-Publication Data
Vance, Eugene, 1934-
Mervelous signals.
(Regents studies in medieval
culture) Includes index.
1. Poetry, Medieval –
History and criticism –
Addresses, essays, lectures.
2. Poetics –History –
Addresses, essays, lectures.
3. Semiotics – History –
Addresses, essays, lectures.
I. Title. II. Series.
PN688.V36   1986
809.1'02   85-21013
ISBN 0-8032-4655-2
(alkaline paper)

To my mother,
a fine reader of poems

CONTENTS

Contents

PREFACE

      This book has been written and re-
written during a period of turmoil and challenge for modern criticism
in general and for modern medievalism in particular. With the rapid
demystification, in the late 1960s, of the idea that structuralism and
semiotics could attain the status of empirical, descriptive, and ahistorical science, critics and scholars began a fresh return to the history
of Western culture with these fundamental questions in mind: in what
ideological, psychological, and metaphysical contexts do texts that we
now call "literary" materialize in the first place? What historical assumptions about signs, language, and discourse governed the production of—or were transgressed by—the medieval poetic text? Over the
past ten years, semioticians have become increasingly concerned to
understand earlier systems and theories of culture that have had a constitutive or generative function in Western tradition.

    Most would agree that this mutation of modern disciplines has been
beneficial to the study of medieval culture. It has shaken orthodox medievalism out of the torpor that set in as the discipline of philology lost
its speculative vision, especially in France. Although structural and
semiotic analyses have only begun to contribute to our understanding
of medieval culture, simply by calling into question the dominant intellectual paradigms of traditional criticism, these modern disciplines
have summoned forth vital interest in those theories of language and
signification that were the very core of medieval culture itself.

    Indeed, if there was any intellectual coherence to what we now so loosely call medieval culture, and if that term applies with any validity to the span of history coinciding roughly with the near-millennium lying between the deaths of St. Augustine in 430 and William of Ockham in the mid-fourteenth century, then it is perhaps not an exaggeration to claim that the major thread of coherence in medieval culture was its sustained reflection, within the three branches of the *trivium*, or the three "arts of discourse" (*artes sermocinales*), upon language as a semiotic system—more broadly, upon the nature, the functions and the limitations of the verbal sign as a mediator of human understanding. A constant reference point in both Jewish and Christian thought throughout the Middle Ages was the problem of the ineffability of God. While Christians believed that Christ was the answer to that problem, the very idea that Christ was a unique and perfect sign—one where signifier and signified, Son and Father, were consubstantial and without difference, and wholly adequate one to the other—only intensified medieval anxiety about the finiteness, the arbitrariness, and the mutability of the conventional verbal signs of fallen, speaking man. Still, it was above all in the disciplines of language and discourse that medieval thinkers were most audacious and resourceful in challenging and extending the wisdom of the ancients.

In contrast with modern linguistics, medieval disciplines of language and discourse scarcely ever tended to become what we would now call an empirical science. Modern linguists commonly take the phonetic stratum of language as their point of departure, seeking from there to describe and explain syntactic and semantic features of speech. Medieval linguistic theory begins at the top: with speculations about the *logos*, with its presentation to the soul, and finally, with the external phonetic and textual dimensions of language, which are the lowest ontological stratum of the Word. With the exception of certain treatises dealing with music or rhetoric, and with the notable exception of Dante—who brought a new and positive emphasis to the fact that the verbal sign, by its very constitution, is not only *rationale* but *sensuale*—the pragmatic analysis of the material dimensions of the signifier was all but ignored.

Nor was the history of language a matter of scientific reasoning. How could it have been without an equally scientific historiographical discourse as its matrix? Unless in the context of biblical and classical myths of cosmic history, and unless in the context of specific problems of translation and exegesis, a concrete historical consciousness of language was lacking in European thought until the rise of Humanism.

Medieval theoreticians of language rarely lost sight, however, of on-tological, psychological, and pragmatic aspects of verbal signification. The verbal sign was commonly understood to be conventional and ar-bitrary, rather than natural, yet the laws of grammar and the ends of discourse were thought to reflect unchanging and universal processes of cognition natural to the human soul as it perceives, understands, and expresses reality, or what truly exists. Perhaps the most beneficial effect of modern semiotic theory for medievalists has been that its highly technical character, exemplified by C. S. Peirce (whose debt to Duns Scotus is well known), has encouraged us to approach the equally technical and abstract theories of medieval semiotics with a curiosity and sympathy without precedent in post-Humanist European culture.

Given that the amorphous body of texts we so loosely call "medi-eval literature" was to a large extent spawned with the *trivium* as its intellectual habitat, medieval poetic texts testify, within their *matière* and conventions, to a refined metalinguistic and semiotic awareness. No important medieval literary text lacks an awareness of language, whether as a medium of consciousness or as the living expression of the social order. Poetic language in the Middle Ages is always in part a metalanguage, and embodies an ethical consciousness which translates into palpable human terms problems of signification that logicians such as Abelard, Peter of Spain, or William of Ockham approached abstractly. For instance, a logician is concerned with the semantic consequences of choosing this or that word to "stand for" (*supponere*) a thing as we construct propositions and arguments; but a poet such as Dante or Chaucer is concerned with the personal, ethical, and historical conse-quences of choosing words to express (or conceal) our thoughts and deeds. The recent book by Judson Boyce Allen, *The Ethical Poetic of the Later Middle Ages: A Decorum of Convenient Distinction* (Toronto: Univ. of Toronto Press, 1982), illustrates very cogently the tendency for medieval commentators to classify poetry as a specifi-cally ethical discourse, one inseparable from ethics as a philosophical discipline. Medieval poetry built into its own performance a critical consciousness that later, with the Renaissance, would become crys-tallized as the autonomous discourse that we now call "criticism."

This book attempts to explore the manner in which poetic texts of the Middle Ages reflect upon processes of language, including those of poetic language itself. I do not mean that I have studied the influence of medieval linguistic theory upon poetic texts. It would be silly to claim, for instance, that the *Chanson de Roland* was "influenced" by *grammatica*, though I will claim that the intrusion of *grammatica* upon an oral discourse and its *episteme* is indissociable from the poem's tragic perspective. Again, I shall not propose that Chaucer's *Troilus* was "influenced" by Ciceronian or medieval rhetoric, but I shall propose that an ethical and historical concern with "rhetoricity" is central to Chaucer's poem. It is surely not an accident that from Bede onward, vernacular literature and linguistic theory evolved together in medieval culture. Such a counterpoint should not, however, lead us to believe that we must subordinate our understanding of medieval poems to that of formal medieval linguistic theory. I am convinced, to the contrary, that poetic language was a major source of philosophical provocation during the Middle Ages—as was sophistry, whose affinities with poetic language are close. In other words, poets share and provoke a metalinguistic consciousness in their time by working *independently* within or through the codes of an inherited *matière*. For that reason, the main purpose of this book is to study the link between medieval poetics and medieval theories of language as a *critical* link, one that also legitimizes our seeking outside of medieval linguistic theory itself for ways of describing what is "going on" in a medieval poem.

In other words, the critical perspectives informing this book are triangular, since I often draw upon the insights of modern linguistic theory in order to speak about poems written in the shadow of another linguistic tradition. I do so with the hope that both medieval theories of language and the responses that poets made to these theories will seem pertinent to the theoretical concerns of our own time. There is scarcely a term, practice, or concept in contemporary theory that does not have some rich antecedent in medieval thought, and I believe more firmly than ever that familiarity with the older culture can help us better to "think" the new.

Since my concerns are as much critical as they are historical, each chapter deals with a specific text and with a specific critical or theoretical problem. Although this book spans the Middle Ages, I have not attempted to write the history either of medieval poetics or of medieval semiotics—which, indeed, would scarcely be writable at the present time. I have, however, made mineshafts into the history of the *trivium*, with the hope that others will carry on. Since we are only beginning to understand a vast but systematically ignored area of the Western intellectual tradition, sweeping syntheses and generalizations would perhaps best be reserved for other decades than the present one.

Given that this book is intended to be read more as an open-ended chronicle of discovery than as a *summa*, each chapter is an initiative in its own right, and I have not provided the kind of rhetorical transition from chapter to chapter that would promulgate the illusion that this book grew as an organic plant from page one to the end. Nor have I attempted to eliminate occasional repetitions of points that gain, for the most part, by being repeated in more than one context. I have given priority to the coherence of argument within each chapter so that it can be read as an independent experiment. Since few readers of a book of this sort will start at the beginning and read in a linear way to the end, I shall describe each of the chapters in a sentence or two in order to assist the reader in finding an entry into the book and a congenial order of reading.

Chapter 1 is a critical examination of Augustine's *Confessions* and of the theory of autobiography in the light of Augustine's own concept of "confession" as a discursive act, which is centered on a notion of sacrifice. From the circumcision of the flesh by the Jews to the "circumcised" heart of the Christian and finally to the "circumcised" tongue of Augustine, there is a progression of ideas that explains Augustine's rhetorical strategies in the *Confessions*, whose unfinished narrative portion is succeeded by a commentary on Genesis.

Chapter 2 is a study of Augustine's "physics" of time and its relationship to the uttering (*énonciation*) of verbal signs as a temporal process. Language may very well allow us to conceptualize about time, but the very act of speaking our thoughts is an expenditure of our being in time that, once apprehended, dialectically demands a movement of transcendence, through degrees of silence, to immediate union of the soul with God as timeless, indivisible, immobile One.

Chapter 3 is a study both of the function of the faculty of memory in what we now identify as an "oral" epic tradition, and of the ethical dimensions of memory (and of forgetting) in a heroic set of values. However, given that the *Chanson de Roland* has survived as a text, and *not* as an oral poem, I have tried to assess the impact of textuality upon its archaic poetics of memory. Only through writing can the very notion of "orality" come into our minds in the first place. To that extent, orality is an obverse fiction of writing. Already in the *Roland* there is a detectable nostalgia for the realm of the voice and of song as a realm of truth, presence, and permanent renewal. Is there not a redundancy between the "myth" of Roland and the scholarly myth of orality that needs further analysis in its own right?

Chapter 4 is a study of the contradictory functions of *je* (and its morphemic equivalents) as a grammatical sign and as an operator of courtly lyric discourse. Proffering itself as an object that rivals the woman's body as an object of desire, the *trouvère* lyric is an inscription of the desire to desire. Considering the presuppositions governing *trouvère* discourse as a latent story, we may compare this "story" with that of other verbal performances: for instance, sexual jokes, where the formal pleasures of speech may be considered as a manifestation, through displacement, of repressed desire. The courtly lyric poem domesticates the passion it evokes.

In chapter 5, I explore certain rhetorical implications of Chrétien's writing under the patronage of the court of Champagne, precisely as that court was also patronizing a new mercantilism that would soon make Champagne not only the most prestigious court but also the most prosperous financial center of northern Europe. Even though mercantilism enjoyed no legitimate, official discourse of its own, the impact of mercantile interests and values on other, prevalent official discourses was massive. In this reading of *Yvain*, I propose that courtly romance, whose discourse was becoming the emblem of an aristocratic elite, incorporates into its traditional *matière* a new ethics of exchange based upon the paradigm of human sexual love, considered as a transactional model that could be inflected to express a shift in the economic patterns of the late twelfth century.

An important feature of thirteenth-century poetics is the tendency to produce hybrid texts, texts constituted by multiple discourses. What are the underlying rhetorical suppositions of this interdiscursivity, and what are its social purposes? In chapter 6 I consider the interference of formally and semantically distinct discourses in *Aucassin et Nicolette* as a manifestation of interfering class consciousness within a social group marked by mobility and by the rise of a new middle class. In other words, the story that mediates between discourses has a *totemic* function within its culture, by which I mean that it expresses intergroup relationships.

In chapter 7, I describe the latent metaphysics of dialogue in the paraliturgical play *Le Mystère d'Adam*, in order to show how this metaphysics is dismantled in the thirteenth-century comedy, *Le Jeu de la feuillée*, by Adam de la Halle. In the earlier play, the instigation of horizontal, human dialogue leads to the Fall and dialectically to the hope of redemption through prophecy. In the later play, the failure of dialogue and of language as a medium of understanding within the social group becomes a symptom of a more absolute regression of man into bestiality and of the macrocosm back to primeval chaos.

In chapter 8, I study Dante's ethical concern with language as a part of his search for principles of rectitude and hierarchy in human discourse that will enable human beings to perfect their desire and direct it toward God as its proper final end. I focus specifically upon the negative example of Brunetto Latini, the great Florentine rhetorician, as Dante's way of pointing to the rhetorical perversion of signs as the close spiritual double of sexual perversion. I attempt to show how Dante's intricate poetic strategies compel readers to evaluate their own responses to Dante's text in terms of its ethical message.

Chapter 9 is a study of Chaucer's critical attitudes toward the conventional rhetoric of courtly eroticism, seen as a subversive political force in the archetypal city of Troy. So given over to the figurative "heart's war" of love are the noble warriors of Troy that they are incapable of responsible civic action. Pandarus personifies an equivocity of speech that engages *Troilus* in a relationship doomed from the start. Chaucer shows us how, principally in and through language, Criseyde perpetrates her betrayals of truth and troth, leading the narrator to a conclusion that is not properly narrative but consists rather in the abandonment of poetic language altogether for higher truths of philosophy and prayer.

As a conclusion to this book, chapter 10 is a study of Humanist ideology of translation, seen as a reversal of medieval attitudes toward flux and change in both language and the creation. I then consider the Paridell-Hellenore episode of Spenser's *Faerie Queene* as a Humanist poet's statement of the relationship between poetic language and the process of history, a statement that vindicates poetic language as a valid foundation for ethical action in the world. A new and positive discursive relationship between the individual and his or her fantasms is expressed in Britomart, one that encourages men and women to respect, obey, and express—rather than deny and transcend—their natural desire for *voluptas*.

This book has been long in the making, and since the time when I began it, many useful studies of all three branches of the *trivium* have appeared. It is now possible for a young scholar to have access not only to many primary documents (and their translations) that were not available when I began, twelve years ago, but also to mature secondary scholarship that gives the medieval disciplines of language their intellectual due. This book falls therefore at the beginning of what promises to be a rich period for medieval literary studies and for the larger Humanities curriculum that is its beneficiary. I hope that once the shortcomings and lacunae of these chapters have been made evident to all, they will still have proved helpful and stimulating to some.

This book has benefited from the influence and criticisms of many colleagues and friends. It gives me deep pleasure to record these debts here. The manuscript was written for the most part during my years as a member of the Programme de littérature comparée at the Université de Montréal. I could not imagine a more congenial atmosphere in which one could write a scholarly book, and every chapter has been marked by the daily debates that transpired there. The late Eugenio Donato was not only my first colleague in that new program but the most influential, and his passing has left an unfillable gap in the circle of his many close friends. Walter Moser and Wladimir Kryzynski were always cordial and supportive of my writing. My close collaboration and friendship with Paul Zumthor has had an incalculable effect on my work, and I have also benefited from many long and cordial discussions of medieval poetics with Marie-Louise Ollier. My relationship with Timothy Reiss, now also of Emory University, has been one of close friendship, one of whose forms has been to be critical when necessary, and my work has profited from this exchange. Of my students, Denyse Delcourt was a valuable, resourceful, and generous reader of several parts of the manuscript. Visiting colleagues at Montréal have also influenced my thought, especially Marcel Détienne, Michel Foucault, Louis Marin, and Jean-Pierre Vernant.

While at Montréal I benefited from several travel grants awarded by the Comité de la recherche, as well from a sabbatical leave fellowship awarded by the Social Sciences and Humanities Research Council of Canada.

Many friends in other universities have been generous with their thought and time: Wlad Godzich, Stephen G. Nichols, Jr., and Kevin Brownlee read the manuscript and made many helpful suggestions for improving it, as did my diligent copy editor for the Nebraska Press, Patricia Sterling. The following friends have engaged in tireless discussions which have made the sharing of ideas a deeply human process and my experience of the academy, in an extended sense, a great privilege: Jeremy D. Q. Adams, Howard Bloch, Robert Benson, Morton Bloomfield, Monique Canto, Terence Cave, Marcia Colish, Sheila Delany, Peter Haidu, Hans Robert Jauss, Victoria Kahn, Daniel Lesnick, Alexandre Leupin, Giuseppe Mazzotta, Jean Pépin, Pietro Pucci, Michael Putnam, Beryl Schlossman, Brian Stock, and Nancy Struever. I, of course, must bear all responsibility for errors or faults in the present work.

Portions of the book originally appeared elsewhere. Chapters 2 and 4 were presented at colloquia organized by the Romance Language Department at Dartmouth College. I wish to thank the following for permission to republish, though with massive revisions, other sections of the material: the editors of *Modern Language Notes* for permission to publish what is now chapter 1; the editors of the University Press of New England for permission to use an essay that originally appeared in *Mimesis: From Mirror to Method, Augustine to Descartes*, ed. Stephen G. Nichols, Jr., and John Lyons (1982), which appears here as chapter 8; the editors of Cornell University Press for permission to republish in chapter 3 portions of my essay in *Textual Strategies: Perspectives in Post Structural Criticism*, ed. Josué Harari (1979), and portions of my essay in *Lyric Poetry: Beyond the New Criticism*, ed. Patricia Parker and Chaviva Hosek (1985), which appear here in chapter 4; the editors of French Forum, Publishers, for permission to include in chapter 6 portions of my essay in *The Nature of Medieval Narrative*, ed. Minnette Gaudet and Robin F. Jones (1980); the editors of *New Literary History*, for permission to reprint portions of my essay in volume 10 (1979) as chapter 9 here; the editors of the *Canadian Review of Comparative Literature* for permission to use part of my essay in volume 8 (1981) in chapter 10 here.

The publication of this book has benefited from a subvention generously granted by the Emory University Research Committee. I wish to express my strong gratitude for this support.

xvii

CHAPTER I

Augustine's *Confessions*
and the
Poetics of the Law

The term "autobiography" is a neologism of modern European culture that originated with romantic myths of subjective expression at the beginning of the last century. As an outgrowth of Romanticism, the concept of autobiography seems to rest on the supposition that conventional verbal signs disposed as a narrative text can serve the writing individual both as a vehicle of subjective consciousness and as the document of an external, objective history whose alterity is also finally his or her own.

The autobiographical undertaking is constituted, then, by two distinct fictions of referentiality, that of an "I" of the "present" whose identity derives from circumstances alleged to prevail "now" during the actual moment of writing, and the "I-as-object" manifested in historical statements cast "then" in a network of past tenses where the first and third persons are collapsed into one. Thanks to the indeterminacy of the sign "I" as a shifter, "I" as a speaking subject enters into a dialectic with an objectified narrative "I," and the moment of consummation of that dialectic, crucial to any autobiographical project, comes when past and present converge: that is, when the "I" of the narrative past catches up with, and becomes identical to, the "I" writing the text. The autobiographical text will be accepted as "true" only on the condition that we subscribe to a circular metaphysics of extroversion and presence-to-self which we not only presume to be achievable by us, but delegate to others as credit.[1]

St. Augustine's *Confessions* is commonly read as if it were an autobiography. Superficially, the *Confessions* seems indeed to lend itself quite aptly to such a classification: as a "confession," it is both a manifestation of an individual consciousness speaking in the *present* (in this case with God as interlocutor) and a narrative history of a life of sin, now *past*. A dialectic between the converted speaking self and the unredeemed self-as-other, the once "dead" *vetus homo* of history, seems to be intact, and Augustine himself declares his intention in Book X to "reveal not what I have been but what I now am and what I still am."[2] However, Augustine also acknowledges here the vanity of man's readiness to take his neighbor as an object of understanding and the impossibility of intersubjective communication. Only charity, where man understands lower things spiritually through what is higher, can truly unite men "by binding them to itself," and the truth divulged by charity is not human, but divine (*Conf.* X.iii.3).

Moreover, the last four books of the *Confessions* (X–XIII) are a radical departure from the story of his life contained in the preceding nine books. The narrative contained in these earlier books extends from Augustine's speculations about his infancy to his rebirth in the Church and the death of his earthly mother, Monica. Book X veers from narrative into an epistemological essay on the faculty of memory in the human soul, and Book XI inaugurates a commentary on the first chapters of Genesis. Here, Augustine explicitly confirms his intention not to return to the story of his external life: since God knows everything, Augustine suddenly asks (*Conf.* XI.i.1), why should he address all of these stories (*narrationes*) about himself to God? Rather than dwelling upon his "present" as a Christian convert and priest in Hippo,

1. Jacques Derrida, "Otobiographies: The Teaching of Nietzsche and the Politics of the Proper Name," in *The Ear of the Other: Transference, Translation. Texts and Discussion with Jacques Derrida*, ed. Christie V. McDonald, trans. Peggy Kamuf (New York: Schocken Books, 1985), 3–38.

2. St. Augustine, *Confessiones libri tredecem*, ed. Pius Knöll and Martinus Skutella (Leipzig: Teubner, 1934), as published in *Oeuvres de Saint Augustin: Les Confessions*, Bibliotèque augustinienne, 2e serie: Dieu et son oeuvre, vols. 13–14, French trans. A. Trehorel and G. Bouissou, notes by A. Solignac (Paris: Desclée de Brouwer, 1962), hereafter cited as Solignac, *Conf.*; *The Confessions of St. Augustine*, English trans. John K. Ryan (New York: Doubleday, 1960), hereafter cited in my own text as *Conf.*

Augustine now elects priorities other than those of autobiographical narrative to command the tongue of his pen (*lingua calami*), above all, his burning desire to meditate upon God's Law—that is, upon the written letter of the Old Testament—so as to share his understanding "fraternally" with other men. Henceforth abandoning the *narratio* of his own life for the *enarratio* of the Law, Augustine concludes his text by explicating that portion of Genesis that narrates the six days of the creation, the seventh day being God's sabbath.

Such transitions are perplexing to the modern reader of fiction, so easily thwarted by the collapse of narrative discourse and by the encroachment of anything didactic. As a result, interest in Augustine's *Confessions* as "literature" often flags at this point. For the reader imbued with the norms of autobiography, the problem is especially baffling, because Augustine appears to lose artistic purpose precisely at the moment when his work is on the verge of fulfilling a project fully sustained, up to that point, by the internal logic of autobiography. As a result of Augustine's radical change of direction, readers of the *Confessions* tend to classify the treatise on memory and the exegesis of Genesis as detachable documents of intellectual history whose objectives are remote from those of autobiography. Scholars react to their unfulfilled expectations in a number of ways: some blame Augustine for his bad judgment; some act as if the final books were not there; some continue to write Augustine's autobiography with their own hand. Only a few have sought formal and rhetorical explanations for Augustine's apparent change of purpose in the *Confessions*, and my purpose here is to add to these explanations some new ones based not on theories of literature, but on Augustine's own statements of purpose.[3]

Before we indulge in "esthetic" judgments of the *Confessions* as an

3. Cf. Georg Nicolaus Knauer, *Psalmenzitate in Augustins Konfessionen* (Göttingen: Vandenhoeck and Ruprecht, 1955), esp 133–61; "*Peregrinatio animae*," *Hermes* 85 (1957–58): 216–48; John C. Cooper, "Why Did Augustine Write Books XI–XIII of the *Confessions?*" *Augustinian Studies* 2 (1972): 37–46; Peter Brown, *Augustine of Hippo: A Biography*, (Berkeley: University of California Press, 1967), 180–81; Eugene Vance, "Augustine's *Confessions* and the Grammar of Selfhood," *Genre* 6 (1973): 1–28, and "Le Moi comme langage: Saint Augustin et l'autobiographie," *Poétique* 42 (1980): 139–55; an earlier version of this chapter, substantially revised here, appeared as "Augustine's *Confessions* and the Poetics of the Law," *Modern Language Notes* 93 (1978): 618–34; Michel Beaujour, *Miroirs d'encre* (Paris: Seuil, 1980), 29–53. For a more general discussion of the literary form of the *Confessions* and a bibliography, see Solignac, *Conf.*, 19–45, 248–50.

autobiography, we should bear in mind Philippe Lejeune's welcome point that the history of autobiography is that of a contract between author and reader which is also historically variable.[4] In the light of such a claim, we should both question those implicit critical models by which we comprehend and evaluate the *Confessions* and be willing to consider Augustine's decision to conclude with an exegesis of the Old Testament as a discursive strategy subtended by a set of assumptions, both metaphysical and rhetorical, not wholly apparent to us today. More important, we need to understand how this exegetical gesture may be seen as a positive fulfillment of the composition of the *Confessions* as a whole. Even if reliable scholars who surmise that Augustine added his study of memory and the commentary on Genesis several years after completing the narrative portion of the *Confessions* are correct, may we not take as our hypothesis that Augustine undertook this addition with a lucid purpose in mind?

Although we may be certain that Augustine's writing of the *Confessions*, like that of the *City of God* and *On the Trinity*, was a continuous experiment in method and style, we know from *On Free Will*, which he completed in Thagaste in 395, shortly before beginning to write the *Confessions*, that the goal of self-knowledge implicit in his project was already insufficient—if not blameworthy, even, as a movement of pride:

> Why does the soul, contemplating sovereign wisdom (which, since it is immutable, is not the soul itself) contemplate itself, being mutable, and bring itself, so to speak to mind? Only because, though it is different from God, it is still something whose nature can be pleasing to God. But it is better when it forgets itself charitably in favor of unchanging God, or else when it utterly condemns itself in comparison to him. If, to the contrary, the soul takes pleasure in encountering itself, in a perverse imitation of God, and seeks to enjoy its own power, then it diminishes itself in the same degree that it desires to be great. Thus, "Pride is the beginning of all sin."[5]

4. Philippe Lejeune, *Le Pacte autobiographique* (Paris: Seuil, 1975), 45.

5. St. Augustine, *De libero arbitrio*, III.xxv.77, ed. Migne, *Patrologiae latinae*, vol. 32, col. 1221–1303, as reprinted and translated in *Oeuvres de saint Augustin: Dialogues philosophiques*, Bibliothèque augustinienne, vol. 6, French trans. and

If Augustine considered self-knowledge an unworthy intellectual goal, he also scorned the esthetic pleasure that the art embodying such knowledge might afford. Art is a human institution whose sole value is to disclose some higher authority. Such is Augustine's judgment in his *De doctrina christiana*, which he began in 395, two years before writing the *Confessions*:

> Where pictures or statues are concerned, or other similar imitative works, especially when executed by skilled artists, no one errs when he sees the likeness, so that he recognizes what things are represented. And all things of this class are to be counted among the superfluous institutions of men except when it is important to know concerning one of them why, where, when, and by whose authority it was made. Then there are thousands of imagined fables and falsehoods by whose lies men are delighted, which are human institutions. And nothing is more typical of men among those things which they have from themselves than what is deceitful and lying.[6]

Even the term "confession" itself had semantic features that would have predisposed Augustine against what we now consider an "autobiographical" performance. "Confession," for him, as for his classical predecessors, implied far more than the admission of sins committed; it meant also the speech act of *praising*, as when Christ says to God, "I confess to you [*Confiteor tibi*], Father, Lord of heaven and earth, since you have hidden these things from the wise . . ." (Matt. 11:25. "Confession" also meant, for Augustine, the profession of faith in a spirit of sacrifice, as in the case of a martyr before a tribunal.[7] The single word "confession" implies, then, at least three distinct speech acts, and as I shall show, Augustine's *Confessions* is constructed in such a manner that its different parts bear out, each in its own way, one sense of the word serving as title of the work as a whole. What interests me in par-

---

notes by F. J. Thonnard (Paris: Desclée de Brouwer, 1941); English translation mine; hereafter cited as *On Free Will*.

6. St. Augustine, *De doctrina christiana*, as published in *Oeuvres de Saint Augustin*, Bibliothèque augustinienne, vol. 11, ed. G. Combès and J. Farges (Paris: Desclée de Brouwer, 1949); *On Christian Doctrine*, English trans. D. W. Robertson, Jr. (New York: Bobbs-Merrill, 1958); hereafter cited as *DDC* in my text.

7. See Joseph Ratzinger, "Originalität und Ueberlieferung in Augustins Begriff der *Confessio*," *Revue des études augustiniennes* 3 (1957), 375–92; see also Solignac, *Conf.*, 13:9–12.

ticular, though, is the manner in which the commentary on Genesis may be seen as a discursive performance which most fully subsumes all the separate meanings of the term "confession."

CONFESSION, LOVE, AND THE LAW

In his prayer inaugurating his commentary on Genesis 1, Augustine employs for us what can only seem like a daring metaphor to describe his hermeneutical objectives, but it is a metaphor whose prehistory tells us a great deal about Augustine's gesture of passing from the narrative to the exegetical, from *narratio* to *enarratio*: "From all temerity and all lying circumcise my lips," he writes, "both my interior and my exterior lips. May your Scriptures be my chaste delights" (*Conf.* XI.ii.3). This metaphor is instructive for several reasons, among them, as we shall see, that it compels reflection about metaphor itself, which Augustine—again in his *De doctrina christiana* (II.x.15)—defines as a kind of sign where "things that we signify by proper terms are usurped by others signifying something else." Thus, a spiritual metaphor is a usurpation and transformation of what is carnal or "literal." We should bear in mind that Augustine's metaphoric circumcision inaugurates an exegesis whose dominant mode in the *Confessions* will be figurative, which is to say that its purpose is to vivify the dead letter of the Law with the Spirit. Indeed, Augustine undertook four different commentaries on Genesis during his lifetime, each with a different purpose in mind, and at the same time as he was writing his figurative or allegorical commentary as a conclusion to the *Confessions*, he was probably writing another very great "literal" commentary on that same text, the *De genesi ad litteram*: the former was probably concluded in 401, and the latter begun in that same year.[8] Augustine had the habit of working on many different texts at the same time, and it is always pertinent to observe what transformations of meaning occur when an idea or theme passes from the discourse of one text into the discourse of another. Augustine's choice of a "figurative" mode of cognition in the commentary on Genesis in the *Confessions* was obviously a clear one,

8. St. Augustine, *De Genesi ad litteram*, Corpus Scriptorum Ecclesiasticorum Latinorum, vol. 28, ed. Joseph Zycha (Pragae: F. Tempsky; Vindobonae: F. Tempsky; Lipsiae: G. Freitag, 1894). For a discussion of its date, see *Oeuvres de saint Augustin: La Genèse au sens littéral en douze livres*, Bibliothèque augustinienne, vols. 48–49, French trans. and notes by P. Agaesse and A. Solignac (Paris: Desclée de Brouwer, 1972), 25–31.

for in his "literal" commentary (III.ix.22), he refers to his previous, and now presumably complete, "allegorical" commentary on Genesis in the *Confessions*, and he recalls that the two modes are distinct. Therefore, if we dwell on Augustine's metaphor of circumcision for a moment, we will perhaps better perceive how his exegetical performance relates to the narrative portions of the *Confessions* that precede it.

In pleading with God to circumcise his lips so that he may gain the chaste pleasures (*casta deliciae*) of understanding God's text, Augustine is on the one hand comparing his tongue to his phallus, and on the other, comparing the hermeneutical performance to erotic love: the word *deliciae* commonly connotes voluptuousness as it is used by Augustine's classical forebears. The "outer" lies that must be circumcised from his lips are lies uttered externally as verbal or written signs, while the "inner" occur in the production of that silent, nonverbal language of the soul which precedes the utterance of outward speech; the foreskin of these inner thoughts must also be trimmed in sacrifice before Augustine may enjoy, as he tells God, the "inside of your words" (*interiora sermonum tuorum*). To possess, and be possessed by, the inner voice of the spirit is to experience something "beyond the flood of voluptuous pleasure" (*ecce uox tua gaudium meum, uox tua super afluentiam uoluptatum; Conf.* XI.ii.3). In expressing here his preference for spiritual over carnal climaxes, Augustine echoes a previous moment in the *Confessions* where he condemned his "flood" (*fluctus*) of semen at puberty on the "shore" or "bank" of conjugality (*ad conjugale litus; Conf.* II.ii.2) and lamented not having become a eunuch of heaven (*absciscus propter regnum caelorum*) in order to enjoy more pleasurable (*felicior*) embraces. Later, Augustine explains how, when he wished to detach himself from conjugal love, he understood (presumably with relief) that the sacrifice of castration demanded by the kingdom of heaven (*regnum caeli; Conf.* VII.i.2) was only metaphorical, not literal.

So, too, the circumcision of Augustine's lips is only a metaphorical one, yet it is a sacrifice nonetheless: "May I sacrifice to you the service of my thought and my tongue, and may you grant what I offer up to you, I who am an indigent pauper" (*Conf.* XI.ii.3). Why, though, and by what license, does Augustine indulge here in such violent metaphors or, rather, in metaphors that presuppose the repression of physical violence?

Let us look at the source of Augustine's metaphor. It derives from St. Paul's epistle to the Romans, a text devoted first to the sin of idolatry—

7

which God has punished, Paul says, by allowing its practitioners to become sexually perverted—and second, to the carnal observance of the
Jewish Law:

> Circumcision, indeed, profits if thou keep the Law; but if thou
> be a transgressor of the Law, thy circumcision has become un-
> circumcision. Therefore if the uncircumcised keep the pre-
> cepts of the Law, will not his uncircumcision be reckoned as
> circumcision? And he who is by nature uncircumcised, if he
> fulfills the Law, will judge thee who with the letter and cir-
> cumcision art a transgressor of the Law. For he is not a Jew
> who is so outwardly; be he is a Jew is so inwardly, and circum-
> cision is a matter of the heart, in the spirit, not in the letter.[9]

St. Paul opposes the written Jewish Law to the "natural" law of the
Gentiles, which is "written in their hearts" (Rom. 2:15).

Augustine further explored Paul's notion of "inner" circumcision in
treatises of his own. In one of his treatises on lying (*De mendacio*), for
example, Augustine considers as a type of lie the gesture of the Jew
who tries to become a non-Jew by covering up "what has been made
bare" with what remains of his foreskin.[10] In *On the Spirit and the
Letter*, however, Augustine elaborates on Paul's "circumcision of the
heart" in such a way as to accentuate Paul's equation of carnal circumcision with the *textuality* of the Law itself and with the *letter* of that
text of stone ("stone" is a favorite example of inanimate being in classical and medieval thought) in which the Law was incised. At the time
of the Mosaic Pentecost on Sinai when the Law was first given to
Moses, we are told, its text was written by God's finger, which is the
Holy Ghost, in tablets of stone; at the Christian Pentecost, by contrast, God's ghostly finger wrote the new Law not in stone but in the
living tablets of the heart: "The Holy Ghost came upon them who
were gathered together in expectation of his promised gift. There it was
written on tablets of stone that the finger of God operated; here it
was on the hearts of men."[11] In a sermon on Exodus, Augustine says

---

9. Rom. 2:25–29, Confraternity-Douay version (New York, 1957).

10. St. Augustine, *De mendacio*, ed. Joseph Zycha (Pragae: F. Tempsky; Vindobonae: F. Tempsky; Lipsiae: G. Freitag, 1894), as published in *Oeuvres de saint
Augustin: Problèmes moraux*. Bibliothèque augustinienne, vol. 2, French trans. and
notes, Gustave Combès (Paris: Desclée de Brouwer, 1948), vii.

11. St. Augustine, *De spiritu et littera*, xxix, trans. P. Holmes, *On the Spirit and*

that because the Jews did not understand grace, the finger of God engraved the Law upon stone in order to imprint fear upon them and to
lead them to grace.[12] Moreover, so long as fear prevails, rather than
charity, true understanding cannot occur. For it is charity, he says,
"which sings the new psalm. The servile fear of the old man may very
well have the psalterion with ten strings—the carnal Jews did indeed
receive the ten precepts of the law—but he cannot sing with this
psalterion the new psalm, because he is under the law and would not
know how to do it."[13] The heart that is both circumcised and transformed by metaphor, and the lips that speak that heart, signify by
virtue of a living text written by the Holy Ghost which abrogates the
killing, stony text of the carnal Law. In his other treatise on lying,
Augustine exempts figurative interpretations of the letter of the Old
Testament from the charge of lying, especially interpretations that rely
on metaphor, which he again defines as the "usurpation" of the proper
by the improper (*hoc est, de re propria ad rem non propriam uerbi
alicujus usurpata translatio*).[14] Since any person who speaks his *own*
mind can proffer only lies, Augustine's plea to be circumcised from
both outward and inward lying (in Book XI of the *Confessions*) is as
much a plea to transcend his own subjective consciousness as it is a
plea to be allowed to speak truly: that is, to comprehend and unveil to
others the spirit of the Law.

In *De doctrina christiana* (III.v.9), Augustine deepens the link between carnal desire and reading, thereby establishing one of the more
complex generative problematics of Western literature, considered as
an open-ended inscription of self-thwarting human desire:

> For at the outset, you must be very careful lest you take figur-
> ative expressions literally. What the Apostle says pertains
> to this problem: "For the letter killeth, but the spirit quick-
> eneth." That is, when that which is said figuratively is taken
> as though it were literal, it is understood carnally [*carnaliter*].

---

the Letter, in *Basic Writings of Saint Augustine*, ed. Whitney Oates (New York:
Random House, 1948), 483.

12. *Epistola ad inquisitiones Januarii* xvi.29, ed. J.-P. Migne, *Patrologiae latine*
(Paris: Migne, 1902). vol. 33, col. 218.

13. St. Augustine, "Sermon 33 on Psalm 143," 9, in *Oeuvres complètes de saint
Augustin*, ed. and French trans. M. Péronne (Paris: Vivès, 1871); English translation
mine.

14. St. Augustine, *Contra mendacium* (see n. 9).

> Nor can anything more appropriately be called the death of the soul than that condition in which the thing which distinguishes us from beasts, which is the understanding, is subjected to the flesh in the pursuit of the letter [*hoc est, intelligentia carni subjicitur sequendo litteram*].

The commentary on Genesis, understood as a "meditation on God's Law" (*Conf.* XI.ii.2), may be seen, then, as the last phase of a spiritual itinerary that involves the passage from the outward Law of the Letter incised in stone, the Law commanding circumcision of the flesh, to another inner Law, a universal Law "written" in the circumcised heart. Though this latter Law is now known through the Gospel, which is inspired by the Holy Ghost, this law is also given by birth as a "natural" Law which is both prior and superior to Mosaic Law because it is universal. A. Solignac, in his notes on the *Confessions*,[15] summarizes Augustine's conception of the two Laws thus: the natural Law is divine, and immutable, and it is written in the souls of the wise;[16] however, that natural Law can be obscured, and perhaps even effaced, by sin. As a consequence of man's sin, a second Law, opposed to the first, the Law of Sin (Rom. 7) was given to man outwardly as a written text. Yet this second Law kills, not only because it condemns the carnally inclined sinner but also because this Law *begets* the very carnal desire that it forbids. As St. Paul had put it, "I had not known lust unless the Law had said, 'Thou shalt not lust'" (Rom. 7:7). The Law, then, instills in innocent men the unlawful and unnatural desire to desire, as Augustine aptly explains with another metaphor of flooding (*On the Spirit and the Letter*, xii):

> Just as the rush of water which flows incessantly in a particular direction, becomes more violent when it meets with any impediment, and when it has overcome the stoppage, falls in greater bulk, and with increased impetuosity hurries forward in its downward course, in some strange way the very object which we covet becomes all the more pleasant when it is forbidden. And this is the sin by which the commandment deceives and by which it slays, whenever transgression is actually added, which occurs not where there is no Law.

15. Solignac, *Conf.*, 669.
16. St. Augustine, *De ordine* II.viii.25, ed. and trans. Robert P. Russell, *Divine Providence and the Problem of Evil* (New York: Cosmopolitan Science and Art Service, 1942).

As Solignac explains,[17] progress in spiritual life consists, for St. Augustine, in overcoming the Law of Sin through the action of grace and in interiorizing the external law so as to discover, on a higher plane, the inner Law. Man ceases, then, to be *sub lege* to find himself *in lege,* and passes at the same time from dependence on society to a condition of freedom. The charity that inhabits him and moves him henceforth allows him to fulfill *freely,* and with both pleasure and love, the precepts of the Law.

Such, then, are the presuppositions that underlie Augustine's plea that God circumcise his lips as he undertakes his commentary on Genesis I. Obviously, here as elsewhere, Augustine's achievements in the *Confessions* are not to be measured by the originality of his ideas—since it is clear that equations between the Law and the letter, and also their dialectical relationship to lust— had already been carefully asserted by St. Paul, but rather by the systematic deepening of these ideas.

In the rest of this chapter I shall indicate a few important passages in Augustine's narrative that illustrate, first, the inculcation of the Law of Sin in his soul, and second, the process by which he purges his soul of that Law and of its intellectual consequences. I shall conclude by suggesting that Augustine considered the commentary on the creation in Genesis as a speech act which is the re-creation (in two senses of that word) of his soul, owing to a relationship of homology between the structure of the soul and the structure of God's creation.

FROM WORD TO WORD

The parameters of Augustine's spiritual itinerary are already clearly set forth in the *exordium* of the *Confessions,* which begins with an exclamation of praise drawn from the Psalms: that is, from songs of praise in the Old Testament composed and written by the Holy Ghost, even before the birth of the historical Christ. But Augustine brings to this exclamation some seemingly unanswerable questions: how can a mere fragment (*portio*), and a sinning fragment besides, possibly presume to praise God as an uncreated totality? Must a mortal first invoke God—call God inside him—before *returning* God's love as praise? But how can he invoke God without already knowing the God he is invoking? Augustine's ontological and epistemological questions are an-

17. Solignac, *Conf.,* 664.

swered with stunning simplicity by the Scriptures themselves: if he seeks, he will find, since God has been forespoken (*praedicatus*) by Christ as Word and mediator between man and his otherwise ineffable God (*Conf.* I.i.11). This debate announces both the beginning and the conclusion of the *Confessions*, understood as the record of an arduous spiritual journey: illuminated by the New Testament, a converted and redeemed Augustine now communicates confidently with the mind of God (and with himself) through the previously opaque letter of the Old Testament. Its language of praise is both God's *and* his own. However, this journey had begun with Augustine's alienation in the Law of sin and of letters, as we shall presently see.

Speculating upon his earliest infancy, Augustine implies that like all children he enjoyed for a brief period a kind of tranquillity within a charitable hierarchy that was possible because, as a newborn child, he was still close to that natural Law into which he was born and which was born in him. Hence, his earliest existence is free of the basic dichotomies of human life—inner/outer (*intus/foris*), self/other, spiritual/corporeal, divine/mortal, and so forth—which do not yet divide and torment his consciousness:

> I myself do not remember this. Therefore, the comfort of human milk nourished me, but neither my mother nor my nurses filled their own breasts. Rather, through them you gave me an infant's food in accordance with your law, and out of the riches that you have distributed even down to the lowest level of things. You gave me to want no more than you gave, and you gave to those who nursed me the will to find what you gave to them. . . . For at that time I knew how to seek the breast, to be satisfied with that pleasant thing, and to cry at my bodily hurts, but nothing more. (*Conf.* I.vi.7)

This moment of earthly bliss in God's charitable justice is short-lived, however, and Augustine himself cannot even remember it. Although he has strongly attenuated the neoplatonism of *On Free Will* in this passage, neoplatonic doctrines still underlie his theory of developmental psychology. In *On Free Will*, Augustine subscribed overtly to neoplatonic theories of the soul's existence prior to birth. The soul is sent, he tells us, to govern our body and to assume its punishment of mortality, guiding it by means of virtue through a just servitude toward a place in incorruptible heaven. The corporeal condition of the soul causes it to forget its previous life and to encounter, instead, the toil of present life:

> When these souls enter into this life and undergo the burden
> of mortal members, they also undergo forgetfulness of their
> prior life and the toil of the present one: from this, ignorance
> and hardship arise, which are the punishment of mortality
> dealt to the first man, so that he might measure the misery of
> his soul and so that these souls may enter into their proper
> function of repairing the incorruptibility of bodies. (*On Free
> Will*, III.xx.57).

Augustine believes that his soul became subject to the passions of his mortal, sinning body very early: not only did the infant Augustine cry immoderately for the breast, and, worse, pale at the sight of other infants being suckled at the breast (covetise, despising of one's neighbor), but he even tried, as best he could, to strike and hurt those around him who would not obey his whims: "Thus it is not the infant's will that is harmless, but the weakness of infant limbs" (*Conf*. I.vii.11).

It is through the acquisition of language, however, that Augustine becomes ensnared in the external, temporal Law. First, he allies his inner thoughts to natural corporeal signs (kicking, crying); next, to indexical signs, when adults point out objects to him; finally, to symbolic verbal signs, as adults pronounce the conventional words that signify those objects. Thus, through his subjection to the laws of language, Augustine becomes caught up in the agitations of human society and subject to parental authority:

> So little by little I inferred that the words set in their proper
> places in different sentences, that I heard frequently, were signs
> of things. When my mouth had become accustomed to these
> signs, I expressed by means of them my own wishes. Thus, to
> those among whom I was communicated the signs of what I
> wished to express. I entered more deeply into the stormy so-
> ciety of human life, although still dependent on my parents'
> authority and the will of my elders. (*Conf*. I.viii.13)

Given that Augustine considered the social and linguistic orders as co-natural (*De ordine* II.xii.36), it should not surprise us that he first encounters the laws of the social world through language. Like Mosaic Law, given to the Jews in order to correct their depravity, social law is temporal and serves the needs of temporal justice. If temporal law is changeable but just, such justice derives from eternal law, which is just but *un*changeable (*Conf.* III.vii.13). Thus, within the laws and customs of temporal society, Augustine's parents and elders express, by their authority, the wrath of a vengeful but just God toward the unredeemed sinning child. Indeed, it is primarily by the whip that Augustine's father Patricius, not yet a Christian, governs the delinquent servants of his household. His mother Monica is a Christian, however, and through her virtues of patience and meekness, she manages to escape being beaten, much to everyone's astonishment. Moreover, Monica regularly counsels other wives to accept their bondage to their husbands and masters: "From the time, she said, when they heard what are termed marriage contracts read to them, they should regard those documents as legal instruments making them slaves" (*Conf.* XI.ix.19).

As the child ceases to be a non-speaker (*in-fans*), he becomes that depraved thing called a "speaking boy" (*puer loquens*) and is sent to school in order to perfect his skills in the disciplines of language. But eloquence is attained in school only through shattering rituals of pain, through the spiritual death of the individual as he is subjected to the laws of language, understood as the living expression of the fallen social order:

> O God, my God, great was the misery and great the deception that I met with when it was impressed upon me that, to behave properly as a boy, I must obey my teachers. This was all that I might succeed in this world and excel in those arts of speech which would serve to bring honor among men and to gain deceitful riches. Hence I was sent to school to acquire learning, the utility of which, wretched child that I was, I did not know. Yet if I was slow at learning, I was beaten. This method was praised by our forebears, many of whom had passed through this life before us and had laid out the hard paths that we were forced to follow. Thus were both toil and sorrow multiplied for the sons of Adam. (*Conf.* I.ix.14)

Since the teacher is the emissary of a vindictive but just God, the dominant relationship between the schoolboy and the teacher is one of fear: "A little one, but with no little feeling, I prayed to you that I would not be beaten" (*Conf.* I.ix.14). The argument for the justice of Augustine's schoolboy beatings is subtle. He tells us (*On Free Will* XIII.xix.54) that children are born into a condition of sin, but what we

14

call sin in the child is rather the consequence of Adam's first sin, committed by free will. The child is afflicted with two punishments for Adam's sin: ignorance and hardship (*ignorantia et difficultas*; *On Free Will* III.xviii.52). Since the child has not altogether lost the "fecundity" for becoming an ornament of the earth (*On Free Will* III.xx.55), by justly punishing the child for the consequences of original sin in him, adults encourage him to regain the goodness he lost when his soul was joined to his mortal body.

Although Augustine was born and raised in a rural, agricultural community of North Africa, nothing could be more characteristic of his mind than for him to define the toil to which fallen man is condemned as the labor of studying language and books. However, the labor of reading will both rescue Augustine from false religion (*Conf.* III.xii.21) and engender truth in him, as he tells us in a sermon:

> To proclaim the word of truth as well as to listen to it is hard work. But it is a labor, brethren, which we endure cheerfully when we remember the Lord's decree and our own circumstances. From the very beginning of our race, and not from a deceitful man, nor from that seducer the devil, but from Truth itself out of the mouth of God man heard the words, "In the sweat of thy face shalt thou eat of thy bread." Thus, if our bread is the word of God, let us exert ourselves in listening, rather than perish from hunger.[18]

Augustine's initiation into the laws of *grammatica* (the science of the "letter," *gramma*, also called *litteratura* in Latin), involves a Pauline paradox: the trauma of mastering these vain laws also engenders lust in the schoolboy, which takes the form of an immoderate, fetishistic love of poetry. Augustine's first poetic love is the story of Dido and Aeneas, two fictive fornicators whose tragedy makes the schoolboy weep at the same time as they harden him against more "useful" learning that might raise him from the city of men (whose "theologians" are poets) to the City of God.[19] Augustine's fornication in the arts of language is reinforced by the false rewards of social ambition:

18. "Third discourse on Psalm 32," in *Saint Augustine on the Psalms*, trans. Dame Scholastica Hebgin and Dame Felicitas Corrigan, Ancient Christian Writers, vol. 30 (Westminster, Md.: Newman Press; London: Longman's Green, 1961), 2:117.

19. St. Augustine, *De civitate dei* XVII.xiv, trans. Marcus Dods, *The City of God* (New York: Random House, 1950), 733.

> I did not love you, and I committed fornication against you,
> and amid my fornications from all sides, there sounded the
> words, "Well done! Well done!" Love of this world is fornica-
> tion against you, but "Well done! Well done!" is said, so that it
> will be shameful for a man to do otherwise. (*Conf.* I.xiii.21)

Augustine seems to be using these events from his Roman educa-
tion to illustrate, by analogy, a moral dialectic in Paul's epistle to the
Romans: if Augustine's torments as a schoolboy are enforcements of a
temporal law that begets transgressions as well as censures, such is the
case with Mosaic Law itself. As Paul had written (Rom. 7:5−7):

> For when we were in the flesh the sinful passions, which were
> accused by the Law, were at work in our members so that they
> brought forth fruit unto death. But now we have been set free
> from the Law, having died to that by which we were held down,
> so that we may serve in a new spirit and not according to the
> outworn letter. . . . Is the Law sin? By no means! Yet I had not
> known lust unless the law had said, "Thou shalt not lust."

Moreover, Paul tells us that idolators have been punished by experiencing unlawful sexual desire; so it follows (again by analogy) that
Augustine's idolatry of the poetic word should also induce lust in him.
His pride in the art of rhetoric makes the letter of the Scriptures
opaque to his mind's eye:

> When I first turned to that Scripture, I did not feel towards it
> as I am speaking now, but it seemed to me unworthy of com-
> parison with the nobility of Cicero's writings. My swelling
> pride turned away from its humble style, and my sharp gaze
> did not penetrate into its inner meaning. (*Conf.* III.v.9)

Even though language and oratory are the basis of secular social
order and justice (just as Christ as Word reveals the truth of *spiritual*
order and justice), pride in oratory leads the citizenry to fetishize the
purely arbitrary laws of language to a point where even so slight an
error as an orator's dropping an aspirate "h" will cause a public outrage,
hence will cause men to transgress the natural Law (and second great
commandment) written in their conscience, which is to love one's
neighbor as oneself. Pride in the changing laws of conventional language leads to social dissension, rather than harmony:

Thus if a man who accepts or teaches the ancient conventional forms of pronunciation violates sounding the "h" in the first syllable, he will offend men more than if, contrary to your laws, he who is a man himself would hate another man. . . . It is as if he thought an enemy more pernicious to him than his own hatred by which he is aroused against the other. Certainly, no knowledge of letters is more interior to us than that written in consciences, since he does to another what he himself does not want to suffer. (*Conf.* I.xviii.29)

Augustine tells us that the study and practice of poetic meter, whose mathematical proportions are (unlike the laws of pronunciation) not conventional, should have led him to perceive, by analogy, a transcendent order that is eternal and true, just as justice is immutable and true:

The very art by which I composed poems did not have different laws in different places, but was always all the same. I did not perceive how justice, to which good and holy men submit, contains in a far more excellent and sublime manner at one and the same time all that it commands, and still is no part at variance with itself, and how, at various times and not all at once, it distributes and commands what is proper. (*Conf.* III.vii.14)

If the rules of grammar and rhetoric, the first two disciplines of what came to be the medieval *trivium*, burden the soul with the vanities of the world and with sins whose consequences are obvious, far more subtle and tenacious are the sinful laws that the third, logic, inculcates in the student's mind. This is what Augustine concludes from his reading of Aristotle's *Categories*. One will recall that the purpose of Aristotle's text is to teach the laws of predicating properly; that is, of correctly asserting, in propositions, the reality of a created thing that we apprehend. The initiation into the *Categories* (and, by extension, into dialectics as a discipline) first induces Augustine to believe that what his mind apprehends of God's substance (e.g., greatness, beauty) is *in* God in the same way that accidents are in substances, as opposed to being *of* God. After his conversion, though, Augustine understands that however we, as creatures in time, apprehend God, his existence is not subject to ontological differences with regard to itself:

In this way, I attempted to understand even yourself, my God, who are most wonderfully simple and immutable, as if you were subject to your greatness and beauty in such wise that they would be in you as a subject, just as they are in bodies. But you yourself are your greatness and beauty. (*Conf.* IV.xvi.29)

Augustine explains later that the "whirlpool" of dialectical fantasms (*turba phantasmatum; Conf.* VII.xvii.23) that his mind has created is inferior to the mental power to create fantasms in the first place, a power which is presumably to be compared with God's own power to create, since we are made in his image: the *Categories*, then, teaches mortals to love *figmenta* derived by the mind from its experience of the material world created on the *third* day, and not from the firmament, which was God's creation of the *second* day and which is a kind of sky that is immaterial and immutable, even though created (*Conf.* XII.viii.8). As was the case with his sufferings as a schoolboy, Augustine considers the labors of Aristotelian logic as the intellectual consequences of Adam's sin and of God's curse (Gen. 3:17) condemning Adam's race to cultivate the ungrateful fields of the created world, as opposed to those of Paradise or of the firmament:

> What I had conceived of you was falsity itself: it was not truth. It was a figment formed out of my own misery; it was not the firmament of your beatitude. For you had commanded it, and so it was done in me, that the earth should bring forth thorns and thistles for me and with labor should I earn my bread. (*Conf.* V.xvi.29)

Indeed, Augustine's tribulations as a student finally lead him to conclude that all the books of the liberal arts (*artes liberales*) are anything but liberating, and that as a student he has been nothing but their slave (*servus*).

When puberty overwhelms Augustine with "dark concupiscence" of the flesh and "unholy desire," his eloquence becomes similarly perverted. Indeed, from this moment forward, sexual desire serves in his narrative as an arch-metaphor for perversions of language. As the art of persuasion becomes his primary goal, the weapon of eloquence turns strongly phallic:

> Then it was that the madness of lust, licensed by human shamelessness but forbidden by your law, took me completely under its scepter, and I clutched it with both hands. My parents took

no care to save me by marriage from plunging into ruin. Their only care was that I should learn to make the finest orations and become a persuasive speaker. (*Conf.* II.ii.4)

Thus, at sixteen, thoroughly seduced by the arts of language, Augustine also begins to frequent brothels, which is to say that his fornication is now also physical. As a young child, he had sinned by ignorance and weakness, but now he recapitulates, by a conscious act of free will, the archetypal original sin that had been innate in him. Intentionally breaking the law (both natural and temporal) that forbids stealing, Augustine vainly tries to please both his comrades and himself by stealing pears from that old garden that we all know. In *On Free Will* (III.xxv.74), Augustine had explained that the fall occurred when Adam chose between the higher commandment of God and the lower suggestion of the devil. But here in the *Confessions*, it is an unworthy social bond that incites Augustine's "fall." Having chosen the creation over its creator, Augustine now becomes completely enslaved to signifiers, rather than to what they signify.

As Augustine begins to teach the seductions of speech, he sets up a household with a concubine. However, his perspectives on mortal love—and on language, which mediates that love—are soon painfully altered by the death of a friend who had become so dear to him that they held each other to be one soul in two bodies. In contrast with purely spiritual beings, who become united or separated merely by similar or dissimilar affections, and in whom union or separation involves neither change nor loss (*On Free Will* III.xi.33), union and separation in mortals are necessarily tempestuous and painful. Augustine's cruelly won awareness, through the death of his friend, that the flesh is mortal leads him to understand that, like all material things, verbal signs too are transient and must be used and not enjoyed:

> They rise and they set, and by rising, as it were, they begin to
> be. They increase, so as to become perfect, and when once
> made perfect, they grow old and die. . . . See, too, how our
> speech is accomplished by significant sounds. There would be
> no complete speech unless each word departs, when all its
> parts have been uttered, so that it may be followed by another.
> For all these things let my soul praise you, O God, creator of
> all things, but let it not be caught tight in them by the love
> that comes from the body's senses. (*Conf.* IV.x.15)

Augustine's grief is so intense that he fears his own death, fears that the vestige of his friend's existence still surviving in his own soul will die. His fear of death (whether his own or that of someone he loves) may be seen, however, both as a low point in man's spiritual life and as a point of departure for spiritual progress. In *On Christian Doctrine*, which he had begun (but not finished) two years before beginning the *Confessions*, Augustine outlined seven steps or degrees in man's progress toward wisdom (II.vii.9–11). The first of these is fear of mortality. Moreover, bearing in mind that *On Christian Doctrine* is a manual for understanding Scripture properly, and bearing in mind also that the story of the *Confessions* will itself culminate in an exegesis of Genesis, we may be tempted to see the life story that follows (or at least what he tells us of that life) as an ascension of this same ladder. Thus, if the second step, piety, is a state of mind where we cease to contradict the Scriptures, Augustine experiences this piety when he meets Ambrose and becomes a catechumen in the Church. The third step involves the proper use of knowledge (*scientia*), by which he means knowledge of created things; such knowledge must lead beyond itself rather than become an obstacle to the apprehension of God. Augustine confronts this problem during his struggle to overcome Manicheism. The fourth step is fortitude, by which he means the unflagging hunger for justice. Such justice transcends, of course, justice in material affairs, and is an attribute of God as creator (through the Son) of the cosmic order. Augustine gains fortitude by withdrawing from his mistresses and from his profession as a rhetorician (*Conf.* VIII.xi.26; IX.i.2), and through the search for inner truth. Augustine experiences the fifth degree, mercy, at the moment of his conversion, when he takes up the Scripture and there finds spontaneous deliverance from his sins, and also when he shares that experience of deliverance with Alypius. The sixth step involves "cleansing the eye" through which we see God, and Augustine achieves this first by examining man's faculty of memory, through which God illuminates his soul, and next by confessing those sins that have been holding his soul captive. The seventh step, or wisdom, is attained in, and expressed by, his exegesis of Genesis.

Such an upward pilgrimage toward wisdom is circuitous, though, and the period following the death of his friend is marked for Augustine by doubt and wandering in an intellectual desert: such is the plight of those who live by "envenomed" language. As we might expect, Augustine also changes mistresses (again, with great torment) at the same time as he encounters dissatisfaction with the materialistic and dualistic doctrines current in the circles in which he moves.

Although Augustine's Manicheism, as well as the burdens of Epicurean and Stoic materialism, were obstacles to his intellection of God as an immaterial substance, his close personal proximity to the great Manichean professor, Faustus, portends very early his future disillusionment with that religion: for all his charm, humility, and semblance of eloquence, Faustus proves to be a man of shallow learning in the liberal arts. However, Augustine is still unable to free himself either from a corporeal understanding of God or from a belief in evil as an autonomous principle:

> I wished to meditate upon my God, but I did not know how to
> think of him except as a vast corporeal mass, for I thought that
> anything not a body was nothing whatsoever. This was the
> greatest and almost sole cause of my inevitable error. As a re-
> sult, I believed that evil is some such substance and that it
> possesses its own foul and hideous mass, either gross, which
> they styled the earth, or thin and subtle, as is the body of
> the air, which they imagine to be a malignant mind stealing
> through the earth. (*Conf.* V.x.19)

Augustine's appointment to a chair in rhetoric at Milan leads to his encounter with Ambrose, a decisive event in his liberation both from the Law and from the sins of carnal understanding that it begot. Not only is he freed from his fear that the New Testament was falsified in a conspiracy to infiltrate Christian teaching with the Jewish Law (*Conf.* V.xi.21), but through Ambrose's sermons he acquires new respect for Christianity because he may now understand certain problematical passages in the Old Testament allegorically, "by which passages I was killed when I had taken them literally" (*Conf.* V.xiv.24). Moreover, certain aspects of Ambrose's personal conduct strike him: first, the man's celibacy; second, his ability to withdraw not only from the society of men but even from the production of vocal signs in his reading. Ambrose is a living portrait of a man who is carnal yet capable of enjoying spiritual knowledge:

> When he read, his eyes moved down the pages and his heart
> sought out their meaning, while his voice and tongue remained
> silent. Often when we were present—for no one was forbidden

to enter, and it is was not his custom to have whoever came
announced to him—we saw him reading to himself, and never
otherwise. After sitting for a long time in silence—who would
dare to annoy a man so occupied?—we would go away. (*Conf.*
VI.iii.3)

Through Ambrose, Augustine's literal understanding of the text of the
Law continues to be overcome:

> I rejoiced also that the ancient scriptures of the law and the
> prophets were now set before me for reading, not with that
> eye which once looked on them as absurdities. . . . I was glad
> when I often heard Ambrose speaking in his sermons to the
> people as though he most earnestly commended it as a rule
> that "the letter kills, but the spirit quickens." For he would
> draw aside the veil of mystery and spiritually lay open things
> that interpreted literally seemed to teach unsound doctrine.
> (*Conf.* VI.iv.6)

By the same token, Augustine illustrates through a curious anec-
dote about his friend Alypius, a Christian, how difficult it is to resist
the tyranny of social pressures that compel the individual soul to forsake the spiritual Law. Alypius was Augustine's lifelong friend and a
man of great integrity, but he had a very Roman penchant for watching
fights between gladiators. Augustine considers such fights a paradigm
of civil society at its most decadent, as crimes sanctioned by temporal
law where the eternal (and Christian) values of justice, peace, and love
of neighbor are deliberately abhorred, and where individuals sacrifice
their inner harmony to be swallowed up in the chaos of the multitude
that erupts at the spilling of human blood. Though Alypius has renounced such spectacles, one day he meets several friends in the street
who urge him to come along to the arena. Alypius boldly seizes the
occasion as a challenge: he *will* go, but will prove his moral superi-
ority and his wisdom by sitting through the entire spectacle with
his eyes shut. When a gladiator finally falls, however, so great is the
clamor that Alypius is conquered by *curiositas* and opens his eyes: his
spiritual fall is worse, Augustine says, than the physical fall of the
gladiator in the ring (*Conf.* VI.viii.13).

That Alypius should join the mob in its applause of evil may be seen
as a dispersion of the oneness of the individual self among the multitude: "We vanished into a multitude, we were dispersed by the many,

and we clung to the multiple."[20] The only way back from the many to the one is Christ: "Thus are they purified by the mediator, so that they may be one in him" (*De trin.* IV.ix.18).

It is above all Augustine's encounter with the writings of the neo-platonists (translated into Latin) that leads him to comprehend the absolute ontological cleavage between the creation, which is the *regio dissimilitudinis*, and its creator. Consequently, he also discovers the need to understand spiritual things (*intelligibilia*): that is, to surpass knowledge (*scientia*) of things existing temporally, knowledge that only clutters the soul with idolatrous fantasms. Augustine at last becomes capable of experiencing supernatural ecstasies in which his soul enjoys unmediated, yet fleeting, knowledge of God, grasped now as the very principle of existence:

> Thus I gradually passed from bodies to the soul, which perceives by means of the body, and thence to its interior power, to which the bodily senses present exterior things—beasts too are capable of doing this much—and thence again to the reasoning power [*potentia ratiocinans*], to which what is apprehended by the bodily senses is referred for judgment [*iudicandum*]. When this power found itself to be in me a variable thing, it raised itself up to its own understanding [*ad intelligentiam suam*]. It removed its thought from the tyranny of habit, and withdrew itself from the throngs of contradictory phantasms. In this way it might find that light by which it was sprinkled, when it cried out. . . . Thus in a flash of its trembling sight it came to that which is [*id quod est*]. (*Conf.* VII.xvii.23)

Although this neoplatonic mystical vision belongs to the narrative portion of the *Confessions*, its sequence of steps reveals why Augustine will become dissatisfied with the narration of his personal life as a source of true wisdom and will consequently invite his soul (as he does in Book X) to reflect upon its own inner, spiritual substance rather than upon the external images of the creation that have until now corrupted his soul by infiltrating his memory.

20. St. Augustine, *De trinitate* IV.vii.11, English translation mine, based on the Latin of the Benedictine edition as published (with French translation) by M. Mellet, O.P., and Thomas Camelot, O.P., in *Oeuvres de saint Augustin: La trinité*, Bibliothèque augustinienne, 2e serie, vols. 15–16 (Paris: Desclée de Brouwer, 1955); cited hereafter as *De trin.*

What follows in the context of this same passage also leads us to anticipate why Augustine saw fit not to exalt, as might a neoplatonist, his unmediated, face-to-face knowledge of God as existence (even though in his famous vision at Ostia he does once again celebrate the mystical potential of the soul to encounter God), but rather to stress the sad but inevitable return of his vision to what is ordinary: Augustine requires, he tells us, a constant and trustworthy mediator to make fast his bond with God. That mediator is of course Christ, who, as both the way and the truth, is a signifier consubstantial with its signified, hence a unique, perfect sign. Yet in the *Confessions* (as in *On Free Will*), Augustine emphasizes his understanding of Christ more as an epistemological instrument than as a historical person in whose passion he might vicariously indulge. This intellectualized Christological bias in the *Confessions* explains to a large extent, as we shall promptly see, why a commentary on Genesis 1 follows the soul's examinations of its own powers in Book X, and not a theophany experienced through the *person* of Christ.

After reading St. Paul (who had been himself deeply marked by neoplatonic teachings), Augustine comes to identify the deep division within his own will as a conflict between the two Laws, the Old and the New: "In vain was I delighted with your law according to the inward man, when another law in my members fought against the law of my mind, and led me captive in the law of sin which was in my members" (*Conf.* VIII.vi.12). Moreover, since the Old Law had come to dominate Augustine through the intimately related forms of an idolatrous love of letters and a passionate attachment to the creation (especially to women, who, through Eve, had wreaked so much havoc in the creation), obviously, only through new experiences both of language and of love could Augustine be redeemed from the Letter and the Law of Sin. Accordingly, in his readings of St. Paul and St. John, Augustine clings above all to the principle of Christ as Word (*Verbum*), not only as Word forespoken in vocal signs to men by a God in and of the flesh, but also as Word "spoken" by God at the creation: "All things were made through him, and without him was made nothing that has been made" (John 1:1–3).

Even after Augustine accepts the notion of the incarnation of the Word, his corrupt will prevents him from throwing off his twin vices of lechery and eloquence and from espousing the church as his spotless bride. However, as he listens to two stories narrated by friends—one dealing with Victorinus, formerly a distinguished rhetorician now converted to Christianity; the other with two civil servants who imitate the ascesis of St. Anthony—these stories recall Augustine to himself and point up the shameful persistence of his own twin evils:

> But the day had come when I stood stripped naked before myself, and my conscience upbraided me. "Where is my tongue? You said, forsooth, that you would not cast off your burden of vanity for the sake of an uncertain truth. See, now it is certain, and yet that burden still weighs you down." (*Conf.* VIII.vii.17)

Augustine's state of mind begins to grow even more turbulent with conflict between his two wills, one of which is spiritual and seeks to accept the Word, the other of which is carnal and resists. Suddenly he rushes out to another decidedly archetypal garden:

> The tumult within my breast hurried me out into it, where no one would stop the raging combat that I had entered into against myself, until it would come to such an end as you knew of, but as I knew not. I suffered from a madness that was to bring health, and I was in a death agony that was to bring life. (*Conf.* VIII.viii.19)

Images of violence now become more and more extravagant: wounds, tearing of hair, beating of forehead, wringing of hands, twisting in chains, fainting, floods of tears. This is not a classical epic of "ships" or "chariots" (*Conf.* VIII.viii.19); this is an inner Christian epic of the soul's fortress struggling to admit the Word. If Augustine's accounts of violence call to mind the tortures inflicted upon him when he was a young man acquiring the disciplines of language, it is because the two violences are nearly identical: each is occasioned by the transgression of his identity by the word of another; each is the single violence of death in language, except that in the latter case Augustine's death to the flesh is the trauma of salvation as rebirth (*Conf.* IX.ii.3).

As we might expect, Augustine's labor to espouse the Word of God is attended by his struggle to transcend the carnal urge to fornicate. The memory of all his mistresses besieges him, and they caress his "fleshly raiment" and tempt him by asking whether it will really be forbidden for him to do "this and that" (*hoc et illud*) with them for the rest of eternity (*Conf.* VIII.xi.26). Is Augustine another Orpheus? As the will to be saved wins out in his mind, the lascivious voices of his mistresses grow fainter: there can be salvation, it seems, in deafness. Now an allegorical vision of chastity floods his mind, comforts him, and chides

25

him for still hearing the solicitations of lust: "Turn deaf ears to those unclean members of yours upon the earth, so that they may be mortified. They tell you delights, but not as does the law of the Lord your God" (*Conf.* VIII.xi.27). At last Augustine is ready to receive the Word, and in a climactic, archetypal moment in the garden with Alypius, Augustine the rhetorician and the fornicator dies as his finger falls providentially on these verses in Paul's epistle to the Romans (13 : 13 – 14): "Not in rioting and drunkenness, not in chambering and impurities, not in strife and envying; but put you on the Lord Jesus Christ and make not provision for the flesh and its concupiscence" (*Conf.* VII.xii.29). Augustine the reader is now liberated from his sinful servitude of the Old Law as he fulfills the first and great commandment, on which hangs the Law and the Prophets, which is to love God with all his heart. Just as spontaneously, Augustine fulfills the second, which is to love his neighbor as himself, when he runs to Alypius to share his excitement. Alypius too finds in the very next sentence of the epistle to the Romans his own liberating self-knowledge: "Love therefore is the fulfillment of the Law."

Augustine's submission not only frees him from lust but simultaneously loosens the grip of classical eloquence on his tongue: "And I babbled]*garriebam*] my brightness, my riches and my health to you, O Lord my God" (*Conf.* IX.i.1). Speaking in tongues, now, and drunk from his discourse with the sublime, Augustine is determined, as he says, to "withdraw the service of my tongue from the language markets" (*Conf.* IX.ii.2). The task of retiring gracefully from his chair of rhetoric is simplified when God sends him a good case of bronchitis (*Conf.* IX.ii.4), rendering the performance of his former duty impossible.

Augustine now retires to the country to read the Scriptures, and one of the first tests of his newfound faith is the death of his good friend Nebridius. In contrast with the death of his earlier friend, when an inconsolable Augustine had discovered mortality in human discourse, he scarcely feels the death of Nebridius as a loss, for he continues to communicate with his friend through the immutable language of the Other:

> No longer does he put his ear to my mouth, but he puts his
> spiritual mouth to your fountain, and in accordance with his
> desire he drinks in wisdom, as much as he can, endlessly happy.
> Nor do I think that he is so inebriated by that fountain of wis-

dom as to become forgetful of me, for you, O Lord, of whom he drinks, are mindful of us. (*Conf.* IX.iii.6)

Now that Augustine is spiritually reborn in the Word, his earthly mother Monica may die in peace. Just before her death, she and her son experience in each other's company a mystical vision in which their spirits, together, momentarily meet their maker in heaven. This famous vision takes the form of a silent, interior dialogue with each other and with God, one which progressively transcends all created things, all signs, and evokes a total, unmediated face-to-face union with God that culminates in something like a spiritual orgasm. Such are the ecstasies reserved for those freed from the temporal bondage of mortal discourse, "where," as Augustine says, "a word both begins and ends" (*Conf.* IX.x.24). Indeed, they imagine salvation as a permanent discourse where the soul's substance, no longer expressed by the ephemeral "I" of the language of carnal man, survives eternally in the Word:

There we said: if for any man the tumult of the flesh fell silent, silent the images of earth, and of the waters, and of the airs; silent the heavens; silent for him the very soul itself, and he should pass beyond himself by not thinking upon himself; silent his dreams and all imagined appearances, and every tongue, and every sign; and if all things that come to be through change should become wholly silent to him—for if any man can hear, then all these things say to him, "We did not make ourselves, but he who endures forever made us"—if when they have said these words, they then become silent for they have raised up their ear to him who made them, and God alone speaks, not through such things but through himself, so that we hear his Word, not uttered by a tongue of flesh, nor by an angel's voice, nor by the sound of thunder, nor by the riddle of a similitude, but by himself whom we love in these things, himself we hear without their aid—even as we then reached out and in swift thought attained to that eternal Wisdom which abides over all things—if this could be prolonged, and other visions of a far inferior kind could be withdrawn, and this one alone ravish, and absorb, and hide away its beholder within its deepest joys, so that sempiternal life might be such as was that moment of understanding for which we sighed, would not this be, "Enter into your Master's joy?" When shall this be? When "we shall rise again, but we shall not all be changed." (*Conf.* IX.x.25)

"What am I doing here?" Monica asks at the conclusion of her vision and promptly dies. And it is also here that Augustine's narrative discourse draws to an end, having exhausted its usefulness. After turning inward to analyze his faculty of memory, which is his link with signification beyond time, Augustine confesses his sins in preparation for explicating the creation as it is told in the Book of Genesis. The act of recall of the self gives way to blame of self and self-expulsion, and these give way to confession of God's glory. As Augustine wrote in *On Free Will* (III.xiv.41–xv.42):

> As I was saying, vice is bad only in opposition to the nature of the thing whose vice it is. Hence, it is obvious that the nature of that thing whose vice is blamed is praiseworthy. . . . If you blame a vice, surely you praise the thing whose integrity you desire. . . . If, therefore, to blame vices is to commend the beauty and dignity of the natures themselves whose vices they are, how much more God, creator of all natures, must be praised even in their vices.

Hence, Augustine's progress as it is expressed in the *Confessions* is not merely the pilgrimage of a sinner and rhetorician ascending the path toward conversion to the Word; it is a progress away from the rhetoric of autobiographical narrative itself, because such narrative is ultimately the mediator of false presences. The *Confessions* may be seen as a sequence not only of events, but of discursive acts which carry us beyond the narrative to the philosophical, and beyond the philosophical to the exegetical. This itinerary of performances exemplifies the spiritual itinerary of a Christian neoplatonist who first records his life of sin and his conversion in narrative (Books I–IX), who then analyzes his inner existence in the rational discourse of the philosopher (Book X), and who finally contemplates God as the principle and source of existence itself through the mediation of Christ and through meditating, with the aid of the Holy Ghost, upon the spiritual meaning of the divine narrative that tells the creation (Books XI–XIII). The passage from autobiography to exegesis is the passage beyond "the book of the life of each man," as Augustine calls the process of self-recollection (in the *City of God* XX.xiv), to the Book of God:

"And another book was opened," it says. We must therefore understand it of a certain divine power, by which it shall be brought about that every one shall recall to memory all his own works, whether good or evil, and shall mentally survey them with a marvellous rapidity, so that this knowledge will either accuse or excuse conscience, and thus all shall be simultaneously judged. And this divine power is called a book, because in it we shall read all that it causes us to remember.

Moreover, Augustine's decision to end his *Confessions* with a commentary conformed very well with his new duty as a convert and priest, for Paul had made very clear that it does not suffice for the Christian who has been visited by the Holy Ghost to babble his praise "in tongues," to praise God in an obscure, private way:

Aim at charity, yet strive after the spiritual gifts, but especially that you may prophesy. For he who speaks in a tongue does not speak to men but to God; for no one understands, as he is speaking mysteries in his spirit. But he who prophesies speaks to men for edification, and encouragement, and consolation. He who speaks in a tongue edifies himself, but he who prophesies edifies the church. (1 Cor. 14:1–4)

In contrast with the mindless labor of the child under the pedagogues, which Augustine compares to the servile understanding of the Jews under the Law (*DDC* II.vi.10), the difficulty of understanding the Scripture is *pleasurable* labor (*DDC* II.vi.8). By returning to the Old Testament in a spirit of grace, Augustine frees both himself and that text from the servitude imposed by the Law of Sin and from a carnal understanding of the letter, of the sabbath, and of the act of sacrifice:

What the Apostle says pertains to this problem: "For the letter killeth, but the spirit quickeneth." That is, when that which is said figuratively is taken as though it were literal, it is understood carnally. Nor can anything more appropriately be called the death of the soul than that condition in which the thing which distinguishes us from beasts, which is the understanding [*intelligentia*], is subjected to the flesh in the pursuit of the letter. He who follows the letter takes figurative expressions as though they were literal and does not refer the things signified to anything else. For example, if he hears of the Sab-

bath, he thinks only of one day out of the seven that are repeated in a continuous cycle; and if he hears of Sacrifice, his
thoughts do not go beyond the customary victims of the flocks
and fruits of the earth. There is a miserable servitude of the
spirit in this habit of taking signs for things, so that one is not
able to raise the eye of the eternal mind above things that are
corporal and created to drink in eternal light. (*DDC*, III.v.9)

Thus, Augustine's "Christian liberty" (*libertas christiana*) accompanies the commentator's victory over his own flesh. Just as the old
text incised in stone is abrogated by a new text inscribed in the living
heart, so too circumcision in the flesh is superseded by grace in the
form of figurative understanding: that is, of a *non*-circumcision of the
heart that heals as it does not cut.

To conclude the *Confessions* by uttering, with lips circumcised by
the Holy Ghost, the spiritual meaning of the story of the creation by
the Word as that Word is written in the Old Testament is to signal, per-
formatively, the repeal of the Law of Sin in him.

Augustine's exegesis of Genesis 1 must be understood, then, as more
than a gesture of charitable pedagogy. Because of the isomorphism between the hierarchy of faculties in the human soul and the hierarchy of
being as the good work of the Word, Augustine's hermeneutical performance is a re-presentation of the Word hidden under the veil of the Old
Testament *narratio*: Augustine's *enarratio* of the creation is a celebra-
tion of his own *re*-creation from the abyss of his sins through illumination by the spirit, through whom God let there be light in Augustine's
soul. Following his rejection of Manicheism, Augustine had come to
conceive of evil in the "formable" soul as man's choice, by free will, of
his own annihilation or formlessness: "Thus, those two creatures,
body and life, being perfectible [*formabilia*], and falling into nothing-
ness [*in nihilum*] by the loss of all perfection [*omnino forma*] show
well enough that they draw their existence from that perfection [*ex illa
forma*] which is always the same" (*On Free Will*, II.xvii.46). However,
man's soul still remains perfectible (*formabilis*), but only with help,
since it cannot perfect itself out of its chosen chaos (*inchoatio*). The
process of time is also a progress of revelation which redeems fallen
souls from the abyss that they chose when they fell through Adam,
and are *still* free to choose:

And you began to accomplish in time the things predestined,
so that you might reveal hidden things and put in place our

disordered parts [*ut inconposita nostra conponeres*]—for our
sins were upon us, and we had departed from you into the
darksome deep [*in profundum tenebrosum abieramus ab te*],
and your good Spirit was borne over us to bring us help in due
season—and you justified the ungodly and divided them from
the wicked, and made firm the authority of your book between
those above who were docile to you, and between those below
who were made subject to them, and you gathered together the
society of unbelievers into one conspiracy, so that the zeal of
the faithful might become apparent, and they might bring
forth works of mercy. (*Conf.* XIII.xxxiv.49)

Thus, Augustine prefaces his exegesis of the creation by praying
that he too will be remade from nothing through the light of revelation: "O Lord, perfect me and reveal to me these things" (*O domine,
perfice me et reuele mihi eas; Conf.* XI.ii.3). During his writing, though,
only the continuing actions of prayer and confession will protect his
mind from the darkness of the abyss: "O may it be the Truth, the light
of my heart, not my own darkness [*tenebrae*] that speaks to me. I fell
away to those material things and I became darkened over, but from
there, even from there, I loved you" (*Conf.* XII.x.10). If there can be re-
creation through such writing, it is because the creation itself is a
manifestation of textuality in a hierarchy of modes. The material
world is that of temporal things, of carnal language and of the dead
letter. The soul's world is one in which divine truth is imprinted in the
living heart or the memory.

Finally, stretched out above both of these texts is the scroll of God's
scripture. This is a firmament of transparent writing that allows mortals to contemplate the heavenly bodies as signs, in such a way as to
understand intuitively—but incompletely—what lies beyond them:
"These things, you, our God, wisely discuss with us in your book, your
firmament, so that we may discern all things in wondrous contemplation although as yet in signs and in times, and in days and in years"
(*Conf.* XIII.xviii.23). This parchment is a threshold that separates mortals from the "sky of sky," where intellection is immediate rather than
semiotic, dialectical, figurative, or temporal:

Meanwhile I interpret the sky of sky as the intellectual sky,
where it belongs to the intellect to know all at once, not in
part, not in a dark manner, not through a glass, but as a whole,
in plain sight, face to face, not this thing now and that thing

> then, but, as has been said, it knows all at once, without
> any passage of time. By the earth invisible and without form,
> I understand an earth without any change of time, which
> change is wont to have now this thing, now that.
> (*Conf.* XII.xiii.16)

In this sky of sky, the angelic and the blessed pass their non-time reading, but not, as sinning mortals do, in language and vexed by the Law of Sin. Instead, they read a language without syllables that does not unfold in temporal sequence, and they read from a text that is unequivocal and eternal because it is the face of the Word itself. And unlike mortals enslaved by the liberal arts, for whom intellectual servitude is a consequence of the Law of Sin, these celestial readers give themselves over to a reading (*lectio*) that they choose of their own free will (*elegendo*) and that is only a source of esteem and delight (*diligendo*), not of difficulty, as is the case for mortals dwelling beneath his spiritual firmament:

> Let the supercelestial peoples, who are your angels, praise you,
> they who have no need to look up at this firmament, or by
> reading, to know your Word. They always behold your face,
> and, without any syllables of time, they read upon it what your
> eternal will decrees. They read your will; they choose it; and
> they love it. They read forever, and what they read never passes
> away. For by choosing and loving, they read the actual immu-
> tability of your counsel. Their book is never closed, nor is
> their scroll folded up, because you yourself are this to them,
> and you are this for eternity. (*Conf.* XIII.xv.18)

In contrast with the unredeemed, for whom the sabbath of Mosaic Law is a mere day of earthly rest, St. Augustine considers the seventh day of the creation as the rest of salvation reserved for those whose good works please God in the same way the creation originally pleased him when he saw that it was good. If Augustine's own story is good (and he thought at the end of his life that it *was*), it is not because he was its author, nor because it was written under God's authority; rather, it is God's gift, as is the sabbath reserved for those who do not turn away from God and from his book:

> But the seventh day is without an evening, and it does not
> have a setting, because you have sanctified it to endure for all

eternity, so that by the fact that you rested on the seventh day, having fulfilled all your works, which are very good, although you have wrought them while still at rest, the voice of your book may proclaim to us beforehand that we also, after our works, which are very good because you have given them to us, may rest in you on the sabbath of eternal life. (*Conf.* XIII.xxxvi.51)

CHAPTER 2

Saint Augustine:
Language
as Temporality

Surely it is not an exaggeration to claim that, following St. Paul, St. Augustine inaugurated what we may call the semiological consciousness of the Christian West.[1] All of Augustine's endeavors in metaphysics, epistemology, and exegesis coincide with a relentless effort to define the functions and limits of human language. Many empirical features of verbal signs, whether pronounced, written, or merely thought, gave rise to analogies that nourished Augustine's speculations about man's relationship to himself, to people and external things, and to God. My specific concern here is to explore Augustine's thoughts about the manner in which processes of language may be said to reflect the temporal world or, more precisely, temporality itself. I should like to expose a bundle of ideas that subsisted in medieval culture, with varying degrees of prominence and explicitness, until the rise of Humanism.[2] I hope to show how

1. A good general introduction to medieval sign theory is Marcia Colish, *The Mirror of Language: A Study in the Medieval Theory of Knowledge* (New Haven, Conn.: Yale University Press, 1968; rev. ed., Lincoln: Univ. of Nebraska Press, 1983). See also R. A. Markus, "St. Augustine on Signs," *Phronesis* 2 (1957): 60–83, and B. Darrell Jackson, "The Theory of Signs in St. Augustine's *De doctrina christiana*," *Revue des études augustiniennes* 15 (1969): 9–49; both reprinted in *Augustine: A Collection of Critical Essays*, ed. R. A. Markus (New York: Doubleday, 1972), 61–91 and 92–148, respectively.

2. Cf. Charles Béné, *Erasme et Saint Augustin* (Geneva: Droz, 1969; also Mar-

these ideas about language determined many features of Augustine's own performative strategies.

To begin, let us recall some of Augustine's thoughts about the nature of time itself. Such thoughts are expressed most succinctly in a famous passage in Book XI of the *Confessions*; I shall summarize them briefly and uncritically.[3] Augustine says that even though God created the temporal world, God remains eternally present to himself as pure Being beyond time. The creation exists in time, but what we call the past and future of that creation cannot properly be said to "exist": only the indivisible present exists, and the past and future may be apprehended only in and through that present. Thus, if we commonly speak of past and future times, these are not objectively extant times: rather, they are experienced subjectively or intramentally: that is, as moments of presence *in* the mind and *of* the mind to *itself*. For the mind has the special power both to make the past "present" through the faculty of memory and to make the future "present" as expectation. Time is apprehended and measured subjectively when the mind "distends" itself in the present toward the past, which is made present by means of the memory, and toward the future, which is made present to the mind as expectation. The mind apprehends time as a synthesis of these three presences within itself. Therefore, if beings may be said to move in time, their movement is not time itself nor is time measured by their actual movement. The measuring of time is an act of synthesis that occurs wholly within the mind.

We shall see that it is strikingly characteristic of Augustine that his physical theories of time and movement in Book II of the *Confessions* rest on concrete observations not of bodies moving in space but rather of speech (in this instance, poetic speech) unfolding as a sequence of measurable, vocal sounds. When we recite a verse of poetry, he says, we measure the length of its syllables by comparing the long syllables with the short ones. But how, he asks, can we measure a sound except by hearing it in the present? Yet once the whole sound has been heard,

---

jorie O'Rourke Boyle, *Erasmus on Language and Method in Theology* (Toronto: Univ. of Toronto Press, 1977).

3. Augustine's theories of time have been analyzed critically by logicians: e.g., Hugh M. Lacy, "Empiricism and Augustine's Problems about Time," *Review of Metaphysics* 22 (1968): 219–45 (reprinted in Markus, ed., *Augustine, A Collection of Critical Essays*, 280–308).

it no longer exists. How, then, can it be compared with a *second* sound that, again, will no longer exist in the present when it too is complete?

> In so far as sense perception is clear, I measure the long syllable by the short one, and I perceive that it is exactly twice as long. But when one syllable sounds after another, and if the first is short and the second long, how will I retain the short syllable and how will I apply it to the long syllable if it does not begin to sound until the short syllable itself has ceased to sound? Do I measure the long syllable itself while it is present, since I do not measure it until it is completed? Yet in completion is its passing away. Therefore, what is it that I measure? Where is the long syllable that I measure? Both of them have sounded, have flown off, have passed away, and now they are not.[4]

Although it may seem surprising that Augustine elects language as the empirical foundation for his physics of movement and time, we should recall that Augustine considered verbal signifiers—*voces*—to be corporeal things, even though what they signify is not corporeal but mental.[5] Moreover, Augustine's attitudes toward things and words (as things) are identical. Since the knowledge of a thing is different from (and preferable to) the thing itself, things are to be treated as signs. Things themselves cannot be known directly by the mind, and knowledge of things must pass through signs: "All doctrine concerns either things or signs, but things are learned through signs" (*DDC*. I.i.2). Augustine's tendency to treat things not for themselves but as signs remained a habit of medieval culture during the centuries that followed.[6]

In Book II of the *Confessions*, Augustine illustrates his analysis of

---

4. St. Augustine, *Confessiones libri tredecem*, XI.xxvii.35, ed. Pius Knöll and Martinus Skutella (Leipzig: Teubner, 1934), as published in *Oeuvres de Saint Augustin: Les Confessions*, Bibliotèque augustinienne, 2e série: Dieu et son oeuvre, vols. 13–14, French trans. A. Tréhorel and G. Bouissou, notes by A. Solignac (Paris: Desclée de Brouwer, 1962); English trans. John K. Ryan, *The Confessions of St. Augustine* (New York: Doubleday, 1960), hereafter cited in my own text as *Conf.*

5. Let us recall Augustine's definition: "A sign is a thing which causes us to think of something beyond the impression that the thing itself makes upon the senses": *De doctrina christiana* II.i.1, trans. D. W. Robertson, Jr., *On Christian Doctrine* (New York: Bobbs-Merrill, 1958), 34, hereafter cited as *DDC* in my text.

6. Cf. Jean Jolivet, *Arts du langage et théologie chez Abélard* (Paris: Vrin, 1969), 14–15.

the soul's apprehension of time by describing what happens when we recite a psalm:

> I am about to recite a psalm that I know. Before I begin, my memory extends over as much of it as I shall separate off and assign to the past. The life of this action of mine is distended into memory by reason of the part I am about to speak. But attention is actually present and that which was to be is borne along by it so as to become past. The more this is done and done again, so much the more is memory lengthened by a shortening of expectation, until the entire expectation is exhausted. When this is done, the whole action is completed and passes into memory. What takes place in the whole psalm takes place also in each of its parts and each of its syllables. (*Conf.* II.xxviii.38)

Augustine's analysis here may be a bit plodding, but what follows is a stunning leap by analogy, reinforced by anaphora, beyond mortal knowledge of corporeal things to knowledge in the divine mind:

> The same thing holds for a longer action, of which perhaps the psalm is a small part. The same thing holds for man's entire life, the parts of which are all the man's action. The same thing holds throughout the whole age of the sons of man, the parts of which are the lives of all men. (*Conf.* II.xxviii.38)

And just as Augustine's mind is capable of holding present within itself the whole psalm that he will recite as a temporal sequence, so too the mind of God knows the totality of time as pure presence to itself. God's knowledge occurs without divisions in the divine mind, without any process of differentiation, and this power distinguishes God's mind from man's:

> Far be it that in such mortal wise you should know future and past. Far, far more wonderfully; far more deeply do you know them! It is not as emotions are changed or senses filled up by expectations of words to come and memory of those past in one who sings well-known psalms or hears a familiar psalm. Not so does it befall you who are unchangeably eternal, that is, truly eternal, the creator of minds. Therefore, just as in the

beginning you have known heaven and earth without change in your knowledge, so too "in the beginning you made heaven and earth" without any difference in your activity. (*Conf.* II.xxxi.41)

If divine knowledge of temporality occurs, unlike man's, without division or difference within the knowing mind, so too God's eternal Word, unlike human speech, produces itself without any succession of syllables unfolding in time:

> So you call us to understand the Word, God, with you, O God, which is spoken eternally, and in which all things are spoken eternally. Nor is it the case that what was spoken is ended and that another thing is said, so that all things may at length be said: all things are spoken once and forever. . . . Therefore no part of your Word gives place to another or takes the place of another, since it is truly eternal and immortal. (*Conf.* II.vii.7)

It is the corporeal nature of the creation that necessitates our knowledge of God as three separate persons with three separate names that must be pronounced in three separate utterances:

> But I would like to affirm plainly that the Father and the Son and the Holy Spirit, being of one and the same substance— God the Creator, the omnipotent Trinity—are inseparable in their works, but it is the creation, so greatly dissimilar and corporeal, which constrains them to become separate in their manifestation, just as, with our words, which are of course corporeal sonorities, the Father and the Son and the Holy Spirit cannot be named except by fractions of duration proper to each, and clearly separated and occupied by the syllables of each word. Indeed, in the substance in which they subsist, the three are one, Father and Son and Holy Spirit . . . free of all temporal movement and of all intervals in space and time. But in my words, "Father," "Son" and "Holy Spirit" are separated, and it is impossible to name them together, and in writing they occupy different spaces.[7]

7. St. Augustine, *De trinitate* IV.xxi.30. English translation mine, based on the Latin of the Benedictine edition as published (with French translation) by M. Mellet, O.P., and Thomas Camelot, O.P., in *Oeuvres de saint Augustin: La trinité,* Bibliothéque augustinienne, 2e série, vols. 15–16 (Paris: Desclée de Brouwer, 1955), cited hereafter as *De trin.*

Augustine's metaphysics of the Word stood in opposition to Epicurean and Lucretian materialism, which was purely stochastic. Lucretius believed that the universe was a cataract of falling seeds or atoms. Existing things arise when a clinamen occurs: that is, when atoms bump each other because of their difference in mass, suddenly diverge from their vertical axis of fall, and form temporary configurations, like eddies or whirlpools; these are the forms of created things.[8] Since atoms are also letters, these configurations also produce words or meanings. However, such things, like their meanings, convey no divine intentionality, no ultimate telos, and they disperse forever when the eddy caused by their clinamen expends itself and its atoms resume their free fall in the cataract.

As opposed to the divine Word, which is always without difference with regard to itself, human speech unfolds as a succession of different sounds, and the capacity of these sounds to signify depends solely on social convention (*DDC* II.i.1–2). This inherent arbitrariness of the verbal sign is a result of God's punishment of man's pride in the catastrophe of Babel. Moreover, this same arbitrariness extends to the relationship between letters and the sounds that they signify:

> But because vibrations in the air soon pass away and remain no
> longer than they sound, signs of words have been constructed
> by means of letters. Thus words are shown to the eyes, not in
> themselves, through certain signs which stand for them. These
> signs could not be common to all peoples because of the sin
> of human dissension which arises when one people seizes
> the leadership for itself. A sign of this pride is that tower
> erected in the heavens where impious men deserved that not
> only their minds but also their voices should be dissonant.
> (*DDC* II.iv.5)

It is only by common consent among societies after Babel that a given sound may signify something, and Augustine considers the conventional verbal sign to be a basic social contract: a "pact," to use his term (*Conf.* I.xiii.22). The laws of this pact should not be allowed to become a tyrannical force. Thus, Augustine decries the readiness of a Roman crowd to go into an uproar if an orator drops his "h" when he utters the word *homo* in a discourse before them (*Conf.* I.xviii.29).

8. Lucretius, *De rerum natura*, ed. Martin Ferguson Smith, trans. W. H. D. Rouse, Loeb Classical Library (Cambridge, Mass.: Harvard Univ. Press, 1975), 216ff.

Clearly, Augustine's insistence upon the arbitrary nature of the bond between signifier and signified went against the grain of that tradition that is commonly called "Cratylism," after the opinion of one of Socrates's interlocutors, who held that words are in some obscure way replicas of the substances that they name.[9] Such doctrines had persisted in movements distinct from Platonism—for example, in Stoic theories of language.[10]

Augustine's belief in the conventional nature of the sign also set him apart from tendencies in Jewish thought to stress the ontological necessity of relationships between Hebrew words and the things they name. The Hebrew root *dabher* gives rise not only to the infinitive "to speak" (*ledabher*) but also to the substantive "word" (*davaar*) and to the identical substantive, "thing" (*davaar*). Jewish midrashic tradition situates the origin of the world in the very words of the Torah, "conceived as a textual object of pure anteriority and pure genetic power. As such, it signifies in two ways, as a discourse and by its visible shape; its letters, words, and layout operate as an iconic and symbolic sign system."[11] If, in the beginning, God spoke the creation through the Torah, it is only through the subsequent words (*dvaarim*) of the Law and the Prophets that the history of Israel will materialize as events.

As we might expect, Augustine himself was intrigued by the problem of explaining how God, whose Word is eternal and without difference, is said in Genesis to have created the temporal world by his verbal commands. Did God say "Let there be light" in the eternity of his Word, or did he say it in time?[12] Augustine resolves this enigma by suggesting that the Creation occurred in four phases. First, there was the

9. Plato, *Cratylus*, trans. B. Jowett (New York: Random House, 1937), 173.

10. R. H. Robins, *Ancient and Medieval Grammatical Theory in Europe with Particular Reference to Modern Linguistic Doctrine* (London: G. Nell, 1951), ch. 1.

11. Gerda Eilata, "'Seeing Voices': Lisibility and Visibility in the Tora," unpublished paper presented at a colloquium, "Lisibilité / Visibilité," organized by Claude Gandelman, Ben-Gurion University of the Negev, April 30, 1981. For a recent study of the persisting medieval desire to imagine the bond between signifier and signified as one of consubstantiality, see R. Howard Bloch, *Etymologies and Genealogies: A Literary Anthropology of the French Middle Ages* (Chicago: Chicago Univ. Press, 1983).

12. St. Augustine, *De Genesi ad litteram* I.ix.15 (hereafter cited as *De Gen. ad litt.*), translation mine from the Latin text of the Benedictine edition published (with a French translation) by P. Agaesse, S.J., and J. Moingt, S.J. in *Oeuvres de saint Augustin: De la Genèse selon la lettre*, Bibliothèque augustinienne, vols. 48–49 (Paris: Desclée de Brouwer, 1972), 48–49.

creation in God's Word (*in Verbo Dei*), where all things were not fully created but were still spiritual and eternal; second, there was the creation in the elements of the world, where all things to come in time were created simultaneously; third, all things were created in time, each thing in its own time, and no longer simultaneously (*De Gen. ad litt.* IX.x.17); fourth, all things were created in seeds (*in semenibus*), by which Augustine apparently means the natural tendency of material being—the Stoic *oikeiosis*. At the same time that God first created the light, which was a purely spiritual light, he created the angels, and God continues to illuminate angels as he speaks. To lesser, temporal beings such as man, God speaks through the mediation of the creation, whether spiritually, as in dreams, or corporeally, as in forms and voices (*De Gen. ad litt.* VIII.xxvii.49).

After the Fall, God walked in the garden in the evening, leaving his light behind him, and henceforth spoke to men by things of the creation (*De Gen. ad litt.* XI.xxxiii.43).

Augustine believed that the meaning of Scripture is strictly autonomous—independent of the temporal, verbal signs by which it is expressed, and such atemporal meaning must be grasped by the reader in a direct process of illumination from within. For this reason, Scripture may be translated from one historical language to another. Thus, if Moses first wrote the words of Genesis in Hebrew,

> he wrote them and he passed away. He passed away from this world from you [God] to you, and he is not now here before me. If he were, I would catch hold of him, and I would ask him, and through you I would beseech him to make these things plain to me. I would lay my body's ears to the sounds breaking forth from his mouth. If he spoke Hebrew, in vain would his voice strike upon my senses, and none of it would touch my mind. But if he spoke in Latin, I would know what he said. Yet how would I know whether he spoke the truth? Even if I knew this, would I know it from him? Truly, within me, within the dwelling place of thought, Truth, neither Hebrew nor Greek nor Latin nor barbaric in speech, without mouth or tongue as organ, and without the noise of syllables, would say to me, "He speaks the truth." (*Conf.* II.iii.5)

If Augustine dwells on the transiency of spoken sounds in order to speak dialectically of a transcendental Word where the bondages of time and space do not pertain, his search for this Word was born of im-

mense personal suffering and loss in his relationship with people—
whether as friend, lover, son, or, finally, as the father of a son whom he
loved but outlived.

Since biographical events in the *Confessions* are often construed as
events of Augustine's life in language, it is entirely in character that he
should first ponder the transiency of verbal signifiers through the despair caused by the death of a close childhood friend shortly after
Augustine's first appointment as a teacher of rhetoric—that most vain
of sciences—in Thagaste. This is Augustine's first experience of mortality, and the effects of losing his soul's other half are overwhelming:
"Wretched was I, and wretched is the very soul that is bound fast by
friendship for mortal things, that is torn asunder when it loses them,
and then first feels the misery by which it is wretched even before it
loses those things" (*Conf.* IV.vi.II). Augustine extrapolates from this
loss a comprehensive vision of the perishability of all things created in
time. All created things

> rise and they set, and by rising, as it were, they begin to be.
> They increase, so as to become perfect, and when once made
> perfect, they grow old and die, and even though all things do
> not grow old, yet all die . . . this is the law of their being.
> (*Conf.* IV.x.15)

Once again the example of spoken language is privileged by Augustine.
Created things that succeed each other in time are parts of a whole,
just as words in an utterance are multiple parts of a sentence whose
meaning is integral: "See, too, how our speech is accomplished by significant sounds. There would be no complete sentence unless each
word departs, when all its parts have been uttered, so that it may be
followed by another" (*Conf.* IV.x.15).

Man's understanding is necessarily fragmentary and sequential because of his original sin. Were it not for that, God would wish for man
to enjoy total, unmediated knowledge:

> But if fleshly sense had been capable of comprehending the
> whole, and had not, for your punishment, been restricted to
> but a part of the universe, you would wish that whatever exists
> at present would pass away, so that all things might bring you
> the greater pleasure. (*Conf.* IV.xi.17)

Augustine is vexed not only by the incommensurability of conventional language with an ineffable God but also by the paradox of even

attempting to utter in temporal, vocal signs a notion such as that of eternity. In his commentary upon Psalm 76, which takes the form of a sermon, Augustine gives brilliant rhetorical emphasis to this paradox by performing, so to speak, a discursive act in the *via negativa*. Commenting upon the verse "I meditated upon days past, and I held in my mind eternal years," Augustine calls into question his own license to speak:

> Consider whether this does not demand, rather, great silence. Let all external sound be far from me, all clatter of human things, when I wish to meditate within me upon the eternal years. . . . In conversation, we say "this year." But what do we possess of this year, except the day in which we exist? For those days which have preceded are past, and nothing remains of them; the days to come are not yet in existence."[13]

But how can we presume, Augustine continues, to speak even of today? Or even of this hour? Or even of this very moment?

> What moment? Even as I utter syllables, if I must utter two of them, the second does not sound until the other is no longer. And even within this syllable, if there are two letters, the second does not sound until the first is no longer. What, then, is our place in those years? (*Comm.*, p. 214)

Augustine denounces, then, the whole attempt to speak in time about eternity in a language which is itself a perfect reflection of the temporal. Instead, we may only speak truly of time and of eternity by speaking with God from within: "For you remain the same, and your years do not disappear. Such are the years that the man who progresses meditates in silence, and not in exterior babbling" (*Comm.*, p. 214).

One may imagine how Augustine's very calculated discursive strategies in this sermon must have stirred his audience. Nevertheless, consummate rhetorician that he was, Augustine held his homiletic art in contempt. In a treatise entitled *De catechizandis rudibus*, which is devoted to methods of instructing newcomers to the Church, Augustine describes what occurs in the mind of an orator who struggles to en-

---

13. St. Augustine, *Commentary on Psalm 76*, as published (with a French translation) in *Oeuvres complètes de saint Augustin*, ed. and trans. M. Raulx (Bar-le-Duc: Louis Guérin, 1871), 9:213, English translation mine. Further references to this work, abbreviated as *Comm.*, are included in my text.

lighten his speakers with spiritual truth.[14] An intellection of the truth originates in the soul as a lightning-like flash that is always already hidden in its secret place. This timeless flash in some marvelous way leaves prints (*impressiones*) in the memory, and these are a kind of mental language distinct from historical or conventional language. These prints subsist during that brief interval of time when we assign to them syllables of historical language (Latin, Greek, Hebrew), which are proffered as phonetic signs (*signa sonantia*) directed at our audience. But "how remote," Augustine says, "is the sound of the voice from the intellectual flash when it does not even resemble the imprint on the memory!" (*De cat.* ii.4). This inadequacy of exterior language to primary intuition is vexing to the orator: "I become sad that my tongue cannot suffice to my heart," and "my discourse is slow, long, and unsimilar to it"; furthermore, "the tedium that we feel with our language when we begin to speak only makes our language even more languid and obtuse than it was before we spoke" (*De cat.* ii.3).

Although Augustine holds that the sequentiality of verbal signs is a necessity of man's status as a fleshly and mortal inmate of the temporal creation, he nevertheless considers that verbal signs may manifest a rational order and that though it is manifested in words as material things, such order transcends the materiality of speech and thereby becomes pleasing to the soul. Such is the case with poetic language. Poetry as form is the art of the muses, or music, and music is the art that teaches how to measure sounds well (*musica est scientia bene modulandi*).[15] Just as a beautiful building pleases us by the harmony of its proportions, which architects call *ratio* (a term that translates the Greek *logos*), so too poetic language displays movements that are properly measured and have a similar capacity to delight us.[16] However, the

14. St. Augustine, *De catechizandis rudibus*, ii.3. Reference is to the Benedictine edition as published in *Oeuvres de saint Augustin: Le magistère chrétien*, Bibliothèque augustinienne, vol. 11, ed. and French trans. G. Combès and M. Farges (Paris: Desclée de Brouwer, 1949), English translation mine; hereafter referred to as *De cat.* in my text.

15. St. Augustine, *De musica libri sex*. I.ii. Reference is to the Benedictine edition as published in *Oeuvres de Saint Augustin: Dialogues philosophiques IV*, Bibliothèque augustinienne, vol. 7, ed. and French trans. Guy Finnaert and F. J. Thonnard (Paris: Desclée de Brouwer, 1947); cited hereafter as *De mus.*

16. St. Augustine, *De ordine* II.vi.34, ed. and trans. Robert P. Russell, *Divine Providence and the Problem of Evil* (New York: Cosmopolitan Science and Art Service, 1942), 139; Henceforth referred to as *De ord.* in my text.

truth of poetry is in its form, not its content: "Our praise of the meter is one thing, our praise of the meaning [*sententia*] is something else" (*De ord.* II.xi.34). The art of poets is therefore that of giving order to speech, and hence is the "power of lying reasonably" (*rationabilim mendaciorum potestas; De ord.* II.xiv.40). The capacity of music to integrate several voices into a harmonic whole is the very model of civic order as well, and on this point Augustine cites Cicero's *De republica*:

> As, among the different sounds which proceed from lyres,
> flutes, and the human voice, there must be maintained a cer-
> tain harmony which a cultivated ear cannot endure to hear dis-
> turbed or jarring, but which may be elicited in full and
> absolute concord by the modulation even of voices very unlike
> one another; so when reason is allowed to modulate the di-
> verse elements of the state, there is obtained a perfect concord
> from the upper, lower, and middle classes as from various
> sounds; and what musicians call harmony in singing, is con-
> cord in matters of state, which is the strictest bond and best
> security of any republic, and which by no ingenuity can be
> retained where justice has become extinct.[17]

Poetic form originates in the foot, which is the basis of meter, and which is composed of short and long syllables. These have a ratio of $1:2$, and this ratio not only corresponds to the relationship between God and the creation but is the basis of "what the Greeks call 'harmony'" (*De trin.* IV.ii.4). This abstract dimension of poetic language is distinct from the terrain of jurisdiction proper to the grammarian. For the rules of the grammarian that determine the lengths of syllables are tied up with the history of the language, and they rest strictly upon authority (*De mus.* II.i.1). By contrast, the actual metrical proportions of poetic line are universal and hence beyond all temporal authority. Though poetry, as language, is corporeal movement and is among the lowest of beauties because "its parts cannot all exist simultaneously,"[18]

---

17. St. Augustine, *De civitate dei* II.xxi, trans. Marcus Dods, *The City of God* (New York: Random House, 1950), 60–61; hereafter referred to as *De civ. Dei* in my text.

18. St. Augustine, *De vera religione* xxi.41, trans. Louis O. Mink, *On True Religion* (South Bend, Ind.: Regnery/Gateway, 1959), 37–38. Henceforth referred to as *De vera rel.* in my text.

yet poetry is capable of manifesting, in time, an order that is not itself temporal:

> A line of poetry is beautiful in its own way though no two syllables can be spoken at the same time. The second cannot be spoken until the first is finished. So in due order the end of the line is reached. When the last syllable is spoken the previous ones are not heard at the same time, and yet along with the preceding ones it makes the form and metrical arrangement complete. (*De vera rel.* xxii.42)

Thus, the *art* of poetry is an ideal distinct from composed poetry, and even more distinct from the actual succession of sounds in the uttered poetic line. Since the art of poetry derives from a purely spiritual competence, such ideal art can only be compromised by the actual performance in material language:

> The art of versifying is not subject to change with time as if its beauty was made up of measured quantities. It possesses, at one and the same time, all the rules for making the verse which consists of successive syllables of which later ones follow those which had come earlier. In spite of this the verse is beautiful as exhibiting the faint traces of the beauty which the art of poetry keeps steadfastly and unchangeably. (*De vera rel.* xxii.42)

Augustine scorns as "perverse" those who prefer the materiality of poetry itself over the *unperformed* rules of art by which poetry is made:

> Some perverse persons prefer a verse to the art of versifying, because they set more store by their ears than by their intelligence. So many love temporal things and do not look for divine providence which is the maker and governor of time. Loving temporal things they do not want the things they love to pass away. They are just as absurd as anyone would be who, when a famous poem was being recited, wanted to hear one single syllable all the time. (*De vera rel.* xxii.43)

Augustine's extremism here may seem a bit fanciful, but it is a springboard for a daring analogy between the temporal process of the recited poem and the temporality of history. It is easy for us, he says, to grasp and judge the totality of a poem, because we are not part of that poem.

However, because of original sin, we labor as part of history; hence we are not able to stand apart from it and grasp its totality:

> There is no one who cannot easily hear a whole verse or even a whole poem; but there is no one who can grasp the whole order of the ages. Besides, we are not involved as parts in a poem, but for our sins we are made to be parts of the secular order. The course of history is made up of our labors. (*De vera rel.* xxii.43)

Man labors, then, in a poem of history that he cannot read as a whole. Nevertheless, God has disposed the *logos* of history as a set of rhetorical oppositions based on the opposition of good and evil,

> thus embellishing the course of the ages, as if it were an exquisite poem set off with antitheses. For what are called antitheses are among the most elegant of ornaments of speech. . . . As, then, the oppositions of contraries lend beauty to the language, so the beauty of the course of this world is achieved by the opposition of contraries, arranged, as it were, by an eloquence not of words, but of things. (*De civ. Dei* II.xxiii)

The Creation, then, is a region of difference (*regio dissimilitudinis*) in more than one sense: not only is it absolutely different from a God who may not be known except through Christ and by the *via negativa*, but the temporal creation is always different from itself. Angels, by contrast, inhabit a spiritual realm where there is no difference and where they understand God's *logos* as a discourse proffered without syllables, without syntax, and without enigma: "They always behold your face, and, without any syllables of time, they read upon it what your eternal will decrees" (*Conf.* XIII.xv.18).

How can we presume to pass from the lower beauties of poetry and music (or of things) to the highest? This question preoccupied Augustine in the final book of *De musica.* Having given an exhaustive (and exhausting) inventory of metrical combinations, both actual and possible, in Latin, Augustine suddenly turns to the epistemological dimensions of poetic beauty. The harmony (*numeri*) produced by the movement of corporeal things is the lowest manifestation in a hierarchy of harmonies. First, then, there is the harmony (*numeri*) of sounds (*sonantes*) produced by physical bodies; second, there is the harmony that is heard by the ear (*occursores*); third, there is the harmony that is proffered (*progressores*), which is actually produced by an activity of the soul from within; fourth, there is the harmony of memory (*recordabiles*), which is either imprinted a priori on the memory or retained by it. Finally, there is the harmony of judgment (*iudicales*), which is that ultimate, innate capacity for man to admire or to reject what is beautiful or ugly (*De mus.* VI.x.28). Although this latter harmony is superior to all the others, it is nevertheless activated by corporeal harmony. This enjoyment by the soul of lower rhythms manifested through and in the body is a consequence of man's original sin, after which the soul became subject to bodily passions (*De mus.* VI.xi.33). Degrading though this may seem to the soul, rhythm and harmony in the body are not in themselves bad, even if the body itself is the soul's prison. To the contrary, all harmonies—within the soul or without—are only manifestations of a universal harmony called reason (*ratio*), and this harmony transcends all others (*De mus.* VI.xi.33). All other harmonies derive from this timeless harmony of reason:

> There, there is no time, for there is no mutability; from there come all times which are formed [*fabricantur*], ordered, and regulated [*modificantur*], like an imitation of eternity, as the revolution of the sky returns to the same point and brings back to the same point the celestial bodies, obeying, by means of days, months, years, and lights, and other astral movements, the laws of equivalence, unity and order. Thus, the things of the earth are subjected to those of the heavens, and by the harmonious succession of their times they associate their movements with a kind of poem of the universe. (*De mus.* VI.xi.29)

Augustine's treatise on music soars into a truly magnificent neoplatonic praise of the "One" and of "He who, alone, proceeded from the One and who is united to the One in Charity," thereby setting spiritual goals for the lovers of poetry and song which invite them, finally, to repudiate their art as we commonly understand it. By moving so dramatically beyond a very mechanical study of metrics to the realm of vibrant spiritual ecstasy, Augustine expressed attitudes toward the body of poetic language that were doubled by his political ideology, opposing the body politic of the city of man to the transcendent city of God. Augustine's hostility toward performed music very nearly carried him to censure even liturgical music, on the grounds that its very beauty, which pleases the body, can easily seduce the mind away from the sacred eloquence that is its very soul (*Conf.* X.xxxiii.49). He did, however, concede that because of some "secret familiarity" (*occulta familiaritate*) between music and the soul, liturgical music should be at least tolerated in church (*Conf.* X.xxxiii.49).

Although Augustine's treatise on music is really a treatise on metrics, its spiritual orientation was similar to that of Boethius, who considered the true musician a speculator and a judge, not a performer:

> Thus there are three classes concerned with the musical art. One class has to do with instruments, another invents songs, a third judges the work of instruments and the song. But that class which is dedicated to instruments and there consumes its entire efforts, as for example the players of the cithara and those who show their skill on the organ and other musical instruments, are separated from the intellect of musical science, since they are servants, as has been said, nor do they bear anything of reason, being wholly destitute of speculation. The second class having to do with music is that of the poets, which is borne to song not so much by speculation and reason as by a certain natural instinct. Thus this class also is to be separated from music. The third is that which assumes the skill of judging, so that it weighs rhythms and melodies and the whole of song. And seeing that the whole is founded in reason and speculation, this class is rightly reckoned as musical, and that man as musician who possesses the faculty of judging, according to speculation or reason, appropriate and suitable to music, of modes and rhythms and of the classes of melodies and their mixtures and of all those things about which there is to be discussion later on and of the songs of the poets.[19]

Together with Boethius (and also with Cassiodorus and others), Augustine implanted in the Western consciousness an esthetics of transcendence that haunted medieval poets of every major genre, as we shall see in the chapters to follow. Medieval poetry is an art whose status as the embodiment of beauty in temporal language was a conse-

---

19. Boethius, *De institutione musica* I.33, ed. Gottfried Friedlein (Leipzig: Teubner 1967), trans. Oliver Strunk, in *Source Readings in Music History: Antiquity and the Middle Ages* (New York: Norton, 1950), 86. I have repunctuated one of Strunk's sentences for the sake of coherence.

quence of chosen *dissimilitudo* from the *logos*, and therefore from God as the only proper object of human love and understanding. We shall also see, in the final chapter of this book, that the Humanist challenge to this particular strain of Augustinianism constituted an important cultural threshold marking the end of a certain medieval poetics of transcendence—though not the end, to be sure, of Augustinianism itself.

CHAPTER 3

Roland and Charlemagne:
The Remembering
Voices and the Crypt

> **T**he science of grammar [gram-
> matica] might now have been complete, except that since by its very
> name it claims to profess letters (whence in Latin it is called "litera-
> ture"), it came to pass that whatever was committed to letters as
> worth remembering necessarily pertained to it. And so history, whose
> name is one, but whose subject matter is unlimited, multiple, and
> fuller of cares than of enjoyment or truth, was added to this disci-
> pline, though it is more burdensome to grammarians than to histo-
> rians themselves. (St. Augustine, *De ordine*)

Throughout its history, medieval culture as we know it granted special
importance to the faculty of memory, in both theory and social practice. My purpose in this chapter is to show how this privileging of
memory determines the *Chanson de Roland*, whether as a deep narrative paradigm according to which reality is ordered and understood,
or as a system of ethical values expressed at the surface of events in
that poem.

I shall also show how, in the second half of the *Roland*, we may discern a radical disruption of its commemorative paradigm and of its
ethics, and I shall evoke some of the cultural forces—among them,
writing—that may have contributed to this disruption.

By "commemoration" I mean any gesture, ritualized or not, whose
end is to invoke, in the name of a social group, some remembered
essence or event that is either anterior in time or ontologically prior to
what is present, in order to animate, fecundate, mark, or celebrate

some moment in the present. Commemoration revitalizes or redeems whatever in the world or in the self has become merely corporeal, deficient, and vacant of meaning.

Christianity, especially Augustinian neoplatonism, is founded on a theology of memory and on commemorative rituals of the purest sort. Its Eucharist is centered upon the gestures of a Son recalling men to his Father on the eve of his crucifixion by breaking his bread and exhorting his apostles thus: "This is my body, which is given for you; do this in remembrance of me" (*in meam commemorationem*; Luke 22:19). In the story of Christ's return to men after his resurrection, his disciples will be unable to *know* Christ until they *remember* him as he breaks bread and eats fishes amongst them (Luke 24).

As one may infer from the two previous chapters, St. Augustine was the principal renewer of classical, specifically neoplatonic, theories of memory in the Christian West. Augustine held that all understanding is recollection. Just as words cannot signify unless their significations are previously known, so teachers cannot teach true things, but can only remind their pupils of what they already know.[1] Intelligible things (*res intelligibiles*) are spiritual things that exist immutably and timelessly in the mind of God, but man can truly know intelligible things in his own mind through divine illumination, which transpires in the memory, in concert with the actions of intellect and will. The triple operation of the soul (memory, intellect, and will) corresponds to the triune nature of God himself, with the faculty of memory being the analogue of the Father, the intellect the analogue of the Son, and the will that of the Holy Spirit.[2] To return to memory is to return to the Father.

Already in classical antiquity it was understood that acts of recollection are complex: how, it was asked, does some object embedded in the memory relate to the object or situation stimulating its recall in the present? Aristotle claimed that retrieval occurs by three types of mental association: similarity, contiguity, and opposition.[3] Hence, the operations of memory are essentially tropological, and this rhetorical dimension of memory leads very naturally into Aristotle's theory of tragic recognition (*anagnoresis*).

1. St. Augustine, *De magistro*, x, xiv.
2. St. Augustine, *De trinitate* XV.xxii.42.
3. Aristotle *De memoria et reminiscentia* 451b18. For a useful analysis of this treatment and a translation, see Richard Sorabji, *Aristotle on Memory* (London: Duckworth, 1972), 1–46.

Following the rediscovery of Aristotle, the scholastics continued to speculate actively about man's faculty of memory. Indeed, Aristotle's *De anima* and his *De memoria et reminiscentia* were major catalysts for speculation about memory in the thirteenth century, especially by Albertus Magnus and Thomas Aquinas.[4] That recollection should involve contrariety is a notion that has been amplified in modern times as a theory of repression. Freud held that the passage of an image from the unconscious to the conscious system and into language involves acts of substitution and changes of valence: such is the transforming process of repression in our mental economy.[5] A violent dialectics of repression and recollection may be perceived, according to Freud, in the Eucharist itself. Freud considered Christ's sacrifice as the transformation of a more primal but still unresolved act of violence against the Father:

> If the Son of God was obliged to sacrifice his life to redeem mankind from original sin, then by the law of the talion, the requital of like for like, that sin must have been a killing, a murder. Nothing else could call for the sacrifice of life in expiation. And if the original sin was an offense against God the Father, the primal crime of mankind must have been a parricide, the killing of the primal father of the primitive horde, whose image in memory was later transformed into a deity.[6]

However, if the process of recollection tends to be articulated by images of violence, such violence may stem not only from ambivalence toward the substance of what is being recollected but also from the very necessities of the mnemonic process itself. As Frances Yates has shown, it was customary for orators, from classical antiquity to the Renaissance, to memorize a speech either by metonymically linking those elements to be retrieved from memory with physical objects located in the orator's immediate presence during the performance, or else by imagining some spatial scene whose details were made as vivid as possible through effects of violence and the grotesque so as to sum-

4. J. Castonguay, O.P., *Psychologie de la mémoire: Sources et doctrine de la memoria chez saint Thomas d'Aquin* (Montreal: Éditions du lévrier, 1963).

5. Sigmund Freud, "Repression," trans. Cecil M. Baines, in *Collected Papers* (London: Hogarth Press, 1957), 4:84–97.

6. Sigmund Freud, "Thoughts on War and Death," trans. E. Colburn Mayne, in *Collected Papers* (London: Hogarth Press, 1957), 4:309.

mon up more easily the points the orator intended to expose.[7] Violence may be seen not only as the "subject" of oral epic narrative, but also as an *aide-mémoire* or as a generative force in the production of such narrative. In a commemorative culture, events of violence (sacrifices, circumcisions, tortures, crucifixions, burnings, etc.) are given great prominence so that the collective memory will be duly impressed with the *pathos* of "history" as it is deployed: violence as semiosis. If the *Odyssey* ends in joyous reconciliations of husband to wife and of fathers to sons, it also ends with a violent, exemplary massacre from which only a bard and a herald are spared, for it is they who will remember and speak in the future.

In a commemorative culture such as that of early Greece or of the Middle Ages, the voice of the "oral" poet is not that of an autonomous, reasoning, individual subjectivity; rather, the "truth" of the oral performance occurs as an invasion of the soul by some divine power residing either outside of time or at its origin. As Jean-Pierre Vernant has written:

> Mnemosyne presides, as is well known, over the poetic process. It was obvious for the Greeks that such a process demanded a supernatural intervention. Poetry is one of the typical forms of divine possession and rapture: it is the state of "enthusiasm," in the etymological sense of that word. Possessed by the Muses, the poet is the interpreter of Mnemosyne, just as the god-inspired prophet is the interpreter of Apollo. . . . The bard and the diviner have in common a single gift of "vision," a privilege that they have paid for with their eyes. Blind to light, they see the invisible. The god who inspires them reveals those realities that escape the sight of

7. Frances A. Yates, *The Art of Memory* (London: Routledge & Kegan Paul, 1966), ch. 1. Among other studies of memory in classical thought, especially in connection with poetry, the following have been useful: Eric A. Havelock, *Preface to Plato* (Cambridge, Mass.: Harvard Univ. Press, 1963), esp. pt. 1; Jean-Pierre Vernant, *Mythe et pensée chez les grecs* (Paris: Maspero, 1965), esp. ch. 2, "Aspects mythiques de la mémoire," 51–78; Bennet Simon and Herbert Weiner, "Models of Mind and Mental Illness in Ancient Greece: 1. The Homeric Model of Mind," *Journal of the History of the Behavioral Sciences* 2 (1966): 303–14; Marcel Détienne, *Les maîtres de vérité dans la Grèce archaïque* (Paris: Maspero, 1967); Berkeley Peabody, *The Winged Word* (Albany: State Univ. of New York Press, 1975). I wish to express my gratitude to Professors Joseph Russo, Vernant, and Détienne who, as colleagues in the past, have generously shared their knowledge with me on this subject.

ordinary men. It is a twin vision that bears in particular upon those parts of time inaccessible to mortals: what once was, what has yet to come. . . . In contrast to the diviner, who must usually answer for the future, the activity of the poet is oriented almost exclusively toward the past. Not his individual past, nor a past generalized as if it were an empty framework independent of the events that have occurred there, but "ancient time" with its own contents and qualities: a heroic age or, still further, a primordial age, the origin of time.[8]

Vernant also underscores the link between memory and resurrection in early Greek culture, an important point for our understanding of the resurrection of Roland. Not only does memory provide a bridge between the individual in time and previous incarnations of his being, but memory becomes the means by which the soul is liberated from time altogether and united with the divine.

Plato describes the psychology of the oral performance in some detail. As Socrates says to a rhapsode who performs the Homeric poems from memory:

This gift you have of speaking well on Homer is not an art; it is a power divine, impelling you like the power in the stone . . . which most call "stone of Heraclea." This stone does not simply attract the iron rings, just by themselves; it also imparts to the rings a force enabling them to do the same thing as the stone itself, that is, to attract another ring, so that sometimes a chain is formed, quite a long one, of iron rings, suspended from one another. For all of them, however, their power depends on that loadstone. Just so the Muse. She first makes men inspired and then through these inspired ones others share in the enthusiasm, and a chain is formed . . . a poet is a light and winged thing, and holy, and never able to compose until he has become inspired, and is beside himself, and reason is no longer in him. So long as he has this reason in his possession, no man is able to make poetry or to chant in prophecy. . . . Herein lies the reason why the deity has bereft these poets of their sense . . . in order that we listeners may

8. Vernant, 53, 73–75. Unless specified otherwise, translations in this chapter are my own.

know that it is not they who utter these precious revelations while their mind is not within them, but that it is the god himself who speaks, and through them becomes articulate to us.[9]

In the oral performance, then, poet, hero, and audience re-create each other in a common, phonic space; yet their presence to each other is consummated only in a magnetic alignment, through speech, with some anterior, originary, sacred presence. As is the case with the *Iliad*, the *Roland* grounds its plausibility in the genealogical consciousness of its audience,[10] since it is presumed that at least some of the twelve peers and the names in the chronicle of Christian warriors in the Baligant episode could be identified as distant ancestors of its twelfth-century listeners.

We have relatively few documents from the Middle Ages which capture the epistemic process of oral epic discourse, yet the following statement by Jean de Grouchy insists precisely on the regenerative effect of oral narrative upon a community of laborers and humble people who have been beaten down by their daily tasks and routines, yet who are revived in a collective regression into "our" heroic past:

> We call a *chanson de geste* that in which the deeds of heroes
> and of our ancient fathers are recited, such as the lives and
> martyrdoms of saints and the adversities that beset men of old
> for the Faith and for Truth. . . . Moreover, this song must be
> administered to the old people, to the laboring folk, and to
> those of humble condition, so that by hearing miseries and ca-
> lamities of others they may bear more easily their own and so
> that their own travails may become lighter. And thus this song
> brings about the conservation [*conservatio*] of the whole
> community.[11]

Although we lack testimony contemporaneous with vernacular medieval epic that might inform us about "what it was like" to perform or

9. Plato *Ion* 533d–534d, trans. Lane Cooper in *The Collected Dialogues of Plato*, ed. E. Hamilton and H. Cairns (New York: Pantheon, 1961), 219–20.

10. Vernant, 55–56. On genealogy as a model of medieval narrative, see R. Howard Bloch, *Etymologies and Genealogies: A Literary Anthropology of the French Middle Ages* (Chicago: Chicago Univ. Press, 1983), esp. chs. 2, 3.

11. Jean de Grouchy, *De musica*, in "Die Musiklehre des Johannes de Grocheo," ed. J. Wolf, *Sammelbände der internationalen Musikgesellschaft* 1 (1899): 90.13.

to hear a *chanson de geste,* we may find in the story of the *Chanson de Roland* itself abundant reflections of the cultural functions of oral epic in general, and of a problematic of memory in particular. Hence, let us now consider certain narrative features of the *Chanson de Roland* as they reflect the mode—rather, the modes—of production that brought this poem (as we now know it) into existence.[12] If we may suppose that the basic function of communication is to make experience intelligible, we may suppose that high in priority of experience to be made intelligible is that of communication itself. We may suggest, in other words, that both the form and content of myth and legend tend to be chosen for and shaped by their mode of dissemination. Thus, if memory is the principal means of preserving sacred history in oral discourse, reciprocally, history in oral discourse serves to consecrate the faculty of memory. Inversely, when writing intervenes in an oral poetics, new priorities are dictated by what Brian Stock calls "textual communities."[13]

Though the *Chanson de Roland* has been considered, since the Romantic age, as being among the most "historical" of epic poems,[14] one may also propose that it is as much a drama of memory as it is a memory of a historical drama. We shall explore later the consequences of the following glaring paradox: if the *Roland* was an "oral" poem, it is nevertheless accessible to us now only as a corpus of written texts, which is to say that a system of writing has already intervened in the process of selection, composition, and transmission of its material.

Nothing definite is known about what we commonly call the "origins" of the *Chanson de Roland* (e.g., who composed it? when? where?), but we may be certain that the Oxford version of the poem as we now possess it is a coagulation of disparate narrative materials that once

12. Rather than dealing with the technical aspects of oral formulaic language in the *Roland* I shall mention several studies that bear upon the question: Jean Rychner, *La Chanson de geste: Essai sur l'art épique des jongleurs* (Geneva: Droz, 1955); Stephen G. Nichols, Jr., *Formulaic Diction and Thematic Composition in the "Chanson de Roland"* (Chapel Hill: Univ. of North Carolina Press, 1961); Joseph J. Duggan, The *"Song of Roland": Formulaic Style and Poetic Craft* (Berkeley: Univ. of California Press, 1973); Ruth Finnegan, *Oral Poetry: Its Nature, Significance and Social Context* (Cambridge: Cambridge Univ. Press, 1977); Paul Zumthor, *Introduction à la poésie orale* (Paris: Seuil, 1983).

13. Brian Stock, *The Implications of Literacy: Written Language and Models of Interpretation in the Eleventh and Twelfth Centuries* (Princeton, N.J.: Princeton Univ. Press, 1983), ch. 2.

14. Cf. Ramon Menéndez Pidal, *La Chanson de Roland et la tradition épique des Francs,* French trans. Irénée-Marcel Cluzel (Paris: Picard, 1960), esp. 481.

propagated themselves (whether separately or together) in oral performances, during which the poetic spirit and its heroes would continually be reborn together, thanks to the memory and the song of the poet summoned forth by his audience.[15] Obviously, the legends and myths from which the *Roland* draws its substance had to be compatible enough with the medium of oral production to be both conservable and renewable in oral discourse through the ages. Thus, exactly as in the *Iliad* and the *Odyssey*, the heroes of the *Roland* speak in the same metrical formulas as the poet; they employ the same epithets, they rehearse the same lists, and they even share his dark foreknowledge of events.

The fact that these heroes live only by the memory and the voice of the poet compels, in other words, a solid cognitive congruence between them, and in the *Roland* this congruence becomes evident in the very motivation that the poet imputes to the heroes themselves. For if it is the antique glory of the hero that animates here and now the voice and the gestures of the poet, reciprocally, it is the commemorative posterity of the future singer's voice that inspires the epic blows of the hero on the battlefield. Thus, as the pagans and Franks gird up for combat, Roland exhorts his peers to wield their swords so as to become the *matière* for future *chansons de geste*, and by his own *essample* Roland constitutes himself as the "author" of the future poem that will celebrate his memory:

> Or guart chascuns que granz colps i empleit,
> Que malvaise cançun de nus chantet ne seit! . . .
> Malvaise essample n'en serat ja de mei. AOI.[16]

> (Now let each man take care to deal great blows,
> Lest a bad song be sung of us! . . .
> A bad example shall never be made of me.)

Yet, as in Plato's magnetic chain, Roland is acting not in his own individual name but in the greater name of Charlemagne, his lord, to whom he has sworn absolute allegiance at the expense of his own flesh:

15. In the discussion that follows, I draw freely on my book *Reading the "Song of Roland"* (Englewood Cliffs, N.J.: Prentice-Hall, 1970), and on a subsequent article, "Roland, Charlemagne, and the Poetics of Illumination," *Olifant* 6 (1979): 20–23.

16. *Chanson de Roland* vv. 1013–16. All quotations are from the Gérard Moignet edition (Paris: Bordas, 1980); subsequent references are included in my text.

Ben devuns ci estre pur nostre rei:
Pur sun seignor deit nom susfrir destreiz
E endurer e granz chalz e granz freiz,
Sin deit hom perdre e del quir e del peil.
(vv. 1009–12)

(We must indeed stay here for our king.
For his lord a vassal must suffer distress
And endure great heat and great cold,
And a vassal must lose both hair and hide.)

And Charlemagne too is acting, his legend holds, as a *vicarius Christi*, just as Christ as Son is sent by the Father, the greatest Other. However, such actions by someone always in the name of some transcendent "Other" involve, in each instance, some kind of violence and mutilation: Christ will die on the cross; Roland will burst his temples calling Charlemagne with his horn; by serving God in Spain, Charlemagne will lose in Roland his "right hand." This is the sacrificial violence of self-effacement before the transcendent Other which transpires in the psychosomatic process of collective commemoration itself.

Put differently, the dialectic of self-assertion and deference that underlies the oral performance tends to restage itself *within* the narrative world of the poem as specific configurations in the relationships of characters, whether to each other or to the physical world in which they move. Such a configuration informs the *Roland* from the start: the Franks have fought in Spain for seven years, an expanse of time easily understood in the Middle Ages as a synecdoche for all the travails of temporal existence. Despite the triumphs of the moment, the Franks are weary of the war and nostalgic for "sweet France," the terrestrial (and political) seat of God's presence among men. Blancandrin, the Saracen ambassador to the council of the victorious Franks, promotes the false peace proposals of the Saracens by exploiting the acute nostalgia of the Franks for their homeland (vv. 134–36), but the very topographical location of Roncevaux makes these feelings of nostalgia much more explicit. Situated in the mountains midway between Spain and France, Roncevaux serves as a threshold of intense recollections for the war-weary Franks who now contemplate their homeland: recollections of abundance, security, and appeased desires. The tantalizing proximity of France is all the more poignant in that a violent (and foreknown) tragedy separates the Franks from their longed-for sabbath:

Puis que il venent a la Tere Majur,
  Virent Guascuigne, la tere lur seignur;
  Dunc lur remembret des fius e des honurs,
  E des pulcele e des gentilz oixurs:
  Cel nen i ad ki de pitet ne plurt.
  (vv. 818–22)

(When they came to the Tere Majur,
  They saw Gascony, the land of their lords.
  Then they remembered their fiefs and their possessions,
  And their maidens, and their noble wives;
  There's not a one who does not weep for pity.)

The passage through Roncevaux stirs up special anguish in Charlemagne, who is already remembering (and grieving for) a Roland destined never to return. Given that Charlemagne is the most powerful
man in the world, why, we may ask, does he not act—or even speak—
in such a way as to alter the course of events? Such foreknowledge is a
condition of that fatalistic, cognitive homology between hero, oral poet,
and audience in which the prophesied future is seen and understood by
all to be as necessary and as irreversible as the remembered past:

Sur tuz les altres est Carles anguissus:
  As porz d'Espaigne ad lesset sun nevold.
  Pitet l'en prent, ne poet muer n'en plurt. AOI. . . .
  Carles li magnes ne poet muer n'en plurt.
  .C. milie Francs pur lui unt grant tendrur
  E de Rollant merveilluse poür.
  Guenes li fels en ad fait traïsun.
  (vv. 823–25; 841–44)

(Among all the others, Charles is most anguished.
  He has left his nephew at the edge of Spain.
  Pity seizes him; he cannot help weeping. . . .
  Charles the great cannot help weeping.
  One hundred thousand Franks show their great tenderness;
  And for Roland they feel strange fear.
  Ganelon the traitor has betrayed them.)

Though as an epic hero, Roland no doubt appealed to medieval audiences on more than one political or ideological score, it may also be
shown that he embodies, in his reflexes and actions, what we may call
an exalted ethics of memory.

Indeed, the ethical dimension of Roland's memorial "logic" is evident from the very moment he appears in the poem. Blancandrin, one will recall, has just delivered Marsile's treacherous proposals to Charlemagne, who now submits the issue, as a good feudal lord must, to the council of his barons. Roland is the first to speak out, and he initiates his speech with a formulaic recital of his previous conquests as Charlemagne's agent: *"Je vos conquis e Noples e Commibles . . ."* (v. 198). Roland's achievements in the past, in other words, entirely determine the validity of his argument in the present. Then, Roland reinforces his a priori opinion with the *exempla*, likewise drawn from the collective memory of the past, of Basan and Basile, two knights who had previously been sent as emissaries to the Saracens—at the price of their heads. Thus, counsels Roland, "Pursue the war as you began it." Whether Roland is also motivated by an excess of zeal or by outright pride, we of the audience know by our privileged perspective upon the Saracens' intentions that Roland, the champion of the *idée reçue*, is "historically" right because of what he remembers so clearly and well.

Ganelon's memory, by contrast, is less acute: eloquent, a good rhetorician, this future traitor persuades the Frankish barons that the present appearance of things suffices as proof that it would be a "sin" to continue the war. Seduced by Ganelon's speech, the Duke of Naimes, ordinarily a paragon of good sense among the Franks, corroborates Ganelon's counsel. "The Duke has spoken well," exclaims the assembly of barons; but the destructive import of their judgment is obvious on more than one level: the rhetoric of appeasement is subversive not only in ethical terms but in artistic terms as well, for without a war, there can be no *chanson de geste*. Courageous though he is, Ganelon embodies a dangerous combination of features: he is a rhetorician, a liar, a traitor, a negotiator of false peace, and a proponent, in germ, of mercantilism and exchange. Ganelon also has a propensity for spinning lies that are gratuitous, fabulous, and even strikingly poetic (e.g., vv. 381–91; 1780–82). The subversive side of Ganelon, like that of his pagan cohorts in conspiracy, always seems to lead him, in one manner or another, to dislocate the signifiers from their natural or proper signifieds, thereby compromising language as a vehicle of proper retrospection. In an ethics of memory, forgetfulness is fatal, and memory is the key to eternal life.

Once Roland and the twelve peers have been named to command the rearguard, a new dilemma arises: in view of the magnitude of the pagan forces, should the Franks summon the aid of Charles? Perhaps because Oliver is a more recent interpolation into the nuclear legend of Roland[17] and is accordingly detached from the archaic commemorative ethic that commands its principal figure, Oliver accepts the empirical evidence of the pagan masses before his own eyes as moral justification for sounding the alarm. Oliver is a champion not of memory and of will but of inductive *judgment* that derives from what is *perceived* in the present, knowledge which has objective truth and which can be treated rationally and even be communicated. Oliver's impulses to act and speak arise from within his own psyche, and are not dictated from without: *"E lui meisme en est mult esguaret"* (Within himself he is very distressed; v. 1036). By contrast, for Roland, true knowledge is always a priori, and language is the codification of a truth that is anterior to the present and immutable. Perhaps it is a generality that as a generative force in narrative plots, the ethics of memory tends to favor creatures of will who engage in relationships of irrational force with whomever or whatever is present; their dominant sentiments tend to oscillate between hatred and nostalgia, and they are often motivated by a spirit of revenge. The ethics of the heroic memory seems to preclude negotiation, exchange, or even communication; its judicial equivalent is the judicial duel, and its economic equivalent seems to be the cult of the hoard. In the relationship between Roland and Oliver, an epistemological cleavage erupts that is soon smothered by the course of events in this poem, yet it is one that will have further ramifications in the intellectual disputes of the decades to follow, such as that between Bernard of Clairvaux and Peter Abelard.

Though Roland invokes against Oliver's more rational empiricism the "good" vassal's unreasoning obligation to obey the earlier orders of his lord Charlemagne at any cost, Roland himself is not beyond reproach. And if his initial display of idealism is founded upon a rectitude of memory, inversely, his pride subsequently manifests itself as a wilful forgetting. Roland will not tolerate Oliver's recalling Ganelon's earlier threats and the gesture—the dropped glove—that portended Ganelon's treason:

> —Tais, Oliver! li quens Rollant respunt
> Mis parrastre est, ne voeill que mot en suns—
> (vv. 1026–27)

17. Menéndez Pidal, 487–91.

("Quiet, Oliver!" Count Roland replies.
"He is my stepfather: say no further word.")

A few lines later, however, once the battle is certain to be engaged,
Roland himself confirms what Oliver and everyone else know but what
Roland has until now wrongly suppressed:

Li quens Rollant apelet Oliver:
"Sire cumpainz, mult ben le saviez
Que Guenelun nos ad tuz espïez:
Pris en ad or e aveir e deners.
Li emperere nos devreit ben venger.
Li reis Marsilie de nos ad fait marchet;
Mais as espees l'estuvrat esleger." AOI.
(vv. 1145–51)

(Count Roland calls to Oliver:
"Noble friend, you understood it well:
Ganelon has betrayed us all
For gold and wealth and money.
Surely the emperor will avenge us well.
King Marsile bargained for us at the marketplace,
But he will have to procure us with swords.")

From the time the battle begins, the poet makes it clear that a victory on the battlefield is a victory of memory over oblivion. Indeed, no
less for the soldier than for the poet, a moment of heroic glory in battle
culminates in an outcry of the remembering human voice, even on the
threshold of death:

Oliver sent qu'il est a mort nasfret,
De lui venger jamais ne li ert sez.
En la grant presse or i fiert cume ber,
Trenchet cez hanstes e cez escuz buclers
E piez e poinz e seles e costez.
Ki lui veïst Sarrazins desmembrer,
Un mort sur altre geter,
De bon vassal li poüst remembrer
L'enseigne Carle n, i volt mie ublier,
Munjoie escriet e haltement e cler.
(vv. 1965–74)

(Oliver feels that he is wounded to the death.
Never can he avenge himself enough.
In the great horde he strikes like a true baron,
He cleaves apart these spears and those shields,
And feet and fists, and saddles and ribs.
Whoever could have seen him dismember Saracens,
Hurling one dead man upon one another,
Would be able to remember a good vassal.
He never wants to forget Charles's ensign.
"Mountjoy!" he cries, loud and clear.)

Time and again the warriors in the poem express the commemorative impulse that spontaneously converts the splendor of violence into epic song. As Oliver exhorts his men to fight and remember, we clearly hear the contrapuntal voices of soldier and poet:

"Seignors baruns, el camp vos retenez!
Pur Deu vos pri, ben seiez purpensez
De colps ferir, de receivre e duner!
L'enseigne Carle n' i devum ublier."
A icest mot sunt Françeis escrïet.
Ki donc oïst Munjoie demander,
De vasselage li poüst remembrer.
(vv. 1176–82)

("Lords, Barons, hold your ground!
In God's name I pray you, take care
To strike good blows, to take and to give them!
We must not forget Charles's ensign."
Upon this word the French cried out.
Whoever could hear them cry "Mountjoy,"
That man would remember the deeds of a good vassal.)

The closer Roland approaches to the moment of his death, the more the action of the poem tends toward pure commemoration. Almost surreptitiously, an unmistakable substitution of priorities takes place as a heroics of memory displaces a heroics of the sword. Indeed, the commemorative performance will ultimately come to dominate the dramatic surface of its own narrative vehicle. We may observe here the manifestation of a priority that outweighs all others in an oral culture: the need to commemorate. During the final moments of Roland's life, we witness a sharp reversal in the action of mimesis: if the oral poet first imitates the voice and gestures of his heroes, in the end it is the hero who imitates the actions of the poet.

Once all twelve peers but Roland have been killed, he interrupts his heroic struggles and begins to gather up the dead bodies of his companions in order to have them blessed by Archbishop Turpin and to commemorate their heroism with his own poetic voice. *Planctus* and prayer, poet and priest, answer together to the single burden of past and future. The spectacle of the bodies arranged before him, like a dead audience, provokes from Roland a *planctus* and a series of mimetic gestures that are unmistakably those of the poet. The hero at this point is actually imitating the poet, though with this difference—slight, perhaps, in the eyes of a remembering Christian: the audience of dead barons within the poem will not rise again except in heaven. By invoking a history that is sacred in order to stage a paradigm of heroic memory, the first half of the *Roland* in effect consecrates the faculty of memory itself by which that history continues to live.

Roland's final act of communication with the heroic community of the Franks is to sound his horn. Heroic language gives way, here, to the yet purer and more ethereal vocalism of the heroic horn. Roland's hyperbolic strength as a wielder of the sword is now fully devoted to the production of a miraculous, musical voice whose fatal but unspoken message resounds through the mountains a full thirty leagues away. Now the poet brilliantly inflects the binary formula "*Halt sunt li pui e li val tenebrus*" (vv. 814, 1830) by substituting the tragic voice of the horn for the "shadowy valleys":

> Rollant ad mis l'olifan a sa buche,
> Empeint le ben, part grant vertut le sunet.
> Halt sunt li pui e la voiz est mult lunge.
> (vv. 1753–55)

> (Roland has put the olifant to his mouth.
> He grasps it well, and sounds it with great force:
> High are the mountains, and the voice is long.)

Moreover, the foreknown tragedy announced by that voice is instantly heard—rather, remembered and understood. It is appropriate, given the reversal of mimetic roles relating hero and singer of tales in this poem, that Roland should die not from wounds in battle but rather from the total expenditure of himself in the performance of this sublime, musical sound:

> Li quens Rollant, par peine e par anans,
> Par grant dulor sunet sun olifan.
> Par mi la buche en salt fors li cler sancs.
> De sun cervel le temple en est rumpant.
> (vv. 1761–64)

> (Count Roland, with effort and suffering
> Sounds his olifant with great pain.
> Bright blood gushes from his mouth:
> His brains are bursting at the temples.)

And it is also perfectly appropriate that Roland's heroic audience should both hear him, even at great distance, and take new heroic action. Indeed, Charlemagne's men already act as if Roland's future example as a wielder of the sword was a thing of the past:

> N'i ad celoi a l'altre ne parolt:
> "Se veissum Rollant einz qu'il fust mort,
> Ensemble'od lui i durriums grans colps."
> (vv. 1803–06)

> (Not a one does not say to the other,
> "Were we to see Roland before he were dead,
> Together with him, we would strike great blows.")

It is perhaps possible to see the great spatial distance between Roland and his audience as a metaphor for the great distance of time that the poet himself must overcome by making *gestes* remembered from ancient, heroic times live anew in his own performance.

Roland's final moments are spent in solitude, however, and they provide insight into what we might call the psychology of poetic commemoration, at least to the degree that an isolated hero appears to be addressing only himself. But Roland's is hardly a subjective consciousness, because his formulaic recital of past conquests expresses a repertory of historical deeds that belong to his lord Charlemagne and to a collectivity. Thus, after his attempt to break his sword Durendal on a stone, Roland discovers in its imperishability a reminder of the numerous conquests that he himself has made in the past as Charlemagne's vassal. The intrinsic, God-given virtue flashing in Roland's sword, which has now become his silent interlocutor, excites, moreover, a sequence of psychic reflexes that tend toward the eschatological. Durendal, one will recall, was given to Charlemagne by God (through the mediation of an obedient angel), with instructions that Charlemagne should bestow it, in turn, on one of his best captains. Thus, Roland's sword shines with good works that originate, ultimately, with the Father in heaven, and this light now illuminates his memory with true poetic history: the list of conquests that Roland recalls undoubtedly corresponds to the boundaries of Charlemagne's holy empire as they would have been imagined by an epic writer at the beginning of the twelfth century. Each name on Roland's list of conquests must have coincided with a whole epic cycle, and in its aggregate, this list is a capsule expressing the totality of a history that was sacred. Though he would hardly pass for an intellectual hero in cultures to come, in the ambience of epic, Roland has only to recite the list of his conquests to show that he knows (and has done) everything.

If it is true that in a commemorative culture the power to recall is also the power to conquer, then Roland's final reminiscences mark a victory not only over the world but also over himself. Likewise, when the poet succeeds in animating his voice with the true, heroic timbre of ancient times, he has overcome, through memory, the opacity of conventional speech. The violence of combat that carries a hero toward rebirth in the kingdom of the saved is the double of a no less primal struggle to reinvest conventional words and formulas with new life, once again overcoming both inertness and oblivion: by the blows of the hero and the incantations of the poet, a heroic culture endures. And if the Saracens are evil, it is not just because they ambush good Christians; it is also because they forget their own sons given as hostages, because they adore graven images only to forget their god Mohammed, and because, in miming true heroes, they turn the traditional poetic formulas of Christian excellence into shadow, parody, and sham. As their terribly strange, uncanny names suffice to show, the Saracens are emanations of oblivion, obscurity, and nonsense, signifying nothing.

Roland's recognizance of his "own" personal glory expands, through incantation and praise of others whom he loves, into a less and less individualized field of presences—memories of his absent lord Charlemagne and finally of the Great Magnet hidden behind all things. Roland's commemorations become *infinitely* regressive. But such regression cannot occur without a certain violence to the historical self: the more the self languishes for communion with the infinite, the more it must confront and surmount its own material finitude. If the self is to liberate its eternal spirit, the historical body, like all corporeal *visibilia* by which we only dimly see the invisible, must give way. The soul, in other words, must come home from its exile among the multiple and disparate traces that constitute the palpable world but point vaguely beyond themselves to an original, redeeming presence whose eternal, uncreated substance is absolutely different from theirs. Such is the dilemma facing the Christian hero who brings to bear the logic of commemoration upon the obstacle constituted by his corporeal being.

But this is a dilemma for which the Christian religion had remedies, and those remedies also stem from the faculty of memory. Thus, having commemorated the glory of Charlemagne and finally of God, Roland engages in another type of reminiscence, the sacrament of confession (whose discourse is equally formulaic), in which he becomes momentarily present to himself. The transition is clearly signaled in the text:

> De plusurs choses a remembrer li prist,
> De tantes teres cum(e) li bers cunquist,
> De dulce France, des humes de sun lign,
> De Carlemagne, sun seignor, kil nurrit;
> Ne poet muer n'en plurt e ne suspirt.
> *Mais lui meisme ne volt mettre en ubli,*
> Cleimet sa culpe, si priet Deu mercit.
> (vv. 2377–84; italics mine)

> (He began to remember many different things,
> So many lands that he conquered as a good baron,
> And sweet France, and the men of his clan,
> And Charlemagne, his lord, who nourished him;
> He could not restrain himself from weeping and sighing.
> But he does not want to forget himself.
> He confesses his sins and prays to God for mercy.)

By an act of memory, Roland now confesses his sins and succeeds in purging himself of the evil that has kept him a captive of the created and spoken world: here the ritual of commemoration brings not the retrieval of something transcendent but the expulsion of sins degrading to the soul. The self willingly discovers within its own citadel a *pharmakon* whose expulsion eliminates the tragic difference between body and soul, or, more generally (but not more abstractly), the difference between *signans* and *signatum* in a universe of the Word. Having purged himself, then, of evil through a labor of memory, Roland recalls the positive *exempla* of Lazarus and Daniel, of two other mortals in the past who were revived by their faith because they too would not forget God. Thanks again to the ministrations of memory, Roland is now free to quit the vassalage of Charlemagne, his uncle and terrestrial lord, in order to rejoice in an unmediated relationship, *facie ad faciem*, with God the True Father (*Veire Patene*), "who never lies." The first half of the *Chanson de Roland* may be read as an exalted, Christian comedy of memory—and of signs.

However, Roland dies in the middle of the poem, and it is Charlemagne who inherits the bitter consequences of Roland's heroic splendor and who brings into the poem a sharp tragic relief. The *Chanson de Roland* is populated by characters who are perhaps static, yet *our* perspective is not so. To the contrary, with the change from a young hero to an old—Charlemagne is a Roland grown old—many of the formulaic values that seemed so absolute in the poem's first half become deeply equivocal. If it is true that the legend of Roland himself is the most archaic "nucleus" of this epic and that during succeeding eras different characters and episodes (e.g., Oliver, Baligant) were added in order to restore symmetries and to renew interest (scholars of French epic call this process "epic *mouvance*"; Lévi-Strauss calls it *bricolage*), then we may consider the *Roland* as a poem in which history is not *represented* by language but rather inscribed into the semantic material of language itself, understood as the temporalization of meaning. Indeed, the displacement of Roland by Charlemagne as the central protagonist of this epic also carries with it a disruption not only of the fundamental epistemic paradigm immanent in the Roland legend but of its very language as well. It is with this cleavage in mind that we now focus upon the story of Charlemagne.

Except at the moment of his initial joy in victory at the beginning of the *Roland*, Charlemagne is strangely remote from the events that develop around him in the first half of the poem, even though it is a matter of agreement among Christians and Saracens alike that Charlemagne is the most powerful man in the world. Charlemagne's detachment from the present world is expressed most obviously in his two centuries of age, a distance from the glory of warlike youth which no doubt coincided with a twelfth-century audience's sense of their own cultural remoteness from a "heroic" age—the age when oral legend was forged—two or more centuries before. Charlemagne is also strangely undetermined, indecisive even, with regard to Ganelon's dispute with Roland, despite his certainty that Ganelon is a "living devil" and that the strat-

egy of dividing his army into vanguard and rearguard can only result in
the destruction of its best heroes. Charlemagne is also passive with regard to the sinister auguries of his destiny in his dreams: *videmus
nunc per speculum in aenigmate* (1 Cor. 13:12). Finally, Charlemagne
seems especially remote from the *discursive* world around him in
which the younger heroes are so quick to argue, threaten, and boast:

> Li empereres en tint sun chef enclin,
> De sa parole ne fut mie hastifs:
> Sa custume est qu'il parolet a leisir.
> (vv. 139–41)

> (The emperor holds down his head.
> In his words he was never hasty;
> His custom is to speak with deliberation.)

Though Charlemagne's royal detachment inspires a certain awe during the first half of the poem, this same remoteness gives rise, in the
second half, to a perspective that is tragic, one that compels us to question, finally, the adequacy of conventional epic language to deal with
the now equivocal nature of human experience.

As we have seen, Roland is a warrior whose motives and gestures are
profoundly compatible with the ethical values that underlie the formulaic language of his poem, and both hero and poet in the poem's first
half invite us to believe that "meaning" is not something abstract or
objective that we contrive and communicate: rather, we assume it in
our own being; we somatize it as deeds that are words and as words that
are deeds, in accordance with an early sense of the word *hermeneuein*,
so palely served by its translation as *interpretatio*.[18] The more violent
and bloody his deeds, the more easily they may be remembered and
uttered. In Roland's actions, both the language and the values of a commemorative culture find adequate realization, and Roland dies assured
that his heart will live on, after his death, in the rhythms of poetic
song. The formulaic *planctus* that tends to follow episodes of violence
doubles, *within* the universe of the poem, the commemorative function attributed *to* the poem by the community of audience and poet
celebrating, through song, their own common heroic origins.

As a different protagonist, Charlemagne initiates profound disruptions in the coherence of the epic imagination. Not only is Charlemagne

---

18. Jean Pépin, "L'Herméneutique ancienne," *Poétique* 23 (1975): 291–300.

impotent to grasp, except dimly, the prophecies of the future revealed to him in his dreams—much less to alter that future by producing alternative "interpretations" in his words and actions—but he will be incapable of reuniting himself with Roland, his resurrected nephew, his "son" and a carnal link with his own heroic past. Indeed, during the entire second half of the poem, the memory of an absent Roland eclipses (even literally, at one point) all apprehension of the present. Not even the vengeance of Charlemagne over the Saracens ("an eye for an eye" is another type of "commemoration") can recover the splendor of young blood irrevocably lost. Hence, for Charlemagne there can be no triumph in revenge.

To the extent that the heroes of this poem are emanations of a poet's voice apart from which they have no separate existence, it should not surprise us that, along with its new hero, the very language of the *Chanson de Roland* should inscribe into itself—into its very formulas—a kind of subtle nostalgia, during which a present moment *in* speech is experienced as a falling off *from*, a de-composition of, a more splendid heroic discourse that was earlier possible in the universe of this poem. In other words, an anonymous vernacular poem whose language has passed into the realm of *grammatica* is carrying its audience to an awareness, verging on Augustine's as evoked in the previous chapter, of language as temporality.

Such is the case, I would propose, in the narration of Charlemagne's exhaustion in his grief for Roland; for if we look closely at the passages evoking the emperor's grief, we will see that they comprise a sequence of formulas—more precisely, of antiformulas—that systematically reverse the content of those earlier formulaic passages where heroes joyfully take up arms in a brilliant sunlight in preparation for the fatal glee of combat. Consider, first, this earlier *laisse* where the pagan and Frankish forces are poised for attack:

> Paien s'adubent des osbercs sarazineis,
> Tuit li plusur en sunt dublez en treis.
> Lacent lor elmes mult bons, sarraguzeis,
> Ceignent espees de l'acer vianeis;
> Escuz unt genz, espiez valentineis,
> E gunfanuns blancs e blois e vermeilz.
> Laissent les muls e tuz les palefreiz,
> Es destrers muntent, si chevalchent estreiz.
> Clers fut li jurz e bels fut li soleilz;

71

N'unt guarnement que tut ne reflambeit.
Sunent mil grailles, por ço que plus bel seit.
Granz est la noise, si l'oïrent Franceis.
Dist Oliver: "Sire cumpainz, ce crei,
De Sarrazins purum bataille aveir."
Respunt Rollant: "E Deus la nus otreit!"
(vv. 994–1008)

(The pagans arm themselves with Saracen hauberks,
Most of which have three layers of chain.
They lace their helmets, the best of Saragossa.
They gird up their swords of Viennese steel.
They bear noble shields, and spears from Valence,
And flags that are white, blue and crimson.
They leave their mules and palfreys;
They mount their steeds and ride in closed ranks.
Clear was the day and beautiful the sun.
There was no armor that did not flame in the light.
A thousand trumpets sound, to make it more beautiful.
The noise is great, and the Franks hear it.
Oliver says, "My comrade, I believe
That we shall do battle with the Saracens."
Roland answers, "Ah, may God grant it to us!")

Consider next how, along with its now exhausted hero Charlemagne, heroic language itself is generated as anti-formulas, which signify even more poignantly because of their counterpoint with a more glorious heroic discourse that now belongs to an irretrievable narrative past. A world of young warriors once teeming with potency, movement, and exuberance, once buoyant with sunlight, color, and fine weapons, has become a wasteland (*tere deserte*) of darkness and the dim pallor of moonlight;[19] here, men and horses are too exhausted even to stand up under the weight of armor or saddle, much less to rejoice in their recent revenge. Does this dark night of the heroic soul not threaten to become a dark night of poetic language as well? Even the name "Joyous"

19. Gerard J. Brault, *The Song of Roland, An Analytical Edition: Introduction and Commentary* (University Park: Pennsylvania State Univ. Press, 1978), 1:265, suggests that the moon in this scene is from the iconography of the crucifixion, where it traditionally stands in opposition to the sun. I would suggest that a similar contrast permeates the semantic substance of the poem itself.

given to Charlemagne's sword becomes invested with the torturesome paradox of a joy born in suffering and death, since we now are told that the tip of the very spear that jabbed Christ on the cross is encased in its handle:

> Li emperere ad prise sa herberge.
> > Franceis descendent en la tere deserte,
> > A lur chevals unt toleites les seles,
> > Les freins a or e metent jus les testes,
> > Livrent lur prez, asez i ad fresche herbe:
> > D'altre cunreid ne lur poeënt plus faire.
> > Ki mult est las, il se dort cuntre tere.
> > Icele noit n'unt unkes escalguaite.
>
> > Li emperere s'est culcet en un prét.
> > Sun grant espiet met a sun chef li ber:
> > Icele noit ne se volt desarmer,
> > Si ad vestut sun blanc osberc sasfret,
> > Laciet sun elme, ki est a or gemmet,
> > Ceinte Joiuse unches ne fut sa per,
> > Ki cascun jur muet .XXX. clartez.
> > Asez savum de la lance parler
> > Dunt Nostre Sire fut en la cruiz nasfret:
> > Carles en ad la mure, mercit Deu;
> > En l'oret punt l'ad faite manuvrer.
> > Pur ceste honur e pur ceste bontet,
> > Li nums Joiuse l'espee fut dunet.
> > Baruns franceis nel deivent ublier:
> > Enseigne en unt de Munjoie crier;
> > Pur ço nes poet nule gent cuntrester.
>
> > Clere est la noit e la lune luisant.
> > Carles se gist, mais doel ad de Rollant,
> > E d'Oliver li peiset mult forment,
> > Des .XII. pers e de la franceise gent
> > En Rencesvals ad laiset morz sanglenz.
> > Ne poet müer n'en plurt e nes dement,
> > E priet Deu qu'as anmes seit guarent.
> > Las est li reis, kar la peine est mult grant;
> > Endormiz est, ne pout mais en avant.
> > Par tuz les prez or se dorment li Franc.

N'i ad cheval ki puisset ester en estant:
Ki herbe voelt, il la prent en gisant.
Mult ad apris ki bien conuist ahan.
(vv. 2489–2524)

(The Emperor has set up his camp.
The French dismount on the barren land.
They have taken the saddles from their horses.
They remove from their heads the reins of gold.
They put them afield, where there is much fresh grass.
They can give them no further care.
Whoever is that tired sleeps on the ground.
On that night they do not set up guard.

The emperor has lain down in a field.
His great spear is by the baron's head.
That night he does not wish to disarm himself.
He wears his great saffron-colored hauberk.
His helmet is laced, which is of gemmed gold.
His sword Joyous is girded at his side,
A sword without peer, which gleams thirty times a day.
We know all about the lance
With which our Lord was killed on the cross,
Charles has the point, thanks be to God,
And has it encased in the golden handle.
Because of that honor and its great goodness,
The name Joyous is given to the sword.
The Frankish barons must never forget it.
And for that they cry out "Mountjoy"
So that nothing can resist them.

Clear is the night and the moon is shining.
Charles lies down, but he grieves for Roland,
And for Oliver he is greatly weighed down,
And for the twelve peers and the Frankish people.
He left them bloodied in death at Ronceval.
He cannot hold back from weeping and lamenting.
And he prays that God protect their souls.
The king is tired, for his pain is very great.
He falls asleep, for he can endure no more.
Now the French are sleeping all about the fields.

Not a horse can stand.
If he wants grass, he grazes lying down.
He who has suffered much has learned much.)

In short, a tragic flourish of counterpoint between joy and grief is expressed, not just thematically but also at the more pragmatic level of poetic language as a medium. Epic language is becoming differentiated or alienated from itself—or, to use the terms of Bakhtin, is passing from the monologic, which is the pre-condition of univocal truth in language, to the dialogic, where truth is at best equivocal and relative.[20] Though knights still put on armor in the second half of the Roland, and though the poem will occasionally fall back into formulas expressing the glee (*joie, baldur;* v. 3682) of combat, the formulas of the heroic idiom of the poem have lost much of their capacity to signify. This vitiation of meaning is an inscription of death into the Word as an immanent force; it can presumably be transcended, as the passage above suggests, only in the paradoxical mystery of Christ's own passion and resurrection.

The amazing and poignant gestures of Charlemagne that follow in the *Roland* dramatize a very real anxiety of the medieval world before the perception of once-sacred signs as arbitrary: the spirit, it would seem, does not always vivify. Unable, for the moment, to regenerate the world (or the word) by a new sequence of heroic actions of his own, Charlemagne withdraws and devotes himself solely to the task of commemorating as meticulously as possible the final gestures of his nephew. No longer a theater of triumphant action, the "present" world reduces itself to the status of a mere trace, a text, of the past glory of Roland; thus, as Charlemagne walks reverently about the spot where Roland died, he becomes less an epic soldier than an epic reader, a hermeneutician who interprets Roland's hieroglyphs of blood on grass, his sublime calligraphy of sword blows incised forever in a monument of stone:

> Quant l'empereres vait querre sun nevold,
>   De tantes herbes el pré truvat les flors
>   Ki sunt vermeilz del sanc de nos barons!
>   Pitet en ad, ne poet muer n'en plurt.
>   Desuz dous arbres parvenuz est . . .
>   Les colps Rollant conut en treis perruns;

20. Mikhail Bakhtin, *Problems of Dostoevsky's Poetics*, trans. R. W. Rotsel (Ann Arbor, Mich.: Ardis, 1973; first published in Russian in 1929), 90, 150.

Sur l'erbe verte veit gesir sun nevuld.
Nen est merveille se Karles ad irur.
Descent a pied, aled i est pleins curs,
Entre ses mains ansdous . . .
Sur lui se pasmet, tant par est anguissus.
(vv. 2870–80)

(When the emperor goes seeking his nephew
He finds the flowers of so many plants in the field
That are crimson with the blood of our barons!
Pity takes him; he cannot hold back from weeping.
He came beneath two trees, and
He recognized the blows of Roland on three stones;
He sees his nephew sprawled on the green grass.
It is no wonder if Charles feels grief.
He goes now by foot and sets out at a full run.
Between both his hands he clasps the count;
He faints over him, so great is his anguish.)

In a sense, Charlemagne is the first "reader" of the *Chanson de Roland*; that is, he must recover the epic voice as it is mediated by visible traces of Roland's martyrdom. Charlemagne attempts to recover the spiritual presence of Roland by embracing his nephew's dead body—that is to say, a thing whose pure thingness is both an irreducible presence and a conspicuous absence. Despite his efforts to invoke a human presence now belonging to his past, regression beyond the inert corporeality of the signifier is impossible for Charlemagne. Charlemagne and the Franks now faint, and their loss of consciousness is a symptom of their loss of Roland as the living center, and as the very voice of heroic epic. Roland's death leads to a vision of the centrifugality of history and of the Holy Roman Empire itself, understood as the ideological telos of the literate, post-Augustinian West. As Charlemagne says,

Encuntre mie revelerunt li Seisne,
    E Hungre e Bugre e tante gent averse,
    Romain, Puillain e tuit icil de Palerne
    E cil d'Affrike e cil de Califerne.
    (vv. 2921–24)

(Against me the Saxons will rebel,
    The Hungarians, the Bulgarians, and
        so many hostile peoples:

> The Romans, the Apulians, all those of Palermo,
> And those of Africa and those of Califerne.")

But Charlemagne is condemned to survive in a world that will neither signify nor vanish: "*Si grant doel ai, que jo ne voldrai estre!*" (So great is my grief that I no longer wish to live; v. 2929). Indeed, the poem's end will merely be another unwanted beginning. Clearly, *historia*, as Augustine referred to it in the epigraph above, is overwhelming the *Roland*, considered as the primal text of France. Thus, the devastation of the Frankish empire has left Charlemagne empty of all desire except the desire to conclude his "exile" in history in order to rejoin the fellowship of his barons, now spiritually present to each other in the timeless kingdom of the saved:

> Morz es mis niés, ki tant me fist cunquere . . .
>> Ki guierat mes oz a tel poeste,
>> Quant cil est morz ki tuz jurz nos cadelet?
>> E! France, cum remeines deserte!
>> Si grant doel ai que no ne vuldreie estre! . . .
>> Ço duinset Deus, le filz seinte Marie,
>> Einz que je vienge as maistres porz de Sirie,
>> L'anme del cors me seit oi departie,
>> Entre les lur aluee e mise,
>> E ma car fust delez els enfuie.
>> (vv. 2920–42)

> (My nephew is dead, who conquered so much for me . . .
> Who will lead my army with such force,
> When he is dead, who each day led us forth?
> Ah, France! How deserted you now are!
> So great is my grief that I no longer want to live! . . .
> May God grant, by Saint Mary's son,
> That before I come to the great gates of Size,
> My soul may be severed from my body,
> And be placed among theirs,
> And my flesh be buried beside theirs.)

Broadly speaking, the vision of death imparted in the first half of the poem by Roland's passion at Roncevaux was ultimately one of compensation, reintegration, and even of fruition, as martyrs on earth blossoming into the "holy flowers" of the saved. Roland and his companions had been absolved of their sins and blessed in advance of their dying. After his peers' death, Roland's last gesture as a good feudal lord had been to gather together their bodies and to commemorate their glory in song; shortly thereafter, Roland would incant his own salvation as well and be borne aloft to heaven by Gabriel and Michael, God's most chivalrous angels. All Christian warriors could be certain, it seemed, of being reunited in heaven's sublimer peerage and of being remembered on earth in song.

But the experience of death that prevails in the wasteland that Charles inherits is quite opposite. Here, death is not a reward or a fulfillment but a punishment that degrades even the punishers. We witness first the tenuous triumph of a skinny, colorless hero of the new establishment, Thierry, over Pinabel, an authentic hero of an archaic, warlike ethos whose values are now in question; then we are told that thirty of Ganelon's relatives are to be hanged for having pledged themselves to his cause; finally, we witness the drawing and quartering of Ganelon, himself a courageous knight who had quite properly defended his honor under the old dispensation only to find himself condemned as a traitor under the new. In contrast with the finally integrative dimension of death manifested earlier in the martyrdom of Charlemagne's troops, death now becomes a centrifugal force, a violent dispersion of human life among inanimate things as Ganelon's limbs are torn from each other in "splendid torment" by four wild, thirsty horses.[21] One last time, chivalric blood spews formulaically onto the green grass, but now it is the unredeemable blood of a traitor. Not only the heroic world, but heroic language has lost its center:

> Trestuit si nerf mult li sunt estendant
> E tuit li membre de sun cors derumpant:
> Sur l'erbe verte en espant li cler sanc.
> Guenes est mort cume fel recreant.
> (vv. 3970–73)

> (Each of his muscles is tightly stretched,
> And all his body's members split apart:
> The bright blood spills onto the green grass.
> Ganelon has died like a hateful traitor.)

Such as it is, the conclusion of the *Song of Roland* points more to unending violence than to forgiveness or consolation. True, there is the

21. I owe this insight in part to a suggestive sentence in a seminar research paper by Lucie Brind'Amour, Université de Montréal, 1975.

baptism of Bramimonde, a woman who forgets the pagan law for that of the true God, yet this is hardly material for a new epic; if anything, it marks the obsolescence of the old. The past hangs over the present only as historical memories that are painfully in conflict with each other. The hardships of Charlemagne, who must set forth once more, this time for the city of Imphe in the perhaps infinitely distant land of Bire, are the hardships of a man who has come to hate the heroic role with which history has burdened him; and it is no less clear that this desolate, two-hundred-year-old man is radically at odds with a poetic language that will neither serve him nor let him die:

> Li emperere n'i volsist aler mie:
> "Deus, dist li reis, si penuse est ma vie!"
> Pluret des oilz, sa barbe blanche tiret.
> Ci falt la geste que Turoldus declinet.
> (vv. 4000−4003)
> (The emperor does not want to set forth.
> "O God," says the king, "how painful is my life."
> He weeps from his eyes and pulls on his white beard.
> Here ends the tale that Turold tells.)

It seems to me that the tragedy of the *Roland* is not primarily that of a poet who has "used" language to express the purgative anguish of noble souls: its language, rather, is used up. The *Roland* is less a tragedy in language than a tragedy of language itself. The loss of force in the heroes of this poem is a way of dramatizing symptomatically a more pervasive loss of signification in the world. Medieval thinkers were clear about equating the power of meaning with vital force. As John of Salisbury put it, "A word's force consists in its meaning. Without the latter it is empty, useless, and (so to speak) dead. Just as the soul animates the body, so, in a way, meaning breathes life into a word."[22] The *Roland* is a poem that transcribes into its very substance a loss of transparency and a fatal discovery of the opaqueness of signs and, by extension, of all created things. A cleavage is produced in the *Roland* between thought and action, between the knower and the known, between the world and language. The seemingly permanent semantic universe of formulaic discourse is disrupted by semantic discontinuities which are those of time itself and which an ethics of memory

22. John of Salisbury, *Metalogicon* II.4, trans. David McGarry, (Berkeley: Univ. of California Press, 1955), 8.

cannot finally remedy. If what we would recognize in narrative as true temporal perspective is lacking in the tense system of the *Roland*, the semantic and cognitive shifts of this poem express temporal perspective in a perhaps more profound and tragic way.

There are many ways in which the ending may be admired and explained; ever since the *Roland*'s discovery a century and a half ago, each generation of readers has found in this poem its own provocations and rewards. By way of conclusion, I should like to return briefly to a problem I deferred earlier—one that quite frankly reflects the concerns of our own time—which is that the *Roland*, for all its marks of an oral tradition, is available to us *not* as an oral performance but as written text.

It is certain that if an oral culture may be said to exist, we as members of a culture centered on the text cannot know exactly what it is like to participate in that "other" culture. But by the same reasoning, how can an oral culture possibly know it is oral unless it has already encountered writing? Does it not follow that the very concept of orality is constituted by the scriptor as a dialectical negative of his own experience? Though orality and writing are each other's "otherness," since we learn to write only after we have learned to speak, our consciousness of ourselves as speaking beings is logically *posterior* to the experience of writing. Since the written letter *stands for* a spoken sound, writing is always a primal metalanguage. In our schools today children are first made conscious of the rules by which they already speak only in the "first" grade, when they learn to write; so too, throughout the Middle Ages, *grammatica* was a term that referred both to the art of making those lines (*grammata*) that we now call letters and to the art of speaking and writing language correctly (*de recte scribendi, de recte loquendi*).

In the Middle Ages, and especially during the post-Carolingian period, learning was possessed by few. Yet people did know how to speak, tell, and sing. If it is true, as scholars surmise, that the most archaic legends of the *Roland* endured and evolved primarily as oral, vernacular narrative during three centuries and more, we may ask what new consciousness came to those legends with the intervention of vernacular writing? If one may assume that both the character and the substance of narrative are at least partly determined by their mode of propagation, is it not possible that the diptych structure of the *Roland*, in some indirect yet forceful way, documents the historical impact of writing upon an oral intelligence—an impact necessarily seen, however, through the experience of a culture of scriptors now contemplating its prehistory as some kind of lost paradise of the oral word?

Admittedly, we still know very little about the way in which a culture of scribes determines which legends it will encrypt from that ocean of legends (and their variants) circulating in an oral tradition; but it is probably safe to assume that, as a rule, writers choose and organize their material in accordance with their own mode of experiencing the world. Perhaps, then, the juxtaposed stories of Roland and Charlemagne fascinated (and still fascinate) a culture of scriptors precisely because these stories delineated, in the juxtaposed successes and failures of their principal heroes, a nascent problematics of signification that had special poignancy for the mind of the scriptor now laboring to subject the spoken marvels of his art to the material of a text certain to become estranged from the circumstances of its production.

I would suggest that, together, the stories of Roland and the story of Charlemagne in the Oxford version of the *Chanson de Roland* express a yet deeper story of alienation from a world of people, things, and language in which the scriptor of songs found a mirror of his own cultural dilemma. Charlemagne's tragic encasement of Roland's lost world—a world of unalien, vocal presence—is a fiction born with the labor of letters, of letters understood as arbitrary signs of arbitrary signs, hence doubly estranged from the reality they are enlisted to represent: the text as crypt of the heroic heart and voice.

Of course, this proposal about the relationship between the tragedy of the Roland and its *mise-en-texte* is not something that can be "scientifically" proved—but neither was it ever proved by earlier scholars that "our" Roland died historically in Roncevaux to survive in a *cantilène*, or that "the" *Roland* sprang during some "sacred minute" into the mind of an inspired "Franc de France." Though it would be silly to insist that the *Song of Roland* is first and foremost a Song of Writing, we have every right to examine its implicit models of self-representation for indices of an epistemological crisis rooted in the competing cultural functions of speech and writing.

Though I believe that there are many such indices, I shall mention but one. It involves a fundamental shift in the conceptions that Roland and Charlemagne express, respectively, about the mode in which the memory of Roncevaux will be preserved and communicated to the future. Roland, one will recall, hurls himself into the fray with the conviction that his legend will live on in song; his epic blows will animate the performance of both bard and hero in generations to come, and his

blood will flow forever in the animate epic word. Charlemagne, by contrast, though he successfully deciphers Roland's last moments and de-
livers the most moving and elaborate *planctus* in the whole poem,
immediately undertakes to monumentalize the glory of Roland and
Oliver not in song but by enclosing their hearts in a more viable edifice
of stone:

> Li emperer fait Rollant costeïr
> E Oliver, l'arcevesque Turpin.
> Devant sei les ad fait tuz uvrir
> E tuz les quers en paile recuillir:
> Un blanc sarcou de marbre sunt enz mis. . . .
>
> Entresqu'a Blaive ad cunduit sun nevold
> E Oliver, sun nobilie cumpaignun,
> E l'arcevesque, ki fut sages e proz.
> En blancs sarcous fait metre les seignurs:
> A Seint Romain, la gisent li baron.
> (2962–66; 3689–93)
>
> (The emperor had Roland's body prepared,
> And Oliver's, and the Archbishop Turpin's.
> He had all three opened right before him,
> And had all of their hearts wrapped in silk,
> And placed inside a coffin of white marble. . . .
>
> He brought his nephew back to Blaye,
> And Oliver, his noble companion,
> And the Archbishop, who was wise and bold.
> He places the lords in white coffins:
> The barons are buried at Saint Roman.)

We may see in Charlemagne's desire to create a marble monument to
the memory of Roland and the twelve peers a fundamental change in
the notion of monumentality itself:[23] a culture once subsisting by virtue of the living word is now becoming a culture of funerary monuments, crypts, and inscriptions. If violence is a kind of "grammar" of
oral epic, the violence of the second half of the *Roland* seems paler and

23. Paul Zumthor, *Langue et technique poétiques à l'époque romane* (Paris:
Klincksieck, 1963), 43–45. For a more recent study of monumentality, Charle-
magne, and Roland, see Stephen G. Nichols, Jr., *Romanesque Signs: Early Medieval
Narrative and Iconography* (New Haven, Conn.: Yale Univ. Press, 1983).

more contrived than that narrated in the first half, and the function of violence as a determinant of truth in the poem's narrative has been subverted. Now, tablets of stone and vernacular epitaphs will convey to posterity the memory not of Roman Caesars but of Frankish, Christian knights. Quite clearly, feudal vernacular culture is in the process of re-defining its status with regard to the patrimony of classical antiquity, whose monuments still testified, thanks to the inscriptions engraved upon them, to the grandeur of past heroes. In wishing to endow his mo-ment of loss with the same monumental glory previously reserved for heroes of earlier empires, Charlemagne is also reviving a relationship between history and writing that had been essentially Roman and clas-sical. John of Salisbury, writing in the mid-twelfth century, expresses that concept well:

> Triumphal arches add to the glory of illustrious men only
> when the writing upon them informs in whose honor they
> have been reared, and why. It is the inscription that tells the
> spectator that the triumphal arch is that of our own Con-
> stantine, liberator of his country and promoter of peace. Indeed
> no one has ever gained permanent fame except as the result of
> what he has written or of what others have written of him.
> The memory of fool or emperor is, after a brief lapse of time,
> the same unless it be prolonged by courtesy of writers. . . .
> Therefore there is no wiser policy for those who crave glory
> than to cultivate sedulously the favor of scholars and writers.[24]

The Oxford manuscript of the Roland is by any standard a humble artifact and not an object of lavish artisanship. But it *is* a *mise-en-page*, a written text, and this textualization of vernacular poetry is a perfectly tangible equivalent of a shift of attitude toward monumen-tality that occurs within the story of the poem when Charlemagne displaces Roland as the central hero. Since we discover suspiciously late in the *Roland* (v. 2955) that Charlemagne's army is fairly swarm-ing with "bishops, abbots, monks, canons and tonsured priests," we may safely infer that by the beginning of the twelfth century these clerical custodians of the written word were eager to declare them-selves as legitimate witnesses of, and heirs to, Roland's legend. More-

24. John of Salisbury, *Policraticus* I.12, trans. Joseph B. Pike, *Frivolities of Cour-tiers and Footprints of Philosophers* (Minneapolis: Univ. of Minnesota Press, 1938), 6.

over, with later written versions of the story of Roncevaux, the account of the burial of the twelve peers became more elaborate (and contradictory),[25] reflecting, it seems, a desire among literate and perhaps clerical poets to appropriate (and to control) Roland's legend by attaching it to the historical patrimony of this or that parish or monastery. In other words, the writing down of the oral epic coincided with the birth of a new "textual community," to recall Brian Stock's term, one whose ethical presuppositions were distinct from those of the poem's audiences during the constitutive period of epic discourse. Moreover, just as in the Oxford version of the *Roland* we find the oral performance staging itself around an oral hero, so too, a generation later, in the Latin chronicle of the Roland legend called the *Pseudo-Turpin* (because it was purportedly written by Archbishop Turpin), we encounter a new and perfectly incongruous feminine presence in this world of male, chivalric heroes, that of Lady Grammatica herself. For when Charlemagne returns to Aachen (so we are told in the chronicle), he builds a splendid basilica and a castle, and on the castle walls are painted not only the stories of his wars in Spain but the allegorical figure of Grammatica, appearing alongside the very heroes whose memory she monumentalizes in writing:

> Bella namque, quae ipso in Hyspania devicit, et VII liberales artes, inter cetera, miro modo in eo depinguntur. Gramathica scilicet que est mater omnium artium, per quam omnes scripturae et celestia et terrestria noscuntur, quae docet quot et qales litterae debent asscribi.[26]

> (Indeed, the wars that he waged in Spain, and the seven liberal arts, among other things, are portrayed here in a wondrous manner. Especially Grammatica, who is the mother of all arts, through whom all writings, both celestial and terrestrial, are born, who teaches how many and what kinds of letters should be inscribed.)

However, if there was optimism in twelfth-century vernacular culture as its languages assumed the status of *grammatica*, we may also imagine that the transition from an oral vernacular culture to a culture

25. Menéndez Pidal, 112–20.

26. *Historia Karoli Magni et Rotholandi, ou Chronique du pseudo-Turpin* ed. C. Meredith-Jones (Paris: Droz, 1936), 223. See also Brault, 1:32, 254–355, n. 188. I am grateful to Professor Brault for his suggestions about this and other points.

of inscriptions and of texts entailed a fresh apprehension of an old problem with the letter: it kills. I am not suggesting that the *Roland* was "influenced" by a Pauline or Augustinian anxiety about the letter's potential to kill, but rather that Charlemagne's personal tragedy captures an experience of life and of the world—or of their *loss*—that any scriptor may undergo as he makes written crypts for spoken words.

To formulate an admittedly mannered question, if Roland is Charlemagne's "right hand" cut off, is this perhaps not also the writer's right hand writing itself off? The substitution of heroes that occurs in the Oxford version of the *Roland* corresponds to two modes of experiencing language, one proper to an oral culture, the other to a culture of writing, *though the former cannot be known except as a dialectical myth of the latter.* Just as the white marble sarcophagus encloses the hearts of Roland, Oliver, and the Archbishop Turpin, so too the written legend of Charlemagne encloses the unwritten legend of Roland. Every writer must bury the word. Charlemagne's nostalgia is the scriptor's as well, as he contemplates, through the memory of Roland, a world of living, vocal presences now lost to a world of opaque letters, now lost to France as the unflowered realm of the text: *E! France, cum remeines deserte!*

CHAPTER 4

The Châtelain de Coucy:
Enunciation and
Story in *Trouvère* Lyric

Ⅰf there is any validity to my proposal that the *Chanson de Roland* inaugurates, in the prestigious "historical" *matière de Charlemagne*, a new but tragic cultural awareness of the radical arbitrariness of the vernacular sign, the question arises as to how other vernacular writers on this (our) side of such a cultural threshold dealt with this irreversible apprehension of their vernacular poetic medium.

The answers to such a question are as diverse as are the principal discourses and genres in this rapidly evolving vernacular culture: for example, epic itself, lyric, romance, fabliau, and religious drama. Nor are the answers always sad. To the contrary, the arbitrariness of verbal signs could also become the ground for artistic play and for a positive pleasure in fiction, as in the cases of courtly lyric and romance.

Such pleasure constitutes itself, however, as a transgression to the extent that it is a rejection of the spiritual transcendence dictated by ecclesiastical letters. We saw, in chapter 2, how Augustine took the transiency of vocal signs as his primary evidence for the transiency of all created things. Bondage to the carnal signifier and to the law of the letter is the soul's death. If Augustinianism censured, along with the seductions of the flesh, those of the letter, it follows that the reverse of such a doctrine will lead to a poetics where desire for the female body would double—rather, compete with—that for the letter, which is the body of the sign. However, desire for the one implies negation of the desire for the other, and the text of the *grand chant courtois* is an expression of an equilibrium of conflicting desires in which satisfaction is an impossibility.

This impossibility is the sine qua non of *trouvère* poetic art. Although it is possible to speak of such a process as "*la névrose courtoise*," as does Henri Rey-Flaud in his penetrating book, I shall consider the courtly erotic *trouvère* lyric of the twelfth-century northern France as a remarkable social experiment with the arbitrariness of conventional verbal signs. I shall consider *trouvère* lyric as an aristocratic sign game that expresses pragmatically (rather than logically) a curious but subtle relationship of redundancy between non-sense in poetic language and self-thwarting libidinal desire. I shall seek out some of the rules of this sign game and suggest in what ways they afford pleasure. Moreover, without denying the perceptiveness of Rey-Flaud's study of courtly desire, I shall draw on a different side of Freud to make a different point about what I have called elsewhere "the joy of the text," and propose that such pleasure is profoundly social in both its origin and its goals.[1]

More precisely, using as my example a lyric poem by a twelfth-century *trouvère*, the Châtelain de Coucy, I shall take what I hope will prove to be a coherent sequence of critical steps. First, I shall attempt to outline what may be called a poetics of "enunciation" (in the sense that Emile Benveniste and others give to that term)[2] that I believe to

1. This chapter was originally written as a sequel to another article on *trouvère* lyric, "Love's Concordance: The Poetics of Desire and the Joy of the Text," *Diacritics* 5 (1975): 40–52. Since the completion of the first version of the present essay, other studies have appeared or are forthcoming on courtly lyric whose affinities with my own work are clear and have for the most part been acknowledged by their authors. See, in particular, Peter Haidu, "Text and History: The Semiosis of Twelfth-Century Lyric as Sociohistorical Phenomenon (Chrétien de Troyes: 'D'Amors qui m'a tolu')," *Semiotica* 33 (1981): 1–62. See also Rainer Warning, "Moi Lyric et société chez les troubadours," in *Archéologie du signe*, ed. Lucie Brind'Amour and Eugene Vance (Toronto: Pontifical Institute for Mediaeval Studies, 1983), 63–100; R. Howard Bloch, *Etymologies and Genealogies: A Literary Anthropology of the French Middle Ages* (Chicago: Univ. of Chicago Press, 1983), esp. ch. 3; Henri Rey-Flaud, *La Névrose Courtoise* (Paris: Navarin, 1983).

2. Emile Benveniste, *Problèmes de linguistique générale* (Paris: Gallimard, 1966); François Récanati, *La transparence et l'énonciation* (Paris: Seuil, 1979). See also these special journal numbers: *Langages* 17 (1970), ed. Tzvetan Todorov, entitled "L'énonciation"; *Etudes Littéraires* 16 (1983), ed. Louise Milot, entitled "Sur l'énonciation"; *Langages* 70 (1983), ed. Herman Parret, entitled "La mise en discours."

characterize *trouvère* lyric as a distinct class of utterance. Second, I shall locate what I will call (with Paul Zumthor and Rupert Pickens)[3] a "latent narrativity," a hidden story, which subtends the process of enunciation in *trouvère* lyric, and I will suggest that the perception of—indeed, the participation *in*—that story by the audience is indispensable to the semantic process of *trouvère* lyric discourse as a whole. Third, since the latent story of lyric discourse has to do with the repression of libidinal desire, I shall demonstrate the relationship of this story to what Freud calls the "psychogenesis" of certain kinds of sexual jokes whose "poetics" strikingly resemble those of courtly lyric. By so doing, I hope to help the modern reader both to find ways of enjoying the remarkable formal beauty of *trouvère* lyric and to *understand* that enjoyment: in short, to see the latent story of *trouvère* lyric as his own.

TROUVÈRE LYRIC AND THE POETICS OF ENUNCIATION

Let me preface this discussion of a *trouvère* lyric with a comment on the term "enunciation": I have favored it here over the more common (and nearly equivalent) modern English term "uttering," because the former is less of a metalinguistic neologism. To the contrary, the term *enunciatio*, as distinct from *enunciatum* ("speaking" vs. "what is spoken"), is a key term of Stoic theories of language; it refers to the act of declaring, of making assertions, or, more precisely, of predicating something about a subject.[4] *Enuntiare* corresponds to the Greek verb *apophainesthai*, which also means "to make known, state, reveal, declare."[5]

However, as a descriptive term of modern linguistics, a science

3. Rupert T. Pickens, "(B)Latant Narrativity and Textual Change in the Early Troubadour Lyric" (forthcoming); Paul Zumthor, "Les Narrativités latentes dans le discours lyrique médiéval," in *The Nature of Medieval Narrative*, ed. Minnette Grunmann-Gaudet and Robin F. Jones (Lexington, Ky: French Forum, 1980), 39–55.

4. Gabriel Nuchelmans, *Theories of the Proposition: Ancient and Medieval Conceptions of the Bearers of Truth and Falsity* (Amsterdam: North Holland, 1973), 107.

5. Nuchelmans, 26–27: "One of the words that Plato uses for giving verbal expression to what one holds true to one's mind is the verb *apophainesthai*. The verb, with *gnomen* or *doxan* as the expressed or unexpressed object, was familiar to every Greek and had the quite ordinary meaning of making known one's opinion. It is this word that plays a central role in Aristotle's treatment of the expression of thought in speech, at least in *De interpretatione*."

heavily influenced by phenomenology, "enunciation" has acquired a different sense; it implies all of those formal mechanisms of language that become significant *in*, or refer *to*, the specific action of producing an utterance. This action is most easily apprehended in the functions of the pronoun system in modern languages—above all, in the function of the first and second persons singular, *I* and *thou*. Emile Benveniste writes:

> What, then, is the "reality" to which I or thou refers? Solely a reality in speech [*discours*] which is a very singular thing. *I* cannot be defined except in terms of "locution," and not in terms of objects, as is the case with a noun [*signe nominal*]. *I* signifies the "person enunciating in the present instance of discourse containing *I*." Such an instance is by definition unique and valid only in its unicity. . . . This sign is therefore bound to the *exercise* of language and declares who is the speaker [*locuteur*] as such. It is this property that underlies individual speech where each speaker assumes, as his own, the whole of language.[6]

However, other classes of verbal signs are also implicated in enunciation as a dynamic process: for instance, all of those "moveable" signs called deictics or shifters (the demonstrative and relative pronouns, adjectives and adverbs of time and place), which are void of semantic content except as they bear upon the *hic et nunc* of the instance of discourse.[7] Even the tense structure of language is centered architectonically upon the present (which is more the mark of the present moment in speech than of a true time) and is therefore implicated in the process of enunciation.[8]

Although the term "enunciation" implies many different features of language in the performance of ordinary acts of communication, it should be obvious that each specific type of utterance—and, by extension, each literary genre—will be governed by its own rules with regard to the way its signs reflect both the process and circumstances of its own begetting. Historiography, for example, is a mode of writing that excludes, through its use of the aorist tense, as much as possible

6. Benveniste, 252, 254. (All translations in this chapter, unless otherwise indicated, are my own.)
7. Benveniste, 262.
8. Benveniste, 242.

the intrusion of such signs of the present upon a "reality" of events belonging to the truth of the irrevocable past, of "what happened."[9] By contrast, we shall see that early French lyric has such extensive and peculiar ways of inscribing the fiction of enunciation into its linguistic substance that the present of enunciation becomes an all-eclipsing "reality." Let us begin, therefore, by considering the text of the Châtelain de Coucy's poem:[10]

I
Merci clamans de mon fol errement,
Ferai de la fin de mes chançons oïr,
Quar trahi m'a et mort a escïent
4 Mes jolis cuers que je doi tant haïr;
Cest mal m'a fait pour le gré d'autre gent.
Tout sunt parti de moi joieuz talent,
Et quant joie me faut, bien est raisons
8 Qu'avec ma joie faillent mes chançons.

II
Bien sai qu'il est lieus et poins et saisons
Qu'a touz les biens d'amours doive faillir,
Quar pourquis l'ai, et moie est l'ochoisons,
12 Et qui mal quiert, il doit bien mal soufrir.
Diex doinst que mors en soit mes guerredons,
Ainz que de moi voie liez les felons!
Maiz pour mon pis vivrai et pour veoir
16 Ma bele perte et pour pluz mal avoir.

III
As fins amans proi qu'il dient le voir:
Li queuz doit mieuz par droit d'amours joir,
Cil qui aime de cuer sanz decevoir,
20 Si ne s'en set mie tres bien couvrir,
Ou qui prie sanz cuer pour decevoir
Et bien s'en set guarder par son savoir?
Dites, amant, qui vaut mieuz par raison:
24 Loiauz folie u sage trahison?

9. Benveniste, 244.
10. *Chansons attribuées au Chastelain de Coucy*, ed. Alain Lerond (Paris: Presses Univ. de France, 1964), 82–85 (translation mine).

IV

S'ainc fins amans ot de mesfait pardon,
Dont m'i devroit amour bon lieu tenir,
Quar je fourfis en bone ententïon
28 Et bien cuidai que me deust merir
Maiz ma dame ne quiert se mon mal non;
Pour ce si has moi et ma guerison,
Et quant mi mal li sunt bel et plesans,
32 Pour ce me haz et me sui mal vueillans.

V

Hé, franche riens, por cui je mur amans,
Faites en vos amors plux biaul fenir!
Sor toute riens est ceu la muels vaillans.
36 Et nonporcant se puis je bien mentir,
Car fins d'amors ne puet estre avenans,
Se mors nes pairt; por ceu morai souffrans
Et chanterai sens joie et sens fineir,
40 Ke nuls ne doit a fin d'amors penseir.

VI

De pouc me set ki me veult conforteir
D'autrui ameir; muelz l'en varoit taisir,
Car je ne puis pais en mon cuer troveir
44 Ke jie de li tornaisse mon desir.
Siens seux, coment ke me doie greveir,
Et se s'amor me fait plux compaireir,
Tout li perdoing en mon definement,
48 Et quant mon cors li toil, mon cuer li rant.

(Crying out for mercy in my insane error, I shall make heard the end of my songs, because my heart has betrayed me and knowingly slain me, my lovely heart which I ought to hate very much; it has done this harm to please someone else. All joyous feelings have left me; and when joy is lacking, it is only proper that, with my joy, my songs should fail.

Well do I know that there is a place and moment and season when all the good things of love must fail, for I have sought love, and the occasion is now my own; and whoever seeks out harm must suffer it for sure. May God grant that death be my reward, rather than that I should see the traitors rejoicing because of me. Yet for my own harm will I live on, and I shall witness my beautiful loss, and thus I shall have even more harm.

To all *fins'amans* I pray that they speak the truth. Which person has more right to have joy in loving: he who loves with all his heart without deception, even if he does not know how to conceal it very well? or he who prays not from his heart but only to deceive, and who knows how to protect himself from it by his rusing? Tell me, lovers, which does reason say is better: loyal folly or shrewd treason?

If ever a *fins'amans* had a pardon for some misdeed, love should reserve a good place for me, for I did wrong with good intentions and I thought that it would surely be to my merit. But my lady seeks nothing but my harm; therefore, she despises both me and my cure; and since my harms are beautiful and pleasing to her, for this I hate myself and am ill disposed towards myself.

Ah, lovely (free) creature for whom I die in loving, bring to your loving a more beautiful end: to do so is worthier than any other thing. Yet, I must not lie so well, because the end of love [*fins d'amors*] cannot be agreeable to lovers unless death separates them; for this I shall die suffering and I shall sing without joy and without end, since no one should think of love's end.

It is no use for anyone to comfort me with the love of someone else; he would do better to keep quiet, for I cannot find peace in my heart by turning my desire away from her. I am hers, however much it must burden and grieve me. And if her love makes me spend more and more, I pardon her for everything in my decline; and when she takes my body, I give her my heart.)

As is usually the case with Old French courtly lyric, this *chanson* is centered grammatically upon an unnamed desiring subject, a perfectly conventional *je* crying out for mercy from the very edge of death or—what is more drastic for singers—of silence. Although the occurrence of the sign *je* (or of its morphological equivalents) indicates not just a process of enunciation but a fiction of human presence in speech, any instance of *je* in a written text, as we have remarked earlier, can carry no identity other than what is bestowed upon it by the text itself in which *je* is contained.[11] Otherwise, *je* is an entirely empty sign, a mere "grammatical" sign or function-word. However, in the case of the Old French *grand chant courtois*, the occurrence of the written sign *je* postulates a speaking subject whose identity is *doubly* denatured: because of its anonymity, and also because the language constituting that sign's written context is made up of words and formulas that are maximally conventional. Hence, the potential of *je* to "refer" to some *specific* extralinguistic reality is minimal, while the inclination of *je* to function as an icon of a specific poetic discourse or code—that is, as an intertextual sign—is maximal.[12] What Roland Barthes has said of the literary "I" in general is especially true of the "subject" of enunciation that we invariably encounter as readers of courtly lyric:

> Subjectivity is the image of a fullness which I supposedly carry to the text, yet this fullness is a sham and is only the wake [*sillage*] of all those codes of which my being is fabricated: thus, my subjectivity has all of the generality of stereotypes. Objectivity is a fullness of the same order: it is an imaginary system like any other (except that its castrating effect is more ferocious); it is an image that is employed so that I will be named more advantageously—that is, to make me known and to make me unknown.[13]

If it is true that the *I* of Old French courtly lyric expresses less a discrete individual selfhood than a terrain of identity determined a priori by the idiom of a discourse belonging to a restricted social group, it may be suggested that the drastic closing of lyric language upon a set of narrowly redundant formal and lexical conventions coincides with a changing social status of the twelfth-century aristocracy, now constituting itself as a closed social caste—not just *de facto*, but *de jure* as well. One is no longer noble because of one's exploits in the world but rather because one is first born noble: indeed, one is now noble because one is.

By the same token, if the identity of the lyric self is predetermined

---

11. Benveniste, 252–53.

12. Paul Zumthor, "Le *Je* de la chanson et le moi du poète," in *Langue, texte, énigme* (Paris: Seuil, 1975), 181–96.

13. Roland Barthes, *S/Z* (Paris: Seuil, 1970), 17.

by a set of conventions that are the emblem of a collective identity, one may suppose that the fiction of erotic frustration so artfully proclaimed at the dramatic surface of this poetry is doubled by a more elementary—and very real—frustration arising from the impossibility of the desiring individual to appropriate even those *social* signs that he invokes to express his *personal* desire. To utter the *je* of Old French lyric is not, finally, to enunciate one's secret desire for another person but, on the contrary, to enunciate before the group the very otherness of one's desire—or, more precisely, to enunciate only the *desire* to desire.

Given the unassumable identity of *je* as a subject of enunciation in the *grand chant courtois*, we should not be surprised to observe that there is also a certain flux or diffuseness in the identity of *tu*, the interlocutor dialectically posited (at least implicitly) with any instance of *je*. Though *je* monopolizes the discourse, at least two "persons" become objects of direct address at different moments in this poem: the lofty *vous* of the lady and the *vous* of sympathetic lovers figuring among the initiates of the poem's audience. However, a field of other potential interlocutors (God, the "poets" of the audience, the arbiters in love's court) are posited indirectly in the enunciation of this poem, even though they remain, finally, outside the axis of direct communication. Obviously, the fiction of enunciation in this poem does not simulate a linear process of intersubjective exchange, much less of dialogue. *Trouvère* lyric discourse dramatizes not its potential as a medium of communication but rather its power to *sustain* desire in a social ritual that precludes such reciprocity in speech as might lead to other, less verbal (and perhaps less social) deeds of amorous exchange; we shall return to this point later.

The distribution of tenses in the Châtelain's poem is interesting because its pattern is a kind of silhouette of the enunciating voice as a principle of reality that eclipses all others. If the sign *je* posits, in ordinary language, a primordial subjective action in discourse, it is the function of the tense system to situate the instance of discourse, the "now" of speaking, in that process of extradiscursive time (supposedly more objective, more "real") that we measure by the clock or calendar. Of course, even the reality of this other "time" is constituted over and against the discursive moment existentially asserted in the process of speech. In this poem by the Châtelain de Coucy, one finds no attempt on the part of the poet to establish anything approximating what we may call, with Harald Weinrich, "locutionary perspective," in which a time of utterance (*Textzeit*) is distinguished from a time of action (*Aktzeit*).[14] To the contrary, all temporal perspective is occulted by a present of enunciation, as we may observe in the distribution and functions of tenses and modes in the poem:

present indicative	35
infinitive	22
present subjunctive	6
past indefinite	5
present participle	5
future	4
imperative	2
conditional	2
imperfect subjunctive	1
imperfect (or past definite)	1

Obviously, three of the four indicative tenses that occur in this poem (the present, the past indefinite, and the future) all have as their common denominator a present constituted by the moment of speaking. Though the past indefinites indicate anteriority, they express this anteriority with an auxiliary cast in the present indicative, thereby subordinating the reality of the past ontologically to the reality of the "present," to the fictive "now" of the text, which is in fact a zero-time.[15] Nor are the four instances of the future so much temporal indicators as they are "modal" expressions of necessity, determination, or resignation, all of which reflect an emotivity centered very much in the present of enunciation.

The one imperfect—or is it a past definite?—occurring in the poem (*ot*, l. 25) has no temporal value because it is part of an "if" clause. Since temporal or chronological perspective, as we know it, is not a constraint upon the verb system here, the occurrence of an *imperfect* subjunctive (l. 44) to express what we would ordinarily express with a *present* subjunctive is unproblematical; conceivably even the metrical demands of a given verse can, within limits, motivate the choice of tenses.

However, the tense system in ordinary language not only asserts temporality but expresses both the modes of existence of things and

14. Harald Weinrich, *Tempus: Besprochene und erzählte Welt* (Stuttgart: Kohlhammer, 1964), 54–55.
15. Benveniste, 244–45.

the basic relationships (activity, passivity, transitivity, intransitivity) that are perceived to prevail between people or things. Finally (and not least important for the discussion that follows), it is ordinarily a property of the verb to posit a factor of truth: that is, to affirm in our utterances "what we hold the case to be." (The utterance "Socrates runs," for example, implies "it is *true* that Socrates runs.") Most noteworthy about the distribution of verbs in this *trouvère* lyric is that over a quarter of the verbs should occur as infinitives, which, grammatically speaking, assert no agent, no time, no truth or reality principle. This high incidence of infinitives reflects a high frequency of modals, which in French are *vouloir, pouvoir, savoir,* and *devoir* (or their locutionary equivalents). The high frequency of modals has the effect of suspending in a timeless present of enunciation all of that potential verbal action that is expressed semantically by the infinitives of the poem. Along with the subjunctives, participles, imperatives, and conditionals, the infinitives constantly refract a universe of objective events through present states of mind in the speaker. Moreover, these states of mind succeed each other in such a throng of mutually exclusive emotions that the whole truth-bearing function of the verb is annulled: error, faulty thinking, and absurdity in *trouvère* lyric are sovereign privileges, it seems, of that noble (or ennobling) folly called love.

Parenthetically, certain discursive patterns generated by this *fol errement* (l. 1) lend themselves to interesting comparisons with clinical observations made of speech patterns of obsessional schizophrenics, which also—according to Luce Irigaray—tend to refract a universe of events and potential actions through a mediating consciousness that maintains only *itself* as a constant and exclusive center of reference. Even the reality of the interlocutor is dissipated:

> His reality as receiver of the message is in effect called into question by the reflexive character of its enunciation and also by the fact that whatever is to be communicated is so entirely mediated by the "I" that it remains, finally, relatively incommunicable. Moreover, as he is evinced in the utterance, the receiver is assigned no function, whether as subject of an action, as agent of a passive, or as object.[16]

16. Luce Irigaray, "Approche d'une grammaire d'énonciation de l'hystérique et de l'obsessionnel," *Langages* 5 (1967): 104ff; see also "Négation et transformation négative chez les schizophrènes," *Langages* 5 (1967): 84–98; and "L'Énoncé en analyse," *Langages* 13 (1969); 111–22.

We shall return to the ambiguous function of the audience of *trouvère* lyric—which includes us as readers of the poem—later.

Anyone who has read even a handful of *trouvère* lyrics will recognize that the basic lexicon and repertory of motifs deployed in this example by the Châtelain de Coucy are perfectly conventional and characteristic of a whole body of poems written by a circle of aristocratic poets in the North of France—several of whom, like the Châtelain, lived in Champagne. Uniformity is much more marked in the *trouvère* corpus than in the corpus of the troubadours, whose poetry is far more individualistic and idiosyncratic. A computer-based study of the *trouvère* corpus by Georges Lavis demonstrates not only the homogeneity of this poetry but the redundancy of semantic patterns generated in the process of enunciation.[17] Taking the lexical binarity *joie/ dolor* as the constitutive paradigm of the lyric semantic field, Lavis illustrates in great detail how lyric poets multiply substitutes for these antithetical terms and amplify them into larger syntagms, which sustain ideas of joy and pain (or their equivalents) yet, as they do so, always conserve a relationship of antithesis or mutual exclusiveness of terms. A marked binarism is also characteristic of this poem by the Châtelain de Coucy, and here, in their grammatical form of occurrence, are some of the obvious pairs: *mal/bien*, *aime/haïr*, *joïr/souffrir*, *toil/rant*, *loiauz/trahison*, *taisir/chanter*, *fol/sage*, *errement/raison*, *greveir/guerison*, *dient le voir/mentir*, *bone entention/mal veuillans*, *mesfait/merir*. Many of these lexical items recur as locutionary near-synonyms: for instance, the series *mentir, bien couvrir, decevoir*, and *prie sanz cuer*.

If a maximally polarized isotopism (in the sense that Greimas gives to that term)[18] is a *precondition* for enunciation in *trouvère* courtly lyric, then we may consider the *actual* process of enunciation as one where, within a given utterance, the positive term of one binarity will be paired with the negative term of a different binarity: *guerredon/mors*, *liez/felons*, *sage/trahison*, *mur/amans*, *loiaus/folie*, *bele/perte*, etc. The referentiality of lyric language is denatured not only by its strict adherence to conventions, which prescribe what *will* be said, but also by the *decontextualizing* effect of coupling negative and positive terms drawn from different binary pairs. This proliferation, within the constraints of convention, of hybrid binarities

---

17. Georges Lavis, *L'Expression de l'affectivité dans la poésie lyrique française du moyen-âge (XIIe–XIIIe s.)* (Paris: Belles Lettres, 1972).

18. A.-J. Greimas, *Sémantique structurale* (Paris: Larousse, 1966), 87–101.

accounts for much of what we now experience as artificiality and abstractness in *trouvère* lyric; yet this combinatory hybridism is perhaps the very terrain of artifice where, within the constraints of code or convention, the talent of the individual poet is manifested most *concretely.*

The more the lexicon of *trouvère* lyric is decontextualized and overdetermined by poetic convention, the more the referrent of *je* becomes the process or code of lyric itself. That is to say, the poem itself becomes an object of pleasure as hybrid binary antitheses of meaning are projected through subsemantic structures of meter, rhyme, hemistiche, and stanzaic patterns of rhyme. In some instances purely formal features of the poem itself enter into binary opposition with the meaning of statements made *in* the poem. Thus, when the poet declares at the beginning (l. 2) that he will "end" his singing, or when near the end he declares that he will sing *sans fineir* (l. 39), form and content are conspicuously at odds. We are close, here, to a poetic phenomenon that Paul Zumthor has described in a well-known article whose title, "De la circularité du chant," serves its content very aptly.[19] Zumthor discerns a peculiar tendency in *trouvère* lyric for the activities of loving and singing (*aimer, chanter*)—activities normally undertaken in opposed states of mind (lyric poets do not sing of success)—to become synonymous: "To sing, which is to love, and vice versa, becomes an action with no end, one which perpetuates its process for the duration of a certain number of strophes by engendering its own substantification: the song, which is love, and vice versa."[20]

The tension between the radical injustice of Amor (designated in stanzas III and IV) and the disciplinary regularity of lyric art is a dialectic of provocation and recovery that constitutes courtly erotic discourse. As Roger Dragonetti writes concerning the *Flamenca*:

> If we argue that the rightness (*droiture*) of Love is to observe neither justice nor measure, this amounts to designating an instance that is heterogeneous with respect to any concept of unity, order or totality: it is to name the very strangeness of what is undoing all calculation and all foresight. Yet it is this chaotic turbulence, which is anterior to all unity, that provokes the necessity of calculating, of measuring, of balanc-

19. Paul Zumthor, "De la circularité du chant," *Poétique* 2 (1970): 129–40; see also his *Essai de poétique médiévale* (Paris: Seuil, 1972), 214–18.
20. Zumthor, "De la circularité du chant," 136.

ing—in short, the desire to discover a network of analogous
relationships, one which is always no doubt precarious and
which is always on the point of undoing itself, but without
which the dazzling cleavages of the Other would never be
perceptible.[21]

Although *trouvère* lyric does not point to the cosmic antinomy of
creative versus chaotic forces, these dimensions of human desire will
become apparent in the material discussed in the next three chapters.

Enunciation in *trouvère* lyric is thus a *formal* artistic activity where
"meaning" is deployed as radical disjunctions, where significations are
aborted as they are begotten, and where words both summon forth and
ultimately come to signify their opposites. As Georges Lavis writes,
"L'effusion lyrique courtoise culmine dans la synthèse de la joie et de
la souffrance, cette fusion des contraires cristallisant autour d'elle la
neutralisation d'autres antinomies: le bon et le mauvais, l'emprisonne-
ment et la liberté, la folie et la sagesse, la vie et la mort, la générosité et
l'avarice, le 'preu,' et le 'damage,' etc."[22]

To observe this process of neutralization and reversal more closely,
let us consider the following utterance from our poem (ll. 31–32) by
the Châtelain de Coucy, in which a tenuous equivalence is established
between the contrary sentiments of love and hate:

> Et quant mi mal li sunt bel et plesans,
> Pour ce me haz et me suis mal veuillans.

This utterance has four basic semantic components: two persons, *je*
and *elle*, and two passions, love and disdain—though the sentiment of
love is represented here by its *effects* (beauty and pleasure) rather than
by the word for love itself. Together, these four components may be
imagined to form a square within which the following transformations
may be diagrammed: *je* "loves" *elle*; *elle* "disdains" *je*; when *je*'s love
encounters *elle*'s disdain, it becomes transformed into *je*'s disdain of
himself. *Elle*'s disdain encounters *je*'s love and is transformed into selfish love (or pleasure at *je*'s expense) on the part of *elle*. If we may schematize the transformations effected in the performance of this utterance, we may localize the process of enunciation ("E") at that zone

21. Roger Dragonetti, *Le Gai Savoir dans la rhétorique courtoise: "Flamenca" et
Joufroi de Poitiers* (Paris: Seuil, 1982), 95.
22. Lavis, 36.

of perpetual semantic crisis where binary oppositions become neutralized and reversed:

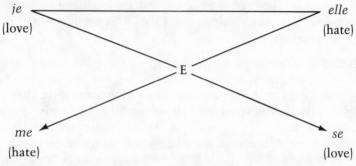

je
(love)

elle
(hate)

E

me
(hate)

se
(love)

Clearly, the succession of utterances in early *trouvère* lyric is governed less by temporal, spatial, or logical priorities than by a principle of negation and sophistical self-falsification that affects every aspect of verbal performance. *Grammatica* becomes the mediator of artful improprieties, equivocations, and contrasts; and such iterations of pure semantic difference may be seen as the transposition, into the semantic process, of desire that is unappeasable because it is the desire to desire. A superficial index of this productivity sustained by negation may be found in the fact that the word heading the frequency list of the lexicon of another *trouvère*, Gace Brulé, is the grammatical function-word *ne* (which in Old French includes the negative conjunction *ni* of modern French).[23] Eleventh on the frequency list is *je*, but when this pronoun is grouped with its graphic and grammatical inflections (*j'*, *me*, *moi*), its occurrences are about equal in number to those of *ne*. However, since the verb in Old French can also carry the morphemic category of person, the actual assertions of *je* as the principle of a desiring self are far in excess of those of any other entity. We are dealing, then, with a poetics of *je-ne* which calls for no other hermeneutical response on our part than a kind of rudimentary formal pleasure in denial.

What motivates us to become an audience to such a performance? Why do we enjoy courtly lyric as a self-thwarting quest for *joi*? We shall ponder these questions in the section that follows.

23. Vance, "Love's Concordance," 49–50.

LYRIC AS LATENT NARRATIVE

If Paul Zumthor is correct in his claim that the "register" of courtly lyric may be defined as a speech act called the *requête courtoise*, then, like any speech act, the *requête courtoise* carries in its conventions a set of roles whose interdependence may be considered as a permanent, deep-structural paradigm subtending lyric as a discursive performance.[24] For reasons that will become apparent, I shall speak of the very special interdependence of these roles as constituting a *latent narrative*, a term once ventured by Zumthor himself and reexamined in some detail in a searching and well-documented study of *troubadour* lyric by Rupert T. Pickens.[25]

When I speak of *trouvère* lyric as latent narrative, I mean quite simply that the lyric performance proffers to its audience a set of implicit roles whose interaction is sufficient to generate a complete story, even though that story is not through-composed in *trouvère* lyric as linear narrative. We are dealing, here, with a critical problem of some importance, for while it is true that we have learned a great deal in the past two decades about the structure of narrative, we have not yet adequately reflected upon the possible modes of existence of narrative.

Must a story be told or "written out" in order to be called a story?

If a story is not told or written out, but latent or repressed, is the repression of the story *part* of that story? Or a new story?

Is the analysis of a story not really the production of yet another story?

Although the discussion that follows will bear upon these general questions, I shall venture two propositions of a more concrete sort about *trouvère* lyric: first, that there is implicit in every typical *trouvère* lyric a complete narrative program, a complete set of the narrative "chromosomes" necessary to form a story; second, that even if the story embedded in lyric is only latent or virtual, it can nevertheless be described in a manner that accounts for the possible ways in which that story might be executed. Indeed, I would suggest that much of what we call courtly romance can be considered as the elaboration, the

---

24. The term first appears in Zumthor's *Langue et techniques poétiques à l'époque romane* (Paris: Klincksieck, 1963), 67–69, but he has since elaborated further on it in "Registres linguistiques et poésie aux XIIe–XIIIe siècles," *Cultura neolatina* 34 (1974): 151–61.

25. Pickens, see n. 3, above.

spelling-out, of a deep narrative paradigm that became available to romance poets in the vernacular only after its economy had been perfected in the Old French lyric. To argue for the centrality of the lyric
paradigm to the code of romance narrative is in effect to speak of lyric
as a pre-narrative *competence* for courtly romance as a genre.

Assuming, then that *trouvère* lyric provides a model for narrative
that is structurally complete, I shall attempt to describe that model by
recourse to the actantial theory of A.-J. Greimas.[26] The heuristic advantage of Greimas's theory is that its generality and simplicity coincide very conveniently with a kind of uniformity and homongeneity
manifested by the lyric tradition of northern France from the twelfth
to the beginning of the fifteenth century. In other words, both the
trouvère lyric, as object, and the descriptive model I am carrying to
that object are abstract, reductive, and stable.

But there are other advantages to Greimas's model as well. Though
the time has long since passed when the structural analysis of stories
(or of anything else) sufficed as a critical goal in its own right, Greimas's
actantial model does put us into a better position to probe the psychic
dimension of certain types of narrative performance and, in the case of
lyric, to speculate upon the psychodynamics in which we ourselves indulge as soon as we become part of the audience of such poetry. Therefore, not only will the Greimassian actantial model provide a fairly
precise narratological calculus for analyzing the formal process of
enunciation in *trouvère* lyric as I have already begun to schematize it,
but this model will lend itself to careful comparisons with a model of
psychic behavior that Freud detects in the enunciation of sexual jokes:
that is, of utterances whose verbal resources have much in common
with those of *trouvère* lyric.

The "structural" portion of the discussion that follows, then, is not
an end in itself but an intermediary phase in an exploration of the congruent social and psychological factors that compel such structures to
manifest themselves in the first place.

Since Greimas's actantial model is now broadly familiar to many
medievalists, I shall not describe it here at length. Suffice it to say that
Greimas proposes that all narrative is constituted by a restricted set of
interdependent roles, even though these roles may be filled by a very
large diversity of people or things. These roles are called actants. There

26. See Greimas, 172–221, for the source of the following description.

are only six actants, which interact in three pairs: the *sujet* and the *objet*, the *adjuvant* and the *opposant*, the *destinateur* and the *destinataire*. These actants are "classes of actors." Though these actantial roles may be filled by an unlimited number of people or things ("actors"), the kinds of relationships that obtain between these people or things tend to be expressed by broad types of action: these are called "functions," and according to Greimas there are only twenty basic functions. The actantial role of the subject tends to be filled by some person or thing manifesting a transitive force or a need, often semanticized as desire and resulting in a quest. (Remember that the register of lyric is a "*request*"). Obviously, the object of this force, need, or desire assumes the actantial role of "object." The *adjuvant* "aids" the subject to fulfill the expression of its force or to satisfy its need or desire, while the *opposant* hinders or obstructs the subject in doing so. The *destinateur* is a person or thing that attributes destinies, arbitrates, and prevails over events; the *destinataire* is the person or thing that receives a destiny or reward, or undergoes the consequence of an arbitration.

Though Greimas does not say so himself, one may suspect that the fundamentally tripartite structure of narrative, of the "minimal story," reflects, if only indirectly, the functions proper to the three pairs of actantial roles that constitute his model.[27]

One particularly important aspect of Greimas's theory is his allowance for the possibility that more than one actantial role may be assumed by a single person. Greimas's example is very pertinent, moreover, to the "situation" of lyric. He writes:

> For example, in a story which is only a banal tale of love, concluding, without the intervention of the parents, in marriage, the subject is also the *destinataire*, while the object is also the *destinateur* of love:
>
> $$\frac{\text{He}}{\text{She}} \sim \frac{\text{Subject} + \text{Destinataire}}{\text{Object} + \text{Destinateur}}$$
>
> The four actants are there, symmetrically inverted, but syncretized in the form of two actors.[28]

---

27. Gerald Prince, *A Grammar of Stories* (The Hague: Mouton, 1973), 31.
28. Greimas, 177.

It is obvious that in the *trouvère* lyric the situation of the *je* crying out for mercy (that is, for the consummation of his love) to a lady who holds the power both to provoke desire in him and also to deny him her favor is identical to that described above by Greimas. Moreover, if we dispose these two pairs of actantial roles of lyric in a square, we may easily see how each role accounts for an aspect of the two persons *je* and *elle* as these persons relate both to each other and, just as important, to themselves:

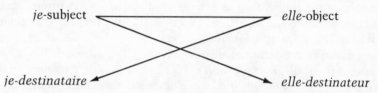

je-subject   *elle*-object

je-destinataire   *elle*-destinateur

In other words, *je* actively loves the lady as subject but hates himself because he is also the passive victim of her denial, or the *destinataire*; *elle* despises *je* and loves herself as *destinateur* (which is to say that she is very proud). Singing is the manifestation of desire in *je*; that is, the body of the song is present as a sign of love because *another* body, more animate, has been denied. That the song should have the power not only to mediate desire but to constitute *itself* as an object of desire that can become the rival of the absent lady is a problem that will call for special consideration in a moment.

The roles of the *adjuvant* and *opposant* in this poem by the Châtelain de Coucy do not function as simply or as obviously as the other four roles. In the vast majority of poems in the *trouvère* tradition, the actantial role of *opposant* is occupied by a figure called the *lozengier* or *médisant*, and not, surprisingly, by a rival suitor or a jealous husband;[29] the latter is an especially rare bird in this verbal habitat of the nightingale. The *médisant* and his band are above all those who turn the supreme powers of the human tongue against the supreme cause of love. They tell lies, they reveal secrets, they denounce lovers in public, they flatter, they boast; worst of all, they even dare mouth the language of true love! In this poem, the role of the *médisant* is not actually named, but it is clearly evoked in three of the six stanzas (II, III,

29. Erich Köhler, "Les troubadours et la jalousie," in *Melanges de langue et de littérature du Moyen Age et de la Renaissance: Offerts à Jean Frappier par ses collègues, ses élèves et ses amis* (Geneva: Droz, 1970), 543–59.

and VI). The *médisant* is that traitor who rejoices in the demise of honest lovers, he who courts women *sanz cuer*, and he who persuades true lovers to swerve from their love merely because they have been rebuffed. Like the *médisant* of convention, then, the *médisant* in this poem is primarily a man of words, but perhaps even a bad singer of songs. The role of the *adjuvant* is even more complex, because it includes all of those people and things who are the poet's real or potential allies; among these are (with the exception of the lady herself) all of those whom I identified above as potential interlocutors of *je*. As long as the basic architectonics of actantial roles remains intact, substitutions can occur without destroying the coherence of *trouvère* discourse, at least in the minds of the initiated audience. The same phenomenon seems to occur in medieval romance, where stories often break off, acquire new heroes, or lend themselves to endless continuation. Medieval narrativity is less oriented, it seems, to the morphology of the story as a discursive unit than it is to a consistent configuration of roles; so long as this is respected, anything (or even nothing) can "happen."

What is most interesting about the actantial roles expressed in this poem, as in *trouvère* lyric in general, is that the *opposant* in the latent story of love is not in the least a sexual rival. As a man of words and letters, the nature of the *médisant* as *opposant* tends very strongly to displace a problem of desire away from the sphere of sexuality and toward the sphere of language. We are dealing here with a fascinating and important presupposition of the lyric register which is perhaps pertinent to all erotic literature and the world that it purports to represent. Given the equivalence of the activities of *chanter* and *aimer* that Zumthor has discerned in the semantic universe of *trouvère* lyric, it makes little difference whether the *médisant* is the enemy of the poet as lover or of the lover as poet. Indeed, the *trouvère* poet seeks an unending suspension between deeds of love and of language, one that calls for a delicate balance between expression and repression. Poetic signs must have the power both to express the prospect of *joie*—which is ultimately that of physical *jouissance*—and to defer it. At the same time, the language of love must constitute an artistic world in which language itself becomes charged with fetishistic desire, which is the joy of the lyric text. Textuality at the expense of sexuality is not a feature of medieval lyric alone, however, but of courtly narrative as well. In his *Lancelot*, Chrétien de Troyes relishes his ambiguous function as narrator—and concealer—of *joie* in erotic love, which he both declines to describe and refuses to pass over in silence.[30]

Thus, *trouvère* lyric expresses what several critics have called a latent story. Such a story is repressed, in that its potential events (consummation, death) have been displaced by (non-) events of a language that constantly renounces its capacity to signify. But how does that story implicate us, as members of the poem's audience?

Clearly, before we may enter into the fiction of the *requête courtoise*—that is, before we may take to heart the secret cause of a despairing *je* so that he may sing our song—we must first become the audience or the reader of his song: that is, an *adjuvant*. Our *opposant* in this role is the *médisant*: he is that abuser of speech, that transgressor of codes, whose false and evil actions are as much the instigators of the song as is the fictive, hostile lady of our desire. To the extent that we enjoy this text itself as an object of desire (we surely would not consent to become its audience if we did *not*), it is the *médisant* as *opposant* who constitutes us dialectically as *adjuvant*. A peculiar oscillation arises in us with the enunciation of the song, however: as creatures of erotic desire who assume the identity of *je*, we hate the *médisant* for spoiling our pleasure; as lovers of the *poem*, we can only applaud him—indeed, we love (as readers) to hate him (as lovers). The fiction that I am a frustrated lover is therefore an occultation of my reality as a reader who is being textually satisfied. By blaming the lady for begetting my unrequited love, I blind myself to my secret connivance with the *médisant*. If I were to enjoy the lady, *je*-audience would die: hence the importance of the *médisant* as the guarantor of my readerly desire—which is to desire.

30. For example:

> Tant li est ses jeus dolz et buens,
> et del beisier et del santir,
> que il lor avint sanz mantir
> une joie et une mervoille
> tel c'onques ancor sa paroille
> ne fu oie et sëue;
> mes toz jors iert par moi tëue,
> qu'an conte ne doit estre dite.
> Des joies fu la plus eslite
> et la plus delitable cele
> que li contes nos teste et cele.

Chrétien de Troyes, *Lancelot*, ed. M. Roques (Paris: Champion, 1958), vv. 4674–84. See also n. 1, above.

There was a time when, at least for a certain type of reader, structural descriptions might have sufficed. Since that time, however, we have become more concerned to find out why, or under what ideological and psychological conditions, structures that we were once content merely to describe have been produced in the first place. What purpose or purposes do such structures (or their analyses) serve?

Accordingly, in an attempt to pass to another level of analysis, I shall assume that the oscillations in the actantial model described above are more than mere rhetorical effects, and that they express or embody the psychodynamics that Freud believes to be at work (or in play) during the enunciation of what he calls tendentious sexual jokes.[31] For our purpose, the chief value of Freud's analysis of sexual jokes is that it allows us to explain in a more thorough way the relationships of interdependence and the transformations that simultaneously implicate all six of the actantial roles manifested by *trouvère* lyric in the process of enunciation.

In having recourse to Freud's theories of wit, I should specify from the outset three points that I am taking for granted. First, I hold it to be obvious (though still worth proving, perhaps) that medieval French lyric draws heavily upon the very same technical resources of language that Freud evokes as characteristics of the verbal joke: replacement of object-association by word-association, discovery of what is familiar, faulty thinking, condensation, displacement, absurdity, representation of the opposite, and so on. Second, I shall take it for granted that the performance of courtly lyric, with its elegance and refinement, is a source of enjoyment for its own sake but that—like the performance of tendentious jokes where an expression of sexual (or hostile) aggression is involved—this performance affords both its performer and its audience some kind of "pleasure" over and beyond that provided by the purely formal aspects of lyric as a verbal artifact. Third, I shall assume that this pleasure is a consequence of our own participation in the dynamics of roles that attends the enunciation of lyric and that this pleasure coincides with some kind of rebalancing of forces within our own mental sphere.

According to Freud, a tendentious joke requires for its performance

31. Sigmund Freud, *Der Witz und seine Beziehung zum Unbewussten* (Leipzig: Deutike, 1905). I have used the translation by James Strachey in the *Standard Edition* (London, 1924), vol. 8, published under the title *Jokes and their Relation to the Unconscious* (New York: Norton, 1963). I am also indebted to Tzvetan Todorov, "Freud sur l'énonciation," *Langages* 17 (1970): 34–41.

three persons.[32] First, there is the teller, and Freud says that his motivation to perform the joke originates in a circumstance where the teller has been an unsuccessful aggressor upon a woman that he desires. Second, there is the woman who is the object of the teller's aggression. Third, there is the interlocutor in whom the teller desires, according to Freud, to instigate pleasure in the form of laughter.

Thus, the performance of a sexual joke implicitly involves the following sequence of events: when a subject finds his libidinous impulses blocked by the woman who is the object of his aggressions, he directs his attention to some third party, who has first been perceived as a spoiler—an intruder or a rival—hence, as some personification of the negative principle displayed by the woman. The teller uses the sexual joke to transform this third person into an ally or confederate by offering him, through verbal representation of the sexual act, easy gratification of his libido. The laughter produced by the joke in the listener results in vicarious laughter in the teller as well, and this coincides with a pleasurable release of impulses (both libidinous and hostile) in the subject which have been repressed but may now be expressed because they have been transformed into a semiological emission that is an acceptable aim in itself. "Since the sexual aggressiveness is held up in its advance toward the act, it pauses at the evocation of excitement and derives pleasure from the signs of it in the woman. In so doing the aggressiveness is no doubt altering its character as well, just as any libidinal impulse will if it is met by an obstacle."[33]

Freud says, however, that the demands of refined culture act as a censorship that forbids the telling of raw sexual jokes, even in the absence of the woman, and in such conditions pleasure can be obtained when the resources of verbal wit are brought into play. The more our aggressive impulses express themselves through the refining techniques of wordplay, the more we lose our capacity to distinguish in the telling of a tendentious joke what part of our pleasure originates in the joke's technique and what part results from the expression of aggression. "Thus, strictly speaking," Freud says, "we do not know what we are laughing about."[34]

To transform thwarted erotic desire into highly refined verbal art (such as the art of *fin'amor*) does not mean, of course, that "innocence"

32. Freud, *Jokes*, 100.
33. Freud, *Jokes*, 99.
34. Freud, *Jokes*, 102.

is being restored: indeed, Jeffrey Mehlman has shown that already in Freud the opposition between innocent and tendentious jokes is perfectly spurious; we may infer that even the seemingly innocent "pleasure from signs" in supposedly nontendentious humor is nothing other than a simulation, in the process of speech, of the fundamentally autoerotic character of human sexual desire.[35] Our pleasure in the refinement of *trouvère* lyric derives from a negation of desire which is also its provocation because it ceaselessly names what is absent.

Though the performance of courtly lyric does not necessarily evince overt laughter (nor, for that matter, do we always roar at the examples that Freud uses to illustrate his theories of sexual jokes), I believe that a fundamentally humorous cast is implicit in its register and that it is therefore worthwhile to pursue a step further the complementarity of enunciation in *trouvère* lyric and sexual wit.

It is obvious that Freud's model implicates three persons but six distinct roles, and that these roles coincide quite precisely in function with the six actants as they are usually expressed in courtly lyric. The speaker is both the desiring subject and the victim of denial on the part of a woman who is both the object of desire and bestower of disfavor; the audience as third party is both rival and potential ally, or *opposant* and *adjuvant*. One advantage of Freud's theory is that it allows us to grasp with more clarity how we as the audience of the poetic performance are related to the *médisant*: as audience, we are his transform. His evil verbal acts have, along with the cruelty of the lady, provoked pain in the speaker, whose relief takes the form of the poem as gratification. To the extent that the *médisant* of *trouvère* lyric provokes the instance of discourse that we as audience crave, we may say that there is a strongly autoerotic character to our readerly desire, though in order to be enacted this textual performance seems to require the fiction that we are primarily lovers. The *je* of the erotic lover is a third party to us in our joy of the text, just as we are the third party in his poetic desire for the woman. The *médisant* is not just a hostile third person; he is the fictive incarnation of that absolute zero-person over and against which the whole axis of communication constitutes itself. In short, he is nothing less than the dialectical guarantor both of the code and of the instance of lyric discourse.

Hence, the *médisant* is no less indispensable to our status as audi-

---

35. Jeffrey Mehlman, "How to Read Freud on Jokes: The Critic as *Schadchen*," *New Literary History* 5 (1973): 443.

ence than is the cruelty of the lady as *destinateur* to the libidinous desire that makes *je* sing (to us).

To perceive the latent story of *trouvère* lyric is not to perceive the fiction of thwarted desire as a motivation of the text but rather to perceive the very fictivization of our libido as precisely the means by which we occult—and thereby sustain—our joy in the signs of the text. Yet the very fictivity of unending erotic desire is also the truth of a textual libido, or a love of signs (and of signs of signs). This fetishistic desire for the sign can never be satisfied because of the dual nature of the sign itself: invested with a signification that is maximally conventional and therefore belongs to everyone and to no one, a signifier of *trouvère* discourse may never be completely possessed by the enunciating individual without the destruction of its capacity to signify. To the contrary, the domain of the verbal sign, even the verbal sign expressing my love, is a public domain whose conventionality (especially in *trouvère* lyric) must be sustained if the sign is to signify. For me to enunciate the *je* of this discourse is less to appropriate this sign than to be dispossessed of my individual fantasms. For me to espouse *trouvère* discourse is to renounce the possibility of enunciating my own personal desires—except, perhaps, my desire to desire. Even ordinary language, poetic or not, can be as cruel and as seductive to *homo ardens* as extraordinary ladies; all the more, then, is the courtly lyric text the elevation of the poet's peculiar *joie d'amor* to its most poignant, enduring, and universal form.

CHAPTER 5

Chrétien's *Yvain* and
the Ideologies of
Change and Exchange

$\mathbb{D}$uring the last few years, a tendency has arisen among certain medievalists to conceive the morphology of feudal society in terms of three "estates," "orders," or "functions" expressed by the actions of prayer, combat, and productive labor. These are performed, respectively, by the *oratores* or the clergy, the *bellatores*, and the *laboratores*: the last category includes not only serfs but certain other social groups as well.

By its very title, Georges Duby's book, *Les Trois Ordres, ou l'imaginaire du féodalisme*, makes it clear that, *à l'état pur*, this triangular structure was in fact only latent in the political consciousness of the medieval West, and that when we try to identify the three estates as social realities at any given moment in history, their functions overlap and blur.[1] Still, the triordinal thesis has a certain heuristic value in allowing us to perceive and express modulations in class structures and social forms, and also to undertake comparisons, not only between moments distant in time but between our own culture and those of ages past.

The triordinal theory also helps us to understand why the value and importance of certain other estates or functions in culture were recognized with such reluctance during the Middle Ages: for instance, those tied to commerce and other more technological activities. Despite the

---

1. Georges Duby, *Les Trois Ordres, ou l'imaginaire du féodalisme* (Paris: Gallimard, 1978).

official reluctance to recognize mercantilism as an estate, a new *class* consciousness *was* provoked by the emergence of the mercantile class. The precision of that consciousness increased as the economic importance of the class itself increased. As Georg Lukács wrote:

> For pre-capitalist epochs and for the behaviour of many strata within capitalism whose economic roots lie in pre-capitalism, class consciousness is unable to achieve complete clarity and to influence the course of history consciously. This is true above all because class interests in pre-capitalist society never achieve full (economic) articulation. Hence the structuring of society into castes and estates means that economic elements are inextricably joined to political and religious factors. In contrast to this, the rule of the bourgeoisie means the abolition of the estates-system and this leads to the organization of society along class lines.[2]

In patristic and scholastic thought, the term *ordo* implied a notion of cosmic hierarchy, and the triordinal theory underlay what we may call a *discursive* hierarchy in medieval culture as well, one that in effect consigned the lowest of the *laboratores*, as an order or class, to official silence. We may see symptoms of this willing neglect in Andreas Capellanus's *De amore*, which was written for the aristocrats of Champagne at a time of intense mercantile initiative.[3] Andreas takes great pains (I.vi) to illustrate how lovers of different social origin ought to address each other, and in the society of those who are worthy to love and speak, he acknowledges only the following class figures: the *plebeius*, who is non-noble but free; the *nobilis*, who is of the lesser nobility, born of vavasors; and the *nobilior*, who is born of high nobles (*a proceribus sumpta*). Above this community of speaking lovers are the male clergy (I.vii), who must remain exempt from love (the female clergy are pushovers, Andreas warns us; I.vii), while below the community of lovers are the servile *agricultores*, or *rustici*, who are simply incapable of the art of love because their destiny is merely to labor and to copulate like beasts. They are incapable even of speak-

2. Georg Lukács, *History and Class Consciousness: Studies in Marxist Dialectics*, trans. Rodney Livingstone (Cambridge, Mass.: MIT Press, 1971), 55.
3. Andreas Capellanus, *De amore libri tres*, ed. Salvatore Battaglia, with two Tuscan translations, under the title *Trattato d'amore* (Rome: Perrella, 1947). See also André le Chapelain, *Traité de l'amour courtois*, French trans. Claude Buridant (Paris: Klincksieck, 1974).

ing of love; hence, if a female serf attracts us, Andreas says (I.xi), we should avoid praising her altogether and possess her directly by force.

The discursive status of the twelfth-century merchant interests me in particular because, on the one hand, here was an unofficial function that was all too often inscribed with contempt and anathema into the official discourses of those whose mandates were to *pray* and to *defend*; on the other, it is undeniable that the *mercator* and his interests became a force that invaded all three orders of the feudal hierarchy of late twelfth-century northern France in ways that we are now only beginning to grasp. If, within the dominant discourses of the clergy and the nobility, the merchant was a shadowy figure at best—a kind of *laborator* without a viable, legitimate discourse of his own[4]—paradoxically, mercantilism and its values began to reverberate in the more established discourses of the late twelfth-century world as a sublanguage promulgating a new ideology of change and exchange. As Lukacs puts it, "The history of (feudal) estates shows very clearly that what in origin had been a 'natural' economic existence cast into stable forms begins gradually to disintegrate as a result of subterranean, 'unconscious' economic development."[5]

It is precisely the problem, both theoretical and historical, of apprehending these ubiquitous yet subtle discursive inflections that interests me in this chapter, and I shall attempt to explore what I believe to be a far-reaching ideology of exchange expressed in Chrétien de Troyes's *Yvain*, a text whose discourse is centered, one may safely propose, on the order of the *bellatores*. However, for reasons that will become clear later, I shall first evoke some of the indirect consequences of mercantilism discernible in the theological discourse of the *oratores* in the closing decades of the twelfth century in northern France— that is, in Chrétien's own culture.

TOWARD A THEOLOGY OF HORIZONTAL EXCHANGE

Although earlier in the century such a mystic as Hugh of St. Victor could acknowledge both the reality of and the necessity for commerce in the body politic (as he does in his *Didascalicon*, about which I shall speak later), Hugh's real interests as an *orator* in matters of change and

---

4. Robert S. Lopez, *The Commercial Revolution of the Middle Ages* (Englewood Cliffs, N.J.: Prentice-Hall, 1971), 123–25.

5. Lukacs, 57.

exchange involve, above all, *spiritual* transactions between the soul and God: that is, mystical transactions upward (or downward) in a hierarchy of being. In his treatise *Soliloquium de arrha animae* Hugh exhorts the human soul to love the material beauties of the world not for themselves but rather as a kind of money by which the soul is mysteriously purchased by God as betrothed:

> All the universe is subject to you and there is hardly anything
> in it which excels in beauty, usefulness, size or quality that
> you do not gladly accept. If you truly love these things, love
> them as being subject to you, love them as objects at your ser-
> vice, as the earnest money of your betrothed, as the offerings
> of a true friend, as the benefactions of a master. In order that
> you may always remember what you owe to him, do not prefer
> these gifts to the giver, but hold them dear because of him, and
> through and above them, love him.[6]

One will recognize here a vertical projection, into the metaphysical realm, of a relatively simple model of exchange founded on gift-giving, barter, and marriage dowries, one where money only measures the value of objects to be given or exchanged. Hugh's idea about the "economy" of salvation was not, of course, new but reflected a long tradition of vertical thought about the Eucharist as a purchase of man's sins and about the saint's relic as *pignus*: that is, pledge money or down payment. Later in the century, the platonist Alain de Lille, writing as Chrétien's exact contemporary, elaborated a cluster of ideas more propitious to an ideology of *horizontal* change and exchange transpiring in and through physical nature, rather than in an axis of vertical ascendance. Alain emphasizes the principle of being (*esse*) less as a process of transcendence than as a process of becoming (*fieri*), conceived as the circulation of life within an economy of forms:

> When the artisan of the universe had clothed all things in the
> outward aspect befitting their natures and had wed them to
> one another in the relationship of lawful marriage, it was his
> will that by a mutually related circle of birth and death, transi-
> tory things should be given stability by instability, endlessness
> by endings, eternity by temporariness and that the series of

6. Hugh of St. Victor, *Soliloquium de arrha animae*, ed. M. K. Mueller (Bonn: A. Marcus and E. Weber, 1913); trans. Kevin Herbert, *Soliloquy on the Earnest Money of the Soul* (Milwaukee: Marquette Univ. Press, 1956).

things should ever be knit by successive renewals of birth. He decreed that by the lawful path of derivation by propagation, like things, sealed with the stamp of manifest resemblance, should be produced from like.[7]

Alain says (*Prosa* 4) that Nature has been appointed as God's substitute in assuring that the creation succeeds itself horizontally in time. Motivated by desire, the proliferation of forms in her womb is carefully regulated, as in the minting of coins. Nature exclaims:

> Accordingly, he appointed me as his substitute, his vice-regent, the mistress of his mint, to put the stamp on the different classes of things so that I should mould the images of things, each on its own anvil, not allow the product to deviate from the form of its own anvil, but that, by my diligence in work, the face of the copy should spring from the countenance of the exemplar and not be defrauded of any of its natural gifts. I obeyed the commander's orders in my work and I, to use a metaphor, striking various coins of things according to the mould of the exemplar and producing copies of my original by fashioning like out of like, gave to my imprints the appearance of the things imaged.

One sees an interesting expression of the tension between vertical and horizontal "moneys" on the romanesque south portal of Saint-Sernin in Toulouse (ca. 1105). The central tympanum shows the resurrected Christ, and to the right we see St. Peter, over whom appear two angels, each holding a coin with a cross on it: this is Christ's pledge money as dispensed, now, through the Church. In contrast, on a corbel at the upper left we see the figure of a woman with lovely hair and a bare breast holding an *unmarked* and presumably very secular coin, one by which man's most secular desires are served.[8]

At a time when the clergy and high nobles of northern France were seeking ways to tame a warfaring, pillaging, revenge-motivated order of *bellatores*—whose God was the *Christus militans*—in favor of a more prosperous, commercial peace, Alain's doctrine of change and succes-

---

7. Alain de Lille, *De planctu Naturae*, ed. N. M. Haring, in *Studi Medievalia*, terza serie 19.2 (1978), 797–879; English trans. James J. Sheridan, *The Plaint of Nature* (Toronto: Pontifical Institute of Mediaeval Studies, 1980).

8. I am grateful to my colleague Thomas W. Lyman for his generosity in discussing these details with me.

sion through carefully regulated love was surely welcome. Moreover, it was in this very same climate of promoting an economy of desire and exchange in the material world that a new, supernatural concept of purgatory emerged. As Jacques Le Goff has recently shown in his book, *La Naissance du purgatoire*, a major mutation occurred in Western theology when, during what Le Goff quaintly calls "the Parisian springtime and the Cistercian summer,"[9] Christian thinkers in northern France—and specifically in Champagne—enunciated, between 1170 and 1200, a forceful new concept of purgatory, conceived now as a specific "third place" midway between the opposite poles of heaven and hell. Here the souls of sinners were believed to spend specific durations of time purging themselves of sins committed while on earth. The carefully quantified labor of penitence (the very notion of *labor* implied punishment in the Middle Ages) was thought to culminate in the just reward of salvation. This spiritual economy allowed even for the vicarious purchase of one man's purgation in the world beyond by the charitable works and prayers of a third party acting here and now in his behalf.

Le Goff is surprisingly cautious about the contribution of socioeconomic developments in northern France to the theological concept of purgatory. However, it seems to me inevitable that the rapid transformation, in the twelfth century, of a barter economy into a profit-motivated monetary economy centered on traveling professional middlemen who bought in order to sell, thereby instigating a kind of protocapitalism, led to a new conception of God as a God of just prices (as opposed, for example, to the more feudal God of gift-giving and judicial duels evident in the *Roland*) and to a new spiritual topography specifying a place where values of time, space, and service could be precisely measured and exchanged. It is well known that thanks to the economic initiative of Henri-le-libéral, Count of Champagne (whose energetic wife, Marie, daughter of Eleanor of Aquitaine, was Chrétien's patroness), the *foires* of Troyes and five other designated fair-towns made Champagne into nothing less than the commercial center of northern Europe.[10] Precisely as this great nobleman and his successors were inaugurating, within the new urban spaces of their territory, a

9. Jacques Le Goff, *La Naissance du purgatoire* (Paris: Gallimard, 1981), 227.

10. The pioneering study of the fairs is by Félix Bourquelot, *Etudes sur les foires de Champagne*, 2 vols. (Brionne: Porgulan, 1865). For a more recent bibliography, see R. Bautier, "Les foires de Champagne, recherches sur une évolution historique," in *La Foire*, Receuils de la Société Jean Bodin, vol. 5 (Brussels: Editions de la librairie encyclopédique, 1953), 97–147.

specific time and place for commerce (as well as a new justice: the provost had one seat within the fair limits, another in the towns),[11] devoted solely to the conduct of trade by professional merchants traveling from Flanders and Italy, so too the Cistercians—quite literally down the road—were hatching a new theological concept of purgatory involving a soteriological economy. While it is true that fire, and not gold, is the dominant medium of exchange in the early theology of purgatory, we should remember that fire is as much a technological force in operations of annealing and refining as it is an instrument of punishment or torture, and the common goal of both *fin'amor* and of alchemy is to ennoble base souls and base metals by mastering the secrets of metamorphosis. Fire and gold, then, are both media of exchange. Such an association is as old as Heraclitus, as Marc Shell reminds us by citing fragment 90: "All things are an equal exchange (*antamoibe*) for fire and fire for all things, as goods (*chremata*) are for gold (*chrysou*) and gold for goods."[12]

Let us consider a second theological concept that underwent a radical reinterpretation during the rise of commerce: marriage. Marriage is a personal relationship but also a social one to the extent that on the occasion of marriage, powers and possessions are exchanged—even now—within the social group. It should come as no surprise that concepts of the marital relationship were also sensitive to new values emerging primarily from mercantile circles. As opposed to exchange (whether of money or of goods) transacted in a feudal context, which generally involves unequal partners in a hierarchy and whose terms are fixed by custom, true commercial exchange demands both the legal *freedom* of partners to negotiate a contract and *equality* as they do so. As the scholastics knew, mutual consent is the basis of true commercial exchange.[13] Previous to the mid-twelfth century, the marriage relationship had been determined not primarily by the exercise of free consent between partners but rather by such exterior considerations as the acquired privilege of a man to possess a woman, or else by such

11. On the justice of the fairs, which was administered jointly by Henri and the religious of Saint-Ayoul, see Bourquelot, 2: 257–59.

12. Marc Shell, *The Economy of Literature* (Baltimore, Md.: Johns Hopkins Univ. Press, 1978), 52.

13. Raymond de Roover, *La Pensée économique des scolastiques, doctrines et méthodes* (Montréal: Institut d'études médiévales; Paris: Vrin, 1971), 58–59; see also *The Cambridge Economic History of Europe*, ed M. M. Postan, E. E. Rich, and Edward Miller (Cambridge: Cambridge Univ. Press, 1971), 3:15–18.

factors as cohabitation or consummation.[14] During the twelfth century (when marriage also became a sacrament), free consent between legitimate partners became the sole basis of the marriage relationship. So, too, the love of friends and of kin was also seen as the union of souls based upon free consent of both wills—as Bernard, in a sermon on the Song of Songs (XXVI.6), understood his love for his deceased brother Girard.[15] It would seem, once again, that mutations in the theology of love and of marriage closely attended social progress occurring in the economic sphere, even though this economic substratum is not, itself, directly expressed in discussions of marriage.

What I am suggesting is simple: the multiple discourses that constitute any given speech community not only develop together; they also act upon and interfere with each other, even though we cannot always be sure in which discourse new concepts first arise, and even though certain innovating discourses of the past are not audible to us now. There obviously *was* a specifically mercantile discourse in the twelfth century, and the *oratores* obviously *heard* it, if from a distance. Here is Hugh of St. Victor describing commerce, which he calls *navigatio:*

> Commerce contains every sort of dealing in the purchase, sale and exchange of foreign goods. This art is beyond all doubt a peculiar sort of rhetoric—strictly of its own kind—for eloquence is in the highest degree necessary to it. Thus the man who excels others in fluency of speech is called a *Mercurius,* or Mercury, as being a *mercatorum kirrius (kyrios)*—a very lord among merchants.[16]

Just as the sociolinguist William Labov gives evidence for the socioeconomic motives underlying linguistic change at the level of pho-

---

14. The best account of twelfth-century shifts in the conception of marriage remains, I believe, that of G. Le Bras, "Mariage," in *Dictionnaire de théologie catholique.* See also John T. Noonan, Jr., "The Power to Choose," *Viator* 4 (1973): 419–34; Marie-Odile Métral, *Le Mariage: Les Hésitations de l'Occident* (Paris: Aubier, 1977); Georges Duby, *Le Chevalier, la femme et le prêtre: Le Mariage dans la France féodale* (Paris: Hachette, 1981); Jean Leclerq, *Le Mariage vu par les moines au 12e siècle* (Paris: Cerf, 1982).

15. *S. Bernardi opera,* ed. J. Leclerq, C. H. Talbot, and H. M. Rochais (Rome: Editiones cistercienses, 1968), vol. 4.

16. Hugh of St. Victor, *Didascalicon: De studio legendi,* II.viii, ed. Charles Henry Buttimer (Washington, D.C.: Catholic Univ. Press, 1939); trans. Jerome Taylor, *The Didascalicon of Hugh of St. Victor* (New York: Columbia Univ. Press, 1961), 91–92.

netic patterns,[17] so I would argue that the socioeconomic basis for mutations, both syntactic and semantic, occurred at the level of discourse. I would further apply Labov's claim that linguistic change occurs most massively in the middle classes, where social mobility is most pronounced, to twelfth-century Champagne, where a powerful bourgeois class was beginning to emerge from the lower ranks, and where the lesser nobles, on their side, were beginning to lose or forsake their inherited martial privileges. Michael A. K. Halliday has written:

> The social context of the linguistic code is the culture. But in order to refer to this we need to represent the culture as an information system, or rather as a network of information systems: that is in semiotic terms. A culture is a configuration of semiotic systems; the central problem is to interpret language in a way which enables us to relate it to other semiotic processes.[18]

Although we still lack a mature general theory defining those principles governing the displacement of concepts from code to code within the social group, no one would deny that such displacements *do* occur; moreover, given the "hybridizing" tendencies of twelfth- and thirteenth-century medieval literature, it is clear that such displacements constitute a generative principle of medieval poetics and, inversely, that medieval poetic texts promulgate such displacements in their social context.

BELLATOR ET MERCATOR

Aspects of medieval texts that we first grasp and articulate through modern critical theory will often become more distinct when we situate them in a historical process. For instance, if we accept the historically grounded contentions of Dumézil, Duby, Le Goff and others that an archaic triordinal theory did indeed inform the ideological consciousness of the Middle Ages, we may infer that this theory also implied certain discursive parameters within which the play of medieval

17. William Labov, *Sociolinguistic Patterns* (Philadelphia: Univ. of Pennsylvania Press, 1972), ch. 1.

18. M. A. K. Halliday, "Language as Code and Language as Behaviour: A Systemic-Functional Interpretation of the Nature and Otogenesis of Dialogue," in *The Semiotics of Culture and Language*, ed. Robin P. Fawcett, M. A. K. Halliday, Sydney M. Lamb, and Adam Makkai (London: Frances Pinter, 1984), 1:8.

literary texts unfolded. Joel H. Grisward has recently published *Archéologie de l'épopée médiévale*, prefaced by Georges Dumézil, in which he proposes that an archaic Indo-European ideology may be found intact in certain French feudal epics. Such studies should not, however, lead us to assume that poetic texts are passive receptacles or simple mirrors of a priori discursive patterns. Perhaps in choosing the *Cycle des narbonnais* for the "autopsy" that he says he has performed, Grisward did perhaps find a corpus compatible with his methods; however, had he chosen the *Chanson de Roland*, which is the most archaic (and in many ways the least typical) of French feudal epics, the corpse for Dr. Grisward's autopsy would have lain less still.[19]

If one accepts the "traditionalist" premise, as most scholars now do, that the discourse of the *Roland* constituted itself during the formation of a dominant warrior class in the two centuries following the collapse of the Carolingian empire,[20] and if one grants a priori that this discourse reflects the institutional values proper to that *ordo*, one will also find (as I have argued in chapter 3) that the seemingly privileged warrior's discourse shows symptoms of being in deep crisis in the *Roland*. This crisis implicates not only a set of traditional ethical values but the most intimate semantic processes of the poem itself. Moreover, it was within the cultural turmoil surrounding the emergence of new economic priorities, I would propose, that a new chivalric discourse constituted itself, entailing a whole new ethics and a new poetics as well: we call this discourse "romance," signaling thereby a new alliance between a vernacular language and writing, *grammatica*, or what at the time was also called *litteratura*.[21] It is with this new discourse that we shall henceforth deal, taking Chrétien's *Yvain* as our example.

By its very name, "romance" may be understood to exist more as a language (*lingua*) and a discourse (*sermo*) than as a form, and in the prescriptive terms of twelfth- and thirteenth-century rhetorical theory, this discourse was to conform to what was called the *stylus nobilis* or *gravis*.[22] Medieval rhetoricians defined the *stylus nobilis* according to

19. Joel H. Grisward, *Archéologie de l'épopée médiévale* (Paris: Payot, 1981), 325.

20. Ramon Menéndez Pidal, *La Chanson de Roland et la tradition épique des Francs*, French trans. Irénée-Marcel Cluzel (Paris: Picard, 1960).

21. See my *From Topic to Tale: Logic and Narrative in the Middle Ages* (Minneapolis: Univ. of Minnesota Press, 1986).

22. Edmond Faral, *Les Arts poétiques du XIIe et du XIIIe siècles: Recherches et documents sur la technique littéraire du moyen-âge* (Paris: Champion, 1924), 86–87.

two main criteria: first, it follows rules of decorum proper to the sphere of the *miles*, or the chivalric nobleman; second, it is marked by an abundance of tropes or "figures of thought." The term used by rhetoricians to designate this resource of the high style is *ornatus difficilis*, which John of Garland equates with the *modus gravis et authenticus*. The tropes that form its arsenal are enumerated by Matthew of Vendôme, Chrétien's probable contemporary, as metaphor, antithesis, metonymy, synecdoche, periphrasis, allegory and its variants, and enigma; as Edmond Faral says of *ornatus difficilis*, "Il a pour principe l'emploi des mots dans un sens différent de leur sens propre: d'où résulte de la part de l'écrivain un effort d'ingéniosité et d'originalité qui justifie l'épithète de 'gravis.'"[23] Although the "noble" style is supreme in a secondary triordinal hierarchy of discourses modeled by rhetoricians on the so-called "Virgilian wheel,"[24] we must not assume that this discourse was based upon the historical reality of the knight as *bellator* or on his true function in twelfth-century political life. Indeed, all three orders of the Virgilian wheel—the *miles*, the *agricola*, and the *pastor otiosus*—are fictions grounded not upon truly extant social categories but on the eminently literary models of Virgil's *Aeneid*, his *Georgics*, and his *Eclogues*. Surely one of the purposes of romance as "fiction" was precisely to accelerate the transformation of twelfth-century chivalric conduct into a class exercise whose archaic warlike function was becoming more an emblem or a sport than a form of direct political coercion.[25] Moreover, as I have proposed elsewhere, the main semantic thrust of metaphor, or *translatio* (understood as the generic term including all figures of thought), in the narrative discourse of chivalric romance is to "translate" warlike impulses into the impulse to love: that is, to subvert the *proprietas* of chivalric war by making it "figurative."[26]

For Chrétien to subordinate the art of war to the art of love in his chivalric fiction is in effect to inculcate a completely new system of values and, more precisely, to inculcate—within a duly decorous "noble" and "difficult" discourse—a new casuistry of exchange whose

23. Faral, 89, 90.

24. Faral, 89.

25. Jacques Heers, *Fêtes, jeux et joûtes dans les sociétés d'occident à la fin du moyen-âge* (Montréal: Institut d' études médiévales; Paris: Vrin, 1971). Heers shows how chivalry from the twelfth century on became ritualized and progressively bracketed by other social rituals.

26. Eugene Vance, "Signs of the City" Medieval Poetry as Detour," *New Literary History* 4 (1972–73): 557–74.

fiction is in reality a transcoded social imperative now suffusing the feudal world from below. The fiction of courtly erotic desire is a metaphorization, I would propose, of a burgeoning new commercial economy that members of the very high nobility of northern France were eager to patronize, though not to practice. The *semiotization* of chivalry—that is, the willingness of courtly poets to make the arms and gestures of the knight into signs or symbols of something *else*—is a process of denaturing the signification of material objects that attended the monetarization of the twelfth-century economy: money summons forth and expresses the significations of things as values so that they can be exchanged. *Translatio,* or metaphor, is the verbal instrument by which Chrétien transacts *mental* substitutions of things for other things. Twelfth-century rhetorical theory considered "artificial disposition" (as opposed to "natural" disposition) as a positive artistic goal, and to the extent that narrative art dislocated things from their "natural" function to "commute" (*commutare*)[27] them into an artificial order, such narrative can, itself, be considered as a kind of economy.

In Chrétien's romances, and in *Yvain* in particular, Arthur's court is portrayed as a place of readily expended (as opposed to hoarded) wealth, and its abundance is the just fruit of adventuring knights who circulate through the world and gather together at Pentecost to exchange not exotic commodities, but marvelous tales:

> Artus, li buens rois de Bretaigne,
> La cui proesce nos ansaingne,
> Que nos soiiens preu et cortois,
> Tint cort si riche come rois
> A cele feste, qui tant *coste,*
> Qu'an doit clamer la pante*coste.*[28]
> (vv. 1–6; italics mine)

> (Arthur, the good king of Brittany, whose prowess teaches us to be bold and courteous, held a very rich, royal court, which cost very much, that we call Pentecost.)

If Arthur's fictional court reflects a utopian ideal of prosperity and abundance characteristic of Henri-le-libéral's own court in Cham-

27. Faral, 56.
28. Chrétien de Troyes, *Yvain,* ed. W. Foerster (Halle: Niemeyer, 1906), vv. 1363–68; hereafter cited in the text (translations are mine).

pagne,[29] the real character of the noble, chivalric *bellator* in that same historical world was far different from that of his fictional counterpart. In general, the second half of the twelfth century was a time of radical change in the technology of arms (for instance, the deadly crossbow, wielded by non-nobles and bourgeois, became important in France after 1185)[30] in both the *technology* of assault and defense (now centered upon the stone fortifications built by towns)[31] and, just as important, in the *sociology* of combat personnel: by that time, not only were non-noble armed horsemen far more numerous than the noble *milites*,[32] but, especially in Champagne, they were in administrative positions of great political prestige[33]—which is to say that functionally speaking, the *bellator* in Champagne was now in the service of the *mercator* and his interests. All of these factors tended to make the conventional rituals and values of chivalry more and more suitable for mere games of war—jousts held within lists—than for effective combat.

The solitary, errant knight of romance who wanders in a marvelous forest in quest of personal honor, fame, and love is a pure fiction, at least with regard to the *miles* as a social creature in the late twelfth century. However, the *fictive knight* of romance is curiously similar in many ways to the *real merchant* as a new and important person in the social horizon of Champagne. If the heroic story of the fictive knight contains disguised applause for the new heroism of the real merchant, an *orator* could be more forthright in his admiration of the merchant as a hero who moves in a world of marvels, and the spirit of Hugh of St. Victor's description (*Didascalicon* II.viii) is strangely consonant with that of chivalric romance:

> Commerce penetrates the secret places of the world, approaches shores unseen, explores fearful wildernesses, and in

29. John F. Benton, "The Court of Champagne as a Literary Center," *Speculum* 36 (1961): 551–91.

30. Philippe Contamine, *La Guerre au moyen âge* (Paris: Presses Univ. de France, 1980), 165.

31. J. F. Finó, *Forteresses de la France médiévale: Construction-attaque-défense* (Paris: Picard, 1977); Contamine, 207–23.

32. Contamine, 159–63. Moreover, as non-nobles gained access to the ranks of mounted combatants, nobles themselves were declining to be dubbed and to participate in combat. Military service by knights with fiefs was being transformed into financial obligation: Contamine, 192–93.

33. For instance, the *gardes* of the fairs were both noble and non-noble, and the mounted sergeants were non-noble: Bourquelot, 1:94. See also Elizabeth Chapin, *Les Villes de foires de Champagne* (Paris: Champion, 1937).

tongues unknown and with barbaric peoples carries on the trade of mankind. The pursuit of commerce reconciles nations, calms wars, strengthens peace, and commutes the private good of individuals into the common benefit of all.

However, if knights gather in Arthur's court at Pentecost, it is not to exchange marvelous commodities from Italy and the Mideast for English wool and Flemish textiles but to exchange marvelous stories of war and love. It is not the just monetary price or wage of an *aventure* that is the major concern in Arthur's court but its truth value, and "aureate" language, not gold, is its medium. When, in fiction, *bellator* becomes *miles amans*, he not only abandons combat as a specific mode of heroic action; he abandons a whole ethics of coercive exchange based upon the wielding of direct force and taking the form of pillage, ransom, and revenge, for another more powerful ethics of exchange founded upon freedom of consent, measure, service, and just prices and wages—and, above all, on the eternally negated (and therefore eternally renewable) hope of *joie*. Chrétien underscores the similarity—and the difference—between the two systems of love and war when Yvain falls in love with the widow of the knight he has just slain:

> Bien a vangiee, et si nel set,
> La dame la mort son seignor.
> Vanjance an a prise greignor,
> Qu'ele prandre ne l'an seüst,
> S'Amors vangiee ne l'eüst,
> Qui doucemant le requiert,
> Que par les iauz el cuer le fiert.
> (vv. 1363–69)

(The lady surely has revenged the death of her lord. She has taken greater vengeance than she would have been able otherwise if Amor had not venged her, who sweetly exacts it when he strikes the heart through the eyes.)

The villain in such a courtly economy is not a cheater or counterfeiter, but a liar and a *médisant* who tampers with and diminishes conventional courtly language as a medium of exchange. Chrétien situates true heroic love in the past, while liars and *médisants* prevail in the present:

> Or est amors tornée a fable
> Por ce que cil, qui rien n'an santent,

Dïent qu'il aimment, mes il mantent
Et cil fable et mansonge an font,
Qui s'an vantent, et droit n'i ont.
(vv. 24–28)

(Now has love become a mere fable, because those who feel it
not at all say that they love, but they lie; and they tell fables
and lies who boast of it without any right to do so.)

In *Yvain*, the counterfeiter of courtly truth is the *médisant* Keu, who
aggresses upon courteous language as a medium of exchange and obstructs the commerce of good stories. Chrétien's concern with the
justesse of language—with the accountability of his language—was a
cultural concern reaching far beyond the sphere of poetic fiction, and
we may be sure that his "literary" concern for the purity and precision
of *li romans* was shared by his patrons, for whom a policy of language
was a properly economic policy as well. Just as there was competition
between political leaders in the twelfth century to promulgate this
or that currency as the dominant currency of commerce (Provins, in
Henri's Champagne, was the seat of an important money aggressively
promoted by the counts of Champagne in Chrétien's time),[34] there
must also have been (as there is nowadays) competition to make this or
that language (or dialect) the dominant language of commerce.[35] Was
not one of the motives of Henri and his wife Marie for so eagerly promoting quality poetry, along with the minting of good money, that of
enhancing the value of their language?

WOMEN, RINGS, AND THINGS

If it is accurate to claim that woman, in Western society as elsewhere,
is central to any system of exchange—whether as an object of ex-

34. Bourquelot, 2:38–64. This Champenois currency was so influential that the
Italians not only used it upon their return from the fairs of Champagne but imitated
it in Rome with a coin called the *provinois du sénat*, which in turn became the official money of the Vatican in 1188 (Bourquelot, 2:59). There was also a coinage in
Troyes (Bourquelot, 2:65).

35. Ian Parker, in an unpublished essay (which he has kindly passed on to me)
entitled "The Rise of the Vernaculars in Early Modern Europe: An Essay in the Political Economy of Language," has probed the "economics" of the emerging vernaculars in the late Middle Ages, and I have gained much from discussing these and
other points with him. For a recent and well-informed theoretical study of the rela-

change, a medium of exchange, or both—the women of Chrétien's romance are no exception. Indeed, the principal heroines of *Yvain* (Laudine, who becomes Yvain's wife, and her servant Lunette) reveal, by their actions in the romance, interesting things about the changing modalities and ethics of exchange as Chrétien seems to have understood them.

Yvain's relationship to Laudine begins on something of an archaic note when he conquers her husband Esclados in combat, thereby depriving the lady and her magic fountain of a defender, and also making her more than simply lawfully eligible to marry another good knight—for instance, Yvain himself. In *Erec et Enide* the Count of Oringle, believing that Erec was dead, had scandalously (but unsuccessfully) tried to compel Enide by force to marry him: Chrétien was already testing and rejecting an older concept of marriage based upon coercion or upon the external right of a man to claim a woman, and was championing consent as the only valid criterion of marriage.[36] In *Yvain*, a marriage will indeed occur between a widow and her husband's slayer, and the acquisition of property will indeed accompany his right to possess the woman's body; however, in this romance, both transactions are made conspicuously subject to the free consent of the woman as marital partner. Even *after* their marriage, their relationship will continue to be mediated by an elaborate economy of measured values of time and services. With this new role of woman in marriage came a new ideal of woman as a creature of constancy, not change. To be sure, Chrétien puts in Yvain's own mouth the old Ovidian doctrine of female changeability—"*Fame a plus de mil corages. / Celui corage, qu'ele a ore, / Espoir changera ele ancore*" (A woman has more than an thousand moods; the mood that she displays now will, I hope, change again; vv. 1437–39)—but it will be Yvain himself who undergoes shameful change with regard to his constant wife Laudine.

Yet even though Chrétien exalts a new relationship of marriage based on the equality and constancy of both partners, and even though the negotiation of that relationship transpires without any consideration of money, an instrument of exchange is hardly lacking. To the contrary, the unmarried, subordinate Lunette figures prominently both as

tionship between money and language as modes of communication, see Genevieve Vaughan, "Communication and Exchange," *Semiotica* 29, 1/2 (1980): 113–43.

36. Chrétien de Troyes, *Erec et Enide* vv. 4770–82, ed. Mario Roques (Paris: Champion, 1955).

middleperson and as designator of *valor* as exchangeable *value*. Let us consider more closely Lunette's role as a mediatrix of change and exchange. After Yvain defeats Esclados by the marvelous fountain in the forest of Brocéliande, Esclados flees—mortally wounded—to his castle, with Yvain in hot pursuit. We were told that Esclados had attacked Yvain "as if he were hunting a stag in rut" (*con s'il chaçast un cerf de ruit;* v. 814), but now, after their clash, the hunter has become the hunted, the pursuer the pursued. Such reversals of roles are easy to narrate in stories of war, but to narrate them in the sphere of love was a subtler artistic challenge that Chrétien was clearly eager to accept.

Having followed Esclados into his castle, where he is now trapped, Yvain finds himself in a room sumptuously decorated with gold and with finely wrought, brightly colored murals: that this is such an eminently artistic spot is already a sign of Chrétien's partisanship to the economy of love. Yvain has scarcely begun to apprehend the danger of his predicament when, quite suddenly, Lunette appears through a narrow door (v. 971) to apprise him of his situation and to bestow upon him a magic ring.

Let us examine the situation in more detail. Although she is the intimate attendant and *confidante* of Laudine, the widow of the man Yvain has just slain, Lunette is curiously indifferent to the grief of Laudine and her subjects:

> Orent ja fet tot le servise,
> Repeirié furent de l'iglise
> Et venu sor la sepouture.—
> Mes de tot ice n'avoit cure
> La demeisele de la chanbre.
> De mon seignor Yvain li manbre. . . .
> (vv. 1255–60)

> (Now the service was finished, and they had left the church to gather at the tomb. But the maiden in the room had no care for all of this: she remembers Yvain. . . .)

Yvain is now Laudine's worst enemy, but Lunette has a long-standing obligation to him that she intends to acquit as *servise et enor* (service and honor; v. 1002) in recompense for the service and honor (v. 1013) that Yvain had rendered her some time before: of all the knights of the court, he alone had deigned to speak to Lunette, who was at the time only a novice in the art of *cortoisie*. By addressing her, Yvain had given

Lunette a kind of credit, a kind of pledge money, in a world of upward social mobility, and now Lunette, who has now "arrived," declares that she is returning his reward: "*Vos randrai ce le guerredon*" (v. 1015).

Lunette is equally devoted, in other words, to two potential partners who have something of value to offer each other, something that each desires or needs, yet who are bitterly opposed. In the story that follows, Lunette will repeatedly function as a go-between and even as a kind of human currency. It should perhaps be pointed out that though Yvain's and Lunette's services to each other are such as to alter radically the status of an individual within a hostile social group, they are hardly equivalent in *degree* of benefit: not only is Yvain's honor now at stake (as Lunette's was not) but so too is his very life, which Lunette will save. Yvain has invested well.

Lunette's *guerredon* to Yvain is a magic ring that allows its bearer to become invisible to others at will. Such a ring, which symbolizes a miraculous power of change and exchange, had many possible sources and analogues in the context of Celtic legend and folklore, but it is probable that Chrétien's classicizing propensity also made him the heir, even if indirectly, of a more distant tradition of magic rings stretching back through the Elder Pliny to Cicero, Herodotus, and Plato. Cicero's *De officiis* (II.38) tells how Gyges went into a chasm, stole a golden ring from a corpse, and discovered that the ring made him invisible at will. Gyges exploited this miraculous power to seduce the queen and assassinate the king, becoming himself King of Lydia. Following a later example of Cicero, Ambrose makes the ring into a symbol of man's hidden inner conscience.[37]

Even if no direct "influence" of this sort can be traced, certain aspects of that tradition are sufficiently instructive in their own right to help us grasp a basic economic pattern not far beneath the surface of Chrétien's own tale. Lunette's ring has striking resemblances, functionally speaking, to the ring of the tyrant Gyges as evoked not only by Cicero but especially by Herodotus and Plato. As Marc Shell has shown, the fable of the talismanic ring of Gyges, which transforms invisibles into visibles and visibles into invisibles, was instrumental as an early (metaphorical) understanding of the power of money at a time when Greek culture was undergoing economic transitions similar to those of French culture in the mid-twelfth century:

37. St. Ambrose, *De officiis*, in *Patrologia latina*, ed. Migne, 16:163–64.

The ring of Gyges controls the opposition of visibility to invisibility, which concerns the definitions of tyranny and economic exchange, especially during the transition from barter to money. Why did Plato choose a ring as the talisman of the person whose way of life he tries in the Republic? If Plato did adopt the ring from previous accounts of the reign of Gyges, he did so with reason. Rings played several roles in the economic development of money and in the opposition of *ousia phanera* to *ousia aphanes*. First, rings were among the most common *symbola* before the introduction of coinage. Second, some of the first coins were ring-coins. Third, the die by which coins were minted was originally the seal of the ring of the king (or *symbolon*, as Pliny calls the royal seal). To some Greeks, a coin (as money) may have appeared to play the same role as a *symbolon*.[38]

Lunette and her golden ring express a similarly terrifying, yet marvelous, power of change and exchange. They not only transform the earlier "service" of Yvain into a spontaneous abundance of new commodities, but they disguise and conceal repugnant actions (Yvain's slaying of Esclados) so that their perpetrator may reappear in a new social context—clean, beautiful, and useful—as potential spouse and protector of Esclados's widow. This new power, which is the secret power of capital, defies earlier customs and norms of justice, yet it also inaugurates a new casuistry based upon the rigorous perception of equivalences of value among people, services, or objects to be metamorphosed or exchanged in an economy of love. It makes little difference to our discussion whether there was any traceable "influence" of Athenian or Roman thoughts about rings and money on Chrétien's intellectual world; the economic forces being explored by thinkers and poets of both worlds were very much the same. Similar, too, are some of the discursive modes and symbols by which these new forces, with all of their terrifying ambiguity, are thrown into relief. The marvels of capital money and commerce are at the very heart of Chrétien's romanesque *merveilleux* in *Yvain*.

Since Esclados's body begins to bleed in the presence of its slayer, the power of Lunette's ring to make Yvain invisible is timely, to say the least, and Laudine's servants, who are trying to capture the killer, cor-

38. Shell, 41.

rectly conclude that the power he possesses is both "marvelous and diabolic" (*Ce est mervoille et deablie*; v. 1202). The ring conceals its bearer, we are further told, exactly as bark conceals the pith of a branch:

> Come a dessor le fust l'essorce,
> Qui le cuevre, qu'an n'an voit point.
> (vv. 1028–29)

> (. . . such as bark that covers a branch
> so that it cannot be seen at all.)

That this metaphor of inner/outer is also a commonplace in medieval thoughts about the relationship between rhetoric and truth is worth emphasizing here, since (as Marc Shell shows) early ideas of rings or money as a social force were likewise inseparable from "the study of other media of symbolization and transfer, such as verbal metaphor. *Symbolon*, in fact, meant not only pactual token but also word; and, as Plato knew, the development of money corresponds to the development of a new way of speaking."[39] An association between *symbolon*, coin and word, was also part of a Boethian legacy to medieval thought. Brian Stock writes of Boethius's commentary on Aristotle's *Peri hermeneias*: "Roughly equating linguistic and material communication, he likened the imposition of meaning onto words to the impressing of the emperor's profile onto an imperial coin. A piece of money, he argued, is not only a metal object; it is also a medium of exchange which represents the value of another thing. Likewise, verbs and nouns are not only physical sounds but also linguistic conventions established for the purpose of what is understood in the mind."[40]

Bearing in mind that the *stylus gravis* was defined by twelfth-century rhetoricians as an "ornate" discourse where *translatio* is prominent,[41] let us follow Shell's arguments further as he situates Gyges's ring in a problematics of rhetoric and logic whose pertinence to Lunette's own sophistical powers (though perhaps not to her motives) will become clear:

> There is a ring of Gyges secretly at work within the minds of men: it is the money of the mind. Sometimes Plato studies

39. Shell, 36.

40. Brian Stock, "Medieval Literacy, Linguistic Theory, and Social Organization," *New Literary History* 16 (1984–85): 13.

41. Faral, 89; Eugene Vance, "Le Combat érotique chez Chrétien de Troyes," *Poétique* 12 (1972): 552–53.

that money by considering his original metaphor that the seal of a ring impresses the waxen or metallic minds of men. More often he studies the money of the mind directly, by considering the thought of the sophists. Plato attacked sophists . . . because they changed money for wisdom (selling their wares and altering them according to the conditions of the market) and because, like the rhetoricians, they made convention, as exemplified in language and money, their universal measure.[42]

Lunette, Chrétien tells us, "speaks with covered words (*parole par coverture*; v. 1938). If one grants that not only Lunette's ring but also her rhetoric and above all her circulating person—with all its timely appearances and vanishings, with its sly powers to conceal and reveal—express, within a fictive economy of love, principles that really do (or should) prevail in an emerging international mercantile economy based on money and middlemen, and motivated by profit and capital gain, how far, we may ask, does this system go in *Yvain*?

From her first appearance in the poem, Lunette is associated with marvels whose economic significance is readily perceptible. For instance, after Yvain receives Lunette's magic ring, he reclines on a couch that is covered with a quilt so lavish (*riche*; v. 1041), we are told, that not even the Duke of Austria could afford one like it. Since we may properly assume that the good duke would indeed want such a quilt even if he did not need it, we may see that mediated consumer desire is now at the heart of a new heroic ethics. Since textiles were also at the heart of the rising mercantile economy of Champagne, and since there were many different kinds and qualities of textiles available in Chrétien's Champagne (wool, silk, cotton, linen), we may assume, first, that these different textiles served also as emblems of social status. Certainly, this *drap* was not made of local Champenois wool, which was reputed to be weak, thin, and very dirty; perhaps it was of English wool, which was the very best; perhaps it was dyed with exotic colors imported from the East, or even decorated with silver and gold; conceivably, it was precious silk brought from Asia Minor by the Italians.[43] Chrétien does not tell us. The main points here are, first, that consumer desire is now a properly heroic sentiment, and second, that like the international trade that excites it, such desire knows no national boundary. If we remember the attitudes expressed in the *Chan-*

42. Shell, 36–37.
43. Bourquelot, 1:216, 258–69.

son de Roland, where the desire for personal profit and foreign luxury was a motive for treason and where few worldly desires other than that of destroying one's enemy held sway, we will realize how massively Chrétien's *roman courtois* is opposed, by its ideology, to the *Roland,* where Roland equates Ganelon's treason with a "sale" (*de nos ad fait marchet;* v. 1150).

Lunette asks Yvain if he would not like to dine, and suddenly Yvain is hungry! Just as suddenly, Lunette vanishes and reappears with a sumptuous meal of capon, cakes, and good wine (*de buene grape;* v. 1050), the latter already a status symbol in feudal France; the accessories include a white goblet and even a tablecloth. The emphasis in this scene is on abundance, decorum, and spontaneity, and Chrétien refuses (here, at least) to take into consideration any questions about who raised the capon, who made the wine, who wove the tablecloth, or who prepared the dinner—in short, questions as to how all these fine commodities found their way into the little room at exactly the right time. The secret of such magic is not hard to guess: isn't money marvelous?

Purveying men to women, however, calls for subtler mediations, all the more because in this case the beautiful woman whom Yvain is about to love (and finally wed) is the widow of the knight he has just slain. Clearly, the honor and valor that have been legitimately expressed by Yvain in the sphere of chivalric combat must undergo some radical change in order to become suitable to a marriage based upon free consent by legitimate partners.

Like valor, beauty in Chrétien's romances is a dynamic concept that sets his world apart from that of epic. In the *Roland,* the word *bel* is extremely limited in semantic range. If we put aside its occurrences as an honorific term used by noble characters to address each other (e.g., "*bel sire*"), *bel* is almost exclusively a word praising weapons, violent gestures, and warlike appearances;[44] "beauty" is practically a synonym either for raw force or for the noble status that is conferred by that force. Even Aude's beauty as a *bele damisele* (v. 3708) is proved when she dutifully falls dead at the news of Roland's death at Roncevaux. In Chrétien's romances, by contrast, we find that the "beauty" of the best knight is complemented by a fully amplified notion of feminine beauty, one that includes the potential for explicitly female modes of

44. For this information, I have used a computer-produced concordance of the *Roland* kindly furnished to me by John R. Allen, of the University of Manitoba.

action equivalent in value (*valor*) to those of men.[45] While beauty in epic is fulfilled in fighting to the finish (and not negotiating), the effect of beauty in Chrétien's romances implies a search for mediations (combat is now only one of them) and for modes of transformation and exchange so that the most beautiful knight will finally wed the most beautiful lady, as in *Erec et Enide* (vv. 1495–96): "*Onques deus si beles ymages / n'asanbla lois ne mariages*" (Never were two such beautiful forms united by the laws of marriage).

Beauty, then, is an attribute of more than power or physical excellence: it instigates a process of becoming and of change in which polarities are effaced, roles are reversed, and differences transcended in some new order. The *concordance* of two bodies (*cors*) in love is like the *concordance*, Chrétien tells us, of several voices in a single song or poem: "*Ausi com maint home divers / Pueent an chançons et an vers / Chanter a une concordance*" (just as many different men may sing in a single concordance in a song or in verse).[46]

Such *concordance* requires mediations of the most subtle sort, at least in this case, and Lunette is entirely competent to perpetrate this improbable transaction between mortal enemies whose modes of action and respective needs are at once specific and different. Not only does her ring absolve Yvain from the brutal justice of revenge that the widow and her club-wielding retinue would customarily exact upon him, but Lunette herself will conceal Yvain in a "little room" (*chanbrete*; v. 1579) in which she provides everything he needs, no matter how much it costs, on credit (*créance*):

> A cest mot aprés li s'an antre
> Dedanz la petite chanbrete.
> La demeisele, qui fu brete,
> Fu de lui servir an espans,
> Si li fist créance et despans
> De tot, quanque il li covint.
> (vv. 1578–83)

> (With this word she follows him into the little room. The maiden, who was sly, expended herself to serve him and gave

45. Karl-Heinz Bender, "L'Essor des motifs du plus beau chevalier et de la plus belle dans le premier roman courtois," *Lebendige Romania: Festschrift für Hans-Wilhelm Klein*, (n.p., 1977), 35–46.

46. Chrétien de Troyes, *Cligès*, (vv. 2803–05, ed. A. Micha (Paris: Champion, 1957).

him credit and the power to spend anything whenever
it suited him.)

Thanks to her slyness, Lunette will spare Yvain the humiliation of
sneaking away from the castle at night (*nuitantre;* v. 1577); she will
orchestrate, instead, a spectacular daylight epiphany of his person before Laudine—precisely at the right time and place. If ever a man's past
was laundered, it is Yvain's; and his appearance, after three days of invisibility in Lunette's *chanbrete*, is a miracle of social and economic
splendor that falls just short of the miracle of Christ's resurrection:

> Si le fet chascun jor beignier
> Et bien laver et apleignier.
> Et avuec ce li aparoille
> Robe d'escarlate vermoille
> De ver foree a tot la croie.
> N'est riens, qu'ele ne li acroie,
> Qui covaingne a lui acesmer:
> Fermail d'or a son col fermer,
> Ovré a pierres precïeuses,
> Qui fot les janz mout gracïeuses
> Et ceinture et aumosniere,
> Qui fu d'une riche seigniere.
> Bien l'a del tot apareillé.
> (vv. 1881–93)

(Thus she has him bathed each day and washed well and
groomed. And she provides him a robe of crimson lined with
powdered fur. There is nothing that she does not lend him
in order to decorate him: a golden collarpin studded with
precious stones, which makes people appear very gracious, a
girdle and a purse made of a rich brocade. She equips him
well with everything.)

Yvain's heroism is above all the heroism of a young and hardy economy,
and we may be sure that any of the fineries that Lunette provides Yvain
could have been purchased right in the fairs of Troyes or Provins.

In Chrétien's fiction, Lunette—not money—is the mediator of marvels. By her very name she is associated with the moon: that is, with a
principle of ordered, cosmic change. The *chanbrete* in which Yvain is
so abundantly fed, clothed, and bejeweled is a kind of womb, or perhaps
even a kind of purse, through whose coinage beings and things pass in

order to be transmuted and reborn. Lunette is in some ways comparable to Alain's Nature. However, as a moon figure, Lunette's light or *san* is reflected light, and her main function in *Yvain* is to reflect or engender images in the desiring minds of those whom she serves. Her repayment for Yvain's earlier courtly "service" to her includes placing him by the little window through which he first glimpses the grieving Laudine: this is a properly courtly payment that brings not *joie* but rather more desire. To experience desire as the perpetual desire for something (or someone) *other* is the fate, Bernard of Clairvaux tells us disapprovingly, of all worldly lovers (*De diligendo dei*, vii.18). Not only does Lunette reflect images of lovers back and forth from one to the other, but when she herself becomes an object of love for Gauvin, who is Yvain's closest friend, we are told that Gauvin's glory is like that of the sun itself and that Lunette is the "moon" of this cosmic couple—hence, Gauvin's mirror, both because of her *san* and *cortesie*, and because her name is "Lunette" (*por ce que Lunette a non*; v. 2414). In my eyes, Lunette looks and acts very much like a coin stamped with a man's noble image: money as *specie, espèce*.

Suffice it to say that Lunette's desire is vicarious, and Chrétien makes it clear that her satisfaction lies in purveying Yvain to Laudine—not once, but twice:

> Or a la dameisele fet
> Quanqu'ele voloit antreset.
> Et mes sire Yvains est plus sire,
> Qu'an ne porroit conter ne dire.
> (vv. 2049–52)

(Now the damsel has done just what she so greatly desired, and now my lord Yvain is more a lord than can be said or told.)

> Ore a mes sire Yvains sa pes . . .
> Et Lunette tres mout a eise:
> Ne li faut chose, qui li pleise,
> Des qu'ele a feite pes sanz fin
> De mon seignor Yvain, le fin.
> (vv. 6799–6812)

(Now is my lord Yvain at peace. . . . and Lunette is fully at ease, and nothing that pleases her is lacking, since she has made unending peace for my lord, the gentle Yvain.)

If Lunette is a mediatrix of exchange, she herself becomes unjustly devalued by Yvain's breach of credit and is condemned by Laudine to be burned as a traitor. Lunette's impending death threatens not only her new role in the more secret economy of love between a knight and a lady but also a more traditional economy of patronage and gift-giving within the court as a social group. Lunette's fellow attendants in Laudine's court lament their mistress's tyranny:

> Ha! Deus, con nos as obliëes!
> Con remandrons or esgarees,
> Qui perdomes si buene amie,
> Et tel consoil et tel aïe.
> Qui a la cort por nos estoit!
> Par son consoil nos revestoit
> Ma dame de ses robes veires.
> Mout changera or li afeires;
> Qu'il n'iert mes, qui por nos parot. . . .
> N'iert mes, qui die ne qui lot:
> C'est mantel ver et cest sorcot
> Et ceste cote, chiere dame,
> Donez a cele franche fame!
> Que voir, se vos li anvoiiez,
> Mout i sera bien anploiiez;
> Que ele an a mout grant sofreite.
> Ja de ce n'iert parole treite;
> Car nus n'est mes frans ne cortois.
> (vv. 4361–81)

(Ah, God! How you have forsaken us! How desolate we are, now that we are losing such a good friend, who gave counsel and aid on our behalf in the court. By her counsel our lady clothed us with her grey and white dresses. Now things will change, since there will no longer be anyone to speak for us. . . . There will no longer be anyone to plead, "This grey and white mantle, this cloak, and this coat, dear lady, give it to this honest woman. For surely, if you send it to her, it will be well used, for she needs it dearly." Surely no longer will such words be spoken, for there is no longer anyone left who is frank and courteous.)

Yvain, for his part, conceives of his discredit more abstractly, more as a debt to be liquidated than as the failure of a feudal patronage system. During his penitential quest for restitution, he conceals himself and circulates in the world with his identity unknown to Laudine and to the other ladies he rescues, except as the *chevalier au lion*. One may consider the anonymous fame that Yvain earns for this emblem as a kind of credit that he accrues by his services until such time as he may rightly be absolved of his disservice to Laudine. After the *chevalier au lion* rescues Lunette from the stake, Laudine asks the nameless lion-knight to tarry longer by her side, but he declines. Laudine pleads with him at least to reveal his name, and then he will be "free" (*quites*; v. 4608) to depart. Yvain quickly overdetermines her notion of "freedom" by bewailing his pending debt to his lady: "Fully paid, lady? I shall not do it: I owe more than I can ever pay" (*Toz quites, dame! Non feroie. / Plus doi, que randre ne porroie*; vv. 4609–70). Finally, at the very end of the story, Yvain's penitence as a sinner against love is deemed complete:

> Dame, misericorde
> Doit an de pecheor avoir.
> Conparé ai mon fol savoir,
> Et je le dui bien conparer.
> (vv. 6780–83)

(My lady, one must have mercy on a sinner.
I have paid, and paid dearly, for my folly.)

Lunette and her ring function as important symbolic mediators of spiritual transactions in the economy of love, but their roles do not preclude other measures of exchange value; thus, Yvain's services to other women's causes as the anonymous *chevalier au lion* give him a new and abstract currency that one can consider as a kind of primitive capital. If the lion doubles in *Yvain* as a heraldic emblem and as an indicator of *valor* as value, one may ask if the different competing moneys of Europe did not also retain some kind of heraldic value for the powerful nobles who promulgated these moneys, all the more since medieval coins commonly bore images (including lions) that also appeared in the repertory of heraldic emblems. Whatever the case, Yvain's services as the *chevalier au lion* give rise to a new and abstract solvency that will make him once again worthy of Laudine's love when the time is right. Yvain performs no less than six honorable services to different causes (including that of his lion) in payment for his breach of contract with Laudine, and Chrétien clearly enjoys putting such an exorbitant price on aristocratic *joie d'amour* precisely to distance his art from the baser casuistry of just prices that preoccupied less courtly souls pondering the ethics of real commerce in Chrétien's milieu. Given that contracts to buy and sell began to mark the financial practices of late twelfth-century commerce, and given that the wardens of the fairs took it upon themselves to enforce such contracts, Yvain's agreement with Laudine enabling him to absent himself from her for exactly one year while he augments his own fame may be seen as a metaphorical reflection of the new contractualism of commerce.

LOVE, CREDIT, AND TIME

The economy of desire that Lunette and her fellow women serve is one where not only the exchange value of people, objects, and services is quantified but so too is time. Time in *Yvain* has precise value, and timeliness is a great virtue. Missed deadlines can kill: Laudine is meticulous in measuring the duration of Yvain's absence from her; when he runs over his limit, Lunette is condemned to die, and Yvain is exiled. As Lunette explains to Yvain:

> Jusqu'a la feste saint Jehan
> Te dona ele de respit,
> Et tu l'eüs an tel despit,
> Qu'onques puis ne t'an remanbra.
> Ma dame paint an sa chanbre a
> Trestoz les jorz et toz les tans;
> Car qui aimme, est an grand porpans,
> N'onques ne puet prandre buen some,
> Mes tote nuit conte et assome
> Les jorz, qui vientent et qui vont.
> Sez tu, come li amant font?
> Content le tans et la seison.
> (vv. 2750–61)

(She gave you your freedom until the feast of Saint John, and you held her in such contempt that you never remembered her. My lady marked in her chamber every one of the days and the whole time; for he who loves is very thoughtful, and cannot rest, but during each night counts and adds up the days that come and go. Do you know how lovers do? They count the days and seasons.)

The notation of precise temporal perspectives originates in the very tense structure of Chrétien's narrative discourse and extends to the surface of narrative events and of heroic motivations as well.[47] Laudine, desiring to meet the knight she loves (but has not yet seen) insists that she cannot *possibly* wait five days for Lunette to convey Yvain to her domain (we, of course, know that he is already there, hidden by Lunette); however, Laudine settles for three. In another episode, when the daughters of Noire Espine quarrel over their heritage, one demands that the other defend herself with a champion *right away;* the king grants her forty days to find her champion. Or again, after he has begun his series of good works to redeem himself from his breach of contract with Laudine, Yvain discovers that he has exactly one day to finish his exploit against Harpin de la Montagne if he is to rescue Lunette from being burned at the stake. How different from the world of the *Roland,* where oaths and promises engage a hero's honor in commitments that are as timeless as the God by which they are sworn, and where the processes of change and exchange are perceived as being tantamount to treason—except in the case of Bramimonde, a woman, who converts to Christianity. Roland's devotion to Charlemagne is coextensive with life itself; so too is Aude's love for Roland, as she proves when she falls dead at the news of his death. In contrast with the world of epic, time is now interesting; good heroes should never be early or late, but punctual. The implantation of this temporal dimension in the mentality of the aristocratic *bellator* of romance reflects, once again, shifts occurring simultaneously on other fronts of twelfth-century culture as well, above all the economic. Jacques Le Goff has described the emergence, especially in Champagne, of what he calls the "merchant's time"; his observations deserve to be quoted here at some length:

> Once commercial networks were organized, time became an object of measurement. The duration of a sea voyage or of a journey by land from one place to another, the problem of prices which rose or fell in the course of a commercial transaction (the more so as the circuit became increasingly complex, affecting profits), the duration of the labor of craftsmen and workers (since the merchant was almost always an employer of

47. Marie-Louise Ollier, "Le présent du récit: temporalité et roman en vers," *Lanque française* 40 (1978): 105; Rupert T. Pickens, "Historical Consciousness in Old French Narrative," *French Forum* 4 (1979): 177.

labor), all made increasing claims on his attention and became the object of ever more explicit regulation. Coinage of gold was resumed, and new monetary instruments were introduced. Exchange transactions became more complex, due not only to bimetalism and the newly created fluctuations in the commercial price of silver but also to the first "monetary disturbances," that is, to the first inflationary and, more rarely, deflationary measures. All this enlargement of the monetary sphere required a more adequate measurement of time. At a time when the new aristocracy of money changers was supplanting that of the early Middle Ages, the sphere of money exchange prefigured the future stock market, where minutes and seconds make and unmake fortunes.

The statuses of corporations, together with such commercial documents as account sheets, travel diaries, manuals of commercial practice, and the letters of exchange then coming into common use in the fairs of Champagne (which in the twelfth and thirteenth centuries became the "clearinghouse" of international commerce), all show how important the exact measurement of time was becoming to the orderly conduct of business.

For the merchant, the technological environment superimposed a new and measurable time, in other words, an oriented and predictable time, upon that of the natural environment, which was a time both eternally renewed and perpetually unpredictable.[48]

In the *Roland*, the verb *creire*, "to believe," tends to express above all a hero's engagements, which are imposed and not chosen, in a vertical hierarchy of being, and such faith is a priori rather than rational or empirical: believing is seeing. To put one's faith in a fellow man or in a material object (except Durendal, Roland's unbreakable sword given by God) is to expose oneself to mortal danger. To believe a pagan is quite simply a contradiction in terms. A notable exception to such prevailing modalities of belief is Oliver, who deduces from the quantities of Saracens before him that a great battle is about to occur: *"Sire cumpains, ce crei, De Sarrazins purum bataille aveir"* (Comrades, I believe that we shall have battle with the Saracens; vv. 1005–06). On the

48. Jacques Le Goff, *Time, Work, and Culture in the Middle Ages*, tr. Arthur Goldhammer (Chicago: Univ. of Chicago Press, 1980), 35.

basis of what he observes, Oliver counsels Roland to sound his horn to summon help: seeing is believing. However, this new empirical voice has no real place as a basis for responsible action in the archaic world of the *Roland*. In *Yvain*, by contrast, we find that believing implies an act of choice on the part of individuals within a horizontal framework of specific dimensions determined by arbitrary but fixed bonds of time, space, and human disposition.

That is to say, *créance* inclines toward a more modern notion of *credit*. Credit depends, to be sure, on the constancy of partners, and the ring that Laudine gives to Yvain as he sets out on his *aventure* is a symbol of that constancy; however, credit also implies futurity, growth, and change, though within limits, and the ring that Lunette gives to Yvain in the *chanbrete* is a symbol of that potential. I have already mentioned Yvain's transgression of his agreement with Laudine as a breach of *créance* that puts him in her "debt," but we find an even clearer expression of *créance* as credit in lending when Yvain, as he awakens from his folly in the forest, asks that a horse be "lent" on credit (*créance*) and makes a clear distinction between such credit and an outright gift:

> Por Deu et por votre créance
> Vos pri, que an toz guerredons
> Me prestoiz ou donoiz an dons
> Ceste palefroi, que vos menez.
> (vv. 3070–73)

> (For God, and by your credit, I pray that you either lend me the means, or that you give me as a gift, the palfrey that you are leading.)

That the once delinquent Yvain deserves such credit is quickly borne out when he finds himself protecting the castle of the palfrey's donor, the Dame de Noroison: he fights, we are told, with an energy surpassing even that of Roland at Ronceval (v. 3235). The inflationary character of the new economy of love is of course spectacular, and it corresponds to a less extreme and yet very real inflationary tendency in the medieval economy of the twelfth and thirteenth centuries, caused in part by manipulations of the currencies; according to Robert S. Lopez, the cost of living in England quadrupled between 1150 and 1325. Moreover, the rise of credit in medieval commerce was directly related to the inadequate quantity and quality of money for the conduct of business. Lopez writes: "Large amounts of debased coins, foreign coins of higher value, or ingots served for substantial transactions when hard cash was absolutely required. A growing proportion of business affairs, however, was carried out more conveniently by credit operations, and these further multiplied the velocity of circulation. Unstinting credit was the great lubricant of the Commercial Revolution. It was altogether a novel phenomenon."[49] Once again, we are encountering an ethical principle not fully approachable in the official discourse of the Church, but one already natural to the fictive discourse of courtly romance.

DEPRESSIONS

If the pursuit of *joie* in love brings abundance in the economy, what happens to the economy when a knight falls out of love's good graces? Right after Yvain breaks his contract with Laudine, Lunette characteristically appears out of nowhere to denounce him, and Yvain promptly goes mad and drops out of circulation—of both love and commodities. First, he loses his speech; next, he forsakes his chivalric arms for a mere peasant's bow; finally, he leaves the company of his fellow men (and women) in order to forage naked and alone in the forest, where he eats his game raw. At this degree-zero of love and of material well-being, Yvain chances upon a hermit dwelling in the forest, and from this moment forward an interesting two-fold process of recovery begins. The first step occurs when the hermit, in a gesture of charity, gives moldy bread and cold water to the wild man; the wild man in turn brings the hermit wild game. Primitive as it is, this exchange marks a threshold between bestial foraging and primitive barter as a minimal social activity. Then the hermit cooks the game that Yvain had previously eaten raw, and the passage from raw to cooked food marks another threshold of human culture, one signaling the mastery of fire as a basis of technology (and, metaphorically, of love). The next step is, for us, truly surprising: the hermit goes to town to sell the skins from Yvains's game in order to buy better wheat and bake better bread. Suddenly, emblems of a divided labor force, money, middlemen, and an economy of surpluses (but not of profit) have emerged before our very eyes.[50]

49. Lopez, 71, 72.
50. Peter Haidu, "The Hermit's Pottage: Deconstruction and History in *Yvain*," in *The Sower and His Seed: Essays on Chrétien de Troyes*, ed. Rupert T. Pickens (Lexington: French Forum, 1983), 127–45.

The role of the hermit in this scene is puzzling: what possible connection can Chrétien see between a hermit, who is motivated only by charity and who has surpassed the ordinary vows of religious poverty, and a nascent profit-motivated urban world? Is not the realm of the *orator* becoming dangerously conflated with the world of the merchant as deviant *laborator*? This is a manifestation of a complicated historical problem that we touched upon earlier in speaking of purgatory, and one may safely propose that Chrétien is doing more, as an artist, than to underscore the analogy between spiritual labor, understood as penitence in an economy of divine love, and material labor in a more horizontal economy of worldly exchange where charity and love are still the ideal ways and means of material well-being.

Indeed, although historians are well disposed to consider texts that we now call "literary" as documents or inscriptions of historical "mentalities," we need a stronger apprehension of these texts as agents *in* history and as *determinants* of "mentalities." A notion of nonmimetic poetic fiction (distinct from the hostile Augustinian notion of poetic fiction as mere lies) obviously developed in the twelfth century, fragile though the notion perhaps was. I have tried to explore elsewhere the intellectual conditions in which that notion began to emerge.[51] However, as poets have always known, the notion of fiction implies rather a different modality of "truth" than does its absence, and I would suggest that the mutations in chivalric discourse that occur in the text of a romance such as *Yvain* were, in themselves, important historical events; indeed, they make *possible* those more palpable "true" events that historians wish to "document" (e.g., the "birth of purgatory"). No one would deny either the primacy of fiction as a resource in the discourse of commercial publicity in our own time, or its efficacy in "moving" an audience in the old Ciceronian sense of that term; so too, I would claim, the patrons of a Chrétien de Troyes promulgated his fictions with definite ideological motives in mind—among them a "true" revalorization, within the dominant codes of the time, of the new "mechanical art" of commerce, in the sense that Hugh of St. Victor gave to those terms.

Indeed, the import of Chrétien's discursive strategies becomes clearer if we look at them not as mimetic (and certainly not as "subversive") but as prophetic of successive developments in the relationship between mercantilism and Christian spirituality that occurred in the century

51. Vance, *From Topic to Tale.*

following the decades of Chrétien's poetic production. Lester K. Little deals very cogently with these developments.[52] Stressing the difficulty that feudal Europe encountered in adapting its social institutions to a new ethics of profitable trade, Little sees the dramatic resurgence of hermitage that occurred in the late eleventh and twelfth centuries not merely as a zealous rejection of material complacency in the monastic orders but as the beginning of a concerted program of ecclesiastical and political reform. Not being cloistered, hermits were commonly itinerant preachers (often feared as heretics) who also clung to the principle of begging from those who inhabited the urban desert—"the new Egypt"—and those to whom they preached. Though such begging could easily become a corrupting end in itself, the hermitage movement nevertheless established a direct bond between spiritual commerce and processes of monetary exchange, and such an encounter obviously reinforced the motive of charity as the ideal basis of both.

One point may have special relevance to Chrétien's hermit. Jews, Little proposes, became scapegoats for Christians because they practiced *openly* the usury that Christians were scarcely willing to recognize as their own goal as well. The ostentatious rejection of profit and wealth accordingly took on anti-Semitic overtones. Given the prominence of the Jewish community of Troyes in the financial life of Champagne,[53] we may ask whether the hermit's charitable commerce is not an attempt dialectically to address issues of profit and usury identified with the Jews by conceiving a positive Christian utopian ethics of exchange founded on charity. The iconography of avarice was of course abundant in Chrétien's culture, but an iconography of capitalism, which was a revolutionary movement in its earliest phases, was not easy to invent. Chrétien's mind was surely hard at work on this problem of his culture as he wrote his romances—not for Mammon but for a very shrewd count and his culturally aggressive wife Marie, daughter of Eleanor of Aquitaine.

Whether or not Chrétien (whom some imagined to have been himself a Jew),[54] was pointing his finger as a convert at the Jewish community of Champagne when he wrote of his charitable hermit as ideal middleman, the fact remains that this romance is a precocious call for

52. Lester K. Little, *Religious Poverty and the Profit Motive in Medieval Europe* (London: Paul Elek, 1978), 70, 56–57.

53. Bourquelot, 2:154–74.

54. Urban Tignor Holmes, Jr., and Sister M. A. Klenke, *Chrétien Troyes and the Grail* (Chapel Hill: Univ. of North Carolina Press, 1959).

a business ethics that led ultimately to the constitution of the Franciscan and Dominican orders, who, as Little says, "brought to fulfilment the quest for a spirituality based upon voluntary poverty. . . . The friars in a sense combined the successful ways of their forerunners into a coherent and workable spiritual programme." The Franciscans were especially determined to reconcile commercial trade with that airier commerce of souls between heaven and earth. Little quotes from a sermon by Federigo Visconti, Archbishop of Pisa, delivered in the 1260s: "How pleasing it must be for merchants to know that one of their cohorts, St. Francis, was a merchant and was also made a saint in our time. Oh, how much good hope there must be for merchants, who have such a merchant intermediary with God."[55]

PROPHECY AND FICTION

If it is possible to consider the *Roland*, particularly the second half, as the failure not only of traditional epic discourse but of both a historical and a prophetic voice, this failure was surely a justification for Chrétien's seeming detachment from history and for his inveterate irony. To link the idea of prophecy with Chrétien's art might therefore seem like an inappropriate echo of Shelley's claim, which was not naive, that poets are the unacknowledged legislators of the world. Yet Chrétien's age was one when other prophetic voices were prominent (especially among the hermits and wandering preachers) and readily heard—or denounced.[56] As the central but highly ambivalent figure of Merlin himself shows, early romance is a genre in whose fiction a concern with "true" prophecy endures, and for all his irony Chrétien too seems aware of the prophetic gesture as a distinct category of human action. He expresses such an awareness in *Erec et Enide* with a mixture of humor and earnestness about his own immortality as an artist:

> Des or comancerai l'estoire
> Qui toz jorz mes iert an mimoire
> Tant con durra crestïantez;

55. Little, 146, 217.
56. See *L'eretismo in occidente nei secoli X e XII*, Pubblicazioni dell'Università cattolica del sacro cuore, serie terza, varia 4, ed. Cincio Violante and Cosimo Damiano Fonseca (Milan: Societè editrice vita e pensiero, 1965); Jean Leclercq, "Le Poème de Payen Bolotin contre les faux ermites," *Revue bénédictine* 67 (1957): 52–86. See Little, *Religious Poverty*, pt. 2, "Avoiding the Crisis: Monks and Hermits," 61–96.

de ce s'est Crestïenz vantez.
(vv. 23–26)

(Now I shall begin a story that will endure in men's memories so long as Christianity endures: this is Chrétien's boast.)

The climactic Château de Pesme Aventure episode in *Yvain*, whose stark economic reverberations include messianic overtones that many readers have noticed, illustrates Chrétien's complex position with regard to prophecy.[57] In this episode, Yvain and his lion deliver three hundred damsels held captive by two sons born of the devil and a woman (v. 5271), and their triumphant release may well have called to mind equally triumphant scenes of the resurrection of the dead in Romanesque tympani. Are Yvain's refusal to take the hand of the daughter of the castle's lord (a point that Chrétien belabors; vv. 5697–770) before resuming his journey back to Laudine, and his promise, as he leaves, to return to the castle at some later time—are these cautiously ludic iconographical allusions to the events surrounding Christ's resurrection (Luke 24)? Whatever the case may be, it does not take a Marxist eye to discern that the economic message of the Château de Pesme Aventure is a thinly veiled criticism of the exploitation of labor in a nascent textile industry lying just to the west of Champagne in Flanders, even though the beautiful damsels to be rescued and the luxurious textiles that they weave (silk, not English wool), are fantasies tailored to the souls and discourses of the chivalrous *bellator* and the reform-minded *orator*, scarcely to those of the *laborator* himself. It would be fatuous to construe Chrétien as a revolutionary spirit; yet he and his powerful patron were quite capable, it seems, not only of revindicating certain commercial values in the dominant discourses of their time (those of the clergy and the knights) but, just as important, of calling for limits in the exploitation of the *laboratores* by a rapacious new middle class. Such coalitions between the very high and the very low are not uncommon in politics, whether ecclesiastical or secular, even now.

The Château de Pesme Aventure addresses, in a coded way, questions that were novel for the time about the social and economic justice of a consumer society built on the powers of money, of profes-

---

57. Julian Harris, "The Role of the Lion in Chrétien de Troyes' *Yvain*," *PMLA* 64 (1949): 1143–63; Peter Haidu, *Lion-queue coupée, l'écart symbolique chez Chrétien de Troyes* (Geneva: Droz, 1972).

sional middlemen, and of employers over a divided labor force. These are questions that Chrétien carefully avoided earlier in the romance when Yvain himself once reclined on luxurious fabrics and freely indulged, without even having to ask, in all the best fruits of a flourishing consumer society. Though the earlier scene stressed the artist's complicity in this economic marvel, in the Pesme Aventure, Chrétien depicts the poet himself as another potential victim of exploitation, a new kind cultural *laborator*, perhaps in Count Henri's and Marie's own chancery or some *scriptorium* where beautiful texts, not textiles, were woven. For in the very same chateau where the three hundred starving, poorly clad damsels weave beautiful silk cloth, an extremely refined and courteous lord and lady recline (on covers of silk!) in a peaceful garden while their ravishing daughter of sixteen reads aloud an anonymous romance (*ne sai de cui*; v. 5366):

> Mes sire Yvains el vergier antre
> Et aprés lui tote sa rote.
> Appoié voit dessor son cote
> Un prodome, qui se gisoit
> Sor un drap de soie, et lisoit
> Une pucele devant lui
> An un romanz, ne sai de cui.
> Et por le romanz escouter
> S'i estoit venue acoter
> Une dame, et c'estoit sa mere,
> Et li prodon estoit ses pere.
> (vv. 5360–70)

> (My lord enters into the orchard, and after him all of his company. He sees a nobleman reclining on a silken cloth, and a maiden was reading before him from a romance, by whom I know not. And to hear the romance, a lady had come to recline, and she was her mother; and the nobleman was her father.)

Refracted through Yvain's eyes, we are encountering in this romance what is in reality a second fictional reader (hence, an image of ourselves) capable of stirring—rather, of troubling—a heroic soul. One will recall that earlier in the romance, Yvain had fallen in love with Laudine precisely when he glimpsed her reading a golden Psalter while she grieved for Esclados. This second fictional reader, however, is a reader of vernacular romance, presumably closer to Chrétien's own authorial fantasies—or phobias—than was the reader of Scripture. This first insight of a European vernacular writer of fiction into authorial fantasies about his readers is worth exploring:

> Et s'estoit si bele et si jante,
> Qu'an li servir meïst s'antante
> Li Deus d'Amors, s'il la veïst,
> Ne ja amer ne la feïst
> Autrui se lui meïsme non.
> Por li servir devenist hon,
> S'issist de sa deité fors
> Et ferist lui meïsme el cors
> Del dart, don la plaie ne sainne,
> Se desleaus mires n'i painne.
> (vv. 5375–84)

(And she was so beautiful and noble that the God of Love, if he saw her, would devote himself wholly to her service, nor would he make her fall in love with anyone but himself. He would become a man to serve her, and would abandon his godhead and strike his own body with that dart whose wounds may never be cured, unless by some disloyal physician.)

This virginal reader of romance is a source of profound ambivalence, both in Yvain's eyes and in the author's own. She is at once perfectly innocent and perfectly threatening: innocent because she rightly loves, and consumes, a well-wrought courtly fiction about desire that is beautiful and seductive in its own right: threatening because she and her audience can remain so wholly unconcerned with the marvels of romance (just as they are with the silken rug) as a product woven by a real but nameless human being with compelling desires of his own. The textile of romance competes with its own weaver when it begins to circulate as an autonomous, nonreferential, intertextual fiction of readerly desire.

Chrétien's sublimely beautiful reader of romance is part of Chrétien's fictive universe and therefore a figuration of his own desire as a writer of stories about desire. The author of such fiction is analogous to *li Deus d'Amors* that Chrétien mentions as another willing victim of the erotic process that the god himself provokes; for the god of love to become a man (rather, the *fiction* of a man) in order to experience his own darts of desire for a (fictive) woman is very much the same gesture as that of the author who stages in his characters his own desires for an equally imaginary reader. I would propose that the underlying terms of reference of Amor's passion (which is now mere "myth") are nothing less than the God of Christianity who created the world, allowed sin into that creation, and then, for love of sinners, translated himself into the supreme fiction of a man in order that he could die for sinners and redeem them with his own passion.

If it is true that Western literature "in general" (if such a thing may be said to exist) is a discourse whose presuppositions about artistic "creation" entail the occultation of a metaphysical horizon, Chrétien's "gentle trivialization" (to borrow a phrase from Karl Uitti) is an important inaugural, downward movement from the true God to mythical Cupid and finally to the poet as "maker" of a fictive world by which he mediates to himself his own autoerotic desire.

Yvain, it would seem, is more intelligent than both Chrétien and Amor, since he spurns adultery with the lord's reading daughter in order to pursue his quest for reunion with his true wife, Laudine. One last ordeal, however, separates Yvain from Laudine, and this is a combat with an "anonymous" knight—who happens to be his best friend, Gauvin. Each knight defends a woman who is litigating with her sister over an inheritance. Since Gauvin seems to function in this romance as a kind of chivalric norm, the stalemate that results from their duel confirms Yvain's worthiness both to be reintegrated into the aristocratic world of the court and to be rehabilitated as Laudine's spouse. The laws of love's economy may be invisible and mysterious, but they do adequately account for good deeds and services rendered. It is fitting to the milieu of Champagne that a fictive chivalric quest should end with a combat that justly mediates between a man and a woman, and that the combat should involve neither fatalities nor even the making of enemies. Indeed, the combat transforms itself into a duel of courtesy where each warrior tries to outdo the other in proclaiming his adversary the true victor. In contrast with the earlier combat between Yvain and Esclados, which involved a process of exchange based on deadly violence, this combat is more like a class activity or ritual that determines which warriors are worthy of becoming breeders. Chrétien is carefully undermining the obsolete ethics of a de facto warrior class in order to promulgate a new ethics based upon the peaceful transfer of wealth through judicial process, and legitimate inheritance and succession. Chrétien's story brackets the chivalric ideal in a principle of higher justice—without destroying, however, those traditional values of courage, generosity, and honor that are still commensurate with the new social order; Chrétien's tact as a partisan of new social values is remarkable. Indeed, Yvain's marriage with Laudine is ultimately restored not (as it was first instigated) by raw victory at arms but by the gentler ruse of Lunette, who tricks her mistress into pledging that she will do everything she can to help the anonymous (but totally creditable) *chevalier au lion* to regain his lady's love—which is of course Laudine's very own.

True to her character as a mediator without desires of her own (except the vicarious pleasure of seeing love's accounts settled so that others can be united), Lunette is duly fulfilled by her final "exploit": "*Or a bien Lunette esploitié: / De rien n'avoit tel coveité. / Con de ce que ele voit fet*" (Now Lunette has performed well; she had never coveted anything so much as what she has just accomplished; vv. 6659–61). However, the conclusion of this debt is only another beginning in the unending (and expanding) economy of charitable love. As Lunette says to a grateful Yvain:

> "Sire", fet ele, "ne vos chaille,
> Na ja n'an soiiez an espans!
> Qu'assez avroiz pooir et tans
> A bien feire moi et autrui.
> Se je ai fet ce, que je dui
> Si m'an doit an tel gre savoir,
> Con celui, qui autrui avoir
> Anprunte et puis si le repaie
> Ancor ne cuit, que je vos aie
> Randu ce, que je vos devoie."
> (vv. 6700–09)

("My lord," she said, "do not be concerned, and do not worry: for you will have both power and time to do good works for me and others. If I have done what I ought, one owes me only the gratitude one owes the man who borrows from another and then repays him. Even now I do not think that I have given back to you what I owed you.")

If there is any warrant for my claim that the economy of desire in *Yvain* is distilled from the values of a nascent mercantile economy in Chrétien's Champagne, then the happy narrative closure of that text is an ideological gesture confirming both the possibility and the means of overcoming depression, whether psychic or economic. This recovery depends upon respect for contracts. Such respect was high among the new ethical priorities of Henri's domain, and he appointed wardens, or *gardes des foires*, whose mandate was to ensure that the merchants made it to the fairs in the first place, and that they settled their accounts once they were there.[58] Chrétien's narrative closure is a fulfillment of his own private contract with his reader as well, to the extent that narrative, by its very structure, involves transformations or exchanges of terms within a determined structure. On that narratological score, Chrétien's credit is high. His closure reinforces an ideology of *success*.

That the rise of commerce was the dominant social feature of twelfth-century Champagne is a fact that few would dispute, and Chrétien himself tells us that he was in the service of those who promulgated that same commercial movement. To be sure, many problems, both critical and historiographical, remain to be solved before we can generalize about the manner in which literary texts may be said to reflect—or occult—a set of values that constitute a given ideological context. We may assume, however, that like most patrons of art, whether ancient or modern, Henri-le-libéral and his wife Marie knew very well where their interests as patrons of a great literary court lay. Hence, if it is true that Yvain and Laudine are only a knight and a lady in Chrétien's story and not merchants, and if it is true that Lunette is only a female servant and not a piece of money, it is just as true that none of these characters acts as husbands, wives, and servants—noble or otherwise—act in the ordinary world. It is precisely their *un*reality that compels us to seek elsewhere than in ordinary affairs of the human heart for the informing paradigms; and if these are still enjoyed by us today, it is no doubt in part because they convey a system of human values which our world still shares with those that motivated Chrétien to become the first great master of vernacular romance fiction.

58. Bourquelot, 2:210–25.

CHAPTER 6

Aucassin et Nicolette

and the

Poetics of Discourse

Modern studies of language and discourse have given rise to what is, in reality, a very ancient tension between disciplines. P. F. Strawson has written:

> Logic, though it may dazzle us with the clarity of its structures, forms only one part—the first—of that modern trivium which now deservedly holds as central a place in liberal studies as ever its predecessor did. The other parts are general syntax-semantics and what, for want of a better word, may be called pragmatics. There is no reason why that dazzling first part, as we have it, should dictate the course of the second, and clearly no possibility of its dictating the course of the third. Rather . . . all three should be held, and viewed in relation to each other and to investigations variously shared by, or apportioned between, metaphysics, epistemology and philosophy of mind.[1]

Even before 1974, when Strawson wrote those words, the imperialism of linguistics had abated, and more basic questions were being raised about those conditions, whether historical, psychic, or ideological, that give rise to certain utterances or classes of utterances in the first place. Many have continued to question the status of modern linguis-

1. Peter F. Strawson, *Subject and Predicate in Logic and Grammar* (London: Methuen, 1974), vii.

tics itself as a discourse: what are its presuppositions and hidden paradigms?

There is nothing more historically or culturally determined than the conviction among modern linguists that their discourse is ahistorical, and a growing awareness of this paradox has renewed interest in the sciences of language that constitute the *trivium* (grammar, rhetoric, logic), which were preeminent among all other sciences during the millennium of Western culture that we call the Middle Ages.[2] Critics today who address themselves to the discourses of medieval texts have interesting alternatives before them: whether to confine themselves to a historical perspective upon medieval discourses and their context, whether to cast their lot with modern analytical techniques, or whether to draw on the insights of both. I believe that the last choice holds the most potential for modern critics, so long as their eclecticism is coherent and lucid.

Given that the art of composing medieval poetry extended, historically speaking, beyond *grammatica* to the discipline of rhetoric and to what came to be called the "second rhetoric,"[3] or what we would now call "pragmatics," I shall add to Strawson's plea for the cause of pragmatics a plea for the study of medieval poetry as the vehicle of a pragmatic metalinguistic consciousness that was not naive but had deep roots in medieval intellectual life.

To attribute a metalinguistic function to what we now call a "literary" text of the thirteenth century is merely to suggest that as practitioners of rhetorical art, poets of that century were reflecting the intellectual priorities of the two other disciplines of the *trivium*, understood as the three "arts of discourse" (*artes sermocinales*). Grammarians were passing beyond the prescription of rightness in reading and writing; they were asking questions as to why and how words in a sentence signify. The thirteenth century saw the rise of grammar as a speculative science whose object was not this or that language but uni-

2. I shall give here only a few pertinent titles: Jean Jolivet, *Arts du langage et théologie chez Abélard* (Paris: Vrin, 1969); *The Cultural Context of Medieval Learning: Proceedings of the First International Colloquium on Philosophy, Science, and Theology in the Middle Ages—September, 1973*, ed. John Emery Murdoch and Edith Dudley Sylla (Dordrecht: Reidel, 1975); Hennig Brinkmann, *Mittelalterliche Hermeneutik* (Tübingen: Max Niemeyer, 1980); *Sprache und Erkenntnis im Mittelalter*, ed. Albert Zimmerman et. al. (Berlin: De Gruyter, 1981).

3. Marc-René Jung, "*Poetria*: zur Dichtungstheorie des ausgehenden Mittelalters in Frankreich," *Vox Romanica* 30 (1971): 44–64; Paul Zumthor, *Le Masque et la lumière* (Paris: Seuil, 1978), 9–23.

versals of language as the vehicle of significant thought construction. As Thomas of Erfurt put it, "The end of a construction is the expression of a composite mental concept" (*Expressio mentis conceptus compositi est finis constructionis*).[4] The "Modists" were less concerned, in other words, with meanings than with the "modes" of meaning implied by different parts of speech (*partes orationis*), which make it possible for the mind to construct statements that are congruous and complete. Logicians, on their side, had been concerned for more than a century with questions about propositions and arguments as they dispose the mind to make judgments that are true or false. "The congruous and the incongruous are to the grammarian what the true and the false are to the logician" (*Sicut se habet congruum et incongruum ad grammaticum sicut verum et falsum ad logicum*).[5] Thus, "Modist" logicians in Paris were concerned to understand the ways in which a "term" (e.g., "man") may signify different things at different times (e.g., "man" as the *species* man; "man" as *this* or *that* man).[6]

In the twelfth and thirteenth centuries, rhetoric may not have been the intellectual front runner of the *trivium*, but it was still important as the discipline most directly concerned with the social and *ethical* dimensions of speech. In other words, the rhetorician would see "congruence" not as a grammatical but as a social problem, as a problem of discursive decorum or of registers corresponding to different social subgroups. The rhetorician would see problems of "supposition"—that is, the question as to how words are invoked to "stand for" (*supponere*) things—as a matter not of syntax but rather of privilege and power within a hierarchy of social forms. Moreover, rhetorically conscious poets were able to deal not only with problems of verbal signification but with the relationship of language to other socially instituted sign systems as well—money, writing, clothing, iconography, and so on.

4. G. L. Bursill-Hall, ed., *Grammatica Speculativa of Thomas of Erfurt* (London: Longman, 1972), 276, as quoted by Irène Rosier, *La Grammaire spéculative des Modistes* (Lille: Presses Univ. de Lille, 1983), 276 (translation mine). See also Bursill-Hall, *Speculative Grammars of the Middle Ages* (The Hague: Mouton, 1971).

5. Martin of Dacia, as quoted (without precise reference) in Rosier, 41 (translation mine).

6. For a recent and excellent survey, see *The Cambridge History of Later Medieval Philosophy*, ed. Norman Kretzmann, Anthony Kenny, and Jan Pinborg (Cambridge: Cambridge Univ. Press, 1983), esp. sec. 4.

My purpose here is to consider the early thirteenth-century text *Aucassin et Nicolette* as a shrewd experiment in the pragmatics of speech. I shall suggest that its narrative syntax is a *mise-en-rapport* not only of lovers but also of socially distinct discourses (*sermones*) or modes of speaking, in such a manner that the ideological and socially determined features of one discourse become defined *functionally*: that is, through contrast with features of other discourses. I shall consider *Aucassin et Nicolette* as a precocious example of what we may call medieval discursive hybridism, by which I mean the tendency for poetic texts to generate semantic problems involving not equivocal *terms* but equivocal *discourses*. The representation of action *by* speech tends to become subordinate to the representation of speech itself *as* action. In the twelfth century, vernacular poets were inclined to homogenize discourses coming from different social or intellectual spheres in accordance with the priorities of a single "discursive hegemony" (to borrow the term of Timothy J. Reiss),[7] however fragile its dominance may have been. In the thirteenth century, "hybridizing" poets display two opposing tendencies: the first is centripetal, and attempts to gather the multiple discourses that constitute the fabric of the body into a hierarchy reflecting that of feudal ideology; the second is centrifugal, and perpetrates an explosion of "meaning" into multiple "meanings" that are as arbitrary as the discourses by which they are expressed.

In suggesting that *Aucassin et Nicolette* exploits a closed narrative structure as a medium for contrastive juxtapositions of distinct, socially marked discourses, I shall take for granted certain axioms advanced by modern linguists or theoreticians of communication that are no doubt valid, as well, for cultures distant from our own in time or place.

(1) I shall assume that any society is constituted by multiple speech groups, and that modes of speaking express, in their encounters, structures that are properly ideological.

(2) I shall assume that a speaker's consciousness that he or she might have alternative modes of speaking at his or her disposal is most acute in the speech groups most subject to, or most affected by, changes of social status among their members.[8] Such was the case, I would pro-

7. Timothy J. Reiss, *The Discourse of Modernism* (Ithaca, N.Y.: Cornell Univ. Press, 1982), 29.

8. William Labov, *Sociolinguistic Patterns* (Philadelphia: Univ. of Pennsylvania Press, 1972), chs. 1, 2, 5; also Michael Silverstein, "Language Structure and Lin-

pose, with the vigorous and precocious bourgeoisie of Picardy (more precisely, perhaps, of Arras) and with the minor nobles, two groups most radically affected (one positively, the other negatively) by the socioeconomic trends of the thirteenth century.[9]

(3) I shall assume that the interdiscursivity reflects social stratification and that discursive action becomes a basis of both evaluation and discrimination on the part of different social groups.[10]

(4) I shall assume that in encounters among members of different speech groups within a given social framework, presentational and avoidance rituals may prevail over the communicative function of language, which is to say that what is finally "communicated" is the agreement not to communicate. Erving Goffman writes:

> Avoidance rituals, as a term, may be employed to refer to those forms of deference which lead the actor to keep at a distance from the recipient and not violate what Simmel has called the "ideal sphere" that lies around the recipient. . . . Any society could be profitably studied as a system of deferential stand-off arrangements, and most studies give us some evidence of this. Avoidance of [the] other's personal name is perhaps the most common example from anthropology, and should be as common in sociology.[11]

(5) Given the radical arbitrariness (perceived during the Middle Ages) with which conventional verbal signs and discourses assign meaning to and order the concepts of things to which they refer, I shall assume that differentiation among speech groups is a manifestation of power structures that have *also* been seen as arbitrary, and I shall as-

guistic Ideology," in *The Elements: A Parasession on Linguistic Units and Levels, April 20–21, 1979,* ed. Paul R. Clyne et al. (Chicago: Chicago Linguistic Society, 1979), 193–247.

9. Cf. M. Ungureanu, *Société et littérature bourgeoises d'Arras aux XIIe et XIIIe siècles,* Mémoires de la Commission Départementale des Monuments Historiques du Pas-de-Calais, vol. 8 (Arras: Imprimerie centrale de l'artois, 1955); Roger Berger, *Littérature et société arrageoises au XIIIe siècle: Les Chansons et dits artésiens,* Mémoires de la Commission Départementale des Monuments Historiques du Pas-de-Calais, vol. 21 (Arras: Imprimerie centrale de l'artois, 1981).

10. Labov, 129. See also M. A. K. Halliday, "Language as Code and Language as Behaviour: A Systemic-Functional Interpretation of the Nature and Ontogenesis of Dialogue," in *The Semiotics of Culture and Language,* ed. Robin P. Fawcett et. al. (London: Frances Pinter, 1984), 1:3–36.

11. Erving Goffman, *Interaction Ritual: Essays on Face to Face Behavior* (Garden City, N.Y.: Anchor Books, 1967), 62–63.

sume that such processes of encoding and decoding preempt other, potentially more violent, modes of structuration: for instance, civil war.

Aucassin et Nicolette has perplexed those who have brought to it the routine questions of orthodox medievalism: questions of origins, of authorship, of genre theory, and of literary "sources and influences." A recent and valuable eighty-three-page bibliography of scholarship devoted to the work, compiled by Barbara Nelson Sargent-Baur and Robert Francis Cook,[12] testifies to both the resourcefulness and the frustration of medievalists wishing to go beyond philological data and to find a satisfying way of accounting for its power to command unceasing interest. The "charm" of *Aucassin et Nicolette* is the only point upon which all critics agree, yet it is this very charm that often blocks readers from seeing that serious cultural and critical issues may also be raised by this text.[13] My purpose not being polemical, I shall not attempt to summarize or weigh here different critical opinions brought to bear on *Aucassin et Nicolette*. Rather, I shall try to suggest certain new historical and methodological guidelines for dealing with the clearly observable features of this text's interdiscursivity.

As is often the case with medieval narrative of several genres, including epic and lyric, the plot of *Aucassin et Nicolette* is constructed upon the fixed nature of its characters, and a permanent change of attitude in any single major character, whether parent or lover, would cause the tale to collapse. Aucassin's love for Nicolette is such that

> De Nicole le bien faite
> nuis home ne l'en puet retraire,
> que ses peres ne l'i laisse
> et sa mere le menace.[14]

12. Barbara-Nelson Sargent-Baur and Robert Francis Cook, *Aucassin et Nicolette*, Research Bibliographies and Checklists no. 35 (London: Grant and Cutler, 1981).

13. For instance, the final item in the Sargent-Bauer and Cook, bibliography, Tony Hunt's "La Parodie médiévale: Le Cas d'*Aucassin et Nicolette*," *Romania* 100 (1979): 351–81, is among the longest and most regressive. Hunt takes on virtually every critic who has attempted to deal with whatever is subtle in the intertextual or intratextual play of this work. For Hunt, "ce charmant poème" is at best a folktale whose poet and audience were without "une conscience littéraire très développée, une sensibilité raffinée et compréhensive en ce qui concerne des procédés allusifs, et un esprit critique éveillé" (p. 380).

14. *Aucassin et Nicolette*, *laisse* III, ed. Mario Roques (Paris: Champion, 1963). All further references to this work are to this edition, with *laisse* numbers included in my text; translations are mine.

> (From Nicolette the beautiful, no man can separate him,
> though his father does not allow it and his mother threatens
> him.)

Nicolette's love is reciprocal, but Aucassin's parents are opposed to
their union on grounds that are at once ethnic, economic, and social, as
his father clearly explains:

> Fix, fait li peres, ce ne poroit estre. Nicolette laise ester, que ce
> est une caitive qui fu amenee d'estrange terre, si l'acata li vis-
> quens de ceste viles as Sarasins, si l'amena en ceste vile, si l'a
> levee et bautisie et faite sa fillole. . . . Et se tu fenme vix avoir,
> je te donrai la file a un roi u a un conte: il n'a si rice home en
> France, se tu vix sa fille avoir, que tu ne l'aies." (II)

> ("Son," says the father, "this cannot be. Let Nicolette alone,
> for she is a captive brought from a strange land, and the vis-
> count of this city bought her from the Saracens and brought
> her to this city, where he brought her up and baptized her and
> made her his stepdaughter. . . . And if you wish to take a wife,
> I will give you the daughter of a king or a count; there is no
> one so rich or powerful in France that you may not have his
> daughter.

This passage is a pastiche of feudal social ambition. If we may fairly
assume that Beaucaire, in the Midi, is not exactly on the same scale as
Ile-de-France, Champagne, Anjou, Burgundy, or even Orange (indeed,
the author himself does not seem to know exactly where it is),[15] and if
we may assume that Aucassin's own social status and genealogical
pedigree are ambiguous (his name is Arabic), we may say that the
Count of Beaucaire is a minor noble who has set his social sights very
high. Jean Dufournet claims that the word *rice* implies power (presumably because of its derivation from the Teutonic type-word implying
"ruler" and because of its possibility as a cognate of *rex*) rather than
wealth.[16] However, I would suggest that this tale illustrates a change in
the notion of power away from that of a landed aristocracy to that of a
moneyed class system. Indeed, we shall see that not only in the count's

15. The author situates it at times inland (*laisses* XXVII and XXXVIII), and at
times by the sea (*laisse* XXXIV).
16. *Aucassin et Nicolette*, ed. and French trans. Jean Dufournet (Paris: Garnier-
Flammarion, 1973), 166, n. 17.

eyes but in the eyes of nearly every other character in *Aucassin et Nicolette,* power is equated with money. Virtually no personal or social relationship in this text is left uncontaminated by monetary considerations.

We have already seen in chapter 5 the tendency in twelfth-century romance to depict an aristocratic chivalric world whose social status is no longer determined by military functions alone but by heredity as well; in *Aucassin et Nicolette* we find a social hierarchy where a class consciousness divorced from function is even more acute, and is shared by high and low alike. An index, in this story, of the divorce between status and military function among the chivalric aristocracy that occurred with the monetarization of social bonds may be observed in the siege led by Bougars de Valence against Aucassin's father, the Count of Beaucaire. Bougars, we are told, disposes one hundred knights and ten thousand *sergens* on horseback and on foot. This is quite a different social mixture from the elite of barons and vassals that made up Charlemagne's forces at Roncevaux. So too have the techniques of combat changed: until Aucassin's decision to fight, the tedious war between Bougar and Beaucaire is distinctly governed by the technology of siege machinery and defense, not by chivalric art. As Philippe Contamine has recently shown, by the thirteenth century non-noble, mercenary *sergens* had become the principal military resource of France and England; and weapons such as the bow and the arbalest, along with the logistics of seiges, fortification, and defense, were making chivalric combat obsolete, stripping it of prestige and consigning it more and more to a realm of class ritual and sport.[17] This new socioeconomic basis of warfare is illustrated with considerable precision in *Aucassin et Nicolette*:

> Entreusque Aucassins estoit en le canbre et il regretoit Nicolete s'amie, li quens Bougars de Valence, qui sa guerre avoit a furnir, ne s'oublia mie, ains ot mandé ses homes a pié et a ceval, si traist au castel por asalir. Et li cris lieve et la noise, et li cevalier et li serjant s'arment et querent as portes et as murs por le castel desfendre, et li borgois montent as aleoirs des murs, si jetent quariax et peus aiguisiés. (VIII)

17. Philippe Contamine, *La Guerre au moyen-âge* (Paris: Presses Univ. de France, 1980), 162–64. See also Jacques Heers, *Fêtes, jeux et joûtes dans les sociétés d'occident à la fin du moyen-âge* (Montreal: Institut d'études médiévales; Paris: Vrin, 1971), 106ff.

(While Aucassin was in his room bewailing his friend Nicolette, Count Bougars de Valence, who had to get on with his
war, did not decline his duty, but when he had summoned his
foot soldiers and horsemen, went to attack the castle. When
the cry of alarm and the clamor arose, knights and sergeants
armed themselves and ran to the gates and the walls to defend
the castle, and the bourgeois mounted the fortifications and
fired arrows and sharpened spears.)

Although Aucassin is a young, chivalric aristocrat, he himself has
no natural vocation whatsoever to fight the good fight. Only in exchange for the permission to wed Nicolette does he agree to defend his
father, and when his father reneges, Aucassin compels Bougars to
pledge henceforth to seek only his own father Beaucaire's harm. If combat on land offers neither glory nor rewards in this story, by contrast,
there are signs of revival of activity on the sea: not only do Saracen
pirates and merchants now ply the coasts, but they transport heroes
and heroines, will or nill; and, thanks to them rather than to the
knights, the story progresses with great efficiency.

The emergence, in *Aucassin et Nicolette*, of an aristocratic class
consciousness divorced from its traditional military functions reflects
the new and all-pervading power of money in the commercial and capi-
talistic context of Picardy. We are dealing, here, with a work embodying
a historical transition between "mentalities" of a kind that Lukács has
described in the passage that I quoted in the introduction to chapter 5.

However much the class consciousness manifested in *Aucassin et
Nicolette* reflects the nascent impact of capital money and trade on a
traditional feudal society, discourse—not the economy—is the primary sphere in which that new social consciousness takes form in this
work. The seeming intractability of characters within a discursive
hierarchy provides an architecture for socially significant stylistic
and rhetorical contrasts. The unidimensionality of characters tends to
empty the plot of emotional impact and invites us to consider them
primarily as icons of discourse and only secondarily as "human beings" whose intentions may be complex or problematical. If Andreas
Capellanus's *De amore* is a reliable index, it is a common feature of
medieval poetry that discourse generates character and motivates the
construction of episodes, though discourse tends to lose its transparency in such works and to move into the center of dramatic interest.

The formal division of *Aucassin et Nicolette* into alternating sung verse *laisses* (whose melody has been preserved) and recited prose is acknowledged by the author in the prologue: *"dox est li cans, biax li dis"* (sweet is the song, beautiful the tale). Thus, the narrative axis of this text is a medium of (and a mediator between) registers whose presuppositions, like their modes of signification, are distinct.

Though the poetry of this text seems to enjoy a wider referential scope than the prose (for example, the number of lexical items that appear only once is proportionally greater in the poetic language than in the prose), the lexical substance of the verse tends to be manifested in nominal and adjectival forms; the prose, by contrast, is proportionally stronger in verbs and adverbs.[18] Such statistically observable differences point up what we might propose as a general claim, that the verse of this text proffers a world that tends to be formal, static, and remote, and one where nominalizing language constitutes its own action; the prose, by contrast, proffers a world where temporal and spatial perspectives pertain, and where movement and action prevail.[19] As modes of signification, the verse and prose of this text posit, though in no absolute way, ontological differences between being (*esse*) and becoming (*fieri*) that have interesting repercussions within the ethical sphere of the tale, since it will be above all Nicolette and the Queen of Torelore (not the male figures of the poem) who will assert the dynamism of becoming (*fieri*) implicit in the verbal axis of the prose.

Although the technique of alternating passages of prose and verse in medieval Latin literature goes back to Boethius and endured as an important feature of rhetorical treatises in the twelfth and thirteenth centuries, I am not aware of previous instances where formal distinctions between prose and verse convey social and ethical connotations of the sort that arise in this work. As nobles, Aucassin and Nicolette seem at first to draw their natures as lovers above all from the idealizing conventions of the aristocratic *chant courtois* (and to some extent from epic and romance), and the prologue nostalgically suggests that Aucassin and Nicolette emanate from a cherished world of values now archaic:

> Qui vauroit bons vers oïr
> del deport du viel antif

18. Simone Monsonégo, *Etude stylo-statistique du vocabulaire des vers et de la prose dans la chantefable "Aucassin et Nicolette"* (Paris: Klincksieck, 1966), 64.
19. Monsonégo, 39–44.

de deus biax enfans petis,
Nicolete et Aucassins,
des grans paines qu'il soufri
et des proesces qu'il fist
por s'amie o le cler vis. (I)

(Who would like to hear good verses drawn from the amusement of ancient times about two winsome little youths, Aucassin and Nicolette, and about the great hardships he endured and of the prowess that he displayed for his friend with the bright face?)

The tension between poetry and prose within *Aucassin et Nicolette* reflects tension between larger intellectual and social forces in thirteenth-century culture. The traditional discourses of twelfth-century vernacular poetry (epic, lyric, romance) had remained, during their evolution, at least more or less superficially constrained by the codes dictated by their aristocratic audience. Vernacular prose, by contrast, was a new and properly textual art that was not a priori marked by the code of any specific social group but surely served the accounting necessities of a newly literate mercantile class, and also the higher aristocracy, for whom the chancery was now an effective instrument of social power in a monetarized body politic. In other words, literacy created new "textual communities," to use Brian Stock's term once more, and with new textual communities came new discourses:

An important consequence of literacy in any human community arises from the area of social organization. Relationships between the individual and the family, the group, or the wider community are all influenced by the degree to which society acknowledges written principles of operation. Literacy also affects the way people conceptualize such relations, and these patterns of thought inevitably feed back into the network of real interdependencies.[20]

Thus, as vernacular prose matured, it not only catalyzed the emergence of new discourses (for instance, that of historiography) but began to rival and even displace poetry as a culturally privileged vehicle of

20. Brian Stock, *The Implications of Literacy: Written Language and Models of Interpretation in the Eleventh and Twelfth Centuries* (Princeton, N.J.: Princeton Univ. Press, 1983), 88.

narrative. Such was the case, for example, with the prose continuations of the Lancelot and the Grail cycle.

The prose text could not, however, presume to contain the discourses of poetry without "rethinking" them—not only because, as I have said, their basic modes of signification were not the same but also because, as a vehicle, prose did not enter vernacular culture embodying the semiotic constraints of any specific social group. Stock's searching scholarship makes it clear that new textual communities were not necessarily restricted to a specific social group. On the contrary, every class in the medieval social hierarchy found itself touched from without and from within by the formation of new textual communities. I would propose, though, that *Aucassin et Nicolette* is basically an "inside job" that reflects the willingness, and perhaps the need, of the aristocracy to articulate for itself (though not necessarily to change) the premises of its social contract, and to do so in the perspective of a larger, englobing social and discursive framework.

This inner/outer group mentality is embodied in the locutionary rules governing the respective spheres of verse and prose. Everybody in *Aucassin and Nicolette* is admissible into the realm of prose, but thirteen of the twenty-one verse *laisses* are reserved for the dramatic presence of Aucassin and Nicolette, and only noble characters (except for the shepherd, who *plays* upon a noble style, and the author) are allowed to speak directly in the realm of verse. Prose is unmarked speech "at large," while verse is the marked speech of a social constituency with precise boundaries.

That Nicolette speaks authentically, like Aucassin, in the elevated discourse of verse probably sufficed to identify her as noble in the audience's mind, despite the seeming disgrace of her origins. For by the thirteenth century, the old Ciceronian criteria for identifying high, middle, and low styles in terms of their functions or ends (to move, teach, or delight) had given way to considerations of style as *decorum* in speech that matched the social standing of the character or speaker. Geoffrey of Vinsauf puts it thus: "When one treats of great people or things, then the style is grandiloquent; when of humble people, humble; when of middle-class people, middle."[21] The term used by the late-thirteenth-century rhetorician John of Garland to designate the re-

---

21. Geoffrey of Vinsauf, *Documentum de arte versificandi*, in Edmond Faral, ed., *Les arts poétiques du XIIe et du XIIIe siècle* (Paris: Champion, 1924; rpt., 1958), 87 (translation mine). See Faral's remarks, p. 87.

lationship that should prevail between social status and speech decorum is *ydioma*.[22] The fact that the decorum of the "low" style is conceived by rhetoricians not according to an identifiable social type among the servile class of northern France but rather with regard to a distinctly artificial pastoral poetic tradition will give rise, as we shall see, to an interesting discrepancy in the modes of verbal conduct of the shepherds whom Aucassin and Nicolette encounter during their adventures.

Nicolette's "idiom" identifies her as a noble and thus justifies, in the mind of the audience, the "noble" love that Aucassin bestows upon her, against the will of his less discerning parents. Indeed, Andreas Capellanus had been very explicit about identifying modes of speaking about love with distinctions of class. Aucassin and Nicolette derive their identity and their motives as nobles, then, from the conventions of a courtly poetic discourse, and through the adventures of these lovers a nuclear style and its presuppositions will be severely tested—though not destroyed—by hardships encountered, and endured, in an uncomprehending world of prose.

The first of these hardships arises when Aucassin's father, who is a count, causes Nicolette to be thrown into a cell by her stepfather, who is his vassal and only a viscount. The viscount's response to the count's threats show how completely he has internalized the rationale of a social hierarchy where class distinctions are both necessitated by and based upon the recognition of money as power. The viscount tells us that he had indeed bought Nicolette with his own money, and even though he had baptized and adopted her, he had never aspired to acquire for her a mate other than a mere "honest breadwinner" (*un baceler qui du pain li gaegnast par honor*; IV); therefore, he agrees that in deference to the count's will and his interests (*vostre volontés . . . et vos bons*; IV), Nicolette will be exiled. Even kin are now mere commodities to be moved or exchanged in a world where monetary interests have the force of law.

However, despite his subordination to the count, Nicolette's stepfather is still a very rich man with a rich palace and a garden (*li visquens estoit molt rices hom, si avoit un rice palais par devers un gar-*

---

22. Traugott Lawler, ed. and trans., *The Parisiana Poetria of John of Garland* (New Haven, Conn.: Yale Univ. Press, 1974), 102. Another pertinent term is *sermocinacio* (p. 132), which is the assignment of discourse to characters in accordance with their station in society.

din; IV). Instead of exiling Nicolette geographically, then, the viscount employs his economic power to make her quite simply vanish from the social world: he imprisons her with an aged companion in a room high up in his rich palace, taking care to provide for bread, wine, and "whatever else they needed" (*quanque mestiers lor fu;* IV). Nicolette is like a bird in a cage. The room has one window overlooking the garden which sufficed, we are told, to give them "a little air" (*un peu d'essor;* IV). An initiated reader will of course recognize here a cliché of the Ovidian romance plot (whose terms of reference are no doubt the story of Pyramus and Thisbe). More important than this intertextual dimension, however, is the following *intra*textual discursive event: the transition here from prose where one "speaks and narrates" (*or dient et content et fablent*) to a register of the lyrical voice (*or se cante*) involves a radical change of presuppositions about the very same reality. From prosaic materialism we suddenly move to a refined world of erotic desire whose iconography and rhetorical program derive from conventional courtly lyric discourse. If Nicolette is imprisoned on the basis of a despicable materialism, suddenly, with a change of register, her prison overlooking the garden becomes an artful place perfectly suited for a lover's complaint, an utterance whose context demands distance (whether social or spatial or both) between lovers, a sense of the hopelessness of their cause in an uncomprehending society, and, above all, the teleological assumptions that art and nature imitate and are adequate to each other. Thus, poet, lover, and bird in the garden as *locus amoenus* vacant of love sing almost as one voice:

> Nicole est en prison mise
> en une canbre vautie
> ki faite est par grant devisse,
> panturee a miramie.
> A la fenestre marbrine
> la s'apoia la mescine:
> ele avoit blonde la crigne
> et bien faite la sorcille,
> la face clere et traitice;
> ainc plus bele ne veïstes.
> Esgarda par la gaudine
> et vit la rose espanie
> et les oisax qui se crient,
> dont se clama orphenine. (V)

(Nicolette is put in prison, in a vaulted room fashioned with great art, marvelously painted. By the marble window the maiden leaned: her hair was blonde and her eyebrows were well drawn, and her face bright and exquisite. She looked at the garden and saw the rose in bloom and the birds which were singing; then the orphan began her complaint.)

Aucassin et Nicolette is a work in which no rhetorical pose endures for long, however, and after a mere eight lines, Nicolette's complaint veers toward unidiomatic rebellion:

> Mais, par Dieu le fil Marie,
> longuement n'i serai mie,
>   se jel puis fare. (V)

(But, by the God born of Mary, I'll not be here long if I can help it.)

Nicolette's sudden resolve to act not only disrupts the relatively stable structure of courtly lyric desire that I described in chapter 4, where we saw how the fetishized song rivals the body of the woman as an object of desire, but also puts Nicolette in a posture of heroic action commonly reserved, in romance and epic, for the man. Aucassin's passive conduct underscores this inversion, for when he learns of the obstacles to his love, he *voluntarily* shuts himself in a room where he effetely allows himself to dissolve in a ridiculous sequence of nominalized infinitives that compel our perception of his lyric preciosity as false action:

> Nicolete, biax esters,
> biax venir et biax alers,
> biax deduis et dous parlers,
> biax borders et biax jouers,
> biax baisiers, biax acolers,
> por vos sui si adolés
> et si malement menés
> que je n'en cuit vis aler,
>   suer douce amie. (VII)

(Nicolette, beautiful when standing, beautiful when coming and beautiful going, beautiful playing and sweet when speaking, beautiful when kissing, beautiful when hugging, because of you I grieve and am so badly treated that I do not believe I can go on living, my sister and sweet friend.)

The inversion of roles makes it clear that, like discourses within the social group, codes of conduct are imposed arbitrarily, *ad placitum*, and not naturally. Indeed, the same Aucassin who has dissolved in effeminate, passive complaints will spontaneously pass from sub- to superhero within a few sentences:

> Il mist le main a l'espee, si comence a ferir a destre et a se-
> nestre et caupe hiaumes et naseus et puins et bras et fait un
> caple entor lui, autresi con li senglers quant li cien l'asalent en
> le forest, et qu'il lor abat dis cevaliers et navre set et qu'il se
> jete tot estroseement de la prese et qu'il s'en revient les galo-
> pant ariere, s'espee en sa main. (X)

> (He puts his hand to his sword and begins to strike to the right
> and left, and cuts helmets and noseguards and fists and arms
> and makes a massacre around himself like a boar when dogs
> attack him in a forest. He slaughters ten and wounds seven
> knights; he hurls himself into the fray and then gallops back,
> sword in hand.)

Just as Aucassin's epic prowess is incongruous, both with his preceding postures of impotence and with the inglorious social context of his exploits, so too is Aucassin's logic, which goes beyond mere satire of the conventional courtly hero's tendency to fetishize language. If his enemy should succeed in cutting off the head, Aucassin reasons, he would never be able to speak to Nicolette again; therefore, he must fight (X). That Aucassin should consider his tongue as his principal organ of love raises interesting questions about his fear of decapitation. Given that Aucassin is fighting a war both for and against his father (he has agreed to fight only to force his father to allow him to wed Nicolette), we are indeed on rich symbolic, perhaps Oedipal, terrain. At this point in his story, the author is clearly teasing our hermeneutical impulses, but he will surprise us later by confronting the supposedly "deep" psychological questions of this text and its discourses very crudely and directly when Aucassin goes to the *fabliau* kingdom of Torelore.

If Aucassin and Nicolette possess (or are possessed by) a noble style, the manner in which they employ language is at odds with the uncomprehending—and obstinate—social world in which they move. Freed from prison, they cheerfully immure themselves in language. Two parallel episodes underscore the opposition between their mode of speaking and that of the surrounding social world. In the first, Nicolette wanders one morning through a forest searching for Aucassin. One of the consequences of urbanism in the twelfth and thirteenth centuries, as we saw in the previous chapter, was to bring a complex perspective to the medieval forest as a mythical place. The forest becomes a locus of noble passion, whether erotic or divine, and when urban aristocrats wander there, marvelous things are bound to happen. Yet when Nicolette chances upon a band of shepherds in the forest, she does not know that they too are city dwellers who commute to the forest early—and dispassionately—each morning for their job. If Nicolette enters a habitat where noble passions are conventionally played out, these shepherds carry to the same forest a *social* identity quite distinct from their *literary* identity as conventional figures of a pastoral landscape. The narrator emphasizes Nicolette's transition from city to forest as a passage into a world of stately pastoral artifice where nature seems to imitate art, and where the poetic imagination is too easily at home:

> Ele n'osa mie parfont entrer por les bestes sauvaces et por le serpentine, si se quatist en un espés buisson; et soumax li prist, si s'endormi dusqu'au demain a haute prime que li pastorel iscirent de la vile et jeterent lor bestes entre le bos et la riviere, si se traien d'une part a une molt bele fontaine qui estoit au cief de la forest, si estendirent une cape, si missent lor pain sus. Entreusque il mengoient, et Nicolete s'esveille au cri des oisiax et des pastoriax, si s'enbati sor aus. (XVIII)

> (She did not dare at all to penetrate far because of the wild beasts and serpents, and she concealed herself in a thick hedge; sleep took her, and she slept until the next morning when, at around eight o'clock, the shepherds came out from the city and turned their animals loose between the wood and the stream. Going off to a very beautiful spring [fountain?] at the entrance to the forest, they spread out a shawl and put their bread upon it. While they ate, Nicolette awoke to the call of the birds and the shepherds, and hastened to them.

Nicolette implores the shepherds to convey a message to Aucassin should they encounter him. The message is highly artificial and figurative, however, and reflects the stylistic procedure called *ornatus difficilis* by thirteenth-century rhetoricians, by which is meant an abundance of tropes or "figures of thought."[23] In Nicolette's figurative discourse, the hunt for a wild beast of nature is transformed into a conventional symbol for the erotic quest in romance (cf. the hunt for the white stag in *Erec et Enide*):

> Se Dix vos aït, bel enfant, fait ele, dites li qu'il a une beste en ceste forest et qu'i le viegne cacier, et s'il puet prendre, il n'en donroit mie un menbre por cent mars d'or, non por cinc cens, ne por nul avoir. (XVIII)

> ("May God help you, my little one," she says, "tell him that there is a beast in this forest and that he must come to hunt it; and if he can take it, he would not offer one of its members for a hundred marks of gold, nor for five hundred, nor for any possession.")

Bearing in mind that *ornatus difficilis* is a criterion of the "serious" or "noble" style, we see here that questions of style pertain no longer to the *communicative* functions of discourse but to the social status of persons concerned by discourse, whether as speaker or subject. As Faral puts it, "What was, for the first critics, a matter of style became, for the school of the twelfth and thirteenth centuries, a matter of social dignity: it is the quality of the person, and no longer that of the elocution, which provides the principle of classification."[24]

As I mentioned earlier, the shepherd was the social type who exemplified the "low" style. However, the shepherd that rhetoricians had in mind was not a real social being but a poetic figure whose origins lay in Virgil's *Eclogues*, and whose medieval afterlife occurred in the *pastourelle*, which was an aristocratic genre. By their answer, these shepherds reveal how remote they are from the traditions of classical pastoral and the medieval aristocratic *pastourelle*. Totally unreceptive to Nicolette's figurative mode of discourse, they respond to her message at the literal level:

> C'est fantosmes que vos dites, qu'il n'a si ciere beste en ceste forest, ne cerf, ne lion, ne sengler, dont uns menbres vaille plus de dex deniers u de trois au plus. (XVIII)

23. Faral, 89.
24. Faral, 88.

(What you are saying is pure fantasy, for there is no beast in
this forest, whether stag, lion, or boar, one of whose members
is worth more than two deniers, or three at the most.)

The shepherds balk at transmitting Nicolette's message and tell her to
get on her way, but Nicolette has a more coercive weapon than native,
aristocratic beauty at her disposal: money. Five *sous* win her the privilege not only to repeat but even to amplify her message, though still in
a figurative mode that the shepherds *appear* not to understand. But
they do willingly understand both the power of money and the necessity to define the precise limits of their contractual obligations:

> —Ha! bel enfant, fait ele, si ferés. Le beste a tel mecine que
> Aucassins ert garis de son mehaing; et j'ai ci cinc sous en me
> borse: tenés, se li dites; et dedens trois jors li covient cacier, et
> se il dens trois jors ne le trove, ja mais n'iert garis de son
> mehaing.
> —Par foi, fait il, les deniers prenderons nos, et s'il vient ci,
> nos li dirons, mais nos ne l'irons ja quere. (XVIII)

("Aha, sweet child," she says, "you *will* do it. The beast has
such medicine that Aucassin will be cured of his wound; and I
have here five *sous* in my purse; take them, and tell it to him;
and tell him that he should come hunting within three days,
and that if in three days he does not find it, he will never be
cured of his wound." "In faith," he says, "we will take the deniers, and if he comes here we will tell it to him. But we will
certainly not seek him out.")

This passage illustrates very clearly a fact of thirteenth-century social
history that scarcely needs to be belabored, that feudal transactions—
indeed, nearly all contractual relationships—are now both motivated
and mediated by money.

More interesting is that if, in this case, money "talks," people don't:
this is an episode in which partners in a social relationship communicate by their salutations and by their mutually deferential conduct
their agreement *not* to communicate. What looks at first like stupid
literal-mindedness in silly shepherds is, on the contrary, a recognition
and assertion of class boundaries that differentiate between social
groups at a moment when the language of *money* apparently speaks
equally (hence, subversively) to all—thus, at a moment when inter-

group relationships require new and emphatic criteria for discrimination. Verbal behavior provides these criteria, though in order to be functional, such criteria must be recognized, at least implicitly, by those parties directly concerned, and especially by those in a subordinate rank.

Such proves to be the case in this story, for in the episode that follows, the shepherds show how very agile they are at playing discursive boundary games. Aucassin has been advised by a knight (that is, by a fellow aristocrat) that if he will mount his horse and go through the forest, he will find flowers and herbs and hear birds singing, and "by adventure you will hear words that will make you better" (XX). Fighting for love is far from everyone's mind. It is with this figural code in mind that Aucassin sets forth on his adventure, and when destiny carries him along the path where the shepherds are gathered, they begin to play at being "literary" shepherds and sing the cutest little *pastourelle* (it is full of diminutive suffixes, which here act as discourse markers) imaginable:

> Or s'asanlent pastouret,
> Esmerés et Martinés,
> Früelins et Johanés,
> Robeçons et Aubriés.
> Li uns dist: "Bel conpaignet,
> Dix ait Aucasinet,
> voire a foi! le bel vallet;
> et le mescine au corset
> qui avoit le poil blondet,
> cler le vis et l'oeul vairet,
> ki nos dona denerés
> dont acatrons gastelés,
> gaines et coutelés
> flausteles et cornés
> maçueles et pipés,
>   Dix le garisse!" (XXI)

(Now the little shepherds gather, Esmerés and Martinés, Früelins and Johanés, Robeçon and Aubriés. One of them says, "Good friend, may God help little Aucassin, in truth a pretty young man, and also the young girl in the blouse with the blonde hair, with the bright face and shining eye, who gave us deniers with which we will buy little cakes, little knives with their sheaths, little flutes and cornets, staffs, and pipes. May God save her!")

Unaware that the shepherds know him not as an errant, adventuring knight but as a local aristocrat, and unaware that they are toying with a mode of discourse that masks both the reality of their origin and what they have perceived about him, Aucassin quite spontaneously thinks of Nicolette when he hears their song. To confirm his intuition, he does not ask the shepherds to decode their song, but rather to *repeat* it. The shepherds are in a foul temper, though, because Aucassin's father is their overlord, and he is selfish with his land. Consequently, though they have just been singing, they have therefore fulfilled their contract with Nicolette and now balk at singing another note. But for a wage exactly double that paid by Nicolette, the shepherd's spokesman does consent to *narrate* Nicolette's message, which he properly does. This crucial moment confirms beyond any doubt that our author is conscious of the socioeconomic basis of the interdiscursitivity of his own *chantefable* and, by extension, of his culture:

> —Bel enfant, fait Aucassins, enne me conissiés vos?
> —Oïl, nos savions bien que vos estes Aucassins nos damoisiax, mais nos ne somes mie a vos, ains somes au conte.
> —Bel enfant, si ferés, je vos en pri.
> —Os, por le cuerbé! fait cil; por quoi canteroie je por vos, s'il ne me seoit, quant il n'a si rice home en cest païs, sans le cors le conte Garin, s'il trovoit mé bués ne mes vaces ne mes brebis en ses pres n'en sen forment, qu'il fust mie tant herdis por les ex a crever qu'il les en ossast cacier? Et por quoi canteroie je por vos, s'il ne me seoit?
> —Se Dix vos aït, bel enfant, si ferés; et tenés dis sous que j'ai ci en une borse.
> —Sire, les deniers prenderons nos, mais ce ne vos canterai mie, car j'en ai juré; mais je le vos conterai, se vos volés.
> —De par Diu, fait Aucassins, encor aim je mix conter que nient. (XXII)

("Good child," says Aucassin, "do you know who I am?" "Yes, we know very well that you are Aucassin, our young lord, but we are not your subjects: we are the count's." "Good child, do sing, I beg you." "No, Corbleu!" he says, "why should I sing for

you if it does not suit me, when there is no rich man in this
country other than Count Garin, who, if he found my oxen
and my cows in his fields or in his wheat would dare drive
them off, even at the risk of having his eyes put out. So why
should I sing for you, if it does not suit me?" "May God help
you, good child, surely you will do it: here are ten sous that I
have here in my purse." "Sire, we will take the deniers, but I
will certainly not sing for you, as I have sworn; but I will tell it
to you, if you wish." "By the Lord," says Aucassin, "I prefer to
have it told than not at all.")

Noteworthy about this episode is that its central area of conflict is
not between meanings but between modes of signifying that are, above
all, markers of group membership. A group consciousness has been
clearly asserted in strategies of discourse in which false or arbitrary
boundaries are first laid down by a speaker and then suddenly withdrawn. Nowhere does a medieval "literary" text bear out more clearly
the following observations by Halliday:

> The interactants in a speech situation treat that situation as
> embodying aspects of the social order—as having a certain po-
> tential in terms of which their own acts of meaning will be
> interpreted and valued. They have to do this in order to be able
> to make predictions about the meanings that are likely to be
> exchanged. . . . The social context of any conversation is con-
> tinuously being created and modified, by the course of the con-
> versation itself as well as by the other processes that might be
> taking place; and those involved unconsciously assess its on-
> going semiotic potential.[25]

However, one will notice that the code-switching occurs *only* in the
speech of the shepherds, and this conduct seems to coincide with a certain ambiguity in their social status as shepherds who "belong" to a
noble overlord whose wealth still lies in rural resources of men, land,
and animals, yet who also "belong" to the life of the town in which
monetary power is creating new alliances, new privileges, new roles—
and new audiences.

A second episode immediately follows where, once again, intergroup relationships are tested through strategies of discourse, and once

25. Halliday, 8.

again we may observe that the systems of money and language function differently: a peasant will succeed in eliciting money from Aucassin, but not meaning.

The episode begins with a narrative cliché of romance, which is that of a young knight passing through the forest on his steed (*destriers*). We are once again in the realm of the "marvelous," and the first "marvel" is that Aucassin is so enraptured by his adoration of Nicolette that he is perfectly numb to the worldly briars that wound his flesh in "thirty or forty places," and this is a spell of hagiographic, otherworldly devotion that the Virgin Mary herself could only envy. Aucassin now encounters a peasant whose grotesque animal features are modeled upon those of the cowherd in Chrétien's *Yvain*. The author of *Aucassin et Nicolette* indicates very clearly that the terms of reference of this beast lie in the marvelous of romance: *grans estoit et mervellex*. The two exchange greetings, and then, curious as to why such a peasant might have wandered into this sylvan locus of adventures of the loving heart, Aucassin asks, "What are you doing here?" When the plowman wants to know why Aucassin even cares in the first place, Aucassin answers that he asked only for the plowman's well-being—a display of good, old-fashioned aristocratic paternalism. But, like the shepherds before, the plowman recognizes Aucassin and cannot understand why such a rich man might ever weep. They agree to exchange stories, and Aucassin initiates the transaction with a highly figurative account that the plowman misunderstands with great vigor:

> —Certes, fait Aucassins, je le vos dirai molt volentiers: je vig hui matin cacier en ceste forest, s'avoie un blanc levrer, le plus bel del siecle, si l'ai perdu: por ce pleur jou.
>
> —Os! fait cil, por le cuer que cil Sires eut en sen ventre! que vos plorastes por un cien puant? Mal dehait ait qui ja mais vos prisera, quant il n'a si rice home en ceste terre, se vos peres l'en mandoit dis u quinse u vint, qu'il ne les eust trop volentiers, et s'en esteroit trop liés. Mais je doi plorer et dol faire. (XXIV)

("To be sure," says Aucassin, "I will tell you very gladly: I came hunting this morning in this forest, and I had a white hound that was the most beautiful in the world, and I have lost it. That is why I weep." "Oh," he answered, "by the heart in the Lord's belly! You weep for a stinking dog? To the devil with anyone who takes you seriously, since there is no one in this land who is so powerful that, if your father asked him for ten, fifteen, or even twenty dogs, he would not furnish them gladly. But as for me, I have reason to weep and grieve."]

The plowman goes on to recount very *literally* his own catastrophe, which is that he has hired himself out to a rich townsman but has lost Roget, his best plow ox. (The name of Roget, uttered so spontaneously, contrasts with that of Nicolette, so artfully concealed in the idolatrous ornaments of the high style.)

Though Aucassin is numb to hardships of the flesh, the plowman explains that he has not eaten or drunk in three days, that he dares not return to town for fear of being imprisoned, and that his poor old mother wallows in straw with nothing more in the world than a rag on her back. Aucassin is swept with compassion, and with a gesture that Dante would surely have admired as an example of *pronta liberalitade*, the young noble spontaneously empties his purse into the plowman's hand. Yet never does Aucassin become concerned that he and the plowman are caught up in separate codes or systems of reference, each of which proffers its own set of values and its own "reality," neither of which we are asked wholly either to approve or to condemn. On the contrary, it may be suggested that by making a lapse of communication the true subject of this episode and by demonstrating so clearly that discourse is a class-bound production of signs whose capacity to refer depends merely on convention, the poet is in effect allowing us to grasp the arbitrary semiotic basis of *all* relationships of political power.

Although the characters of this episode remain completely circumscribed by their separate modes of signifying and by their separate ideological frameworks, we of the audience experience a set of ideological transvalorizations that attend the shift of "human" or ethical perspectives mediated by this tale. If we assume that this episode takes as its point of departure a set of implicit (or even explicit) values or prejudices which a priori are positively marked from the standpoint of a traditional aristocratic poetic code (hence, whose opposite terms, within that same code, are negatively valorized), what occurs in this encounter is a drastic mise-en-cause of this initial axiological input. Valences are suspended, disrupted, and even reversed, if only momentarily, as we are compellingly drawn into the plowman's sphere. Though it is somewhat arbitrary to establish such lists, here are some axiological polarities that are called into question in the duration of this episode:

Positive (+) valorization	Negative (−) valorization
knight	serf
fin'amor	appetition
beauty	abjection
magnanimity	need
wealth	poverty
desire	satisfaction
adventure	flight
hunt	labor
forest	field
steed	plow ox
asceticism	materialism
figural discourse	literal discourse
folly, *démesure*	moderation

There are deep ideological repercussions in this verbal confrontation between a secret, aristocratic, and nearly ineffable erotic passion and the obvious hunger afflicting a terrified peasant burdened by a feeble mother. However, it would be facile to interpret this encounter between lower and higher classes of speech action as an example of emerging bourgeois "realism" daring to dispute the presuppositions of literary discourses that had traditionally served only the *oratores* and the *bellatores*. A challenge is certainly there, yet we must not lose sight of the fact that Aucassin emerges unchanged from his encounter with the starving peasant, even though Aucassin's own tyrannical father is both detested and envied by the lower classes. True, Aucassin's aristocratic magnanimity has allowed him to hear the plowman with compassion and even to relieve his problem merely by opening his purse, yet neither his genealogically rooted position of power nor his manner of apprehending reality or of speaking are affected. On the contrary, the peasant is effectively silenced by Aucassin's paternalism and magnanimity within the social group as an extended family, and the deeper causes of his plight remain ignored as Aucassin resumes his ultimately successful adventure of love.

Nicolette's role as quarry in Aucassin's metaphorical hunt is in reality a role of her own making. Indeed, in an incisive study of Nicolette's function in the story, Kevin Brownlee proposes that though we are told in the prologue of Aucassin's *prouesces* in his pursuit of Nicolette, such *prouesces* are achieved thanks to Nicolette's far more subtle *prouesce* as a shaper of the fictive world in which Aucassin moves, and in this sense Aucassin is as much a quarry as he is a hunter:

Nicolette decides to "test" Aucassin's love by, in effect, constructing a text which he must correctly interpret. This is the *bele loge* (XIX, 5) which she herself builds out of material that she herself has gathered. . . . Metaphoric and literal discourse are programmatically mixed. Nicolette is, of course, identified as the object of his search and it is her beauty and her speech (*vos dox mos*) which *"ont mon cuer navré a mort"* (vv. 14–15). The hunt, which is literally on horseback, in a forest teeming with "real animals," is of course a metaphoric hunt (though a literal search). In the context of the drama of interpretation and discourse that is here unfolding (even, it would seem, becoming thematized) I would suggest that the tracks, the traces (*esclos*) that Aucassin follows are verbal traces, those left by Nicolette's deft deployment of metaphoric discourse. In section XXIV Aucassin comes across the other *esclos*, the other trace of Nicolette's discourse left in the forest: the *bele loge*.[26]

So absolute is the usurpation of *proprietas* by metaphor in this utopia of love—rather, of love's signs—that even when Aucassin's conventionally figurative erotic "wound" becomes literal as he falls off his horse and dislocates his shoulder, the young lover clings steadfastly to the *ornatus difficilis* of the noble style as he utters, from the ground to which he has just fallen, a soliloquy to a star in the sky that is "brighter than all others":

> Estoilete, je te voi,
> que la lune trait a soi;
> Nicolette es avuec toi,
> m'amiete o le blont poil. (XXV)

(Little star, whom the moon draws to itself, Nicolette, my little friend with the blonde hair, is with you.)

Not only does Nicolette, as if by chance, overhear Aucassin from her bower, but she also cures (in this order) both his figurative wound with a kiss and his literal wound by putting his shoulder back in joint. Aucassin has all the luck: as in the previous episode, he retains the closely related privileges of dispensing money and of imposing mean-

---

26. Kevin Brownlee, "Discourse as *Prouesces* in *Aucassin et Nicolette*" (forthcoming). Brownlee has acknowledged points made in my previously published versions of this chapter, but has extended them with insights of his own. These I cheerfully acknowledge in turn.

ing upon what we vaguely call "reality" by means of verbal signs that he deploys in his own aristocratic way. In this instance, if "reality" momentarily threatens to reconstitute itself in the terms of another code (for instance, the medical), such a "reality" remains strictly subordinate to the semiological rules of an absurd yet aristocratic fetishism of words and of *ornatus*. *Aucassin et Nicolette* is a story where the verbal signs, things, events, and characters that it comprises constantly beget uncanny doubles and warped mirror images of themselves: images of what they are not supposed to be. Such pleasure in impropriety and in otherness is an outgrowth of *ornatus difficilis*, understood as an economy of displaced significations based on *translatio*, or metaphor.

However, when an image or signification proffered in one discourse stages itself again in another discourse, we cannot fail to perceive such disfigurations of reality as tears in that textile of significations that we call a story. The more closed the syntax of the story, the sharper its discursive disjunctions become. When Aucassin, "the courtly and the noble" (*li cortois et li gentis*; XIX), arrives in the kingdom of Torelore, he enters the alien discursive realm of the fabliau. Like *Aucassin et Nicolette*, which calls itself a *chantefable*, the fabliaux are neither easily defined nor classified. Individual fabliaux tend to be adapted to different styles or discourses, for instance, which suggest that as shifters between discourses they both embody and beget a metadiscursive consciousness. Neither noble nor popular, these tales seem to haunt above all the courtly world, and their absurdity implies as its target those very impulses that ordinarily afford us pleasure in the fictive marvelous. As R. Howard Bloch has recently written, "The disreputableness of the fabliaux is not that they contain dirty words, that they celebrate the body in all its concavities and protrusions, that they portray lecherous priests and insatiable women, but that they expose so insistently the scandal of their own production; they uncover explicitly not so much a moral as a poetic derogation, poetry as derogation."[27] To this one may add that the fabliaux uncover the scandals of *other* discourses with which they interact as well, whether by refracting their privileged images through a smoky prism or by revealing with too sudden clarity their concealed presuppositions.

Bearing in mind Aucassin's troubling and repeated lack of that prowess which the prologue so unequivocally attributes to him, we need

27. R. Howard Bloch, "The Fabliaux, Fetishism, and Freud's Jewish Jokes," *Representations* 4 (1983): 7.

not look hard to see a relationship between this lack and the absurd scene that now confronts Aucassin in the kingdom of Torelore: the king lies in bed, sore from giving birth to a son, while the queen is out commanding the troops on the battlefield. If we follow Bloch's reasoning a step further when he claims that the humor of the *fabliaux* calls attention to and dispels certain fetishizing impulses, we will perhaps begin to understand Aucassin's sudden and excessive rage as he tears up the sheets of the maternity bed and nearly beats the defenseless king to death with a club. Basing his notion of fetishism on Freud's, Bloch writes:

> Fetishism, a forgetting of what is known from the beginning, implies the displacement of a proper designation by a "second trace," a castration of language and a substitution for the proper par excellence: "The fetish is a substitute for the penis . . . a substitute for the phallus of the woman (the mother) in which the child once believed and which, as we well know why, he does not want to give up."
>
> Fetishism is synonymous with hiding, obfuscation, a scotomization or blindness associated at least in Freudian terms with a specific blind spot—the disavowal of knowledge of the mother's castration, the dismemberment of the original "Dame escouillée" as well as the forgetting of a mother tongue. The fetish is a *stigma indelebile* of repression, a cover whose own source lies not only in the magic of the supernatural coat (a *mantel mautaillié*) but in the very notion of fiction.[28]

The king of Torelore confronts Aucassin with an image of effeminacy that angers him so intensely precisely because it serves as an extreme example of what he has tended, himself, to become. Indeed, the king has threatened the troping prince with an image of himself as a castrated mother, an image whose status is only confirmed by the symmetry of a very phallic queen of Torelore who is out leading the king's troops in battle while he lies sore in his maternity bed. Such perceptions by Aucassin explain why he attacks both the maternity bed and the king with a violence that the sore king himself perceives as folly:

> Quant Aucassins oï ensi le roi parler, il prist tox les dras qui sor lui estoient, si les houla acal le canbre. Il vit deriere lui un

28. Bloch, 20.

> baston, il le prist, si torne, si fiert, si le bati tant que mort le
> dut avoir.
> "Ha! biax sire, fait li rois, que me demandés vos? Avés vos le
> sens dervé, qui en me maison me batés?" (XXX)

> (When Aucassin heard the king speak thus, he took all the
> sheets that were upon him, and threw them around the bed-
> room; he saw a club behind him, he took it and came back and
> struck him and beat him almost to death. "Ah, good sir," said
> the king, "what do you want of me? Have you gone out of your
> mind by beating me in my own house?")

The king's transvestitism may be seen not only as the image of a
troubled genealogy, but as a grotesque emblem of the *ornatus difficilis*
of the noble style: that is, of a discourse that systematically denatures
reality by its prevalence of figures of thought, where "usurpations" of
proper by improper meanings occur.[29] Yet this *chantefable* does not
lead us to infer that Aucassin's zeal to vindicate *proprietas*, whether
sexual or semantic, is any kind of a victory. Although Aucassin compels the king to promise to restore *proprietas* to his land, Aucassin's
own return to "straight" chivalric heroism fails to achieve its proper
social goal; on the contrary, his prowess is considered deviant by all
fighting around him, who throw soft cheese, rotten apples, and mush-
rooms at each other. Moreover, one may surmise that many in the
story's audience were ethically alert enough to recognize that though
the wasteful ethical norms of Torelore are an absurd mirror image of
those of chivalric epic, they make just as much sense:

> Sire, fait Aucassins, sont ce ci vostre anemi?
> —Oïl, sire, fait li rois.
> —Et vouriiés vos que je vos en venjasse?
> —Oïl, fait il, volentiers.
> Et Aucassins met le main a l'espee, si se lance en mi ax, si
> commence a ferir a destre et a sensetre, et s'en ocit molt. Et
> quant li rois vit qu'il les ocioit, il le prent par le frein et dist:
> Ha! biax sire, ne les ociés mi si faitement.
> —Conment? fait Aucassins, en volés vos que je vos venge?

29. Augustine defines metaphor as a "usurpation" of a proper by an improper
meaning: *De doctrina christiana* II.x.15. The term has a judicial sense closely tied
to legitimate rights of rule, possession, and kinship.

—Sire, dist li rois, trop en avés vos fait: il n'est mie costume que nos entrocions li uns l'autre. (XXXII)

("Sir," says Aucassin, "are these your enemies?" "Yes, sir," said the king. And Aucassin draws his sword and hurls himself in their midst and begins to strike right and left, and kills many of them. And when the king sees that he is killing them, he takes hold of his rein and says, "Ah, good sir, don't kill so many." "What?" says Aucassin, "do you want me to venge you?" "Sir," says the king, "you have gone too far: it is not our custom to kill each other.")

Although Aucassin puts the enemies of Torelore to rout, his reward as warrior and peacemaker is to be despised by the people, who petition their king to throw Aucassin out of their land: here is an inverted image of the ceremony of welcome customarily reserved for victorious or conquering warriors when they enter or return to a town, a ceremony not only often described in medieval literature but one that gave rise to a body of "occasional" poetry celebrating royal entries.

Clearly, the ethical relativism of this story invites us to see beneath the events of the narrative itself to the subjacent conventions of genres and discourses that generate the story as semiosis in the first place. Indeed, the anonymous author even calls into question his own power to construct a world of meanings and values in discourse. Aside from taking other successful initiatives in this story, Nicolette also becomes (as Brownlee and others have noted) a transvestite when she dresses up as a black male *jongleur* and sings her way back to her beloved Aucassin, who languishes in Beaucaire:

Si prist une herbe, si en oinst son cief et son visage, si qu'-
ele fu tote moire et tainte. Et ele fist faire cote et mantel et
cemisse et braies, si s'atorna a guise de jogleor; si prist se
viele, si vint a un marounier, se fist tant vers lui qu'il le mist
en se nef. Il drecierent lor voile, si nagierent tant par haute mer
qu'il ariverent en le terre de Provence. Et Nicolette issi fors, si
prist se viele, si ala vielant par le pais tant qu'ele vint au castel
de Biaucaire, la u Aucassins estoit. (XXXVIII)

(So she took an herb and rubbed her head and face until she
was colored all black. And she had made a coat and cape and
shirt and pants, and took on the guise of a wandering poet. She

> took her *viele* and came to a mariner and prevailed upon him
> to take her aboard his ship. They hoisted their sail and sailed
> on the high sea until they came to the land of Provence. And
> Nicolette disembarked and took her *viele* and played her way
> across the country until she came to the castle of Beaucaire,
> where Aucassin was.]

A woman has "figured" her *figure* as a man's, white skin has been "colored" black: in short, a character with a face like ink has eclipsed an author. Given that Nicolette becomes the *jongleur* who successfully brings to closure the story in which she herself is a figure, should we follow Brownlee's suggestion that the surrogate author of the story is underscoring not only Aucassin's distinct lack of *prouesce* but the author's as well? To the failures of a phallic club and a phallic sword to restore *proprietas*, must we add that of the pen?

Surely not. *Aucassin et Nicolette* is the creation of an aristocratic establishment that has gaily assumed the posture of questioning the grounds of its power, but only in order quietly to reendorse its most cherished ideals—with the conviction, moreover, that destiny is on its side.

Thus, even though later medieval social theories conceded that a person could be intrinsically noble by virtue of natural or inborn virtues, and even though most of us are obviously pulling for poor little Nicolette from the start, this is a story with a doubly happy ending: the lovers are united, and it turns out that Nicolette is as noble a woman by birth as any aristocratic bumpkin from Beaucaire could ever hope to win. Not only does the story celebrate a happy succession of power through primogeniture (Aucassin's parents die on time, and he seems not even to have any younger brothers to trouble his inheritance), but we emerge with every reason to suppose that the system will perpetuate itself by these very same means: who could doubt that the new lady of Beaucaire will breed little heroes and heroines, sure to inherit, govern, and replenish the world when their time is ripe?[30] Here is the image of an aristocracy that not only rectifies its own transgressions but at the same time succeeds in satisfying the needs of all those in lesser social ranks as well. In this poem everyone finally gets exactly what he or she is looking for—love, money, heirs, food, plow oxen, or whatever. The arbitrariness of conventional signs, and of the power

---

30. R. Howard Bloch, *Etymologies and Genealogies: A Literary Anthropology of the French Middle Ages* (Chicago: Univ. of Chicago Press, 1983), esp. chs. 2, 3.

structures that they mediate, is made evident but never horrible. The successful reunion of Aucassin and Nicolette is the victory of a myth of love over the obstacles of real life, and of poetic language (an overprecious one to be sure) over more common, roguish parlances. The successful closure of its narrative is all the more valorized by the numerous failures, imbalances, and dissymmetries of communication and exchange that are narrated in the story: messages given that are not understood, sums of money disbursed without goods or services in return, broken promises, disregard of contractual obligations, and so on.

Aucassin et Nicolette displays a kind of extreme liberalism whose model is that of a law which allows for transgressions of itself, and its art encourages us to believe that words, people, and things will always somehow cohere. This belief is most powerfully asserted as charm, and by giving himself over to his own heroine, the author is the first to testify to its force. In the chapter to follow, we shall witness the violent dispersion of charm of every sort, especially charm that is embodied in poetic signs. Everything unpleasant in life that the art of *Aucassin et Nicolette* invites us to forget or deny will surge forth on the hallucinatory, gyrelike stage of *Le Jeu de la feuillée*.

CHAPTER 7

The Apple as Feather: Toward
a Poetics of Dialogue in
Early French Medieval Theater

Written dialogue is as old as Homer, but as a written form and as a mode of verbal action, dialogue has been a relatively neglected object of theoretical analysis among literary critics. When critics do think about dialogue, they instinctively reinforce the notions that language is a positive alterity and a mediator of presence (whether divine or human) or of truth. Such a reflex is inherent to the very concepts of literature and criticism as we have inherited them from the early Romantics.

Indeed, the most serious modern critical tradition where reflection on dialogue has been sustained is the "hermeneutical" movement that began with Schleiermacher and the early Romantics such as Novalis and which endures now in the works of Hans-Georg Gadamer, Paul Ricoeur, Hans-Robert Jauss, Wolfgang Iser, and others. Dialogue is central to hermeneutics as the "art of understanding," and hermeneutics, in turn, is indissociable from criticism. If "criticism" implies, etymologically, "judgment," Schleiermacher held that the thought which produces judgment is dialectical and cannot operate independently of language: "There is no thought without discourse" (*es gibt keinen Gedanken ohne Rede*).[1] Thus, personal identities, systems, and discourses may be understood only through positive encounters with what is other (*fremde*); only together do self-knowledge (*Selbstbewusstsein*) and knowledge (*Bewusstsein*) become complete.

1. F. D. E. Schleiermacher, *Hermeneutik und Kritik*, ed. Manfred Frank (Frankfurt: Suhrkamp, 1977), 77.

184

Even self-knowledge, according to Novalis, is mediated through the collective soul (*das grosse Ich*), and You and I are only "supplements" of that soul even as we strive for selfhood: "Every You is a supplement to the collective soul. We are not I—we may and should, however, become I. We are seeds of I. We should all be transformed into a second I—only thereby may we gather ourselves up in the collective soul—the one and the all is the same" (*Jedes Du ist ein Supplement zum grossen Ich. Wir sind gar nicht Ich—wir können und sollen aber Ich werden. Wir sind Keime zum Ich werden. Wir sollen alles in ein Du—in ein zweites Ich verwandeln—nur dadurch erheben wir uns selbst zum Grossen Ich—das Eins und Alles zugleich ist*). Art, for Novalis, must be the "principle of external signs—above all, the influence of what is foreign—relationship to the foreign" (*das Princip des äussern Kennzeichen seyn—überhaupt Fremde Einwirckung—Beziehung auf das Fremde*). Intellectual growth occurs when "we study foreign systems in order to find our own system" (*Man studirt fremde Systeme um sein eignes System zu finden;* p. 278).[2]

For Gadamer, dialectically discovered truth is possible not, finally, because our logic is systematic but rather because it is manifested through the human process of horizontal dialogue: "As dialectic, philosophy never ceases to be tied to its origin in Socratic discussion. What is mere talk, nothing but talk, can, however untrustworthy it may be, still bring about understanding among human beings—which is to say that it can make human beings human."[3]

As a modern science, "general" linguistics continues to discourage us from imagining the action of dialogue as an effect of distancing between beings, one of rupture, abysses, and absences rather than as one of successfully mediated presences. In the thought of Emile Benveniste, for example, a notion of intersubjective dialogue is a categorical necessity underlying his description of the pronoun system in language:

> Self-consciousness is possible only if it is experienced through contrast. *I* do not employ I except in addressing someone, who will be *you* in my speaking. This condition of dialogue is what constitutes a *person*, because it implies reciprocally that I be-

2. Novalis, *Schriften*, ed. Paul Kluckhohn and Richard Samuel, (Stuttgart: Kohlhammer, 1968), 5:278, 314, 272.

3. Hans-Georg Gadamer, *Dialogue and Dialectic*, trans. P. Christopher Smith (New Haven, Conn.: Yale Univ. Press, 1980), ix–x, 123.

come *you* in the utterance of the person who in his turn desig-
nates himself as *I*. . . . It is in a dialectical reality which
encompasses both terms and defines them in a mutual relationship that we discover the linguistic basis of subjectivity.[4]

In parallel trends that have arisen in linguistics around or after Benveniste, the a priori notion prevails that communication or dialogue
between speaking subjects is always possible, if not necessary.

Contemporary speech-act theory is also predicated on the notion of
what J. P. Searle calls, with alarming complacency, the "principle of expressibility," which is that "whatever can be meant can be said." This
principle has "wide consequences and ramifications," among them
that "cases where the speaker does not say exactly what he means—
the principal kinds of cases of which are nonliteralness, vagueness,
ambiguity, and incompleteness—are not theoretically essential to linguistic communication." Like Searle, M. A. K. Halliday's "real life"
study of the "ontogenesis" of dialogue in his infant son Nigel points
compellingly to a process of successful entry and integration of the
child into the "adult system of dialogue."[5] Even when the notion of
dialogue is extended beyond the linguistic, as it is by Bakhtin, to express discursive modalities of a social consciousness (presumably
something like Novalis's *grosse Ich*) rather than an individual one, the
finally metaphysical assumption still holds that the "dialogical" text
is one where the otherness of interfering discourses is only relative:
"polyphony" is a musical metaphor suggesting a world that is ultimately "tuned"—an ordered cosmos, which is to say that the poly-
phonic novel sustains discourses that ultimately relate to each other
within a whole. Such were the premises, moreover, of Dostoevsky's
Christian humanism.

A POETICS OF DIALOGUE?

The formal linguistic apparatus of dialogue may very well be shown to
exist; however, as often as not, instances of what we commonly call
"poetic" or "literary" discourse structured by dialogue call into ques-

4. Emile Benveniste, *Problèmes de linguistique générale* (Paris: Gallimard,
1966), 260 (translation mine).
5. J. P. Searle, *Speech Acts* (Cambridge: Cambridge Univ. Press), 20; M. A. K. Halliday, "Language as Code and Language as Behaviour: A Systemic-Functional Interpretation of the Nature and Ontogenesis of Dialogue," in *The Semiotics of Culture
and Language*, ed. Robin P. Fawcett et. al. (London: Frances Pinter, 1984), 17, 32.

tion the assumption that language is a valid medium, whether of self-understanding or of intersubjective communication. What Searle deliberately marginalizes as a philosopher—"nonliteralness, vagueness, ambiguity, and incompleteness"—is the very stuff of the poetic. Poets as pragmatists are capable of practicing in their art something quite different from what they themselves say about language. For example, Diderot's definition of dialogue in the *Encyclopédie* is banal and complacent when it is compared with a far more complex poetics of dialogue in his *Le neveu de Rameau*.[6] Dialogue, he writes in the *Encyclopédie*, is an "entretien de deux ou de plusieurs personnes, soit de vive voix, soit par écrit." Quite clearly, poets and novelists (Diderot among them) are more disposed than linguists and philosophers to insist upon the opacity of written verbal signs, upon the radical rhetoricity of speech, and upon dialogue as a vitiation of self-awareness rather than its fulfillment.

What criticism needs, therefore, is a less tautological approach to the problem of dialogue, at least as it occurs in literature. Some years ago, in a brief but stunning article entitled "La Douleur du dialogue," Blanchot discerned in the novelistic dialogues of Malraux, James, and Kafka three distinct paradigms of communication that he believes are broadly representative of the modern novel: in Malraux there is a spirit of dialogue that is essentially Socratic, even though Malraux's fiction never depicts the actual attainment of absolute truth by human reason; in the novels of James there is a kind of communion of men and women that occurs around a hidden and finally ineffable center; in Kafka there is always an impossible distance between interlocutors, one sustained both by an implacable law existing over and beyond language and by attempts to subvert that Law through deeds of ruse, evasion, and deceit. Blanchot's purpose in extrapolating these paradigms of human interaction from the modern novel is to expose a new practice of dialogue that he finds in the writing of Marguerite Duras, where speakers speak, Blanchot says,

> but without concurring. They do not quite understand each
> other; they do not have between them a common space where
> understanding is realized, and all of their relationships are
> based only on the intense and utterly simple sense of being
> outside of the common circle of relationships. . . . This creates

6. Christie V. McDonald, *The Dialogue of Writing: Essays in Eighteenth Century French Literature* (Waterloo, Ont.: Wilfred Laurier Univ. Press, 1984), 73–104.

an instantaneous proximity and a kind of complete understanding without understanding.[7]

Ten years later (1969), in *L'Entretien infini*, Blanchot undertook to
deconstruct more thoroughly the metaphysical and cultural presuppositions in what we ordinarily perceive as horizontal dialogue. He ex-
plores the "pure interval between man and man" as a space without
horizon, where we encounter not another subject or object but rather
an infinitely estranging *Autrui*, whose character is perfectly neutral
and is posited in and with the body of language itself:

> Does this mean that communication with the "Other", as it
> marks our speech, is not a transsubjective or intersubjective
> relationship, but that it inaugurates a relationship that is nei-
> ther one of subject to subject nor of subject to object? . . . I
> believe that we must decide to say that this is so. When the
> "Other" speaks to me, it does not speak to me as I speak, to a
> self. When I engage the "Other," I answer something that
> speaks to me from nowhere, and I am separated from it by a
> caesura such that it forms with me neither a duality nor a
> unity. It is this fissure, this relationship to otherness, which
> we once dared to characterize as an interruption of being, and
> to which we may now add this: between man and man, there is
> an interval which is neither that of being nor non-being, and
> which is sustained by the Difference of the word, a difference
> which precedes any difference and any singleness.[8]

It is certainly valid for Blanchot to explore the modern novel in
order to challenge the metaphysics underlying commonplace assumptions about the exercise of dialogue. However, he has raised issues that
are not new to Western culture, whether in its discursive practices or
in its *conceptualizations* of these practices. To the contrary, Blanchot
has drawn attention to questions central to medieval culture which
call for exploration, both pragmatic and theoretical, within the terms
of that culture. It is with this purpose in mind that I shall sketch in
this chapter what might be called a poetics of dialogue in early French

7. Maurice Blanchot, "La Douleur du dialogue," in *Le Livre à venir* (Paris: Gallimard, 1959), 234.
8. Maurice Blanchot, *L'Entretien infini* (Paris: Gallimard, 1969), 98–99. Interesting parallels between Kafka's model of dialogue and that of the Old Testament could
perhaps be made. See Roger Lapointe, *Dialogues bibliques et dialectique interper-
sonnelle* (Paris: Desclée; Montréal: Bellarmin, 1971).

medieval theater, and attempt to anchor this poetics in a medieval intellectual context. I shall deal with two vernacular plays, the anonymous prescholastic *Ordo representationis Ade* (more commonly known as *Le Mystère d'Adam*), written in the mid-twelfth century, and *Li Jus Adan* (more commonly known as *Le Jeu de la feuillée*), written by Adam de la Halle in the burgeoning scholastic climate of the last quarter of the thirteenth century.[9] Since theater, medieval or otherwise, consists mainly in dialogue, these plays will perhaps be useful in allowing us to isolate tendencies in literary dialogue pertinent to other medieval and modern genres as well. We shall see that, different though these plays are (one is paraliturgical and serious, the other liturgical and comic), they address themselves, whether benignly or perversely, to the same metaphysical issues.

LOGOS AND THE LANGUAGE OF MAN

Given that the intellectual habitat of early vernacular theater (and of early medieval literature in general) was heavily Augustinian,[10] it will be useful to recall here at least the outlines of Augustine's conception of dialogue.

Man's condition as a sign-making animal reflects his ontological position in the universe. In the beginning, God created the cosmos in an act of the Word: the world is his utterance. Yet God remains distinct and *different* (*dissimilis*) from the substance of his creation—*absolutely* different from it: "I asked the whole mass [*molem*] of the world about my God and it replied to me 'I am not he, but he has made me.'"[11] Given that man is part of the material creation, and that even his spirit is different from the God in whose image he is made,[12] how

9. The following editions have been used: *Le Mystère d'Adam*, ed. Paul Aebischer (Geneva: Droz, 1964); *Le Jeu d'Adam*, ed. Willem Noomen (Paris: Champion, 1971); *Le Jeu de la feuillée*, ed. Ernest Langlois (Paris: Champion, 1964). I have also benefited from the modern French translations by Jean Rony, *Le Jeu de la feuillée* (Paris: Bordas, 1969), and by Jean Dufournet, *Le Jeu de la feuillée* (Gand: Editions scientifiques E. Story-Scientia S.P.R.L., 1977). The English translations are mine.

10. The major Augustinian sources close in time and cultural milieu to the *Jeu d'Adam* were probably Anselm of Laon, Bernard of Clairvaux, and especially Hugh of St. Victor.

11. St. Augustine, *Confessions*, X.vi.9, trans. John K. Ryan (New York: Doubleday, 1960). Subsequent references are to this translation, cited as *Conf.*

12. St. Augustine, *Oeuvres de saint Augustin, De Genesi ad litteram*, Bibliothèque augustinienne, vols. 48–49, ed. P. Agaesse and A. Solignac (Paris: Désclée de Brouwer, 1972). VII.ii.3. Cited hereafter as *De Gen. ad litt.*

can man (especially *sinning* man) presume to know—much more, to *speak* to—an incorporeal, uncreated God by means of created signs? "He alone is ineffable, who spoke, and all things were made. He spoke, and we were made."[13]

Before the Fall, Augustine speculates, it was possible for Adam and Eve to communicate with God without recourse to signs, just as God still speaks to angels by illuminating their minds (*inlustrans mentes*) instantaneously with truth that in ordinary language would have to be revealed in and through time; perhaps, too, God spoke to man by created (though at that time still spiritual) things, either during ecstasies of the soul or through the bodily senses (*De Gen. ad litt.* XI.xxxiii.43). But after the Fall, and especially after the diaspora of signification that occurred at Babel, man's corrupted nature was totally alienated from God in the "region of difference" until the advent of Christ, who was God made man and who gave man the capacity to "speak" God: "His Word, by whom we were spoken, in his son; in order that He might be spoken by us in his weakness, He was made weak."[14] Thus, Christ is a unique sign, in that both Son as signifier and Father as signified are perfectly consubstantial and adequate to each other in a bond of eternal truth: "I am the way and the truth . . ."[15] All other signifiers are inferior to what they signify.

By its very existence and nature, the conventional sign of human language (*lingua*) implies, for Augustine, a relationship of horizontal dialogue. As opposed to natural signs (e.g., smoke that signifies fire), conventional signs (*signa data*) imply a social disposition and a common will in man to signify (*voluntas significandi*; *DDC* II.i.2). If man were a solitary animal, he would not need signs, but since man is a social species, he cannot be bound to his fellow man unless they speak together and exchange thoughts by means of external signs:

> Since man could not be firmly bound [*firmissime sociari*] to his fellow man unless they spoke to each other, and poured their thoughts and minds back and forth, so to speak, reason saw that it was necessary to give names to things, that is, cer-

13. St. Augustine, *Commentarium in Psalmum 99*, as quoted and translated by Marcia Colish in *The Mirror of Language* (New Haven, Conn.: Yale Univ. Press, 1969), 35.

14. St. Augustine, quoted in Colish, 35.

15. St. Augustine, *De doctrina christiana* (I.xxxiv.38, trans. D. W. Robertson, Jr., *On Christian Doctrine* (New York: Bobbs-Merrill, 1958), 29; henceforth referred to as *DDC* in my text.

tain sounds bearing meanings, so that, since they could not reach each other's minds by the senses, men still used the senses as interpreters [*interpretes*] in order to be joined together [*ad eos sibi copulandos*].[16]

Language, then, is the most basic of all social contracts, and the order of discourse is nothing less than the living expression of the social order. By the same token, language is also a primal instrument of subversion for those who *will* it to be so. The original community of man, understood as a community of speech, was destroyed when the people of Babel became imperialistic and were punished by God: "These signs could not be common to all peoples because of the sin of human dissension which arises when one people seizes the leadership for itself. A sign of this pride is that tower erected in the heavens where impious men deserved that not only their minds but also their voices should be dissonant" (*DDC* II.iv.5).

If, at one level, Augustine clearly grants that verbal signs offer humans a potential for horizontal communication (*DDC* II.iii.4), when we probe Augustine's understanding of *how* signs signify, we encounter deep skepticism with regard to dialogue as an instrument of what we would call intersubjective action. The vocal sign (*vox*) is a purely external thing, a material *signans* whose *signatum* is an inner "word," a *vox interioris* that belongs to no specific language and is "natural" to the soul. This interior word is therefore the *signatum* of a *vox*; yet it is also, at the same time, another *signans* whose truth is some God-given intuition, a flash whose presence we cannot maintain in our memory except by *supplementing* it: that is, by assigning to it an inner word produced by the mind itself, different though this trace (*vestigium*) is from its original and always already absent referent.

Augustine is aware that this process of supplementation condemns spoken language as a mode of truly intersubjective communication. In a treatise where he tried to console a young preacher who despairs because his language does not convey to his listeners what is in his mind, Augustine gives the following account of enunciation (in the sense Benveniste gives to that term), or the passage of thought to words in speaking:

16. St. Augustine, *De ordine*, IV.xii.35, ed. and trans. Robert P. Russell (New York: Cosmopolitan Science and Art Service, 1943). I have modified Russell's translation.

My own discourse [*sermo*] is almost always displeasing to me
as well. I am eager to improve it, since I first savor it [*fruor*]
within myself before I begin to unfold [*explicare*] it by audible
words. But when I realize that they are inferior to my idea
[*notus*], I become sad that my language does not suffice with
regard to my mind. I wish my listener to understand everything that I understand, and I feel that I do not speak so as to
achieve this. The reason is mostly that my conception [*intel-
lectus*] floods my mind with the speed of lightning, while my
speech is long and slow and very different from it. Moreover, as
my speech is produced, already my conception hides itself in
secret. It leaves, in some miraculous way, however, traces
[*vestigia*] in my memory, and these persist in my memory during the brief expression of syllables and allow us to produce
those audible sounds that we call language [*lingua*], be it
Greek, Latin, Hebrew, or some other, whether these signs are
merely thought by the mind or proffered vocally. But the traces
themselves are neither Latin nor Greek nor Hebrew nor are
proper to any people. They are a production of the mind just as
facial expressions are of the body. . . . It is certainly not possible for us to express [*educere*] or to manifest [*exporrigere*]
these traces which the conception imprints [*imprimit*] in the
memory to our listeners in the same way that our facial expressions are open and manifest. . . . Thus we may imagine
how different the sound of the voice is from a flash of the intellect, since it does not even resemble the impressions it
leaves on our memory.[17]

It follows that verbal signs are only to be used, not enjoyed. He who
cherishes signifiers for their own sake becomes ensnared in carnal
understanding:

If it is a carnal slavery to adhere to a usefully instituted sign
instead of to the thing it was designed to signify, how much is
it a worse slavery to embrace signs instituted for spiritually
useless things instead of the things themselves. Even if you
transfer your affections from these signs to what they signify,
you still, nevertheless, do not lack a servile and carnal burden
and veil. (*DDC* III.vii.11)

17. St. Augustine, *De catechizandis rudibus* (see ch. 2, n. 14); my translation.

With regard to horizontal human relations, such a metaphysics of speech has poignant consequences, since it disposes us to consider the world of people and things as mere signs that are to be used, not enjoyed. It is not proper, Augustine believes, for us to love our fellow man—or even an angel, for that matter—for *his* own sake or for *our* own sake, but only for God and in God:

> There is a profound question as to whether men should enjoy themselves, use themselves, or do both. For it is commanded to us that we should love one another, but it is to be asked whether man is to be loved by man for his own sake or for the sake of something else. If for his own sake, we enjoy him; if for the sake of something else, we use him. But I think that man is to be loved for the sake of something else. In that which is to be loved for its own sake the blessed life resides; and if we do not have it for the present, the hope for it now consoles us. But "cursed be the man that trusteth in man." (*DDC* I.xxii.20)

Purely human love exiles us from God, and to desire horizontal intercourse with our fellows, verbal or otherwise, is to incur the punishment of passions that come with—and lead to—mortality. This was the hard lesson that Augustine learned as a youth when he lost a childhood friend whom he loved to a point where "I thought that my soul and his soul were but one soul in two bodies" (*Conf.* IV.vi.11). The discourse of friendship was not true, but "a huge fable and a long drawn-out lie, and by its adulterous fondling, our soul, itching in its ears, was corrupted" (*Conf.* IV.viii.13).

The true Christian must not, however, shun dialogue with his fellow man in order to withdraw into a world of private babbling, or speaking in tongues. To the contrary, as we saw in chapter 1, Augustine's goal as a reformed rhetorician was not to speak to or about himself in a private language with God but to lead others to vertical dialogue with God through an understanding of the Scripture—in short, to follow Paul's injunction (I Cor. 14:1−4: "Make love your aim, and earnestly desire the spiritual gifts, especially that you may prophesy (*dihermeneuin*). For one who speaks in a tongue speaks not to men but to God; for no one understands him, but he utters mysteries in the Spirit. On the other hand, he who prophesies speaks to men for their upbuilding and encouragement and consolation. He who speaks in a tongue edifies himself, but he who prophesies edifies the church." Although Augustine's mode of prophecy was not primarily to predict future historical events (though there is a prophetic strain in his *City of God*), he did "prophesy" by preaching in a spirit of sacrifice and by interpreting, both activities being proper to the notion of *hermeneuin*. Such is the exalted goal of the spiritual orator who, by imitating Christ and by prophesying, best redeems his nature as a creature made in God's image.

UPRIGHT SPEECH AND (ITS) REPRESENTATION

As the word *representationes* in its Latin title indicates, the problem of dialogue in the *Mystère d'Adam* unfolds within a broader metaphysics of signs. Staged, probably, beneath the facade of a Romanesque church, the play is *on* a threshold between inner and outer—between liturgical truth that belongs inside the church and art that belongs outside—and the play is *itself* a threshold between the original forgetting of ourselves as creatures in God's image by Adam and Eve and the *re*–cognition of ourselves through remembrance in Christ, whose first coming is prophesied in the play and whose second coming is perhaps prophesied by the iconography of the Romanesque facade, which at that time was commonly centered upon the figure of Christ in majesty at the last judgment.

The *Mystère d'Adam* is also internally, by its bilingualism, a threshold between spheres of language. Latin was, of course, the language of the liturgy and of teaching and learning. Latin was the universal, timeless medium of *grammatica* itself and therefore closest to truth; Romance was a mere historical accident, a degraded, tarnished image of its Latin prototype, perfecting itself mainly as the artistic vehicle of man's worldly desires.[18] In a brilliant article, Rosanna Brusegan has studied the *Mystère d'Adam* as a play centered upon a problem of representation: if liturgical language is an ideal sphere in which word and action, together, properly express the Word, this is a *paraliturgical* play whose liturgical elements and didactic instructions in Latin, and human intercourse unfolding—with amplifications—in the vernacular, are in a precarious relationship of metaphorical double. Hence, the play is also by its very constitution necessarily a deviation from its "original." It is a dramatic fiction, a troping, of liturgical truth.[19] If Au-

18. Paul Zumthor, *Langue et techniques poétiques à l'époque romane* (Paris: Klincksieck, 1963), 27–121.

19. Rosanna Brusegan, "Verità e finzione nel *Jeu d'Adam*," *Cultura neolatina* 40 (1980): 79–102.

gustine defines a trope as the "usurpation" of a proper by an improper signification, the *Mystère d'Adam* is a *mise-en-scène* of primeval metaphor as Satanic usurpation of the proper.

In the opening Latin stage instructions, we are told that we are to gaze upon a Paradise that must seem, to its audience, like an *amenissemus locus*, hence a Paradise perfectly different from the man-made garden of erotic courtly passion, the *locus amoenus* of the vernacular, toward which the coded language of the devil will later point. The two languages delineate, in other words, distinct ontological levels of referentiality, one of which is a degraded double of the other. Moreover, we will be invited to perceive in the events of this play how vernacular language helps to produce the reality of the original Fall that it now reproduces as fiction before the audience watching the play—just as this same language later helps, inversely, to prepare through prophecy the spiritual future of Christ's coming. The relationship between the worlds proffered, respectively, in Latin and Old French is a negative one that must ultimately be understood in terms of a theology of the *via negativa*. The human order first arises out of a denial of God and a fall, through passion, into what Augustine calls the "region of difference" (*regio dissimilitudinis*)—that is, a region both different from God and differing from itself. Yet thanks to the incarnation of Christ and to the comfort of the Holy Spirit, man now has the possibility of experiencing divine difference positively, as hope. Tragically, as heirs of original sin, we must transcend the passions of the lower if we are to contemplate the higher.

As a discursive space, the setting in which we are to remember our Fall is an *ordo* in which, we are emphatically told by the Latin stage directions, the actors must utter and refer properly. Adam and Eve stand together before *Figura*, God's "emanation" (or his "face," or his "metaphor"), though Adam is a bit closer to Figura and has a composed expression; Eve is just a little lower (*parum demissiori*) than Adam (is she not also, perhaps, a little abject?). We are told that "Adam" (and not the actor playing Adam—the differences between author, actor, and spectator are not yet distinct) must be well instructed (*bene instructus*), that he must speak neither too fast nor too hesitatingly (*nimis sit velox aud nimus tardus*), and that his gestures, or what Cicero calls *corporis motus*, must conform to his words. All of the players must respect the poetic meter, we are told, neither adding nor dropping syllables, and whenever they mention Paradise they must look back to it and indicate it with their hand (*respiciat eum et manu demonstret*).

The very first words in the play will not come from the actors but are a lesson from Scripture, in Latin borrowed from the office of Septuagesima: "In the beginning God made heaven and earth," to which comes the dutiful choral response, "And God made it."

The musical element of this antiphonal dialogue is hardly a neutral element in the play, whether on intellectual or purely theatrical grounds. As we saw in chapter 2, Augustine insisted upon the musicality of classical poetry as its truest dimension; here, however, the music is sacred and is verbalized with the truest and, even for the medieval logician, the most self-evident statement imaginable, and this truth is perfectly acknowledged in the response to that statement. The creation truly knows its creator, and such knowledge is reflected as praise. Dramatically, the musical dimension of the *Mystère d'Adam* can be, even today, extremely powerful. In a production at Yale and Cornell universities in which I participated in 1962, particular attention was given to the performance of the chorus. It was my impression, as a performer, that the sustained presence of this music established a kind of minimally representational ground—ordered, serene, beautiful— upon which the suffering that attended the Fall acquired intense poignancy. In any case, in terms of dialogue, the play opens with a type of liturgical semiosis in which the gap between signifier, signified, and referent—and also the spiritual difference between interlocutors—is absolutely minimal, at least in a perspective of medieval theory of signs.

Here is a space where the rules and the substance of horizontal dialogue, as we ordinarily conceive of them, are a priori proscribed; that is to say, exchanges between Figura and humanity will consist wholly in speech acts that reflect and affirm a vertical hierarchy of being. God being omnipotent and omniscient, his speech downward to man is a sequence of speech acts corresponding to man's changing states: before the Fall, commands, reminders, consents, warnings; after the Fall, reproaches, anathemas, and, finally, renewed covenants. Reciprocally, man's responses to Figura are largely displays of recognition, deference, duteousness, intimidation, and gratitude—and, after the Fall, of denials, regrets, self-accusations, and lamentations.

To open the dramatic dialogue, Figura imperiously names his subordinate, "Adam!" Naming with proper names is, of course, a privilege that comes with power (whether political or divine), and Adam himself exercises this power as a namer of the lower birds and beasts in his dominion (Gen. 2:19). However, Adam must respond upward to Figura not with a name but with deference, as prescribed by feudal code: "Sire!"

Figura now informs Adam of his creation from the dust of the earth, and Adam *confirms* that he always already knows that he must know: "I know it very well" (*bien le sai*; v. 3). Figura warns Adam that since he is made in God's image, he must never dispute with his creator. "I made you in my resemblance . . . in my image I made you from dust: you must never wage war against me!" (Je t'ai fourmé a mun senblant / . . . A ma imagene t'ai fait de tere: / Ne moi devez ja mais mover guerre; vv. 3–5). Adam *promises* to believe and obey God.

Figura has opened the dialogue by expressing what had become, by the twelfth century, an ample theology of representation, though at this point in the drama the Augustinian problem of difference (*dissimilitudo*) in the creation is still minimal. However, the hierarchy of representation—and the potential for difference—does not stop with Adam at the bottom. Figura explains that Eve is Adam's wife, that she resembles him ("*ta femme et tun pareil*"; v. 11), and that God formed her from Adam's body ("*Je la plasmai de ton cors*"; v. 19). This scene confirms the Augustinian doctrine (*De trinitate* XII, vii. 9) that Adam (as man) is made in God's image but that Eve (as woman) is not; for that reason, woman's role is to serve the husband from whom her substance derives. Figura orders that Adam, in turn, govern Eve with "reason" (*raison*; v. 21). Eve must not only "serve" Figura, who is her lord (*seignor*; v. 30) but must "love" Adam, respect his "discipline" (*discipline*; v. 36) and "serve him" (*lui serf*; v. 37)—though not necessarily like a serf; to the contrary, the prelapsarian relationship of Adam to Eve prefigures the relationship of Christ to the Church.[20] Eve swears the appropriate oaths in which she recalls each of her obligations, both to Figura and to her husband. Adam, too, recites the instructions given by Figura, though, unlike Eve, Adam may in addition presume to praise his creator for his freedom of will at the same time as he promises obedience: "Great thanks to your goodness, who formed me and did such a good thing for me when you put good and evil in my power" (*Grant graces rend a te benignité, / ki me formas e me fais tel bunté / Que bien e mal mez in ma poësté*; vv. 73–75).

20. Robert Javelet, *Image et ressemblance au douzième siècle, de saint Anselme à Alain de Lille* (Paris: Letouzey et Ané, 1967), 1:244.

At the bottom of this hierarchy is the Satanic underworld. Since evil "represents" nothing, and since the devils' choice of evil is a free choice of what does not exist, their evil difference is to be understood above all as a lack, as a privation of what exists and of what is therefore good. Without evil substance of their own, the devils cannot signify anything but nonsense; they cannot be serious, much less grieve, but can only laugh, parody, and sneer. Their discourse is without *proprietas*, and their ability to charm is only rhetorical—that is, derived from the (future) eloquence, poetic or otherwise, of postlapsarian, courtly men and women who will (to) forget the Word in order to celebrate their wordy desire for each other in courtly vernacular songs. We will speak later of Satan as the principle of perverse representation, an Augustinian theme that had great currency in the twelfth century. Suffice it to say for now that the Fall of the creation is Satan's perverse re-creation.

In short, in the prelapsarian world of Paradise, to know is to remember, not to think for oneself. The action of dialogue in such circumstances heavily implies, whether explicitly or implicitly, that class of verbs that linguists call modals. In French, these are *savoir, vouloir, devoir,* and *pouvoir,* all of which tend to convey hierarchical relationships based upon force (or deference to force). Even the future tense functions as a modal, expressing the positive necessity of what is to come or, after the Fall, inaugurating the negative Law that will prevail until the age of Grace, when the Law will be abrogated by the Spirit.

Adam's dialogue with Satan is less a process of communication than a logomachy in which we discern not personalities at work but a tension between larger forces of good and evil. The encounter is preceded by Adam's reiteration of God's commandment not to touch the fruit, and Adam makes it conveniently clear that his obedience is the key, as well, to civic order in the feudal world of the play's spectators: "He must be judged by law of treason who perjures himself and betrays his lord!" (*Jugiez doit estre a loi de traïtor / Que si parjure e traïst sun seignor;* vv. 111–12). The exchange that follows is more a test of Adam's memory and will than a true dialogue predicated upon the desire for mutual understanding. Since Adam is good, he rebuffs Satan's evil at every turn, though in ways not obvious to us. For instance, when Satan asks Adam if he would like to know how to improve his lot, Adam, who is already in Paradise, says that he would. This is not pride but what Hugh of St. Victor calls "the desire for the beneficial," which is a legitimate desire so long as it is allied (and we see that it is in Adam) with the "desire for the just."[21] Adam's responses to Satan communicate, at first, his will *not* to communicate:

(DEVIL: Are you well off?
ADAM: I feel no trouble.
DEVIL: Things could be better.
ADAM: I don't know how.
DEVIL: Do you want to know how?
ADAM: Of course I would like to.
DEVIL: I know how.
ADAM: What's that to me?
DEVIL: And why not?
ADAM: I couldn't care less.)

    DIABOLUS
Estas tu bien?
    ADAM
        Ne sen rien que m'enoit.
    DIABOLUS
Poet estre mielz!
    ADAM
        Ne puis saver coment.
    DIABOLUS
Vols le tu saver?
    ADAM
        Bien in iert mon talent!
    DIABOLUS
Jo sai comment!
    ADAM
        E moi que chalt?
    DIABOLUS
Por quei non?
    ADAM
        Rien ne me valt.
(vv.114–20)

21. Hugh of St. Victor, *De sacramentis* I.vii.11, trans. Roy J. Deferrari, *Hugh of St. Victor on the Sacraments of the Christian Faith* (Cambridge, Mass.: Medieval Academy of America, 1951), 125.

But Satan knows rhetorical strategy, and he tells Adam that he is, after all, in no hurry to reveal how Adam might improve his lot. Satan strikes Adam's *curiositas* with this bait, but only for an instant:

> (DEVIL: I'm in no hurry to tell you how.
> ADAM: Yes, tell me now!
> DEVIL: I won't do it before you're tired of begging.
> ADAM: I don't need to know at all.)

> DIABOLUS
> Ne te dirrai pas en curant.
> ADAM
> Or le me di!
> DIABOLUS
>   Non frai pas
> Ainz te verrai del preer las.
> ADAM
> N'ai nul besoing de ço saveir.
> (vv. 120–23)

Now Adam retaliates. First he pledges to believe everything that Satan will tell him—and here suspense in the audience grows—except for one thing:

> (DEVIL: *What* thing?
> ADAM: I'll *tell* you: I will not offend my creator.)

> DIABOLUS
> De quel chose?
> ADAM
>   Jol te dirrai:
> Mon creator pas ne offendrai!
> (vv. 133–34)

Satan's last resort is to promise Adam a utopian life without a feudal lord, and even peerage with the creator, if he will only eat the forbidden apple. However, Adam's memory of God's precepts and his will hold fast, and he abruptly breaks off his dialogue with Satan in these words:

> (You want to deliver me to torment; you want me to rise up
> against my lord, take away my pleasure and put me in pain. I

will not believe you! Get out of here! Don't you dare appear
before me again! You are a traitor without faith!)

Tu me voels livrer a torment;
Mesler me vols o mun seignor,
Tolir de joie, mettre en dolor.
Ne te crerrai! Fui de de ci!
Ne soies ja mais tant hardi
Que tu ja viengez devant moi!
Tu es traitres, e sanz foi!
(vv. 198–204)

If memory guided by will, not rational thought, is the key to Adam's
righteousness (as it was to Roland's), one will note that Adam himself
afterward underscores the Fall as a forgetting: "Where was my sense?
What happened to my memory?" (*Ou fu mon sens? / Que devint ma
memoire?* v. 531).

THE POETICS OF THE FALL

As we might expect, the dialogue leading to Eve's seduction and to the
Fall proceeds quite otherwise. Adam is told (v. 25) to govern Eve with
reason because Eve, as woman, embodies the passive—or passionate—
side of the human soul. In Adam's absence, Eve welcomes Satan as her
interlocutor from the very start, and the "profit" and "honor" that
Satan offers appeal to her from the start:

> SATAN: Eve, I have come here to see you.
> EVE: Tell me now, Satan: why?
> SATAN: I seek for you profit and wealth.
> EVE: May God grant it!)

> DIABOLUS
> Eva, ça sui venuz a toi!
> EVA
> Di moi, Sathan, or tu pur quoi?
> DIABOLUS
> Je vois querant tun pru, tun honor!
> EVA
> Co dunge Deu!
> (vv. 205–08)

During the next five exchanges, Satan's sole objective remains that of securing Eve as his credulous and secret interlocutor. As the axis of communication passes from the vertical to the horizontal, truth and rectitude (which, for Anselm, are synonymous) are promptly destroyed: Satan slanders Adam, gaining immediate concessions from Eve, and then Satan flatters Eve herself, summoning up pride and vainglory in her through metaphors drawn (as the poet's audience surely recognized) from the conventions of aristocratic courtly lyric. Satan is a shadow of the conventional courtly *médisant*. By troping his discourse with wordy images of worldly beauty, the father of lies turns Eve away from God as well as from her husband, and toward herself as an improper object of love:

> (You are a frail and tender thing, and fresher than a rose; you are whiter than crystal or snow covering the ice in the valley.)

> Tu es fiebelette e tendre chose,
> E es plus fresche que n'est rose;
> Tu es plus blanche que cristal,
> Que neif que chiet sor glace en val.
> (vv. 227–30)

Poetic simile introduces perverse, adulterous alterities into human discourse in opposition to God's Word, which, according to Anselm, is always integral and simple, and always the *same* as He. The devil's equivocal poetic images subvert God's image in man, not to speak of man's image in woman.[22] By copulating improperly in language, Satan tries to disjoin the first couple and to deny the goodness of the creation: "The creator made a bad couple of you: you are too tender, he too hard" (*Mal cuple em fist li criator: / Tu es trop tendre, e il, trop dur*; vv. 231–32).

A passage in some *miscellanea* attributed to Hugh of St. Victor helps us to situate Satan's subversive semiosis in a broad twelfth-century theology of representation:

> Resemblance by equality is one thing; resemblance by imitation is another; yet another is that of contrariety. The first is proper to the son of God, for it is said that he did not consider it a theft to be God's equal. The second is proper to man, who was indeed created in God's image. The third is proper to the

22. St. Augustine, *De trinitate* XII.vii.10 (see ch. 1, n. 19).

Devil: indeed, while God is the author and the principle of
good, the Devil is the author of evil by resemblance in
contrariness.[23]

Before coming to the specific terms of the temptation, Satan once again
engages in a series of exchanges with Eve to confirm her as his *confidante* over and against Adam. Eve's imminent revolt against Adam is
also a revolt against God. As Hugh of St. Victor puts it, "Evidently
Scripture wished to show that woman, who was subject to man, was
not to receive the divine command except through the medium of
man, so that God's statement was first made as it were immediately to
man, then through the medium of man it came to woman also, who
was subject to man and was to be instructed by man's counsel" (*De sacramentis* I.vii.5). Satan then denies the goodness of God's provisions
for man in Paradise and promises her life, power, lordship, and knowledge of good and evil if she will only eat the forbidden fruit. Hugh of
St. Victor is very sensitive to what we would now call the illocutionary
forces at work in Satan's discourse:

> But we must consider this carefully, how cleverly the enemy
> first by denying removed the evil which woman feared, and
> then freely persuaded her of the evil which he himself in-
> tended. Now, lastly he added a promise to support his persua-
> sion, and, that the same persuasion might be received the more
> readily he doubled the promise. For he who persuaded a single
> eating only, setting up two things one by one as a reward,
> promised likeness of God and knowledge of good and evil. So
> in the persuasion to food he tempted man by gluttony; in the
> promise of divinity and knowledge, by vain glory and avarice.
> (*De sacramentis* I.vii.6)

The subversion of God's image in man proceeds, in other words, precisely as horizontal dialogue is successfully instigated by Satan with
Eve. Given that Eve's extroversion leads to her mortality, we may say
that the theological matrix of dialogue in this play is diametrically opposite that of a Romantic such as Novalis, when he writes, "Death is
nothing but the breakdown of exchange between inner and outer stim-
uli—between soul and world" (*Tod is nichts, als Unterbrechung des*

---

23. Hugh of St. Victor, *Miscellanea*, in *Patrologiae latinae*, vol. 177, col. 804
(cited by Javelet, 1:251); translation mine.

Wechsels zwischen innrem und ausserm Reitz—zwischen Seele und Welt).[24]

Goaded by *curiositas,* Eve begins to ask Satan real, rather than merely rhetorical, questions: "What does it taste like?" *(Quel savor a?* v. 252). "Is this the fruit?" *(Est cel li fruiz?* v. 259). Suddenly Adam reappears and asks what Satan wanted, and though he successfully wards off Eve's infatuation with Satan for a brief moment, when the Serpent slithers down the tree and begins to whisper false counsel in her ear, her defenses fall altogether: "Eat, Adam. You don't know what it is. Let us take this good thing that is so near us!" *(Manjue, Adam. Ne sez que est. / Pernum ço bien que nus est prest;* vv. 293–94).

Horizontal discourse between the parents of man is instituted in revolt against God and perfected in a climate of postlapsarian reproach: language is both the instigator and embodiment of difference. In postlapsarian dialogue with God, questions are not proffered by an omniscient God to obtain information that he (always) already knows but rather as perlocutionary acts of reproach: "Where is your brother Abel?" *(U es ton frere Abel?* v. 723). Man's questions to God are acts of evasion: "How do I know, Lord, where he has gone?" *(Que sai jo, sire, ou est alez?* v. 727); or of repudiation: "When he took that rib from my side, why didn't he burn it and kill me?" *(Quant cele coste de moi prist, / Pour quei ne l'arst et moi oscist?* vv. 363–64).

The more man becomes different from God, the more such differences cleave man from himself and from his fellow man. Not only does Adam suffer internal remorse after the Fall, but he blames Eve for his temptation. Likewise, in the scene between Cain and Abel that immediately follows the expulsion from Paradise, we witness a repetition of the subversion of the language of vertical commemoration of God, as horizontal dialogue arises between two brothers. Here the contest of paradigms is economic, as well, since Abel displays both verbal and fiscal rectitude that Cain finds tedious and burdensome. Surely the common folk of the play's audience were able to see the legacy of fiscal discord arising from the Fall as something close to home, since tithing was a common subject in medieval sermons of the time.[25] Cain begins with an assault on Abel's preachiness and concludes with an assault on his monetary servitude to God:

24. Novalis, *Schriften,* 5:314.
25. Michel Zink, *La Prédication en langue romane avant 1300* (Paris: Champion, 1974), 419–25.

(Good brother Abel, you certainly know how to preach, how to practice reason and how to demonstrate what is right. Whoever listens to your teaching will have nothing left for himself in just a few days. I never liked paying tithes!)

Beal frère Abel, bien savez sermoner,
Vostre raison asaer e mustrer.
En poi de jorz avra poi que doner!
Disme doner ne me vient anches a gré!
(vv. 611–14)

Though the *Mystère d'Adam* does sound this one financial chord, for the most part the play's social tensions are refracted through a traditional military structure far less threatened by the radical power of urban money than is the later feudal structure of the worlds of the *Jeu de la Feuillée* or of *Aucassin et Nicolette*. In any case, Abel breathes his last words not in dialogue about money with his brother but, like a future saint about to be martyred, in prayer to God.[26]

PROPHECY

Following Cain's anathema by Figura, horizontal dialogue in this play gives way to prophecy, which, as we saw in our discussion of Augustine above, implied not only prediction of things to come, but the practice of homiletics and exegesis as well. All three dimensions of the notion of prophecy are expressed in the third part of the play. That the Romance vernacular should be invoked, after the Fall, to prophesy the redemption and final judgment of man is, in a sense, at least a partial redemption and revalorization of the language itself; indeed, one may read this play as an attempt to indict *subversive* uses of the vernacular precisely in order to *legitimize* it as a vessel of sacred truth and justice.

At only one point does a fiction of human dialogue intrude upon inspired prophetic discourse; this occurs when "someone rushes from the synagogue" (*quidam exurget de sinagoga;* v. 882) and begins to dispute with Isaiah. Recalcitrant and mocking, the Jew questions above all the status of Isaiah's discourse: Is it true? Is it a joke? A slave to the carnal letter, the Jew clings stubbornly to the *verba* of his book for his certainty, while Isaiah reads nothing less than the book of life whose *res* emanate from God himself:

26. Willem Noomen, Introduction to *Le Jeu d'Adam* (Paris: Champion, 1971), 10.

(THE JEW: Is it written in the book?
ISAIAH: Yes, the book of life. I did not dream it: I saw it.
THE JEW: And how?
ISAIAH: By the power of God.
THE JEW: You seem to me like an old fool: your mind is very
disturbed. You are overripe. You are too good at looking in the
mirror. Now look at my hand, and tell me if my body is sick or
well!)

> JUDEUS
> En livre est escrit?
> > YSAIAS
> > > Oïl, de vie.
> Nel sonjai pas: ainz l'ai veu.
> > JUDEI
> Et tu coment?
> > YSAIAS
> > > Par Deu vertu.
> > JUDEI
> Tu me sembles viel redoté:
> Tu as le sens tot trublé!
> Tu me sembles viel meür!
> Tu sés bien garder al miror:
> Or me gardez en ceste main
> Tunc ostendet ei manum suam:
> Si j'ai le cor malade ou sain!
> (vv. 890–900)

Depending on when the *Mystère d'Adam* was written, it is possible that
the figure of the Jew speaks beneath a statue of *Synagoga* standing blind-
folded on the church facade (beside a victorious *Ecclesia*). In any case,
the dialogue between the Jew and Isaiah echoes certain theological assumptions about Judaism as a refusal to interpret divinely instituted
signs. Augustine had argued that if the Gentiles committed idolatry, the
Jews simply refused to interpret divine signs altogether, thereby subjecting themselves to the bondage of the letter (*DDC* III.vi.10). Such
notions are evoked in the Latin pseudo-Augustinian sermon whose in-
cipit ("*Vos inguam, convenio, O Judei . . .*") opens the prophetic conclusion of the *Mystère*.[27] Ideas about the recalcitrance of the Jews be-

27. The sermon is published in part in the Noomen edition, p. 64.

fore divine signs were current in the twelfth century; John of Salisbury, for example, interprets the destruction of Jerusalem as the just punishment of the Jews' choice to ignore the signs forewarning them of what was about to happen.[28] In this dialogue, however, the Jew does become intimidated by Isaiah's threats, to a point where he bids Isaiah resume his prophecy. At this moment in the play, horizontal dramatic dialogue as such comes to an end.

In short, the discourse of prophecy in its several modes—predicting, interpreting, preaching—may be considered a proper end of natural language. The play tends, therefore, toward the rhetorical goal exemplified by Augustine when he concluded his spiritual itinerary in the *Confessions* with a return to the previously opaque events of the Old Testament through illumination in the New. To proffer such redeemed scriptural wisdom is to participate in God's dialogue with himself.

But what about man's *own* part in the gift of prophecy, his gift of human eloquence, his *suavitas*? If the *Mystère* seemed at first to dismiss outright the claims of the poetic on man's affective life through an implicit (but strong) censure of Satan's courtly lyric discourse, the Procession of Prophets ends in this play with a stunning endorsement of poetry that is uttered in *praise* of God in a spirit of *sacrifice*—one will recall that these are both notions proper to the Augustinian concept of "confession." Thus, the poetry sung by Shadrach, Meshach, and Abednego from the flames of Nebuchadnezzar's furnace is extolled in terms surpassing any classical notion of the sublime: "There, from the burning fire, they sang out such beautiful verses that it seemed like angels from the sky" (*La ou il furent al fouc ardant, / Chantoient un vers si bel / Sembloit li angle fuissent del ciel*; vv. 938–40). So powerful is the song that Nebuchadnezzar sees the mysterious "fourth man" (*le quarz*; v. 941) as if he were the "son of God." The perfection of the human poetic word proffered in sacrifice points to the coming of the divine Word.

It is interesting that the *Mystère d'Adam* censures most emphatically the conventions of vernacular courtly eroticism. This is an idiom rooted in oxymorons of suffering and hope of *joi d'amors* whose rhetoric, albeit profane, is closest to that of praise for the creator and hope of salvation in the moment of martyrdom. Clearly, the quests for vertical and horizontal *joi d'amors* draw upon the same semantic resources of

28. John of Salisbury, *Policraticus* II.iv, ed. C. J. Webb (Oxford: Clarendon Press, 1929).

language, and it should come as no surprise that of the three major discourses of twelfth-century vernacular literature—epic, romance, and lyric—lyric was the one that most deeply infiltrated the discourse of early vernacular sermons, though commonly as condemnation. The desire for spiritual *gaudium* is articulated, within a twelfth-century discursive horizon, through *denegation* of courtly *joi d'amor*.[29] In such instances, the process of dialogue is based less upon a confrontation of distinct *personae* than upon the deployment of contrary illocutionary forces within a given semantic field. As Michel Zink has written of early romance preachers and of the courtly:

> Ils savent, pour la condamner, recourir à ses images et user de ses attraits. Mais, là encore, ils sont pris entre leur désir de condamner l'univers courtois et la fascination qu'il exerce sur eux. Quoi qu'ils fassent, ils ne peuvent lui échapper dès lors qu'ils utilisent la langue romane, qui a été forgée comme langue littéraire par les poètes courtois. Comme dans le cas des citations empruntées au lyrisme profane, ils s'en tirent soit en décrivant avec complaisance les vices qu'ils condamnent, soit en appliquant aux choses de Dieu les expressions et le vocabulaire courtois.[30]

However, a second major genre, epic, is also openly censured in the appended sermon. King Nebuchadnezzar completely forgets his place in history to complain that the heroic passions of Roland and Oliver are wrongly preferred to the passion of Christ, a theme that became dear to medieval preachers:[31]

> Mult est plain de coveité
> Que de Deu n'a nul pitié.
> Plus volontiers orreit chanter
> Come Rollant ala juster
> E Oliver son compainnon.
> Qu'il ne ferrait la passion
> Que suffri Crist a grand hahan.
> (vv. 965–70)

29. Zink, 370.
30. Zink, 376.
31. Zink, 9.

(He is full of covetousness who has no pity on God, and would sooner hear how Roland went out jousting, and Oliver, his friend, than he would the passion that Christ suffered with great pain because of Adam's sin.)

But what about the *merveilleux* of the third major genre, romance, which was now coming into vogue in Anglo-Norman culture? If one accepts Aebischer's arguments (which I find convincing) that the *Quinze Signes du jugement dernier* was intended by the scribe of the Tours manuscript to be a conclusion to an otherwise defective original, perhaps there are explanations for the nature of this conclusion other than that some scribe with doubtful taste felt compelled to fill in the ending as best he could. Indeed, with regard to the *merveilleux* of romance, the *Mystère d'Adam* seems to take the tack not of censure but of emulation. This stunning appendage to the Procession of Prophets replaces the speech traditionally reserved for the pagan prophet, the Erythrean Sibyl, as evoked by Augustine in the *City of God* (XVIII. xxiii). In its content and by its lack of action, the *Quinze Signes du jugement dernier* has no direct relationship with the dramatic action that precedes it, yet it is at once the most brilliant writing in the whole play and the most autonomous from the sacred, from *auctoritas*, since it amplifies no specific biblical or liturgical text. It is perhaps for this very reason that the *Quinze Signes* displays a virtuosity of the marvelous that no writer of romance could possibly have surpassed; Zink's remark that "un sermon peut être plus romanesque qu'un roman" certainly pertains here.[32]

LEAVES OF FOLLY

The *Jeu de la feuillée* is among the most perplexing vernacular texts to have survived the Middle Ages. Almost every utterance harbors an enigma, whether at the level of unintelligible words and expressions drawn from the jargon of its day, or at the level of broad dramatic purpose. Critics respond to such provocation in several ways. The safest and easiest way is to dismiss the play as an improvisation by students—something amusing, but scarcely more.[33] Other critics reso-

32. Zink, 386.
33. Philippe Menard, "Le sens du *Jeu de la feuillée*," *Travaux de linguistique et de littérature publiés par le Centre de philologie et de littératures romanes de l'Université de Strasbourg* 16, 1 (1978): 381–93.

lutely read it as a drama of its author's self-consciousness, carrying to it a set of presuppositions that are as appropriate to a romantic novel as they are to this medieval play.[34] A third possibility, more speculative, is to consider the work the embodiment of a crisis originating in the tensions between speech and writing, a crisis extending beyond the soul of Adam de la Halle, beyond the city of Arras, to the metaphysical foundations of medieval culture itself.[35] Given that the *Jeu de la feuillée* is a dramatic work, I shall continue to study the action of dialogue as it symptomatizes the deeper metaphysical crisis that makes the *Jeu de la feuillée* the radical (and very medieval) play that it is.

If we may safely assume that the theatrical space of a learned anticlerical thirteenth-century play, whose alternate title is *Li Jus Adan*, vibrated with intertextual ties to a century-old tradition of vernacular religious drama, then we cannot escape seeing that the *Jeu de la feuillée* perpetrates, from the start and throughout, a brutal flattening of metaphysical hierarchies. Adamic nostalgia for innocence in the transcendent *amenissimus locus* of Paradise—or, in the vernacular of the *Mystère*, of *paraïs* (vv. 210, 927, 1069)—has given way, in the *Jeu de la feuillée*, to the horizontal, terrestrial desire of a perhaps historical Adam to flee the faded joys of an aging marriage with Maroie in the city of Arras in order to regain the supposedly purer life of the intellect as a student in Paris. The stern, scriptural, otherworldly presence of Figura will be usurped, in the middle of the play, by the visitation of conventional literary fairies (who turn out to be ill-tempered strumpets and witches) and by the Boethian philosopher's arch-enemy, Lady Fortune. The choir that responds so piously to the liturgical lessons of the *Mystère* will be succeeded by *Li communs*, an unruly mob perhaps drawn from the audience. The fiery mouth of Hell to which devils drag sinners and prophets alike is displaced by a tavern full of wet, noisy gullets of ordinary men governed by an anticlerical tavernkeeper. The voices of prophecy are supplanted by those of a psychotic Fool and a

34. The most prominent of these are Alfred Adler, *Sens et composition du "Jeu de la Feuillée"* (Ann Arbor: Univ. of Michigan Press, 1956); and Jean Dufournet, *Adam de la Halle à la recherche de lui-même, ou "Le Jeu dramatique de la feuillée"* (Paris: Société d'édition d'enseignement supérieur, 1974).

35. Alexandre Leupin, "Le ressassement (sur le *Jeu de la Feuillée d'Adam de la Halle*," *Le Moyen Age* 89 (1983): 239–68). My own reading of the play converges at many points with Leupin's and is indebted to Leupin's on others. I have greatly benefited from discussions with Leupin about this play and the problems that it raises, and wish to record here a debt that is considerable, even if its form is not always in evidence.

drunken, simoniac Monk. The *Jeu de la feuillée* (whose title may mean "the play of folly") construes the daily life of Arras as that of a world that is not only lost and fallen but still falling—every moment people speak.

In Adam's opening declaration of his decision to renounce the *grant maladie* of marriage in order to take up the clerk's habit in Paris, language seems to serve its author-speaker as a vehicle of truth both adequate to his judgments of the world and capable of communicating these to the social group that he now yearns to transcend. Language is initially proffered, however briefly, as a kind of human *logos* that successfully mediates between inner and outer, between the rational soul of man and the world, and such a "principle of expressibility" corresponds to the scholastic confidence that the world can indeed be properly intellected and that our intellections are also "sayable" (*dicibiles*) in propositions.[36]

However, the beginning speech is also an ending to the extent that language will not be allowed to function in such a manner for long. Adam closes his opening declaration with a much-discussed proverb: "It still appears from the pieces what the pot was" (*encore pert il bien as tes queus li pos fu;* v. 11). The thrust of Adam's rhetorical turn seems clear: despite the shattering effect of life with Maroie in Arras, Adam's spirit is intact. However, both pots and men are fashioned from earth, and both are fragile; given that Adam never will follow up his ostentatious decision to leave Arras, and given that the motif of the broken pots will return with stark literalness later in the play, Adam's invocation of the broken pot as a metaphor for oneness-of-self will prove to be an unintentional prophecy of bad things, including folly, to come.

The pot is more than a simple household object when it is employed by a medieval writer as a metaphor for the self. The pot is a symbol with a rich metaphysical tradition, and its demetaphorization in the course of the play amounts to a *mise-en-cause* of that tradition. Alfred Adler was the first to underscore the theological tradition of the pot as a metaphor expressing the contingency of man.[37] As St. Paul wrote (Rom. 9:20), "But who are you, a man, to answer back to God? Will what is molded say to its molder, 'Why have you made me thus?'" Augustine, however, invokes the breakable pot as something to be

36. Gabriel Nuchelmans, *Theories of the Proposition: Ancient and Medieval Conceptions of the Bearers of Truth and Falsity* (Amsterdam: North Holland, 1972), 116–18.
37. Adler, 20.

gathered up by God's grace: "The vessels (*vasa*) that are filled by you do not restrict you, for even if they are shattered, you are not poured forth. When you are poured upon us, you are not cast down, but you raise us up; you are not scattered about, but you gather us up" (*Conf.* I.iii.3). For Hugh of St. Victor, the sacraments are *vasa* which contain the grace necessary as a remedy for original sin (*De sacramentis* I.ix.3). Adler points to a passage at the conclusion of Matthieu de Vendôme's *Ars versificatoria* as a more contemporary metaphor of the pot, and what I find most remarkable is the metaphor's context. Medieval ideas often form associative bundles not always apparent to us, and in his example of rhetorical conclusions where he offers his art to the glory of God, Matthieu provides a rich bundle of concepts that will be contested together in the *Jeu*: "I, the mere pot, give thanks to the potmaker; the object made to its maker; the servant [or serf] to the king; the shape to the shaper, the offspring to the father" (*Do grates figulo vas, fabro fabrica, regi / Servus, plasmanti plasma, propago patrit*).[38] I subscribe to Dufournet's suggestion, echoed by Alexandre Leupin, that the broken pot serves as a metaphor for the trajectory of the play itself,[39] and in a forthcoming essay, Leupin aptly calls the proverb of the pot a "shifter prophesying the destiny of writing playing itself out in the play."

A progressive undermining of Adam's self, considered as an integral consciousness where meanings converge and cohere, begins with the dialogue immediately following Adam's initial declaration. Rikeche Auris ("Wealth of gold") attacks Adam's decision to flee what he had called the "enchantment" (v. 7) of Arras by claiming that no good clerk has ever come out of Arras, and that his hope is a "big illusion" (*grans abusions*; v. 15). Arras takes on here an almost theological dimension as an emblem for the despair of fallen man longing in exile for *paraïs*— so close in name to, yet so distant from, Paris. Still clinging to his resolution, Adam retorts with the example of Rikier Amion, "a good clerk, careful with his book" (*Boins clers et soutieus en sen livre*; v. 17). Here is a second privileged symbol of the medieval spiritual world in which Adam takes refuge, and one whose treatment now engages our own motives as readers of Adam's play. As proffered here, "book" is another "shifter" oscillating between several semantic fields. On the one hand, the intellectual bond between the rational soul and the book points to

38. Adler, 20; Matthieu de Vendôme, *Ars versificatoria*, IV.51, in Edmond Faral, ed., *Les Arts poétiques du XIIe et du XIIIe siècle: Recherches et documents sur la technique littéraire* (Paris: Champion, 1924), 192.

39. Dufournet, 69.

the infinitely truer relationship between God and his two books, of life and of Scripture.[40] The book symbolizes, as well, man's own integrity of spirit, his own readable conscience. Commenting on John's expression, "the book of the life of each man" (Rev. 20:12), Augustine writes that "the book of the life of each man is to show what commandments each man has done or omitted to do. . . . We must therefore understand of it a certain divine power, by which it shall be brought about that every one shall recall to memory all his own works, whether good or evil, and shall mentally survey them with a marvellous rapidity, so that this knowledge will either accuse or excuse conscience."[41] As imagined by Adam, then, the book is an emblem of authority, of totality, of method—and of redemption, to the extent that Rikier got to Paris by working with his book. Suddenly, however, a third interlocutor, Hane le Mercier, "shifts" the word for "book" in other unwanted ways, turning the word against the sacred object just named and making it a pun on *livre* as "pound," whether a "pound" of weight or a "pound" of money. If the goal of the medieval logician is to master the equivocity of terms in speech, in this play it is the equivocity of terms that dominates consciousness:

> (Yes, "for two deniers for a pound."
> I don't think he knows anything but that.)

> Oïl: "pour deux deniers le livre."
> Je ne voi k'il sache autre cose.
> (vv. 18–19)

In other words, the book-centered spirituality of Arras's best clerk is denounced as mere mercenarism, a charge that perhaps shows the darker side of the emerging theology of purgatory, whose overlappings with nascent capitalism I stressed in chapter 5. Hane adds that he, Adam himself, is too changeable of mind (*muavle kief*; v. 21) to be reckoned with, and abruptly breaks off the dialogue: "No one dares answer you" (*Mais nus reprendre ne vous ose*; v. 20). This is a dialogue not between kindred speaking subjects but between a tenuous, individual consciousness and a collectivity whose multiple voices not only misrepresent and denounce his intentions but promptly drop Adam

40. Thomas Aquinas, *De veritate, quaestio 7, art. 1–8.* See also Ernst Robert Curtius, *European Literature and the Latin Middle Ages,* trans. Willard R. Trask (New York: Pantheon Books, 1948), ch. 16.

41. St. Augustine, *City of God* XX.xiv., trans. Marcus Dods (New York: Random House, 1950), 753.

from the dialogue in order to speak in puns *about* him, right before his face. Rikier says to Hane,

> Cuidies vous k'il venist a kief,
> Biaus dous amis, de chou k'il dit?
> (vv. 22–23)

> (Do you think, my dear friend, that he will actually do what he says?)

Suddenly the magisterial "I" of the clerkly first person is no longer even a speaker, but is being *spoken*: "I" has become denigrated and reified as the excluded third person in speech, the "zero-person," in Benveniste's terms. We are very far from that encounter with positive alterity which, for the Romantics, leads back to reflexivity—far, for instance, from Novalis when he says: "We naturally understand whatever is foreign only through self-estrangement—self-otherness—self-observation" (*Wir vestehn natürlich alles Fremde nur durch Selbstfremdmachung—Selbstveränderung—Selbstbeobachtung.*[42] Dialogue in the *Jeu* is not circular, not linear, not even zigzag, but aleatory and centrifugal. Having just compared himself to a pot whose whole is still visible in its fragments, and having just proffered the book as a symbol of spiritual integrity, Adam now finds himself protesting against the scattering of his intentionality in the centrifugal language of the group:

> Cascun mes paroles despit,
> Che me sanle, et giete mount loing.
> (vv. 24–25)

> (Each of you holds my words in scorn,
> it seems to me, and scatters them far abroad.)

Once again, Adam asserts his God-given autonomy of judgment and his freedom of will as he repeats his intention to leave Arras and the lower *joie* of marriage:

> Mais, puis ke che vient au besoing,
> Et ke par mi m'estuet aidier,
> Sachiés je n'ai mi si kier
> Le sejour d'Arras ne le joie
> Ke l'aprendre laissier en doie.

42. Novalis, *Schriften*, 5:49.

Puis ke Dieus m'a donné engien,
Tans est ke je l'atour a bien.
(vv. 26–33)

(But, since the necessity has come, and I must count on myself
for help, let me say that I do not hold so dear life in Arras or
joie [in marriage] that I must drop my goal of learning. Since
God has given me the means, it is time that I put them to
good use.)

However, Adam himself is curiously disposed toward the equivocal,
and he ends his second declaration, as he did his initial one, with a rhetorical figure which lays bare semantic threads that he neither intends
nor can prevent: "I have shaken out my purse here long enough!" (*J'ai
chi assés me bourse escousse;* v. 34). Meanings begin to surge up as
much from a collective unconscious in language itself as from the individual minds who wield it. By mobilizing a familiar fabliau metaphor for his testicles—as one fabliau puts it, "The name of that purse
is balls!" (*Ceste borse a non coilles*)—Adam has invited a second
metaphor of dissemination comparing spent semen and coins; and,
sure enough, another interlocutor, Gillos li petis, promptly "shifts" to
the economic charge of Adam's metaphor with this troubling question:
"And what will become of your old broad, my lady Maroie?" (*Que de-
venra dont li pagousse, / Me commere dame Maroie?*" vv. 34–35).
Adam answers that he will place his wife with his father, evoking the
prospect of an improper coupling, not of words but of kin; later, Adam's
father Henri will indeed praise Maroie's sexual acumen (v. 503), presumably on the basis of firsthand knowledge. Indeed, improper couplings
pass back and forth between *verba* and *res* with great spontaneity in
this play; at one point the fool will try to bugger his father in public,
thinking he is a cow (v. 418).

Adam's first metaphor of dissemination is now extended even further: from the testicular purse first came the series "semen," "coin";
now comes "seed," then "mill," and finally "word." When Gillos warns
Adam that his insatiable wife might follow him to Paris, Adam threatens to put mustard on his member in order to thwart her lust and
thereby safeguard his seed. This is good fabliau strategy, but there is
something doubly shocking about mustard, whose seed is celebrated
by Scripture as a metaphor for faith and charity (because of its capacity
to beget so much out of little; Matt. 13:31), being smeared on a man's
sexual organ to preserve his seed. The semantic chain speeds on:

Gillos retorts with a reminder of Adam's duty as a man lawfully wedded to *la chose*, and invokes a frightening (at least in this context) proverb to express Adam's moral obligation to be fruitful and multiply: Adam must be careful, Gillos tells him, to feed his grain into the mill to be ground (*"Warde estuet prendre a l'engrener"*; v. 50). Adam's captivity is not merely to the body politic of Arras, which scatters his words far and wide, but to the female vagina which grinds and devours his seed.

In the retrospective monologue that follows, however, Adam tells at length how he first became infatuated with Maroie and shows us that his captivity began not in the flesh itself but in words—more specifically, in the labyrinth of courtly erotic discourse whose semantic processes (which we studied in chapter 4) blinded him to the truth of Maroie as its all-too-human referent. As any initiated reader will detect, Adam not only exhausts the rhetorical convention of the courtly female portrait (the one that Satan had invoked in the *Mystère d'Adam*) but, even now, still compulsively amplifies it—at the same time as he joins to it an anti-courtly idiom drawn from the *sotte chanson* and the *fatrasie*. [43] Both discourses are merely twin visages of his misogyny; they are rooted not in the reality of Maroie as a woman but in Adam's unbridled indulgence in his own contrary fantasms. That we see Adam still hard at work overelaborating the ideal portrait, carrying it too far, shows that he remains captivated by the *derverie* of conventional courtly poetic signs; that is to say, like Dante's sinners in Hell, Adam still actively chooses his affliction—in this case, idolatry of the poetic sign—even as he bewails that choice:

> Est é faisoit bel et seri,
> Douc et vert et cler et joli,
> Delitavle en cans d'oiseillons;
> En haut bos, près de fontenele
> Courant seur maillie gravele,
> Adont me vint avisions
> De cheli ke j'ai a feme ore,
> Ki or me sanle pale et sore;
> Adont estoit blanke et vermeille,
> Rians, amoureuse et deugie,

43. Lambert C. Porter, *La Fatrasie et le fatras: Essai sur la poésie irrationnelle en France au moyen-âge* (Geneva: Droz; Paris: Minard, 1960).

Or le voi crasse et mautaillie,
Triste et tenchant.
(vv. 63–74)

(It was a beautiful and peaceful summer,
Sweet, and green, bright and beautiful,
Delightful with the songs of birds,
In the middle of the forest, near a spring
Flowing over shining stones
When a vision came to me
Of the woman who is now my wife,
Who now seems pale and sour.
Once her form was white and crimson,
Laughing, loving, and elegant of build;
Now I see her as fat and ill-shaped,
Sad and quarrelsome.)

In both the *Mystère d'Adam* and the *Jeu de la Feuillée*, the same power of courtly language to misrepresent reality is under attack, with this difference: in the latter play, Satan is no longer to blame, but only Adam for his autoerotic dialogue with himself. However, Adam abandons the language of disillusionment less than halfway through his evocation of Maroie as the desire to desire sweeps over him *yet again*. Adam underscores the radical (and un-Romantic) dispossession of self that accompanies his spiritual investment in the poetics of desire:

Et plus et plus fui en ardeur
Pour s'amour et mains me connui.
(vv. 161–62).

(More and more I burned for her love, and I knew myself all the less.)

Adam at last interrupts his running battle with the seductions of poetic language by returning, now literally, to his original monetary concerns:

S'est droiz ke je me reconnoisse
Tout avant ke me feme engroisse
Et ke li cose plus me coust,
Car mes fains en est apaiés.
(vv. 171–74)

(Thus it is right that I come back to my senses before I get my wife pregnant and her "thing" costs me even more; for my hunger for it has been cured.)

Adam's verbal indulgence had begun with an unsympathetic Rikier as his interlocutor. Rikier had interrupted Adam's reminiscence with an economic metaphor explaining why he has "forgotten" (v. 77) Maroie's delightful features: she has flooded his market, he says, with her wares. Adam spurns this insight, once again blaming the illusions of *Amor*, which make one believe that a wretch is a queen (v. 87), and once again repudiating such illusions by invoking the present horrors of Maroie. But desire, it seems, can migrate everywhere with the language of courtly lyric, even into the souls of hostile speakers. Indeed, to declare one's desire negatively—in what we may call courtly denegation—can be erotogenic: Adam's repudiated portrait of the absent Maroie begins to activate not only his own desire but that of Rikier as well. If only Adam would leave his wife to *him*, Rikier exclaims, he would be satisfied:

Maistre, se vous le me laissiés,
Ele me venroit bien a goust.
(vv. 175–76)

(Mister, if you left her to me, she would suit my taste very well.)

It is essential to the progress of illusion in this dialogue that Maroie be absent. Such dialogue flourishes most when it is least constrained by the presence of any referential reality. Indeed, Maroie is absent throughout the play. Her existence to us is purely a verbal one, tossed indiscriminately from mouth to mouth and from discourse to discourse. Maroie is at once remembered and dismembered in a courtly game of words that is endless because it is, finally, a zero-sum game. Another of the most important characters in the *Jeu*, Robert de Someillon (this time a documented historical personality of Arras),[44] also participates in the dialogue only by hearsay, all of it malevolent. An important bourgeois in real life, Robert is named in the play as the new Prince of the Pui—which is the title bestowed upon the person

44. Roger Berger, *Littérature et société arrageoises au XIIIe siècle: Les Chansons et dits artésiens*. Mémoires de la Commission Départementale des Monuments Historiques du Pas-de-Calais (Arras: Imprimerie centrale de l'artois, 1981), 21:439.

who is in charge of the poetic contests peculiar to thirteenth-century Arras. Robert is also the unlikely object of the love of a supernatural being, the fairy Morgue. Morgue has spurned the love of Hellequin (a supernatural knight drawn not from history but from legend) in order to bestow her hyperboles of chivalric honor and courtliness on this very local mortal. When Morgue is informed that her beloved knight, who supposedly adventures *amont et aval* in the land of the Round Table, is in fact a cheat who trips up his adversary's horse in the list (v. 739), and, worse, that Someillon's errantry leads him in pursuit of other—mortal—skirts (v. 752), Morgue summarily orders Hellequin's herald, Croquesot, to convey to his master her renewed *amistiés* (v. 765). Arrageois scuttlebutt has completely undone Morgue's delusions, nourished until now in her native language of the marvelous; and scuttlebutt has perhaps undone a contemporary historical reputation as well.

The *Jeu de la feuillée* is a tissue of scandals gratuitously divulged by characters who materialize on the stage at random and speak out with no bidding. The play's goal seems to be to show that scandal alone is the primary substance of civic history. Potentially endless lists of misers, gluttons, fornicators, and insane citizens of Arras, recited by the physician, the monk, and others, form a vast and purely vindictive documentation, a dark anti-history contesting the more laundered, mendacious accounts of those who wield (and abuse) official power. Moreover, for all its brevity (it is a mere 1,099 lines long), the *Jeu de la feuillée* sets as its target the social corruption of Arras in its totality. No less than fifteen different trades, vocations, or professions are represented in this play, whether by actual characters or by pejorative allusions to living Arrageois who do not appear. The language of the play comprises multiple discourses (e.g., the scientific, the homiletic, the judicial, and the poetic in all of its major genres); in their aggregate they symbolize the speech group of Arras and perhaps of *homo garrulans* as a species. Within this tissue of mutually disrupting discourses, the very notion of truth becomes unthinkable. the arbitrariness of conventional verbal signs extends, as well, to other classes of objects that also function as conventional signs in the social group: the body of the woman, the coin, the relic—all of which are objects of fetishistic desire, and all of which demand the violation, the disfigurement, the fragmentation of some host substance in order to acquire or bear signification. Nothing serves as a more apt emblem of man's ab-

surd will to construct meanings in an aleatory world than the visitation of Lady Fortune, who appears miraculously, like a sinister parody
of Pentecost, during the visitation of the fairies. Like the Holy Spirit
descending upon all the pious men and speaking to each in his own
tongue, Morgue says of Lady Fortune that "she inhabits us all" (*Cas-
cune nous appartient;* v. 770). Deaf, dumb, and blind, Fortune either
exalts men or harms them *sans raison* (v. 811), bestowing or denying
wealth, political favor, or the female *bele cose* (v. 826).

The one person in the play who seems to stand outside the perverse
economy of empty verbal signs is the Physician: his epiphanies, both
medical and moral, are rooted not in arbitrary conventional signs but
in natural signs, and these cannot lie because existence does not lie.
What exists *truly* exists.[45] Thus, the scandals that men's mouths will
hide, their urine betrays, and no one on the stage doubts the physician's
diagnoses of gluttony, avarice, mendacity, and fornication in those
around him. A cross appears on his assistant Rainelet's thumb as he
dips it in Dame Douche's urine:

> RAINELÈS
> Dame, je voi chi c'on vous fout
> Pour nului n'en chelerai rien.
> LI FISICIENS
> Enhenc! Dieus! je savoie bien
> Comment li besoigne en aloit.
> Li orine point n'en mentoit.
> (vv. 266–70)

> RAINELET: Lady, I see here that you've been laid; for nothing in
> the world would I hide it.
> THE PHYSICIAN: Aha! By God, I knew very well how the test
> would come out! Urine never lies.

But even the Physician, for all his clairvoyance in diagnosing—and
judging—the scandals of men and women around him, gives himself
over, near the play's end, to the all-encompassing deluge of drink
(v. 1010).

45. Marcia Colish, "The Stoic Theory of Verbal Signification and the Problem of
Lies and False Statement from Antiquity to St. Anselm," in *Archéologie du signe,*
ed. Lucie Brind'Amour and Eugene Vance (Toronto: Pontifical Institute for Mediaeval Studies, 1983), 17–44; Jean Jolivet, *Arts du langage et théologie chez Abélard*
(Paris: Vrin, 1969, 66–80.

Dialogue in the *Jeu de la feuillée* seems, finally, to emanate not from reason but from whatever is bestial, involuntary, and convulsive in human beings: their rages, their spasms, their distensions, and their climaxes. Given that the species man, logically speaking, belongs to the genus animal, it is in keeping with the perverse logic of this play that as *homo loquens et politicus* regresses into the *charivari* of his generic bestiality, both the players and the audience of the play should moo together like calves as a kind of anti-prayer for some unloved fellow citizen of Arras who is reputed to be sick of mind (v. 376).[46]

Only the Dervé, the crazy boy, remains true to himself and immovable in his nonsense, which at certain times approaches a sublime speaking-in-tongues and at others embodies language as the play of pure difference (in the Augustinian sense of that term). If Adam is hopelessly ensnared by the implacable language of desire in Arras, why, inversely, should the Fool not declare himself the prince of poets, add an "l" to the word for "apple" (*pume*, v. 1042), and make the apple he is eating in Picardy into a "feather" (*plume*) that has flown off like a mere word to Paris? If the power of verbal signs to signify is arbitrary, and if all men are hypocrites, why should the Fool not go right to the top and declare himself king (v. 395)? If women are nothing but by-products of fantasy and language, why should the Fool not pronounce himself a wedded man (v. 1093)? The Fool illustrates by his madness more than the mere failure of the human will to signify: he expresses somatically an active and progressive will to degrade man's sign-making capacity. First, he sounds off on the stage like a trumpet (v. 400); next, he barks like a dog (v. 424); finally, at the end of the play, having been "pissed upon" (*compissé*; v. 1087) by his own father, he farts—bearing out, in one resounding deed, all of those ancient and scholastic treatises informing us that the word (*vox*) in itself, is nothing but struck air (*aer percussus*).[47]

PLAYING DOWN THE DIVINE

There has been a tendency for the ablest readers of the *Jeu de la feuillée*, notably Alfred Adler and Jean Dufournet, to consider the play a dialectical quest for self-knowledge on the part of an author, Adam

46. Jacques Le Goff and Jean-Claude Schmidt, eds., *Le Charivari* (Paris: Mouton, 1983).

47. Jolivet, 22–26.

de la Halle. Adler writes: "L'acheminement vers ce but de la *recon-naissance* de soi-meme, c'est bien là que nous plaçons le sens de la pièce." He believes, moreover, that the play achieves this goal of self-knowledge, though the attainment of this *esthetic* goal passes dia-lectically through the *ugly*: "Désireux de *se reconnaître*, de 'meüer,' le poète jet un regard sur ceux qui l'entourent, et il les voit ou prétend les voir sous l'aspect de la *laideur*. Poète comique et satirique, il profite de l'occasion qui lui permet de faire payer à ses braves concitoyens les frais de son désir de *se reconnaître*."[48]

The links between such a reading, where "tout se tient," and the imperatives of a somewhat caricatural German idealism are inescap-able. They extend, as well, to Jean Dufournet's brilliant reading of the play, whose title, we should recall, is *Adam de la Halle à la recherche de lui-mème, ou "Le Jeu dramatique de la feuillée."* A closer and less cheerful reader of the play than Adler, Dufournet proposes that the fool is an ironic image of the poet Adam de la Halle himself: "Le dervé nous paraît être la face nocturne d'Adam de la Halle qui l'attire et lui fait horreur—fruit d'une curiosité morbide pour quelquechose qui l'obsède." Dufournet brings to the *Jeu* a critical template just as appro-priate to an ironic *Bildungsroman* (e.g., F. Schlegel's *Lucinde*) as to this medieval play: "Mais ce qui nous attache sans doute le plus à cette pièce, c'est qu'elle nous livre les hantises du poète, retrace son itiné-raire moral et spirituel, raconte son histoire de façon fragmentaire en la coupant de scènes d'actualité et de la vie quotidienne, pour finale-ment conclure à son échec."[49]

By claiming that an authorial self-consciousness is the true circum-ference of the action of the *Jeu de la feuillée*, Adler and Dufournet have raised critical questions that are important to the discipline of medi-eval studies at the present time. One will easily discern at work in their readings the presuppositions of early Romantic medievalism, which found in medieval poetry a Christian esthetics that was alleged to have justly triumphed over the false unities of classical art and its materialism in order to reveal the higher, subjective, and self-reflexive nature of inner man.[50] I would argue that the priorities of Romantic medievalism, however compelling they may remain, are basically a de-

---

48. Adler, 37, 12.

49. Dufournet, 339, 342.

50. M. H. Abrams, *The Mirror and the Lamp* (New York: Oxford Univ. Press, 1953).

graded metaphysics, a displacement into the concept of "person," of transcendental principles that exalt the consciousness of man at the same time as they eclipse a speculative tradition that had come falsely to be perceived, with the rise of humanism, as oppressive and dehumanizing. I would argue, further, that for us to impute such limiting parameters to this or any other great medieval poetic work is to deny precisely that dimension of metaphysical awareness which alone gives meaning to the most lucid rhetorical strategies and to the semantic events of medieval literature at its best.

To be sure, the *Jeu de la feuillée* does begin by positing the fiction of an individual consciousness, bearing the proper name "Adam," shown in a moment of crisis and decision. However, the parameters of the crisis quickly dilate to become located in social (as opposed to internal) relationships and in dominant cultural codes (for instance, that of courtly poetics), thereby inviting us to see beyond the horizon of any individual consciousness ("Adam"), and even beyond Arras, into a sick microcosm bearing the name of the species "man." The multiple voices of this play are like threads in a loosely woven textile—burlap, let us say—which is that of language itself, considered as the living but flawed fabric of the human order. Not only do we observe a collective failure of the human will to signify or to understand properly, but we witness the subversion of privileged intellectual symbols (the pot, the book, the seed, the word, etc.) as cognitive instruments permitting man to speculate comfortably by analogy about the unknown and invisible world beyond. Adam speaks in only 169 verses of the poem's 1,066, and already by verse 194 (after his father has declined, out of avarice, to support his studies in Paris), Adam shows signs of folly when he screams out *K'i a! K'i a! K'i a! K'i a!*—which could be either an unanswerable interrogative exclamation similar to "Why? Why? Why? Why?" or an enraged interjection implying a notion of excrement, or, finally, a bird cry such as that of the jay (which is Maroie's surname) or magpie. In any case, we have come very far from the rationally disposed Adam of the play's beginning, and his assertion in the following verse that he is now "sure" he is a student certifies that he has lost his grip entirely. After this moment, Adam becomes a mere background figure, except for his final brief exchanges with Hane le Mercier and with his father, when it becomes clear that the son's morale is completely broken and he will never leave Arras. His only recourse is extreme passive aggression in dealing with a father who, on his side, is triumphally sarcastic:

HANE LI MERCHIERS
Vois ke maistre Adans fait le sage
Pour chou k'il doit estre escoliers,
Je vi k'il se sist volentiers
Avuec nous pour desjuner.
　　ADANS
Biaus sire, ains couvient meurer,
Par Dieu! je ne le fach pour el.
　　MAISTRE HENRIS
Va i, pour Dieu! Tu ne vaus mel.
Tu i vas quant je n'i sui.
　　ADANS
Par Dieu! sire, je n'irai hui
Se vous ne venés avoec mi.
　　MAISTRE HENRI
Va dont, passe avant, vés me chi.
(vv. 949–59).

(HANE LE MERCIER: See what a wise man Adam has become
Because he's supposed to be a student! I've seen him deign to
sit with us at lunch.
ADAM: Good sir, it is better to be mature. By God, I don't do it
for any other reason.
MASTER HENRI: Go ahead, for God's sake. There's no harm; any-
way, you're going off without me.
ADAM: By God, sir, I'll not leave today unless you come
with me!
MASTER HENRI: Go, then: here I am!)

　　Adam has confidently declared in a proverb at the beginning of the
Jeu that the pot's whole is still visible in the fragments; later we learn
that the Fool's father is a potmaker and that the Fool has just broken
two hundred of his pots. Finally, in the tavern, a pot of wine is set up
prominently before all (whether at the center of the stage or on a win-
dowsill), where it is no longer an exalted symbol but a very literal con-
tainer of man's power to alienate himself in drink (v. 918). The cre-
scendo of public drunkenness in the *Jeu* may be seen as the last and
most degrading "enchantment" in the play. As Alfred Adler remarks,
"*L'enchantement* des Dames et *l'ebrietas* de la taverne ont quelque
chose en commun, de même qu'il y a entre les deux états d'âme un

contraste non sans intérêt dramatique."[51] As the Fool, in his last apparition, begins to drain the pot, Henri's cry spurring on the Fool's gluttony ("*Boi bien! Le glout! Le glout! Le Glout!*" v. 1054) is almost as terrifying to the mob as the original deluge:

> Pour l'amour de Dieu, ostons tout,
> Car se chieus sos la nous keurt secure. . . .
> Pren le nape, et tu, le pot tien.
> (vv. 1055−57)

> (For the love of God, let's grab everything, for if this fool descends upon us. . . . Take the tablecloth, and you, take the pot!)

Like the pilgrims "Dante" and "Chaucer" (as opposed to Dante and Chaucer as real persons), "Adam" is one fictive character among many in the play; however, the play's action is not refracted through that fictive consciousness as it is in Dante's or Chaucer's works. The *Jeu de la feuillée* is not an inner crisis of self-consciousness but rather a study of failed relationships, whether within the lines of family (husband/wife, father/son) or within the social group (count/commune, clergy/faithful, physician/patient, tavernkeeper/customer, etc.). Moreover, in all these relationships, whether vertical or horizontal, the twins rhetoric and money are the principle forces of subversion.

However, one relationship in particular, that of father and son, remains painfully central throughout the play, beginning with Henri's plea of poverty as an excuse for forsaking his son's intellectual cause. But among the problems of paternity expressed in the *Jeu*, it is the Fool's relationship with *his* father that commands the most attention, on several scores. Not only is the dialogue between them more ample than that between any other two characters of the play, but even when the father speaks to others, he speaks almost exclusively and poignantly about his son. Also, the relationship between them comes to prevail dramatically because of its brutal physical violence: the play culminates in a terrifying struggle where the Fool tries to choke his father, while the father tries to beat sense into his son with a club. The son makes the father regress into a figure of the "wild man" whose stereotype we saw in *Yvain*.

In her psychoanalytical study of the comic effects of the *Jeu de la*

51. Adler, 36.

feuillée, Claude Mauron proposes that the sons represent the pleasure principle and that the fathers represent the reality principle. The dramatic tension arises as a conflict between these two forces, she believes, and the comic pleasure derives from fantasies of the triumph of the former over the latter. Mauron's thesis has the distinct merit of leading us to perceive in the play a principle of filial revolt not as one confined to specific personalities but as a *relational* one that moves toward higher and more abstract forms. Mauron writes:

> Les fils sont donc vainqueurs, tout au long du *Jeu*. Par "fils" il faut entendre, ainsi que nous l'avons montré, les partisans du plaisir qui affrontent, à travers les personnages paternels, la réalité contraignante. Le morcellement de la pièce en une succession de tableaux permet en effet à certains Pères (Maître Henri, le Père du Dervé) de jouer également, par la suite, un rôle de fils face à une autorité plus haute (le médecin, le Pape, le Moine). Dans ces cas le père et son fils du tableau précédent se rapprochent jusqu'à se confondre: Maître Henri et Adam sont complices en bigamie, le Dervé et son père provoquent ensemble la défaite du Moine, l'un étant ramené par l'autre à la taverne. C'est à une telle ambivalence que l'on doit, entre autres choses, la construction "par paliers" de la partie initiale. Nous avons en effet apprécié l'ingéniosité avec laquelle l'auteur réutilise le père d'Adam comme fils en face du médecin (et plus tard contre le Pape), ce dernier personnage n' étant lui-même qu'une transition vers le niveau définitif, à caractère principalement social, des grandes figures paternelles (Moine, Pape, notables d'Arras).[52]

Nevertheless, there are two important problems in Mauron's reading of the *Jeu*: first, it is simply not the case that sons (any more than fathers) are always "winners"; second, it is wrong to suppose that in this play the "definitive level" of contestation is "the social." The Monk, the Pope, the Physician, and the ruling nobility of Arras are mediators of knowledge and power that are all based upon a common metaphysical principle, that of a divine Father whose paternal aspects of truth, goodness, and power are embodied in the Son as Word. To miss this ultimate referential dimension of the violence between father and son is

---

52. Claude Mauron, *Le Jeu de la feuillée: Etude psychocritique* (Paris: Corti, 1973), 112.

precisely to miss what is both radical and peculiarly medieval about the *Jeu de la feuillée.*

Indeed, the father-son relationship was major speculative terrain among medieval theologians. For instance, it is possible to see a double tendency in speculation throughout the Middle Ages, from St. Augustine to the scholastics, about the Father-Son relationship in the Trinity: that of considering God and Christ first as persons who express a relationship; and that of considering divine paternity and filiality primarily *as* a relationship, one where the mode of being of persons is not distinct from their functional relationship in the pair Father/Son.[53] One may propose that the *Jeu* participates in this cultural ambivalence, inviting us not only to perceive a crisis of human paternity and filiality as implicating distinct persons but to transcend that perception to perceive also a more radical crisis in the metaphysical relationship of Paternity and Filiality, and of Creator and Creation.

If one entertains the proposal that the *Jeu* shares a basic epistemological trajectory with the theological world of its time, then the play's final moments gain a significance reaching far beyond a crisis either of an authorial consciousness or of a corrupt social milieu: the *Jeu* engages us in a metaphysical crisis of the most radical sort. May we not see beyond the human father of the Fool to the Great and Reasonable Potmaker in heaven? And may we not look beyond the Dervé, his son, to a *Logos* that is eternally patricidal and berserk? If there is violence in the way in which men impose meaning on things—whether coins, kings, women, relics, sounds, or sons—then the Fool embodies another kind of centrifugal violence: the violence of matter breaking the laws of mind, and ultimately of creation, that impose order upon things and force them to cohere, bear meaning, and signify. The Dervé is a human expression of a more primeval recalcitrance of atoms (which were also conceived as numbers and letters) before the imperative of the Father who commands that there be light, just as mortal words perpetually defy the philosopher who declares that there shall be truth in speech.

It is interesting that the Monk, who pretends to cure folly with his relics, is more scandalized by the Fool than by anyone else in the play, including even the tavernkeeper who mocks and cheats him. Thus, when the Fool reappears near the end of the play, as if by chance, the Monk lashes out in a paroxysm of wrath, calling him an emissary of the devil:

53. M. Bergeron, O.P., "La Structure du concept latin de personne," *Etudes d'histoire littéraire et doctrinale du XIIIe siècle* 2 (1952): 121–61.

Le chent diavle aport vous ont!
Vous ne me faites fors damage.
(vv. 1031–32)

(A hundred devils have brought you here!
You do me nothing but harm!)

The irreducible folly of the Dervé scandalizes the Monk on more than one ground. Because he is beyond the recuperative power of the Monk's relics, the Fool reveals to all that the Monk is an impostor. However, to the extent that the Fool is beyond the recuperative power of *any* relic, false or true, he points beyond the spiritual impotence of the Monk to a collapse of divine power itself.

Although the *Jeu* is a play whose characters ceaselessly choose their own afflictions, the Monk is strangely impervious to despair, despite his humiliation on every level, social or spiritual. Having burst out in rage at the Fool's return to the stage, the Monk suddenly adopts the Fool as his companion (if not as his spiritual son) and quite simply declares that the time has come for them to move onward to a new spot in quest of treasure—and they are followed, perhaps, by the rest of the crowd (including, maybe, even the audience). However, the Monk moves on not to another town but apparently to a church and to another dramatic spectacle, the *Jeu de St. Nicolas*, written by Adam's fellow Arrageois poet, Jean Bodel. As the Monk vanishes at dawn from one stage to another with the bells tolling behind him, we can scarcely fail to discern an emblem of the Devil gaily leading a procession of sinners off to Hell. One has the impression that much besides salvation has been renounced in a world that has become a seamless, nonsensical, vernacular intertext. If, at the opening of the *Jeu*, Adam claims to wake up at last from the *derverie* of love induced by the rhetoric of poetic art, by the play's end all power to distinguish between art and reality, between rhetoric and truth, between outer and inner, between beginnings and endings has been definitively lost—if ever such distinctions were encouraged by actors and playgoers in the first place.

LI MOINES
Je ne fach point de men preu chi,
Puis ke les gens en vont ensi,
N'il n'i a mais fors baisseletes,
Enfans et garchonaille. Or fai,
S'en irons; a saint Nicolai

Commenche a sonner des cloketes.

Explicit li Jeus de le Fuellie.
(vv. 1094–99)

(THE MONK: I'm not making any profit here, since people are leaving like this; there's nothing left but little girls, children, and young rowdies. Let's go! Onward to Saint Nicholas: the bells have begun to ring!

Here ends the *Jeu de la Feuillée*.

CHAPTER 8

The Differing Seed:
Dante's
Brunetto Latini

In the two previous chapters, we encountered differing degrees of doubt about the capacity of vernacular poetic texts to constitute, in the multiple discourses which are their substance, legitimate artistic forms whose principles of coherence might be extended into a vision of social and cosmic order as well.

In the case of the *Mystère d'Adam* and *Aucassin et Nicolette*, we are shown the rhetorical consequences of human vice, but we are also given either theological or ethical remedies for them. These remedies depend on man's willingness to observe the ordained functions and limits of his natural place in a hierarchy of being. In the *Jeu de la Feuillée*, by contrast, Adam de la Halle assaults every pretext for confidence either that the human soul can avoid vice and folly in its own fragile sphere or that the social order will sustain the soul from without. Adam de la Halle systematically subverts those symbols and cognitive procedures by which the intellect might construct the belief that the universe has been justly framed by a provident Christian God.

In the later Middle Ages, a shift occurred as poets began to experiment more positively with modes of signification and to construe in their art hierarchies both of discourse and of human understanding. Poets also began to draw the reader into the subtle processes of poetic invention itself. They began to make fictions of their writing that compelled the reader to encounter *himself* as a fiction, to see his reading (*lectio*) as something "made" whose nature and value, like those of art itself, were products of constant choice and decision. The choices by which good is made were shown to be not only determined *by* history but determinants *of* history.

Thus, choices made within the sphere of discourse came to be seen as both artistic and ethical. Not only did examples of evil artists and readers now lend themselves to the matter of poetic fiction, but subversive art became the subject of art that aspired to be good.

In this chapter and next, we shall follow the concerns of Dante and Chaucer with what we may call either the ethics of poetics or the poetics of ethics. Each poet dramatizes choices made within the sphere of discourse, conceived as man's highest capacity to act, which are not always apparent to us today. In the present chapter, I shall consider Canto XV of Dante's *Inferno* as a brilliant poetic clustering of three notions commonly associated in the Middle Ages, from St. Augustine forward: those of erotic desire, rhetoric, and text.

Canto XV deals with the example of Brunetto Latini, the distinguished Florentine rhetorician, politician, and poet whose juxtaposition with the sodomists in the *Inferno* has never been justified on historical grounds but has been accepted by modern scholars with a certain intellectual complacency. The notable exception to this statement is of course André Pezard, whose remarkable book, *Dante sous la pluie de feu*, has influenced my reading of this canto.[1]

In the case of Brunetto Latini, Dante does not seem to be concerned specifically with sodomy as a perversion of those organic sexual duties that humans share with all other animals that must be fruitful and multiply in order to replenish the earth with their species. It is a matter of historical record that Brunetto did, in fact, acquit himself of that gentle duty.[2] Dante seems concerned, rather, with what were for him yet graver perversions of two higher and more specifically human properties: to be *social*, and to be a maker of signs—especially *verbal* signs, thanks to which individuals may engender truth in one another's souls. The link between the perversion of man's capacity to make signs and sexual perversion was asserted starkly by St. Paul in his letter to the

1. André Pezard, *Dante sous la pluie de feu* (Paris: Vrin, 1950). A summary of the debate about Dante's portrayal of Brunetto and its historical validity may be found in the essay by Franco Mazzoni, "Brunetto in Dante," in his edition of Brunetto's *Il tresoretto, Il favolello* (Alpignano: A. Tallone, 1967). References to Dante's *Commedia* are to Charles S. Singleton's edition (Princeton, N.J.: Princeton Univ. Press, 1970–75).

2. See J. Carmody's introduction to his edition of Brunetto's *Li livres dou trésor* (Berkeley: Univ. of California Press, 1948), xx.

Romans where he says that God punished idolators by making them sexually perverted:

> For the wrath of God is revealed from heaven against all un-
> godliness and wickedness of men who by their wickedness
> suppress the truth. For what can be known about God is plain
> to them, because God has shown it to them. . . . Claiming to
> be wise, they became fools, and exchanged the glory of the
> immortal God for images [*eikōnos*] resembling mortal man or
> birds or animals or reptiles. . . . For this reason God gave them
> up to dishonorable passions. Their women exchanged natural
> relations for unnatural, and the men likewise gave up natural
> relations with women and were consumed with passion for one
> another, men committing shameful acts with men and receiv-
> ing in their own persons the due penalty for their error. (Rom.
> 1:18–27, Revised Standard version)

The equation between idolatry, including idolatry of the letter, and sexual perversion became a subtle force in medieval poetics. Not only did Augustine bequeath to the West a "sexualized" theory of herme-neutics (to read literally is to read carnally), but he gave dramatic clar-ity to such ideas when he spoke of his own father, who was ambitious for his son's career in letters and who became ecstatic at the discovery of his son's adolescing member at the baths. Augustine reads Patricius's conduct harshly through Paul:

> When my father saw me at the baths, he noted how I was
> growing into manhood [*pubescentem*] and was clothed with
> stirring youth [*adolescentia*]. From this, as it were, he already
> took pride in his grandchildren, and found joy in telling it to
> my mother. He rejoiced over it in that intoxication, wherein
> this world, from the unseen wine of its own perverse will,
> tending down towards lower things [*perversae atque inclinatae
> in ima voluntatis suae*], forgets you, its creator, and loves your
> creature more than yourself.[3]

In Canto XV of the *Inferno*, Dante is situating Brunetto, as poet and rhetorician, in a perspective that is political rather than ecclesiastical (though for Dante, civic and religious histories are ultimately one), and

3. St. Augustine, *Confessions* II.iii.6, trans. John K. Ryan (New York: Doubleday, 1960).

he is asking us to ponder, through Brunetto, what ethical parameters must prevail in that delicate bond between the individual and society, insofar as that bond may be seen as a linguistic and discursive one. In the later Middle Ages, as in many cultures today, different languages were seen to fill distinct discursive functions.[4]

However, in exploring the capacity of medieval intellectuals to identify perversion as a social and discursive evil rather than a sexual one, my purpose is hardly to vindicate Brunetto. On this point, I differ somewhat from Pezard, even though I understand the pertinence of many of his arguments to the problems posed by this canto. But I differ more markedly from Pezard on questions of method. I shall rely less than he on a priori cultural and ideological models that may have "influenced" Dante's poetics from without; to the contrary, I shall concern myself with Dante's manipulation of these models in complex rhetorical strategies within this canto. Dante is a poet whose art is constantly both asserting and calling into question the legitimacy of poetic signs, and such speculative dimensions of his art place him in the same intellectual horizon as that of the *Modistae*, those speculative grammarians of his century who were also concerned with the different modes of signification of verbal signs.[5]

It was generally held in Dante's time, and by Dante as well, that the political order was situated midway in a hierarchy of being between the natural order and the divine. In his *Commentary on the Politics of Aristotle*, Thomas Aquinas affirmed that the city (*civitas*) is the most important (*principalissimum*) work of human reason,[6] and in Aristotle we read that those who by nature remain outside the political order are either superhumans or violent men given to war:

> Hence it is evident that the state is a creation of nature, and
> that man is by nature a political animal, and he who by nature
> and not by mere accident is without a state, is either a bad

4. Such is the lesson Dante's *De vulgari eloquentia*, bk. I, in *Le opere minori*, ed. Enrico Bianchi (Florence: Salani, 1938). For a modern treatment of such questions, see Michael G. Clyne, "Some (German-English) Language Contact Phenomena at the Discourse Level," in *Advances in the Study of Societal Multilingualism*, ed. Joshua A. Fishman (The Hague: Mouton, 1978), 113–28.

5. G. L. Bursill-Hall, *Speculative Grammars of the Middle Ages* (The Hague: Mouton, 1971); Irène Rosier, *La Grammaire spéculative des Modistes* (Lille: Presses Univ. de Lille, 1983).

6. Thomas Aquinas, *Commentum in libros politicorum Aristotelis Expositio* I. proemium, ed. R. Spazzi (Turin: Marichi, 1955).

man or above humanity; he is like a "tribeless, lawless, heart-
less one," whom Homer denounces—the outcast is forthwith a
lover of war.[7]

If, for Aristotle, political exile is closely linked with a penchant for
physical violence, in this canto Dante will explore the spiritual violence of exile as it is wrought above all within the realm of language, of
language considered as the living expression of the political order.

From St. Augustine onward through the Middle Ages, it was commonly held that the orders of language and of society are co-natural,
and that *grammatica* as written language embodies the social order as
it extends across time.[8] Thomas Aquinas states very succinctly both
the social origin of verbal signs and their social function:

> Now if man were by nature a solitary animal the passions of
> the soul by which he was conformed to things so as to have
> knowledge of them would be sufficient for him; but since he is
> by nature a political and social animal it was necessary that
> his conceptions be made known to others. This he does
> through vocal sound. Therefore there had to be significant vo-
> cal sounds in order that men might live together. Whence
> those who speak different languages find it difficult together to
> live in social unity.[9]

In the same passage Thomas refines Augustine's idea about the text as
supplement to the vocal word and about the textual order as the mediator of society's continuous presence to itself:

> If man had only sensitive cognition, which is of the here and
> now, such significant vocal sounds as the other animals use to
> manifest their conceptions to each other would be sufficient
> for him to live with others. But man also has the advantage
> of intellectual cognition, which abstracts from the here and
> now, and as a consequence is concerned with things distant in
> place and future in time as well as things present according to
> time and place. Hence the use of writing was necessary so that

7. Aristotle, *Politics* I.ii, trans. B. Jowett, in *Introduction to Aristotle*, ed.
Richard McKeon (New York: Random House, 1947), 556; cf. Dante's *Convivio* IV.iv,
ed. Bruno Cordati (Turin: Loescher, 1968).

8. St. Augustine, *De ordine* II.xii.36.

9. Aristotle, *On Interpretation: Commentary by St. Thomas and Cajetan*,
lesson II.2, trans. J. Oesterle (Milwaukee: Marquette Univ. Press, 1962), 24.

he might manifest his conceptions to those who are distant according to place and to those who will come in future time.

Thomas says that social order reigns by virtue of laws whose purpose, as the etymology of the word "law" suggests, is to "bind together" (*ligare*) individuals in the body politic.[10] These same ideas are extended by Dante to a yet broader notion of authority, which, he says, remains centered upon the action of the proper "binding of words together" (*legare parole*), and which may therefore be understood, for etymological reasons as well, to include the notion of "author" as someone whose words are of "highest authority" (*altissima autoritade*)—as is the case, Dante says, of Aristotle himself (*Convivio* IV.vi).

Not only does Dante conflate the notion of "author" with the authority of civic life ("Be it known, then, that 'authority' is nought else than the act of an author"),[11] but he sees writing in the life of the individual soul as a device of reason which allows men to govern their wills. Writing, then, is what controls subversive passions, whether in the life of the soul or in the life of the body politic:

> Wherefore Augustine says: "If it [equity] were known of men, and when known were observed, there would be no need of written reason [*raggione scritta*]." And therefore it is written in the beginning of the Old Digest: "Written reason is the art of good and of equity." It is to write, to demonstrate, and to enforce this equity that the official is appointed of whom we are discoursing, to wit the emperor. (*Convivio* IV.ix)

By the same reasoning it follows that the written text could be seen as an instrument of social perversion as well, and I shall suggest at the end of this chapter that it is in the perspective of Dante's ideology of the vernacular text that we must finally understand the motive for his judgment of Brunetto Latini and the deviant *litterati* in his company in Canto XV of the *Inferno*.

In the Middle Ages, the concept of sodomy included not only homosexuality and copulation with animals but any other sexual practice deemed "unnatural" because it turns the seed away from its proper

10. Thomas Aquinas, *Summa theologica*, quaestio XC.1, as published in *Aquinas: Selected Political Writings*, trans. J. G. Dawson and A. P. D'Entreve (Oxford: Blackwell, 1959), 109.

11. *Convivio* IV.vi, trans. A. G. Ferrers Howell, in *Latin Works of Dante Alighieri* (London: Dent, 1903), p. 271.

place, which is the womb, and from its proper function, which is to procreate and renew the species. Though it is a matter of historical record that sodomists were occasionally burned by Catholics and Protestants alike, in accordance with God's exemplary punishment of the Biblical city which gave sodomy (if it must be considered a vice) a name, it is also true that (with some exceptions) acts of sodomy tended to be treated in canonic law rather as occasions for excommunication—that is, for exile from the Christian community—or, in the case of clergy, for removal from their clerical functions.[12] Moreover, Canto XV may be considered as a profound meditation on human exile in all of its various modes.

Such a flexible notion of exile—including the sexual, the political, and the spiritual—was possible in the Middle Ages only because the concept of "nature," over and against which sodomy was conceived of as a class of corruptive behavior, had become such a broad philosophical construct by Dante's time that sodomy could easily be seen as but one of a whole cluster of more subtle—and, for poets, perhaps more interesting—perversions. Following the twelfth-century platonists Bernard Sylvester and Alain de Lille, the concept of nature as a *mater generationis* or a *mater procreatrix* not only had come to valorize and integrate the erotic element of human desire into a comprehensive cosmology of procreation, but had been expanded to include, rather than to oppose, human culture and social order: culture was now seen as the perfection of nature, and "culture as nature" was conceived in dialectical opposition to Chaos as a kind of nonbeing where the seeds (*semines*) of things, or atoms (which, in Lucretius, were also letters), swirled in confusion and waged war with each other until order was imposed by the divine intellect during creation. This creative process occurred in the womb of Silva, or "Forest":

> The seeds of things, too, warring with one another in the chaotic mass—fiery particles with icy, the sluggish with the volatile—dissipated the material or substantial qualities of things of their common subject matter by the clash of their contrary tendencies. Accordingly, divine Providence, to remedy this condition by the promised transformation, reviewed the resources of her mind, mustered her faculties, and summoned up her imaginative powers. Since the reconciliation of discord, the ag-

12. Albert Gauthier, "La Sodomie dans le droit canonique médiéval," in *L'Érotisme au moyen-âge*, ed. Bruno Roy (Montréal: Belarmin, 1977), 111–12.

gregation of incongruities, and the yoking of mutually repel-
lent forces seemed to be the only principles of arrangement,
she resolved to separate mixed natures, to give order to their
confusion and to refine their unformed condition.[13]

In other words, God as *maggior fattore,* to use a term of Dante's, is
to nature what human reason is to the body politic. As Brian Stock
writes, "More emphasis is placed on man's role as creator than as the
object of creation."[14] Robert M. Durling has demonstrated how Dante
himself drew on theories relating man's bodily functions to the order of
the macrocosm as a whole.[15] One may also recall with profit that these
analogies extend no less to man's capacities to act upon the physical
world *around* him. For Hugh of St. Victor, as we saw in the previous
chapter, philosophy now included the seven mechanical arts. As Brian
Stock writes of the *Asclepius:*

> Hermes says that mortal things not only include the two ele-
> ments, earth and water, which Nature has placed under man's
> government, but everything which man makes in or out of
> these, including agriculture, navigation and social relations:
> "This earthly part of the world is preserved by the knowledge
> and use of arts and disciplines, without which God would not
> have wished the world to be completed."[16]

Similarly in Bernard Sylvester, the disciplines of music and poetry are
invoked as crucial implements to aid the cause of nature against the
tumultuous war of seeds in Chaos, or Silva:

> Silva, intractable, a formless chaos, a hostile coalescence, the
> motley appearance of being, a mass discordant with itself,
> longs in her turbulence for a tempering power; in her crudity
> for form; in her rankness for cultivation. Yearning to emerge
> from her ancient confusion, she demands the shaping influ-
> ence of number and the bonds of harmony. (*Cosmographia* I.i)

13. Bernard Sylvester, *The Cosmographia* I.ii, trans. Winthrop Wetherbee (New
York: Columbia Univ. Press, 1973), 71.
14. Brian Stock, *Myth and Science in the Twelfth Century* (Princeton, N.J.:
Princeton Univ. Press, 1972), 201.
15. Robert M. Durling, "'Io son venuto': Seneca, Plato and the Microcosm,"
Dante Studies 93 (1975): 95–129.
16. Stock, 211.

Dante's readiness to exploit such analogies as an ethically minded poet led to a conceptual opposition in his mind between the urban and rustic as applied to the past history of his own city, which he saw as a tragic admixture of the two. This historical vision was not original to Dante but reflects an ancient classical theory that had found its fullest and most tragic expression in the epic poem of Dante's own guide, Virgil.[17] This is implied in the complex political message of Caccia-guida's chronicle of Florence's origins and decline in *Paradiso* XVI. There is a close doctrinal affinity, in any case, between Bernard's concept of Silva and Dante's notion that there is a class of words called the *sylvestria* because of their roughness of sound: it is the duty of the poet to banish the *sylvestria* from the lyric art of the *canzone*, whose proper discourse is *urbana* (*De vulgari eloquentia* II.viii). Nor is it difficult to see an affinity between Bernard's Silva and Dante's *selva oscura* as a locus of disruptive passion whose proper remedy is a return to the *dritta via*, the "straight path," by means of a straight moral epic. *Grammatica*, as the *ars de recte scribendi*, was an art of the "line" (*gramma*) or, rather, of *rectilinearity*; and rectilinearity, or uprightness (as opposed to what is bent or "*curva*"), was an important metaphor for describing man's spiritual state.[18] In the context of Canto XV, which is merely one of three cantos (XIV–XVI) dealing with violence in its different forms, one will remember that the suicidals have not been allowed the annihilation of their being that they sought by their deeds but have been punished by being transformed into the timeless trees of an infernal Silva; only God prevails over the principle of Being.

Against such a philosophical and ideological backdrop, we may readily understand how the order of the *polis* could be seen in the later Middle Ages and by Dante as a natural manifestation, within the sphere of *homo microcosmus*, of generative forces operative in the macrocosm of God's creation. And it will follow, I hope, that we may also see how Dante, in juxtaposing Brunetto with the sodomists, chose to deal with the problem of sodomy in its most extended sense: that is, as

17. Eugene Vance, "Sylvia's Pet Stag: Wildness and Domesticity in Virgil's *Aeneid*," *Arethusa* 14 (1981): 127–38.

18. John of Salisbury says that *grammatica* is the "scientia recti loquendi scribendique et orise omnium liberalium disciplinarum." Grammar is therefore a "linear" art: "*Grama* enim littera vel linea est, et inde litteralis, eo quod litteras doceat; quo nomine tam simplicium uocum figure quam elementa, id est voces figurarum, intelligentur; aut etiam linearis est": *Metalogicon* I.13, ed. C. J. Webb (Oxford: Clarendon Press, 1929), 37–38. On the theme of rectilinearity, see St. Bernard's *Sermons on the Song of Songs*, no. 24.

a problem involving not just an individual's *natural* physical relationship to his species but his natural relationship to the body politic and, by extension, to letters. Sodom, after all, was a city before it became the name of a vice; in this case, however, the relationship is embodied above all in the order and the process of discourse.

That the order of language, understood as a system of conventional signs, might be conceived as the living expression of the social order was an idea central to the Ciceronian tradition that Brunetto himself espoused in his *Trésor* and in his *Rettorica*, the latter being a liberal translation of Cicero's *De inventione*; moreover, Dante had explored many of these same assumptions with great originality in his *De vulgari eloquentia* and the *Convivio*. Though I shall not attempt to summarize here his abundant thoughts about the equation between the orders of discourse and of culture, let us recall for our immediate purposes that Dante considered verbal signs to be the "seeds of actions" (*seme d'operazione*), seeds that must be discretely sustained and dispensed (*lasciare*) by individuals in the social order if they are to be properly received (*ricevute*) and come to fruition (*fruttifere vegnano*); otherwise, the "seeds" of words will be undone in sterility (*difetto di sterilitade; Convivio* IV.xx.8). The word as seed can also be sown in malice, as the case of Ugolino (*Inf.* XXXIII.8–9), who speaks out his horrible sins of the past solely in the hope that his words will become "seeds" (*seme*), the fruit of which will be infamy for Archbishop Riggieri, whose corpse he still devours.

Dante is exploiting a long exegetical tradition centered upon the powerful parable in Matthew 13 where Christ compares the revelation of the Word of God to the sowing of seeds, a parable that gave rise in the Middle Ages to daring analogies between speaking and the ejaculation of semen.[19] (Such ideas will perhaps seem less extravagant if we recall that it was thought during the Middle Ages that semen flows from the brain through the spinal column into the loins during copulation; what is not used up goes back to the brain.)[20] Among Dante's more recent predecessors, Alain de Lille had gone especially far in underscoring the analogy between laws of copulation that must govern the proper regeneration of natural species and laws of grammar, dialectics, and rhetoric as those disciplines of language (*artes sermocinales*) by

19. Pezard, 303ff.
20. Stock, 218. Alain de Lille compares the flow of semen to the flow of thought in the mind: verboseness is the seed (*semen*) that does not fructify but leaves its audience sterile: see Pezard, 303, n. 5.

which we combine verbal signs to engender true and proper intellections. In his *De planctu naturae*, Alain elaborates upon the equivalence of errors in speech with the vice of sodomy. In the following passage, where Nature bewails the generalized prevalence of sexual perversion among men, Alain conflates sexual with grammatical perversion:

> Man alone turns with scorn from the modulated strains of my cithern and runs deranged to the notes of Orpheus's lyre. For the human race, fallen from its high estate, adopts a highly irregular [grammatical] change when it inverts the rules of Venus by introducing barbarisms in its arrangement of genders. Thus man, his sex changed by a rueless Venus, in defiance of due order, by his arrangement changes what is a straightforward attribute of his. Abandoning in his deviation the true script of Venus, he is proved to be a sophistic pseudographer. . . . Of those men who subscribe to Venus's procedures in grammar, some closely embrace those of masculine gender only, others those of feminine gender, others those of common, or epicene gender. Some, indeed, as though belonging to the heteroclitic class, show variations in deviation by reclining with those of female gender in Winter and those of masculine gender in Summer.[21]

Alain extends his analogy to cover all three branches of the *trivium*. He is no less forceful in depicting the relationship between the misdirected seminal flows of phallus and pen, an analogy that would later be made more famous by Jean de Meung.

Not only the misuse of language could be imagined in Dante's time as a kind of spiritual sodomy; so too could the misuse of money. In his recent book, R. A. Shoaf has made a penetrating study of subversion in language and money as sign systems in the writings of Dante and Chaucer.[22] Thinkers were agile in their applications of sodomy as a metaphor. Simony, or the selling of spiritual favors, could be seen as a form of sodomy; such was the claim of William Peraldus, Bishop of Lyons and a contemporary of Dante, who wrote a work on the virtues

21. Alain de Lille, *De planctu naturae* prosa IV, ed. N. M. Haring, *Studia Medievalia*, terza serie, 19 (1978), trans. James J. Sheridan (Toronto: Pontifical Institute of Mediaeval Studies, 1980).

22. R. A. Shoaf, *Dante, Chaucer, and the Currency of the Word* (Norman, Okla.: Pilgrim Books, 1983).

and vices, *Summa virtutem et vitiorum*. Here is how John Wyclif exploits Peraldus:

> For just as in carnal sodomy contrary to nature the seed is lost by which an individual human being would be formed, so in this sodomy the seed of God's word is cast aside with which a spiritual generation in Christ Jesus would be created. And as sodomy in the time of the law of nature was one of the most serious sins against nature, so simony in the time of the law of grace is one of the most serious sins against grace.[23]

It is not difficult to understand why Dante considered Brunetto Latini perverted because he turned against his "natural" language and against all *carità del natio loco*, to use Dante's expression from another context, for Brunetto himself declares his preference for French, in which his major work was written, over all other languages:

> And if anyone asked why this book is written in French [*roumanc*], according to the custom of the French, since we are Italian, I would say that it is for two reasons: one, that we are in France, the other, because that language [*parleure*] is the most delectable and the most common of all languages [*langages*]. (*Trésor* I.7)

Just as the sodomist turns carnal love away from its proper end, so too those who renounce their language turn from its proper end the first gift that God gave to man by his love—a gift made for the purpose of love, since the community of language is the primary spiritual bond of the family and of the nation. Thus, Brunetto Latini, a writer and a deserter, by refusing to give life to his language, denies its purpose and takes away its means of giving life to new beings: literary works as daughters of the intellect which must grow on the soil of one's native land. At the very least, he deprives his language of the hope to make viable, through the intellect, the sons of Italy, both born and unborn, since he refuses to communicate his knowledge to all of the "famished poor" who do not know French. He has frustrated his idiom with regard to its natural end, which is to disseminate and multiply the spirit.[24]

23. John Wyclif, *On Simony*, trans. Terrence A. McVeigh (forthcoming). I am grateful to Professor McVeigh for allowing me to read his translation.
24. Pezard, 302 (translation mine).

If such notions are indeed Dante's, inversely—and on a more cheery note—just as Aristotle saw the state as prior to the family (*Politics* I.2), so Dante saw language, which is the living expression of the social order, as the mediator of his own very existence. It was thanks to the Italian language, he tells us, that his mother and father first knew each other, were united in marriage, and subsequently begot him: While it is true that in his *De vulgari eloquentia* (I.x) Dante recognizes the established claims for each of the languages of *oc, oïl,* and *si,* based on the different uses to which these languages had best been put (French was reputedly the most suitable for translations and compositions in prose), I would suggest that in the present context languages are taken by Dante above all as emblems of political groups: hence, he sees Brunetto's choice of French as a political choice that is also gravely immoral.

In other words, though Brunetto was accidentally exiled in France by political circumstances, he *voluntarily* exiled himself from his culture through language. Similarly, if sodomists were punished by spiritual exile, it was because their lust was, in itself, already seen as a manifestation of exile. Alain de Lille says (*prosa* III of *De planctu naturae*) that reason "enables man to hold converse [*disputare*] with angels, the other [lust] drives him to wanton with brute beasts; one shows the man in exile how to get back to his fatherland, the other forces the one in his fatherland to go into exile." André Pezard summarizes the equation between sexual and discursive perversion in the Middle Ages thus:

> Now this my vernacular it was that brought together them
> who begat me, for by it they spoke; even as fire disposes the
> iron for the smith who is making the knife; wherefore it is
> manifest that it took part in my begetting and so was a certain
> cause of my being. (*Convivio* I.xiii)

Though Pezard has distilled from the historical and intellectual background what I believe to be the proper intellectual matrix for an understanding of the Brunetto Latini episode of the *Inferno*, much remains to be said about Dante's strategies in the dramatization of his inherited models. That he chose to emphasize the political backdrop against which we are to witness Brunetto's life as an example of violence against social order is already strongly indicated by the sequence of metaphors at the beginning of Canto XV. There Dante compares the firm dikes of the divine but not-yet-namable "masterbuilder" ("Whoever he is," as Dante says of God), which hold back the river of blood from the burning sand, with the constructive efforts of organized social groups to preserve, through their common labor, the physical existence of their cities from the chaos of the unbridled natural elements. Dante mentions, in particular, the Flemish of Bruges and of Wissant who must erect dikes against the sea, and the Padovans who must build fortifications *per difender lor ville e lor castelle* against the Brenta River and against the meltoff of the snows from the mountains in the spring, the season of Aphrodite, goddess of moisture and of love.

The opposition between the constructive labors (or what were called the "mechanical arts") and the subversive forces of unbridled desire had already been strikingly celebrated by Virgil in the example of Dido, Queen of Carthage, who gave up her city-building to fornicate with Aeneas in the forest (*silva*). But in a more specifically medieval context, if we may properly assume that Dante was conscious (as was Chaucer) of those astrological myths that allegorize the lifegiving period of spring as the result of the cosmic union between Venus and Mars, then we may see the floods of spring as a kind of cosmic orgasm that must take place, yet whose excess must be controlled, as must all passion, in order to be properly lifegiving. As Nature says in Alain de Lille's *De planctu naturae* (*prosa* IV):

> For I am the one who formed the nature of man according to
> the exemplar and likeness of the structure of the universe so
> that in him, as in a mirror of the universe itself, Nature's linea-
> ments might be there to see. For just as concord in discord,
> unity in plurality, harmony in disharmony, agreement in dis-
> agreement of the four elements unite the parts of the structure
> of the royal palace of the universe, so too, similarity in dis-
> similarity, equality in inequality, like in unlike, identity of
> four combinations bind together the house of the human body.
> Moreover, the same qualities that come between the elements
> as intermediaries establish a lasting peace between the four
> humours.

That Dante posits elsewhere the analogy of the flood with orgasm seems clear. Robert M. Durling shows in great detail how in the first of his *rime petrose* Dante draws on the same mythical tradition as Bernard Sylvester, who calls the flow of semen during intercourse a flooding, a "little death," during which nature "survives the world" as she "flows into herself and yet remains unchanged: to that extent she is nourished by her own flux."[25] The same process of regeneration occurs in the macrocosm, though without the need for those genital members that are necessary to humans as animals. I am suggesting, in other words, that there is a latent analogy between the "heat" (*caldo*) that gives rise to floods in the spring and the human erotic passion—the fire of Mars in man—that excites man's animal being to overflow its bodily limits in the act of procreation. Each flood of passion must occur but must be contained, just as the *duri margini* of the "master-builder" contain the river of passionate blood that flows through Hell. Dante's metaphors are involved in a triple process of analogy (a process called *proportionalitas* by medieval philosophers), and he is telling us that *reason* is to *passion*, as *construction* is to *flooding*, as *God's creative power* is to the warring elements of *Chaos*. Analogy, one will recall, is a comparison not of things to each other but of relationships.

If the metaphors at the outset of Canto XV stress the fragility of man's social order before the physical violence unleased upon it by the natural elements from without, Dante also shows us that man's culture is no less fragile with regard to the forces of alienation and subversion that may overwhelm it from within. His conception of the inner life of the city reflects, moreover, a distinction between two opposed yet necessary tendencies: first, that of the centrifugal division of labor into specialized groups, each of which provides some necessary service to the whole; second, that of the centripetal integration of separate groups of language and by law, put to the service of authority and justice. Indeed, Dante's interpretation of the Babel episode in Genesis proposes, basically, that the linguistic confusion affected first and foremost the integrity of the body politic, whose division into different labor groups became an obstacle to understanding between those groups (*De vulgari eloquentia* I.viii). The division of labor became, in other words, a division of speech against itself. Political science has as its object not the material or technological aspects of the body politic but rather those relationships that must prevail between individuals and groups, relationships that depend above all upon language. Thomas Aquinas (*Commentam*, lectio 1) distinguishes political art from the mechanical arts:

> Furthermore, reason can operate about things either as making something [*per modum factionis*], in which case its action passes on to some external material, as we see in the mechan-

25. Durling, 108–10; see also Stock, 216–19.

ical arts of the smith and the shipwright; or by doing something [per modum actionis], in which case the action remains intrinsic to the agent, as we see in deliberation, making choice, willing, and all that pertains to moral science. It is clear that political science, which is concerned with the ordered relationship between men, belongs, not to the realm of making or factitive science or mechanical art, but rather to the realm of doing or the moral sciences.

In this politically oriented canto of the *Comedy*, Dante's own poetic discourse is clearly no neutral agent, and we should be aware that in those same metaphorical gestures, those *signa translata*, in which Dante posits the fragility of organized culture before the tumult of the elements, he is enlisting his own poetic discourse as a potentially regenerative force in the contest for the survival of the body politic. A metaphor (*translatio*) is a "trope," that is, a "turning" of verbal signs from their proper to an improper signification. Technically speaking, the later scholastics saw metaphor (whether the motives behind it were good or evil) as an act of "improper supposition."[26] Good metaphors (for instance, the *signa translata* of Scripture or of theological discourse) have a potential to edify us and to make us fecund with the truth; bad metaphors, on the other hand, are tropes that subvert truth by turning the polysemous word from its appropriate end in such a way that it leaves us barren of the truth. This is a moment in Dante's text where the crucial question arises: what are the political consequences of Dante's own poetics of desire? The theologians' prejudice against poets in the Middle Ages is well known, and because we are dealing with a region in Hell populated by *litterati grandi e di granda fama*, Dante was no doubt unusually sensitive to the possibility that his own poetic metaphors, if not his whole fiction of human love, might themselves somehow be considered subversive. Joseph Mazzeo describes the problematical status of the poetic sign:

> Poetry is merely the lowest of the kinds of knowledge (*est in-fima inter omnes doctrinas*). Its function is to make pleasing pictures of representation, since man, by nature, is pleased by such pictures. St. Thomas thus maintains that the use of meta-

26. Claude Panaccio, "Guillaume d'Occam: Signification et supposition," in *Archéologie du signe*, ed. Lucie Brind'Amour and Eugene Vance (Toronto: Pontifical Institute of Mediaeval Studies, 1983), 264–86.

phor is common to both poetry and theology, but in the former
it obscures a lower truth, whereas in the latter it discloses a
truth which would not otherwise be known.[27]

Though Dante both questions and vindicates in many ways the
methods of the poets in the *Comedy* and in his other treatises, in this
instance I would suggest that he has already begun to dramatize the
problem in a deliberate and interesting way in the *Inferno*, Canto XIV,
of which XV is—narratively speaking—a prolongation. One will recall
that the *vendetta di Dio* reserved for the sodomists, as well as for their
contiguous co-sinners of the seventh circle (the blasphemers and the
usurers, each of whom in his distinct way violates some intellectual
faculty bestowed by God upon man), is a rain of fire that falls down
upon the sterile sand and burns the naked sinners. To postulate the
oxymoron of *rain* that is also *fire*—of heat that is moisture—is to postulate, of course, a supremely "unnatural" and even chaotic occurrence, all the more so since it is a property of fire not to fall but rather
to rise to its "natural place," as both neoplatonic and Aristotelian
teachings agreed. So long as transgressions of natural law could be
understood as supernatural events produced by God, they were not especially problematical to the medieval mind. In the case of rain-that-is-
fire, we are dealing with a "literal" event actually recorded in Scripture: hence the legitimacy of this example of God's *orribil arte di
giustizia*, as Dante calls it, in Canto XIV. However, we may suspect
that Dante's motives for punishing the sodomists with a rain of fire
included more than an appeal to scriptural authority. As Mazzeo
writes about the later medieval tradition:

> The notion of natural place was extended to the spiritual
> realm so that appetition or love became simply the desire of all
> things, corporeal and spiritual, to attain the "place" in the uni-
> verse, material or immaterial, that was proper or "natural" to
> them. Thus as air and fire go up and earth and water naturally
> go down, so all things seek their place and man seeks his "true
> place" in heaven. It is in this form, not in the more properly
> Aristotelian form that St. Thomas expounds, that we find the
> doctrine of love as a cosmic principle in Dante; his "spiritual

27. Joseph Anthony Mazzeo, *Medieval Cultural Tradition in Dante's "Comedy"*
(Ithaca, N.Y.: Cornell Univ. Press, 1960), 67–69. See also the chapter "Dante's Con-
ception of Expression" in Mazzeo's *Structure and Thought in the "Paradiso"* (Ithaca,
N.Y.: Cornell Univ. Press, 1958), 49.

gravity" is the correspondence between states of soul and their proper or natural place in the universe.[28]

What could be more supernaturally "natural" than to punish with fire that falls on those who turn love from its proper end?

Such conjectures about Dante's intentions cannot be proved. However, what follows his scripturally motivated example of God's justice (however "poetic" such justice may *also* be) allows us to grasp the complexities of his rhetorical strategies with somewhat greater certainty. Dante deigns to supplement an Old Testament God's "horrible art" specifically with the art of the poets when he compares the falling fire to "snow falling in the Alps without wind," now an oxymoron of fire and ice that is both stunning and—seemingly, at least—gratuitous, all the more because the "snow" in the comparison harks not to Scripture but rather to an erotic *canzone* in the illustrious vernacular by Guido Cavalcanti.[29] In this poem (a remarkable piece in itself) Cavalcanti generates a whole sequence of images of worldly beauty surpassed, he declares, by the beauty of his lady. If one is willing to assume that Dante's use of sources is always deliberate and strategically motivated, his conversion of Cavalcanti's line about falling snow into a metaphor for falling fire is a perfectly "unnatural" erotic oxymoron that functions as an icon, so to speak, of a new poetic discourse based upon the principle of poetic metaphor that is at once impassioned, rational, and spiritual. Quite clearly, a poetic discourse in the *dolce stil nuovo* expressing a movement of charitable love that is both human and divine is being brought by Dante into a spiritual counterposition with the vindictive and unredeemed letter of the Old Testament, and specifically with the text dealing with the perversion of Sodom.

If there is any warrant for my claim that Dante's performance here is one that both asserts and vindicates the fiction-making capacity of poets—the faculty of inventing what Augustine, as we saw in chapter 2, calls "reasonable lies—by contrast, Dante continues by demonstrating, in the encounter with Brunetto Latini, how easily *litterati* may stray in their writings (*in scriptis errare*, as Alain de Lille put it) or deviate from the straight path, *la dritta via*. Though there is a strong tendency for critics of Dante to be moved by the terribly "human" sentiments exchanged between Dante and Brunetto, it seems to me that

28. Mazzeo, *Structure and Thought*, 51.
29. Guido Cavalcanti, "Biltà di donna e di saccente core," in *Poeti del duecento*, ed. Gianfranco Contini (Milan: Ricciardi, 1960), 2:494.

these exchanges are mined with traps intended to snare us, too (as men and women of letters), in affections that we are subsequently led to repudiate in ourselves as we progress through the canto. Dante frequently demands that we read backwards.

One will recall that Brunetto's band of *litterati grandi et di granda fama* (Brunetto's insistence on *their* grandeur betrays his ambition for *his* grandeur) wander eternally and without direction (like seeds of Chaos) about the desert of burning sand, dramatically in contrast with Dante and Virgil, who must walk prudently along the narrow dike separating the river of blood (in which the violent are being boiled) from the burning desert where the sodomists wander. Brunetto turns back (*ritorno in dietro*) in order to converse with Dante. This is but one of several motifs of turning, wandering, delaying, and dispersion in this canto that may possibly be linked with tropes as a dangerous art of "turning" (*tropare*) and not inconceivably even with the figure *tourn* mentioned by Brunetto himself in the *Livres dou trésor* (XXX.xiii.2–3) as a strategy of rhetorical amplification achieved through substitution: "*Tu changeras les propres mos e remueras les nons des choses et des persones en plusors paroles tot belement environ le fait.*"[30] The potential for perversion in such "turns" of the tongue is high, and Alain de Lille had already compared this "turning" with the act of turning one's desires toward members of the same sex. One may perhaps see Brunetto's own ingenious *tourn*, in which he calls the death of the sodomist Franceso D'Accorso a "quitting of his sinfully distended muscles" (*lascio di mal protesi nervi; Inferno* XV.114), as a speech act dangerously close in its rhetorical effects to the perversion that it both names and conceals. In the case of the sodomist, Alain says, "Grammar does not find favour with him, but rather a trope [*tropus*]. This transposition [*translatio*], however, cannot be called a trope. The figure here more correctly falls into the category of defects (*De planctu naturae*, metrum 1).

The horribly sooty appearance of Brunetto contrasts violently with Dante's memory of the man in real life, but aside from its stunning dramatic effect, this scene no doubt harbors deeper allusions. To St. Augustine, for example, Sodom was a real city, one that subsisted even

---

30. If rhetoricians and sodomists are driven by compulsions to "turn," Dante tells us that Paradise is a place where man's appetitive self is *not* twisted or turned, *là dove appetito no si torce* (*Paradiso* XVI.5).

after its punishment by divine fire and, even though infertile, continued to produce apples that were deceptive because they were filled not with fruit but with ashes:

> The land of Sodom was not always as it now is; but once it had the appearance of other lands, and enjoyed equal if not richer fertility; for, in the divine narrative, it was compared to the Paradise of God. But after it was touched by fire from heaven, as even pagan history testifies, and as it is now witnessed by those who visit the spot, it became unnaturally and horribly sooty in appearance; and its apples, under a deceitful appearance of ripeness, contain ashes within.[31]

Sodomists, then, are people whose perversion extends even to agriculture as a mechanical art, but Dante is less concerned with the false fruit of the bad farmers of Sodom than with the false spiritual fruit of the sodomist as rhetorician.

Dante's reply to Brunetto's greeting reveals, to be sure, a high degree of reverence for his achievement, a reverence that the reader can at first scarcely refrain from sharing. However, at the very same time that Dante acknowledges Brunetto as a *buona inagine paterna*, a father-figure to whom he was once, therefore, a spiritual *figluol*, Dante also reveals that for selfish reasons he too has been vulnerable to passions that would turn him away from his culture, passions therefore improper to the *grammaticus* as a man of letters. Brunetto not only blasphemes the people of his native Florence, calling them beasts that devour each other, but opposes the crudeness of their rustic origins to the "holy seed" (*sementa santa*) of classical Roman culture, a culture that Brunetto no doubt understood as consisting primarily in the literary achievements of rhetoric—therefore, a culture that he now yearns to endow with his own fame. The model of the poetic word as a sowing and fructification is invoked a second time by Brunetto (again, perversely) when he bids Dante believe that the sweet "fig-tree" of his poetic talent is incompatible with the bitter fruits of the "sorb–apple tree" that is the culture of Florence. Ambition, then, has caused Brunetto to *flatter* Dante by slandering the society that begot them both. I believe that there is a political lesson embedded in this exchange

---

31. St. Augustine, *The City of God*, XX.18, trans. Marcus Dods (New York: Random House, 1950).

that may be clarified by St. Thomas, who says in his *De regimine principium*:

> The desire of human glory [*cupido gloriae*] destroys magnanimity of soul. For whoever seeks favour of men must consider their desires in all that he says and does; thus, because of his desire to please men he becomes the servant of individuals. For this reason the same Cicero in his *De officiis*, warns us to beware the desire of glory. It is this in fact which destroys liberty of spirit [*animi libertatem*] which should be the greatest aspiration of the magnanimous man.[32]

Dante does not openly reprove either Brunetto for uttering such thoughts about Rome and Florence (we must remember that Virgil is beside him) or himself for hearing them. However, we know that his real attitudes toward his culture are quite the opposite: though Dante himself will later excoriate the vainglory of certain Florentines, especially those who take pride in the ancestry of their families (Paradiso XVI), and though he too has been a political exile from Florence, he obviously continues to see the bond between individuals and their native society as a sacred one. Implicit in the contrasting cultural attitudes of Brunetto and Dante is also a contrast of doctrines of history: as had Horace and Ovid, Brunetto subscribes to an ideal of the permanent cultural supremacy of the Romans, and he ignores the contrary possibility, that the temporal succession of cultures is also the unfolding, in time, of a revelation that could not be known until the vehicle of human language had matured to a point where such a truth could be accommodated and expressed. Dante, however, saw in the reality of historical change the ontological necessity for the individual to acknowledge and respect the primacy of his native language in the acquisition of all other languages, including Latin. Dante was also aware of the potential of a new language (especially the language of *si*) both to rival the old and, what is more, to express certain moral values (for instance, the virtue of humility, the worthiness of passion, and the value of erotic love based on charity) whose expression had remained yet unfulfilled in the languages of the ancients (*De vulgari eloquentia* II.ii–iii). Even Cicero himself, as Dante reminds us (*Convivio* I.i.) had

---

32. Thomas Aquinas, *De regimine principium* I.vii, trans. J. G. Dawson, in *Aquinas: Selected Political Writings* (see n. 10), 37.

once remonstrated with those who "found fault with the Latin of the Romans and commended the Grammar of the Greeks, for the like reasons for which these others now make the Italian speech cheap and that of Provence precious."

In this encounter, Dante reveals that he has at least momentarily put aside Brunetto's incurable pride in worldly fame—*come l'uom s'eterna*—a pride compulsively reiterated in Brunetto's plea at the end of Canto XV that Dante remember him on earth for his *Trésor*. Brunetto is still laying up treasures for himself on earth, and not beyond. Dante considers the achievement of earthly fame to be false creativity, a vain fiction. *Fama* is a rumor that flourishes, he tells us in *Convivio* I.iii, because it is "dilated" by men's minds as it passes from mouth to mouth, just as Brunetto himself dilates the *vecchia fama* of Florence's avarice and pride as he speaks to Dante and Virgil (XV.68). Opposed to this false goal of earthly fame is Dante's more humble desire to invent a text worthy of being glossed (*chiosar*) by a higher intelligence moved by charitable and transcendent love—that is, by Beatrice, *la donna che sapra*, whose intellect already dwells among the saved. As Dante uses it here, the model of text and gloss now implicates the word as "seed" in a more theological sense, although with this interesting variant: normally the hermeneutical gesture is undertaken by someone living in time who must discover the hidden truth of the word that has been obscured by vice and by time; but in this instance, a being in time is planting the seed of his individual historicity in a text whose beloved hermeneutician is in heaven, and whose charitable *operazione* will redeem this seed so that it may fructify, not in this world but beyond.

The encounter between Dante and Brunetto now situates the problem of improper love in a context of hermeneutical action. A hermeneutics motivated by charity induces us to read beyond the carnal letter, and beyond the individual consciousness that produced the letter: hence Augustine's insistence (*Conf.* X.iii.3) that we read his *Confessions* exactly as we read the Scripture, with charity. To believe in Augustine is to believe in God. A concupiscent hermeneutics leads us to a carnal knowledge of both the letter and its maker. It causes us to hope, in vain, that a text can be the vehicle of a human consciousness that will truly survive in the mind of another. As we shall see shortly, Brunetto's love for Dante and for his companions in Hell is uncharitable in the extreme (again, in Augustine's sense of the word) in that he loves people or things (words too are things) for their own sakes or for his own sake, but never for God's sake. Indeed, it is with this point in mind that I shall venture some concluding remarks about the notion of *litteratus* that Brunetto evokes with regard to the company of sinners in which he appears, and I shall also comment upon the presence of the grammarian Priscian in that group.

The term *litteratura* was the Latin equivalent of the Greek *grammatica*, as Augustine had said of the art of *grammatica*, "By its very name it proclaims that it knows letters—indeed, on this account it is called *litteratura* in Latin" (*De ordine* II.xii.37). As a vehicle of culture, then, *litteratura* is not first and foremost a corpus of texts or a norm of correct writing but rather a signifying operation that begins with the special type of sign that is called the *littera*, or letter. The letter is nothing but a line, a *gramma*, which signifies merely because of an arbitrary association with a spoken word (*vox*) whose sounds are no less arbitrarily related to their significations than a sound is to a letter. Written signs never signify necessarily, as do natural signs (e.g., smoke that signifies fire) but only where there is a shared will to signify (*voluntas significandi*) and to understand on the part of those who exchange them. Moreover, understanding is an experience that occurs strictly within our minds, not corporeally.

Obviously, the written, corporeal letter is only the most extrinsic dimension of meaning: it is meaning in exile. Although such problems had been articulated primarily with regard to the search for a true understanding of the Scripture, already St. Augustine, as I have indicated, had begun to deal with them as problems of communication involving mortal readers and writers of other texts, including what we now call autobiography. Hence, we may safely imagine that no writer could have been more aware than Dante that, as love's vernacular scribe, he too was begetting dangerous hermeneutical problems by seeming to invest the previously empty zero-sign "I" of the medieval lyric tradition with the plenitude of his own singular, historical intelligence. A similar problem was obviously apparent to Chaucer, who created a fictive "I" who understands far less than his readers do, and whose "presence" only makes Chaucer "himself" all the more inscrutable. Although Dante's strategies in dealing with the alluring but dangerous fiction of the "I" in the body of his text are not always easily grasped, the example of Brunetto does illustrate pragmatically some of Dante's ambivalence about *litteratura* in its relationship to the individual writing self. Indeed, we may suggest that Brunetto goes quite far, however unwittingly, to make himself a focal point for such a problem: though he can speak of his *magnum opus* as a "treasure" that serves princes like *deniers contans por despendre tousjours es coses besoignables*, and can further compare the parts of his book devoted to rhetoric to "fine gold," now Brunetto wants to keep this treasure for himself. Dante understood very well that inordinate love for such verbal gold was no better than that for a golden calf.

The moral consequences of such idolatry of himself and his writing are displayed in Brunetto's own conduct at the end of the canto, where he vaingloriously pleads not only that Dante intercede for him in Heaven but that he recall to those on earth his *Book of the Treasure*. Suddenly, Brunetto wheels compulsively (*si revolse*) away from Dante to greet some unknown new arrival in Hell—as if, Dante says, he were a footracer competing for a prize. As the willing emblem of the classical rhetorician, Brunetto is enacting all the vices for which rhetoricians since Plato had been censured—love of appearances, love of money, opportunism, and so on—vices that persist in Brunetto even though he is now suffering for them in Hell. Brunetto's self-adulation and ambition lead us retrospectively to suspect his motives for praising Dante so warmly when they first met in Hell. Was it flattery whose purpose was to evince reciprocal praise from the younger poet? Was it a desire to corrupt yet another Italian writer with a perverted love of letters?

With hindsight, the very moving meeting of Dante and Brunetto becomes disturbingly ambiguous, all the more so because it invites us, as readers, to reevaluate the motives behind our *own* responses to the event in Dante's text.

The presence of the grammarian Priscian among the *litterati grandi* of the *Inferno* has puzzled generations of Dante scholars, with good reason: not only was Priscian, with Donatus (who is in Paradise), one of the most important pillars of the medieval *trivium*, but strictly nothing seems to have been known about the person of Priscian during the Middle Ages—much less about what may have been his sexual proclivities. However, there was a legend that circulated about him—an apocryphal one, yet one that explains his presence in the *Inferno*. Priscian had dedicated his *Institutiones grammaticae* to a certain "Julius, Consul and Patricus," and this Julian later came to be confused with the Emperor Julian the Apostate, who decreed that Christians did not have the right to sign their names to any published text. On this basis it was surmised during the Middle Ages that Priscian had renounced his religion in order to sign his grammar. In his *Anticlaudianus*, Alain de Lille berates the memory of Priscian in the following terms:

> Our Apostate strings out tracts on grammar, and, somewhat tiresome in style, is the victim of sluggish dreams. As he strays [*errans*] far and wide in his writings, he is thought to be drunk or insane or to be drowsy. He falters in his faith to prevent the reputation [*fama*] of his book from faltering and he sells his faith not to lose the sales from his book; his faith goes astray to prevent popular fame from straying away from him.[33]

Alain goes on to say that Priscian is one of those "base grammarians who rejoice in mere husks, whom the richness of the marrow within does not set apart: if they seek chippings [*fragmenta*] from the outside [*foris*], content with mere shells, they cannot taste the flavour of the nut [*nuclei*]." Though Pezard is aware of this legend, he attributes the presence of Priscian in Hell to prejudice in certain medieval circles against those who considered *grammatica*, as a science, a precondition for all rational knowledge.[34] Such a prejudice is not prevalent in Alain, however, since he also bestows lavish praise on Donatus in the very same context; nor is such prejudice in any way proper to Dante, who not only situates *grammatica* in the first sphere of the "cosmos" of human understanding (in the *Convivio*) but puts Donatus in Paradise. Yet if we conceive of grammar as the law of the *gram(m)a*, of the letter as an external, corporeal object and as the exteriority of speech in its most extreme form, then we may understand that Dante is ascribing to Priscian an idolatry of the text that is fatal to meaning as the inner life of the soul. Such attitudes, if they may be said to exist in Dante, reflect, of course, the longstanding doctrinal fear of idolatry among Christians that I mentioned at the beginning of this chapter, a fear that St. Augustine amplified with great eloquence in his famous treatise *On the Spirit and the Letter* (xxiii–xxiv).

There is an interesting case of possible wordplay in the line in which Priscian is mentioned in this canto: "*Priscien sen va con la*

---

33. Alain de Lille, *Anticlaudianus: Texte critique avec une introduction et des tables*, ii,vv.500–513, ed. R. Bossuat (Paris, 1955); trans. J. J. Sheridan (Toronto: Pontifical Institute of Mediaeval Studies, 1973), 90.

34. Pezard, 160ff.

quella turba grama" (Priscian goes off with the miserable crowd). If we may presume, with Pezard,[35] that Dante was alert to the similarity of the adjective *grama* (a word of Germanic origin cognate with "grim") to the word *gramma*, which one might also spell (as did John of Salisbury) as *grama*,[36] then there is an interesting semantic contiguity here of the notion of the letter of the improper text with the notion of a dismal, milling crowd, a confused crowd of bad seeds in which one may become eternally lost. Whether or not this semantic trick is being played by Dante, the *figluol*, on an unsuspecting "father," Brunetto— that is, upon a *litteratus* who was patricidal with respect to his native culture, and who suddenly deserts his former spiritual son in order to greet some unknown newcomer to the crowd of wandering rhetoricians and sodomists from which he had earlier turned away—we are witnessing a vivid dramatization of the potential for rhetoric to become, finally, a self-defeating art and a process of deception whose first victim is none other than the deceiver himself.

35. Pezard, 162.
36. Cf. n. 18, above.

CHAPTER 9

Mervelous Signals: Sign Theory and the Politics of Metaphor in Chaucer's *Troilus and Criseyde*

Dante's stance as a poet was to mark his autonomy with respect to the theologians but to emulate their goal of transcending what is temporal and material in human understanding (as well as what is discursive) in order to prepare the loving soul for its reunion with God. Chaucer's instinct as a poet was, by contrast, always to explore the horizontal, ethical dimensions of language, understood as the living expression of the social order, without pretending to dramatize the inward processes of spiritual transcendence or to practice what Novalis called *Seelenconstructionslehre*. Unlike the theologians and mystics of his age, Chaucer did not try to apprehend the inner life of the soul separately from the medium of conventional language and from the multiple discourses that determine the social life of individual man.

In this chapter, I shall consider Chaucer's *Troilus and Criseyde* as a projection of his concern with the relationship between the order of discourse and the social order into a tragic historical vision that calls not for the perfection of human love (and of the language that mediates it) in a process of ascendance but rather for its rejection. In what follows, I shall first set forth some notions broadly held in the later Middle Ages about the relationship between discourse and the body politic, and I shall attempt to show how Chaucer directed the metalinguistic consciousness of his age into strategies of poetic composition.

SPEECH AND SOCIETY

The notion that the order of discourse is the living expression of the social order was already central to a tradition of classical oratory that any poet such as Dante, Petrarch, or Chaucer knew very well. Centered upon the explicitly discursive spaces of the *agora* and the *forum*, the classical city (like the Humanist city to follow) was thought to owe its very existence to the operations of speech. In the *De oratore*, for example, Cicero says it is speech that has the power to unite men in a single place, to extract them from their bestial and savage condition, to bring them to civility, and to sustain laws and justice (I.viii.53).

The Bible brought yet other dimensions to the classical understanding of the congruence of the orders of discourse and of culture. The story of Babel taught that the linguistic dispersion of humanity was a consequence of its pride; conversely, the story of Pentecost taught that the Holy Spirit, by its visitation upon all the tribes of Israel, allowed persons to transcend political divisions through direct, spiritual knowledge of the Word. The Bible is also laced with an ethics of speech lacking in classical oratory but essential to good poetry (e.g., "Through the blessing of the righteous the city is exalted, but through the mouth of the wicked it is overthrown"; Prov. 11:11). In St. John, where the whole of existence is equated with the Word, sign theory took on an ontological dimension whose consequence was that Christ as Son and perfect sign of the Father, as sign admitting no difference (*dissimilitudo*) between signifier and signified, became the negative reference point for all human discourse in its radical equivocity. But it was no doubt St. Paul, in whom neoplatonic and Stoic doctrines of signification received their most urgent scriptural articulation, who established the necessity for a specifically Christian semiological consciousness in the West.[1]

As doctrine, medieval theories of signification tended to revolve around certain enduring questions: If God is ineffable, how can we properly presume to name God? How, inversely, does God's grace act through the words and gestures of men when they perform the sacraments? Do vocal or written signs ("book," "man," "tree"), which are only conventional, stand for (*supponere*) things that truly exist as uni-

---

1. For a general study of medieval sign theory, see Marcia L. Colish, *The Mirror of Language: A Study in the Medieval Theory of Knowledge* (New Haven, Conn.: Yale Univ. Press, 1968; rev. ed., Lincoln: Univ. of Nebraska Press, 1983).

versals? or exist only as individuals? or as individuals and as abstractive concepts? Is there a correspondence between the parts of speech (*partes orationis*) and the structure of reality? By what rules do we judge whether an argument is true or false? Such questions gave rise to reflection about every aspect of man as a *relational* creature, particularly about the fragility of language as a mediator between man and God, between man and man, between man and things, and between individual man and his knowledge of himself.

A sign, according to Augustine's definition, is "a thing that causes us to think of something (*aliud aliquid*) beyond the impression that the thing itself makes upon the sense."[2] Natural signs—such as smoke that signifies fire, a blush that signifies shame—signify "naturally" or automatically, without there being any *will* or *intention* to signify. However, conventional signs (bird calls, speech) do involve a will to signify (*voluntas significandi*). Because people of the Middle Ages were basically anti-Cratylistic in their conception of verbal signs (which are the signs proper to the human species), holding that the bond between signifier and signified (*signans* and *signatum*) was merely conventional, medieval thinkers grasped not only the relationship between free will and signification but also the *contractual* basis of signification (*secundum id pactum et placitum, quo inter se homines ista signa firmarunt*)[3] and, by extension, the idea that the order of discourse could be considered as the living expression of social or political order.

The twelfth-century English schoolman and friend of Becket, John of Salisbury, conceived of the bond between the linguistic and social orders as follows: In the beginning, we are told (following Augustine), Hebrew was man's natural language which "mother nature gave to our first parents and preserved for mankind until human unity was rent by impiety, and the pride which presumed to mount to heaven by physical strength and the construction of a tower, rather than by virtue, was leveled in a babbling chaos of tongues."[4] In his *Policraticus* John of Salisbury embarks upon a careful classification of the different kinds of signs.[5] Though speaking man disposes only of shifting and conven-

2. St. Augustine, *De doctrina christiana* II.i.1, trans. D. W. Robertson, Jr., *On Christian Doctrine* (Indianapolis, New York: 1958), p. 34; cited hereafter as *DDC*.

3. St. Augustine, *Confessions* I.xiii,35.

4. John of Salisbury, *Metalogicon* I.8, trans. David McGarry (Berkeley: Univ. of California Press, 1955).

5. John of Salisbury, *Policraticus*, esp. Bk. II, ed. C. J. Webb (Oxford: Clarendon Press, 1929).

tional signs in his discourse, John nevertheless equates the operations of this discourse with the very existence of the body politic:

> Deprived of their gift of speech, men would degenerate to the condition of brute animals, and cities would seem like corrals for livestock rather than communities composed of human beings united by a common bond for the purpose of living in society, serving one another, and cooperating as friends. If verbal intercommunications were withdrawn, what contract could be duly concluded, and what instruction could be given - in faith and morals, and what agreement and mutual understanding could subsist among men? (*Metalogicon* I.1)

John says further that the union of reason and speech "has given birth to so many outstanding cities, has made friends and allies of so many kingdoms, and has unified and knit together in bonds of love so many peoples" (*Metalogicon* I.2). In a less positive vein, he speaks of the fall of Jerusalem as an example of the catastrophes that beset societies whose members abuse or ignore signs—in this case, supernatural, rather than natural or conventional, signs (*Policraticus* II.4). St. Bernard, John's contemporary, tended to base his understanding of the opposition between chaos and signification on his conception of women, and it all hangs on poor Eve: "She spoke but once and threw the world into disorder."[6] The thirteenth-century rhetorician John of Garland is more florid, but not less contemptuous, about female speech: "In death's eternal kingdom Woman is enthroned forever; from her mouth flows gall that is taken for nectar, and kills [*necat*] body and soul."[7]

Like Augustine and John of Salisbury, Thomas Aquinas also held that the orders of society and of speech are co-natural. Vocal sounds, according to Thomas (following Aristotle) are exterior signs of passions in our soul: that is, of effects that the experiences of things cause in our minds. Vocal sounds that are also *verbal* signs become so by human "institution," and the "institution" of signs is a sine qua non of social order.[8]

6. Attributed to St. Bernard by Humbert of Romans, *De eruditione predicatorum*, trans. Dominican students, Province of St. Joseph, *Treatise on Preaching*, ed. W. M. Conlon, O. P. (Westminster, Md.: Newman Press, 1951), 48.

7. John of Garland, *Poetria parisiana* VII.1909–10, ed. and trans. Traugott Lawler (New Haven, Conn.: Yale Univ. Press, 1974).

8. Aristotle, *On Interpretation: Commentary by St. Thomas and Cajetan*, Lesson II.2–5, trans. Jean T. Oesterle (Milwaukee: Marquette Univ. Press, 1962), 24–25.

St. Thomas elaborates further (II.5) upon the relationship between *written* language and social order. Since society, in its most extended sense, is constituted as an order existing not here and now but abstractly, it was necessary for man as a social creature to find a means of abstracting his speech in order to satisfy the needs of society as an abstraction of the here and now. Writing is precisely such an instrument, and it follows that social order in its most extended sense exists as an intertextuality.

In the Middle Ages, the imagined homology between the political and linguistic orders permeated even descriptive grammatical theory. Honorius of Autun (d. 1136) explored the allegorical possibilities of the "city" of grammar, a very feudal one in structure: those parts of speech that have the power to refer (the noun and verb) are masters; those that do not are slaves.[9] According to G. L. Bursill-Hall, the speculative grammarian Siger de Courtrai likened "government" among words in a sentence to the "state of affairs in natural things, i.e., in the natural kingdom we find one animal, e.g., man, who is fit (*dignissimus*) to govern all the other animals, and similarly in the human body, there is one member, i.e., the heart, which governs all other members. Therefore there will be among the partes orationis one pars which will properly govern the other partes but will not itself be governed, i.e., the verb."[10]

That the body politic may be characterized not only by a plurality of competing social and economic groups but also by a plurality of speech variants, or discourses (*sermones*), was a prominent notion in medieval theories of language, especially theories of style or *genera dicendi*. The most elaborate reflection upon such questions is to be found in preaching manuals emanating especially from the Franciscans and Dominicans, of which the treatise by Humbert of Romans, fifth master-general of the Dominican order, is a good example. "Without preaching, which scatters the word of God like seed," writes Humbert, "the world would be sterile and produce no fruit."[11] However, in order for the seed to be fecund, the discourse of the preacher must be accommo-

9. Honorius of Autun, *De animae exsilio et patria*, trans. Joseph M. Miller, *Readings in Medieval Rhetoric*, ed. Joseph M. Miller, Michael H. Prosser, and Thomas W. Benson (Bloomington: Indiana Univ. Press, 1973), 200.

10. G. L. Bursill-Hall, *Speculative Grammars of the Middle Ages* (The Hague: Mouton, 1971), 64.

11. Humbert of Romans, *Treatise on Preaching*, p. 5.

dated to the character of a specific audience; hence, to preach properly calls for an acute discursive awareness. Humbert sets himself the task of making a complete inventory of the different groups within society that the preacher might have to address, and the second part of his *De eruditione praedicatorum* undertakes as its task to describe the *sermones ad status* (or codes) that the preacher must master if he intends to preach to any given group. Humbert's classification of social groups by *status* provides no less than one hundred different categories of audience to be found among the species man.[12]

In less elaborated form, an analogous preoccupation with *genera dicendi* is to be found in late medieval rhetorical theory as well. As Douglas Kelly reminds us, we are not dealing here merely with superficial questions of style but with questions of content, too.[13] The decorum of each *genus dicendi* commands not only the style or level of our discourse but the choice of an appropriate subject matter. Moreover, a speaker's choice of audience and discourse is a moral choice. Thus, the fourteenth-century Dominican, Domenico Cavalca, declares that those who preach only to high or noble persons and to the well-educated (*litterate*) are "adulterers of the word of God" (*adulteri della parola di Dio*).[14] The pertinence of such questions to the homiletically oriented *Canterbury Tales* is obvious.

Although most of the ideas to which I have so far referred are elaborated within and about the sphere of Latinity, such ideas were not irrelevant to poets laboring in the vernacular, especially since later medieval theoreticians insisted that the concepts they were elaborating in Latin were universals belonging to a *general* grammar of human speech and not to any specific language. As Roger Bacon put it, "Grammar is

12. For a penetrating semiological study of Humbert, see Maria Corti, "Structures idéologiques et structures sémiologiques dans les *Sermones ad status* du XIIIe siècle," *Archéologie du signe*, ed. Lucie Brind'Amour and Eugene Vance (Toronto: Pontifical Institute for Medieval Studies, 1983), 145–64.

13. Douglas Kelly, "*Matière* and *genera dicendi* in Medieval Romance," in *Approaches to Medieval Literature*, Yale French Studies 51, ed. Peter Haidu (New Haven, Conn.: Yale Univ. Press, 1974), 150ff; see also Kelly's "La spécialité dans l'invention des topiques," in Archéologie du signe (n. 12, above), 101–26.

14. Domenico Cavalca, *Frutti della lingua da fra Domenico Cavalca, ridotti alla sua vera lezione* (Rome, 1354), 206–07. I have benefited from conversations about medieval preaching with Daniel R. Lesnick, who called to my attention the edition of Cavalca. See also Lesnick's "Dominican Preaching and the Creation of Capitalist Ideology in Late-Medieval Florence," *Memorie Domenicane*, n.s., 8–9 (1977–78): 199–247.

one and the same by substance in all languages, though it may vary accidentally from language to language."[15]

Moreover, every genre of continental vernacular poetry embodies almost invariably some immanent doctrine of signification—or what we may call a "poetics" of the sign. Dante believed that verbal signs are proper to the nature of man as a social creature situated midway in a hierarchy of being between angels and beasts. Angels enjoy total knowledge of each other, whether directly or through God, and so do not need verbal signs (*signa locutionis*); beasts, on the other hand, are guided wholly by the instincts of their species, and may know one another adequately through *themselves* (*per proprios alienos cognoscere*). But man is both a rational and an individual being. Being corporeal, he cannot enjoy the purely spiritual knowledge of angels; being individual, he cannot know his fellow creatures through himself: hence the necessity of signs.[16] Vernacular speech (as opposed to Latin) is a determinant of the historical self in its relationship to other selves composing society.[17]

Although medieval grammarians and logicians tended to ignore the primacy of the phonetic or subsemantic structures in the production of meaning, Dante's grasp of the "noble subject" (*subiectum nobile; De vulgari eloquentia* I.iii) of signs begins right there, albeit at the level of the syllable and not the phoneme. The syllable, for Dante, is that basic unit of sound that combines with other syllables to produce a meaning separate and different from those sounds yet structurally homologous with them. According to their combinations of sound, polysyllabic words may be classified hierarchally as "childish," "feminine," or "manly." The manly category of sounds is superior, but this category itself comprises two subtypes that Dante calls "rustic" (*sylvestria*) and "civilized" (*urbana*). When properly realized, "urban" discourse is a harmony of contraries: that is, of "groomed" (*pexa*) and "hairy" or "shaggy" (*irsuta*) sounds which, together, produce a "fair harmony of structure" (*pulcram armoniam compaginis; De vulgari eloquentia* II.viii). For a poet to compose a song (*cantio*) of words is to "bind up" (*ligare*) sounds, and in this operation the poet's function as "author" joins that of the monarch as "authority." One binds up vowels, which

15. "Grammatica una et eadem est secundum substantiam in omnibus linguis, licet accidentaliter varietur": quoted by Bursill-Hall, 38.

16. Dante, *De vulgari eloquentia* I.ii–iii, ed. Enrico Bianchi (Florence: Salani, 1938).

17. Dante, *Convivio* I.xii, ed. Bruna Cordati (Turin: Loescher, 1968).

are the "soul and juncture" (*anima et legame*) of the word, while the other binds up the souls of individual men into a harmonious civil order (*Convivio* IV.ii). Just as medieval rhetoricians like Geoffrey of Vinsauf and John of Garland equated the high, middle, and low styles of poetic discourse with the functions proper to the supposedly distinct social classes of their time,[18] so Dante, too, stipulated (*De vulgari eloquentia* II.iv) that the poet of the high or "tragic" style (*stylus tragicus*) should write on noble subjects that are most fitting to the activities of the ruling class: these are love (*amor*), defense or public safety (*salus*), and virtue (*virtu*). These ethical concerns are central to Chaucer's *Troilus*.

Especially important for our purpose is the fact that Dante brought to vernacular poets a consciousness of the *historicity* of their own speech—indeed, with Dante the historical doctrine of the *translatio empirii* is refurbished, as it were, into what might be called a doctrine of the *translatio linguae*. Adam was the *primus loquens*, and his language was Hebrew, which was the universal language until the fall of Babel, after which Hebrew was preserved by the Jews only until their dispersion. Man being a most unstable and variable animal, his speech cannot be any more enduring or continuous than his customs or clothing; hence, grammar was invented, with Latin as its manifestation, to provide stability to the order of speech so that the different societies of history might communicate with the past (*De vulgari eloquentia* I.vi–ix). This was a broadly taught notion in the Middle Ages, but what is particular to Dante is his insistence, despite the universality of Latin, upon the "nobility" of the vernacular: it is only through the vernacular, he argues, that the individual may gain access to Latin, or *grammatica* (*Convivio* IV.ii).

In England, attitudes among poets toward discourse as a political foundation were ambivalent. As Lois Ebin has shown, John Lydgate is very positive in his conviction about "goldyn" language and the well-being of the state; and his political poetry, including the *Troy Book*, makes explicit the connections between eloquence and political virtue. Ebin writes of Lydgate's theories:

> Like the sun, the poet illuminates his matter and makes it "goldyn." Like Nature, he creates works fairer than the ordi-

---

18. Edmond Faral, ed., *Les Arts poétiques du XIIe et du XIIIe siècle: Recherches et documents sur la technique littéraire du moyen-âge* (Paris: Champion, 1924), 86–89.

nary and more enduring. By his use of the terms "elloquence" and "rethoric," Lydgate sums up this function of a poet and defines a standard of good writing toward which the poet repeatedly strives. His ideal is a "sovereign style" in which artistic skill is linked with prudence, wisdom, and discretion.[19]

In Chaucer, by contrast, the "rhetor" is usually seen as a powerful and dangerous figure who subverts the well-being of society: such is the case with the Summoner, the Pardoner, and the Wife of Bath, all of whom are answered by the Nun's Priest, a paradigm of Christian eloquence, not in the high but in the "mixed" style.

In either case, medieval attitudes toward the relationship between language and history are not far from those of the modern linguist, Emile Benveniste, who writes, "History . . . is not necessarily a dimension of language; it is only one of its possible dimensions. Nor is it history that makes language live, but rather the inverse. It is language which, because of its necessity and its permanence, constitutes history."[20]

LANGUAGE AND TROY

Among the numerous legends that medieval poets inherited from classical antiquity, the legend of Troy seems best to have lent itself to a narrative in the "tragic" style (in Dante's limited sense of the word), whose themes were most properly love, war, and virtue. The legend of Troy not only brought to poets such as Chaucer a repertory of thematic material fully consonant with medieval criteria of the high style but was a narrative whose authoritative tragic form could bring artistic finality to all the deepest potential of medieval courtly poetry—a poetry otherwise yet lacking (with the exception, perhaps, of the story of Tristan and Iseut) the dignity of mature tragic vision in the broad sense. The story of Troy, supposedly the first in an open-ended sequence of great cities of classical antiquity to "fall" (Troy, Thebes, Alexandria, Rome . . .), had nourished in the medieval consciousness an understanding of the principle of macrocosmic history itself, seen as a

19. Lois Ebin, "Lydgate's Views on Poetry," *Annuale Mediaevale* 18 (1977): 76–106.

20. Emile Benveniste, *Problèmes de linguistique générale* (Paris: Gallimard, 1966), 31 (translation mine).

cyclical violence of becoming.[21] Such beliefs were reinforced by the Boethian theory of tragedy, centered on the figure of Fortune's wheel, whose cycles catch up the proud, exalt them, then work their fall. An awareness of this principle compelled every medieval political establishment (including England) sooner or later to ask itself this ominous question: when, if ever, must *we* become the next Troy?

Troy, Chaucer writes in his translation of Boethius, was destroyed in a just war of revenge when Agamemnon "recovered and purgid in wrekynge, by the destruction of Troye, the loste chambirs of mariage of his brothir."[22] However, to a good poet, the archetype of Troy's fall exemplified much more than a drama of political revenge, for only at its most superficial level does the *historia* of Troy deal with the sacking of the city at the hands of the Greeks. Indeed, from Homer onward, the real fascination that the life and death of Troy held for poets was less the clash of strong men on the battlefield than that network of more subtle forces of destruction at work *within* the city's walls: for instance, breakdowns in fundamental laws upon which man's survival as a political creature depends. By refusing to punish or expel Paris, the *polis* reveals its inner corruption, its negligence of justice, and finally its weakness. Especially in Chaucer, as we shall see, the spatial disposition of Troy as a dramatic setting—as a town sick with love from within, besieged by hostile forces from without—gives rise to a plot whose structure is basically contrapuntal, in this sense: though Chaucer's narrator recounts only the erotic tragedy of Troilus (the narrator shares most of the blindness of his unheroic heroes), we of the audience are always capable of seeing beyond the told violence of erotic passion, of the "hertes werre," to that larger, *untold*, and seemingly forgotten violence of the martial realm unfolding outside the city's walls. In Chaucer's *Troilus*, walls prove to be only false boundaries, since they do not, in the final analysis, protect the knights and ladies of Troy from answering to the harsh claims of history. Such a counterpoint of plot is not, of course, unique to Chaucer. Already in Virgil (who was himself following Greek models of epic and tragedy) there is a constant pairing of sexual delinquencies and civil calamities—or, more rarely, a pairing of their opposites: continence and peace.

21. Michelle A. Freeman, *The Poetics of "Translatio studii" and Conjointure: Chrétien de Troyes's "Cligès."* (Lexington: French Forum, 1977).

22. Geoffrey Chaucer, *Boèce*, metrum 7, in *The Works of Geoffrey Chaucer*, ed. F. N. Robinson (Boston: Houghton Mifflin, 1957), 372. Subsequent Chaucer references are to this edition and are included in my text.

Finally and more importantly, however, the legend of Troy offered to poets an occasion to explore their consciousness of language—of language as the living expression of the social order, and even of language as the medium of poetic art. Once again, such a consciousness is already acute in Virgil. Recall, for instance, that in the *Aeneid* the fall of Troy is instigated not by a battle but by a very moving speech: specifically, the deceitful narrative of Sinon that persuades the Trojans to open the city gates to the wooden horse. Similarly, Aeneas's own narrative of the fall of Troy is delivered before Dido, Queen of Carthage, and however innocent his intentions, the effect of his discourse is catastrophic: as his story unfolds, Dido falls fatally in love with its winsome teller. Once again, a city (this time Carthage) will fall heir to all the violence of human nature as that violence is communicated through (if not incited by) speech—and, more specifically (if Aeneas's narration may properly be called "epic"), through epic language itself.

If the social and historical consciousness of language, including narrative language, embedded in Virgil's story of Troy was both heightened and refined (as I will shortly show) by Chaucer, this is no doubt in part because of certain historical perspectives that came to prevail in late medieval Europe. As is well known, the legend of Troy nourished the political identities of newly emerging European nations faced with the task of inventing their own historical past. As early as the eighth century the *Historia Britonum* speaks of the Trojan origins of Britain, but only in the twelfth century—with the *Historia regum britanniae* of Geoffrey of Monmouth in England and the chronicles of Saint-Denis in France—did myths of Trojan "origins" really begin to grip the political imagination of Europe. It was claimed that Brutus, son of Priam, passing through Gaul, arrived at the Island of Albion and founded there *Troja Nova*; similarly (though in a less direct sequence of events), Francion, another Trojan prince, posthumously gave his name (France) to Gaul. The modern historian Bernard Guenée reminds us that during the Hundred Years War the French and English quarreled over the identity of Brutus. In the *Débat des hérauts de France*, the Englishman argues that the wars of Brutus in Gaul justify the undertakings of his modern heirs; to which the Frenchman replies that the Bretons are descendants of Brutus but the English are not.[23]

It is interesting to speculate whether Chaucer might have seen in

23. Bernard Guenée, *L'Occident aux XIVe et XVe siècles: Les États* (Paris: Presses Univ. de France, 1971), 126.

the relationship between the Trojans and the besieging Greeks some deep analogy with the relationship between English and a more prestigious Continental eloquence, or, even more specifically, between the competing languages of English and French in his own country (for example, only in 1362 was it decreed—in French—that lawsuits would henceforth be conducted in English.[24] Whatever the case, we may safely venture that at a time when the several vernaculars of Europe had become emblems of new political entities, Chaucer's project of writing Troy's story "out of Latyn in my tonge" was no empty ideological gesture. To the contrary, one may infer from many features of Chaucer's artistic relationship with his pagan forebears that he was capable of grasping clearly, and even of exploiting, the fundamental ambiguity of his cultural role as a Christian *translateur*, as Eustache Deschamps called him. This is to suggest that as he wrote Troy's fall into the English tongue, Chaucer perceived both the triumph and the danger of proclaiming, with a newfound but tenuous Englishman's pride, that his culture was not only heir to but perhaps even a rival of the revered classical "auctours" of the past. This is a rivalry that Chaucer at least superficially abjures at the end of his poem:

> But litel book, no makyng thow n'envie,
> But subgit be to alle poesye;
> And kis the steppes, where as thow seest pace
> Virgile, Ovide, Omer, Lucan and Stace.
> (V.1789–92)

Still, merely for Chaucer to activate in his own tongue an intertextuality of poetic "tragedies" is to assert not just the vitality but also the fragility of English culture: "Pride goes before destruction, and a haughty spirit before a fall" (Prov. 16:18). Cannot history as a cyclical violence of becoming "translate" itself into one more terrible English cycle? Is not England, as heir to Troy, now in line to have a great fall? Machaut, as a Frenchman whose country had been long at war with England, had, of course, his own prophecy to give to the English:

> Destruiz serez, Grec diront et Latin:
> *Ou temps jadis estoit ci Angleterre.*[25]

24. Albert C. Baugh, *A History of the English Language* (New York: Appleton-Century-Crofts, 1957), 177.

25. Guillaume de Machaut, *Ballade* 211, as quoted by Daniel Poirion, *Le Prince et le poète: L'Évolution du lyrisme courtois de Guillaume de Machaut à Charles d'*

Clearly, later medieval poets had deep convictions about the inter-action between poetry and history: poetry is not a passive mirror of reality, but an agent *in* reality. Judson Boyce Allen has attempted to define the medieval understanding of the relationship between the inner life of the poem and that of the social world that is its context by exploring the medieval term *assimilatio*, which has been translated, however weakly, by the English term "likening." What is important in this term is that it includes the notion of *mimesis* of the external world (as in the process of description), the notion of metaphor or simile (comparisons that occur as relationships between things *internal* to the poem), and the notion of universals outside of time (and poetry) which the poem as an instance of discourse evokes. In other words, medieval poets subscribe not to the ontological autonomy of the poem but rather to its deep relational networks within a larger field of being. Allen's remarks go far, I believe, in defining Chaucer's supposition about poetry as action within multiple relationships and *planes* of reality:

> I recognize in this term, which denotes not the state of the existence of an entity but the result of the achievement of a relation, the same demand which I have repeatedly emphasized throughout this book—that is, that what we call poetry exists in the Middle Ages only because of and in terms of some larger complex of relationships and significances. The very stuff of which poetry is made—the stories and descriptions which are, literally, the words which poems are—cannot be taken as merely and in isolation themselves. The key definition of the words, stories, figures, and statements of which poems compose themselves is a definition, not of a thing, but of an act— an act, moreover, whose actors and objects inhabit a larger world than that of the poem itself. Considered as texts, poems are, as it were, locations within a tissue of assimilatio larger than themselves.[26]

As I shall try to show in this chapter, the tragedy of the *Troilus* is not merely that of a relationship between two lovers but of *assimilatio*

Orléans (Paris: Presses Univ. de France, 1965), 109: "You will be destroyed. The Greeks and Latins will say, 'In times gone by, here was England'" (translation mine).

26. Judson Boyce Allen, *The Ethical Poetic of the Later Middle Ages: A Decorum of Convenient Distinction* (Toronto: University of Toronto Press, 1982), 179–80.

on every level of being, and of *assimilatio* as the notion even of coherence in the realm of speech itself. For whatever Chaucer's personal view of history may have been, by drawing the story of Troy from the remoteness of the past, he was able not only to emphasize the coincidence between diachronism and linguistic change but above all to show, dramatically, what are the underlying social causes of that very historical process by which speech continually becomes different from itself:

> . . . in forme of speche is chaunge
> Withinne a thousand yeer, and wordes tho
> That hadden pris, now wonder nyce and straunge
> Us thinketh hem, and yet thei spake hem so.
> (II.22–25)

SPEECH AS ACTION

Chaucer shared with many other major authors of the late Middle Ages what may be called a "performative" linguistic consciousness: that is, an acute sense that speech is a kind of behavior by which many different types of social acts are achieved. It may seem inappropriate to impute to a medieval poet concerns about language as "performance" that are current in modern "speech-act theory," which is a branch of contemporary analytical philosophy,[27] yet a long tradition in medieval theories of language included the attempt to classify and define many nondeclarative utterances, such as exclamations, commands, oaths, prayers, greetings, curses, suppositions, "exhibitions of particular instances" (*ekthetikon*), and explanations.[28] Moreover, medieval treatises of rhetoric deal by example with many different discursive acts that lend themselves very well to modern analysis, and one may add that modern speech-act theory would prove itself very parochial if it refused to recognize the pertinence of its own history, especially in deal-

27. John R. Searle, *Speech Acts: An Essay in the Philosophy of Language* (Cambridge: Cambridge Univ. Press, 1969), and J. L. Austin, *How to Do Things with Words* (Oxford: Oxford Univ. Press, 1962). I accept Searle's argument that *no* speech act is not *some* kind of performance, and that constative utterances, which I shall equate with narrative utterances telling us "what happened," do not enjoy a neutral, detached status.

28. Gabriel Nuchelmans, *Theories of the Propositions: Ancient and Medieval Conceptions of the Bearers of Truth and Falsity* (Amsterdam: North Holland, 1973), 63–64.

ing with texts which have been *marked* by that history. Though the pragmatic and rhetorical strategies particular to poets such as Dante, Petrarch, Machaut, and Boccaccio differ greatly in detail, each poet constantly obliges his reader to become aware of the encoding and decoding of utterances as radically distinct acts corresponding to distinct sets of motives in interlocutors.

Since intramural relationships are exclusively favored in the *Troilus* until the last book, it is hardly surprising to discover that the principal sphere of action of the story's characters should be words—as opposed, for example, to sword blows or even kisses. A locus of the body politic, Chaucer's Troy is a locus of speech. Beyond the fact that the narrator of the poem speaks to his audience as a discrete persona, an "I" whose mediating awarenesses and intentions are always equivocal, even *within* the story the primacy of speech over all other forms of action becomes obvious if we observe how much of the poem's substance is devoted explicitly to conveying the utterances of its characters, or else to describing the delivery or reception of these utterances. Although it is not possible, in the case of the *Troilus*, to establish truly rigorous metalinguistic classifications with regard to what follows, but only to indicate poles or tendencies within the discursive composition of the poem as a whole, I have found, first, that only about three-eighths of the *Troilus* consists of supposedly "straight" narrative where the narrator simply informs us about the deeds or events that constitute the action of the poem: these may be called, with J. R. Searle (and hence, with qualifications, with J. L. Austin), propositional or constative utterances.[29] But, as I have already implied, a considerable amount of this propositional or constative discourse is indirect discourse or is devoted to the reporting of *how* or *why* utterances are delivered and received by interlocutors *in* the poem; hence, its function remains strongly metalinguistic.

Second, I have found that about one-half of the poem is composed of the direct discourse of characters in dialogue with each other, or else in implicit dialogue: prayers, oaths, invocations, vows, exhortations, admonitions, invectives, deliberations, etc. Since these utterances constitute the main body of an erotic tragedy—which is to say that the narrative fulfills itself through speech as action and reaction—we may propose, again with Searle and Austin, that these utterances are always *illocutionary* or *perlocutionary*. In the former, a speaker does not

29. Searle, 68.

merely refer or say but performs some *other* action as he or she speaks, such as to declare, describe, assert, warn, order, promise. In the latter, as Searle puts it, "is the notion of the consequences or effects such acts have upon the actions, thoughts, or beliefs, etc. of hearers": persuading, angering, seducing, repressing, convincing, inspiring, edifying.[30]

Third, there is a small proportion of utterances (less than one-eighth of the poem) which, for lack of a better term, I shall call "exclamatory," since they do not postulate a fiction of dialogue or of intersubjective communication but function, rather, as lyrical "cores" that mark the main "stations" in the progress of erotic passion. They occur in the main vocalizations of emotion (joy, grief, fear, despair, etc.), which accomplish little outside the action of their execution. Paradoxically, although these outpourings are presented dramatically as though they were spontaneous with—and entirely personal to—the character who is exclaiming, the lyrical cores in the *Troilus* are generally examples of conventional lyric types drawn from the high courtly vernaculars of Italy and France: the *aubade*, the *planctus*, the *canzone*, the hymn, etc. During such pivotal moments, all other action is suspended, and "pure" speech moves to the center of the stage in order to speak *itself* across the lips of the individual: in Chaucer's *Troilus* it is at moments of most intense passion that man is at his most conventional, a paradox that I shall explore in a moment.

Though by line count these lyrical cores are a minimal portion of the poem, they are nevertheless all-important in their command over the events that lead up to or grow out of them. That Chaucer, compared with his French and Italian sources, heightened the lyric element of his art has long been recognized by his critics, but what has not been properly understood is that these lyrical cores are not merely ornamental but generative with regard to the narrative in which they occur.

That courtly erotic lyric gives rise to semantic structures which can be amplified into the larger discursive units we call "narrative" is obvious, and the centrality of lyric discursive structures to structures of narrative was fairly clear, it seems, to Dante. There is a primacy of poetry (*metrice*), Dante says, over prose (*prosaice*), since prose writers derive both their examples and language from poets; but even within poetry itself, the lyric *canzone* is quintessential:

> Since, therefore, poems are works of art, and the whole of the
> art is embraced in *canzoni* alone, *canzoni* are the noblest

30. Searle, 22–26.

> poems, and so their form is the noblest of any. Now, that the
> whole of the art of poetic song is embraced in *canzoni* is
> proved by the fact that whatever is found to belong to the art
> is found in them; but the converse is not true. *De vulgari elo-
> quentia* II.iii)

Put in other terms, one may conceive of the *Troilus* as a complex
texture of different kinds of utterances that tend to distribute themselves between the constative as narrative, the illocutionary, the perlocutionary, and the exclamatory, as in the following schema:

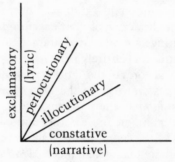

Although in practice these axes of speech performance constantly dis-
rupt each other—as when the voice of the narrator "exclaims" or the
speakers in the poem "narrate," or when exclaiming is "narrativized"
in indirect discourse—such disruptions are precisely a major source of
the metalinguistic consciousness that the *Troilus* provokes in its readers: *whenever utterances are dislocated from their proper functions
and rearticulated in new speech acts, a problematics of meaning passes to the foreground.* Each time a speech act is transposed out of its
original or proper context or code, a whole set of new intentions and
referential factors is necessarily introduced, and we of the audience are
caught in a movement that simultaneously compels and frustrates a
hermeneutic reflex: if meanings of utterances can be transformed into
their contraries, are not meanings from the very start perhaps also
non-meanings?

Chaucer often carries his experiments in problems of signification
very far. Consider, as an example, Pandarus's "reporting" of Troilus's
lyrical complaint to Criseyde, originally uttered in solitude, we are
told, to an *absent* Criseyde. What was in the first instance a single
speech act supposedly grounded on a pragmatic "I" is refracted, in its

textual manifestation, through at least five different intentional and interpreting consciousnesses. If we may assume that no speech act as an *encoding* by one speaker is identical to the speech act that is a *decoding* by a receiver, it is possible to schematize the transformations of meaning or intention that occur when Troilus's single utterance is refracted through a multiplicity of different voices, discourses, and consciousnesses. Since the "I" of Troilus's speech, however "sincere" its motives may have been, is already that of a *very* conventional lyric voice, I shall assume that the first "instance of discourse" is only virtual, given a priori as code; let us assume, also, that Chaucer's poem was composed with the understanding that it *too* would become a viable part of the tradition from which it derives. We may call this network of utterances that extends from the "present" moment in speech both backward and forward in time the *axis of intertextuality*.[31] The axis of intertextuality cuts across all the different levels of fiction of the *Troilus*, making apparent to what extent the conventional nature of verbal signs preempts the "reality" of the instance of discourse in any speaking subject, whether he be writer, character or reader. Poetic language does not *express*, by its conventions, the consciousness of the desiring individual but *determines* the operations of that consciousness.

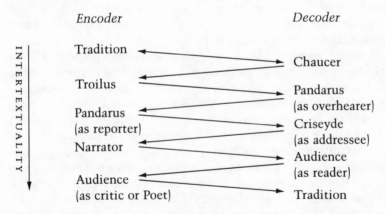

The power of courtly poetic discourse—a power deriving at once from its prestige as a traditional emblem of the aristocracy and from

31. Julia Kristeva, *Semiotikè, recherches pour une sémanalyse* (Paris: Seuil, 1969), 113ff.

its intrinsic beauty—is such, then, that its conventions dictate the structure of Chaucer's *historia*, to be understood as both story and history. Speaking individuals do not appropriate courtly discourse; rather, it appropriates them. As they relinquish their autonomy from poetic signs, individuals lose their capacity to refer: their reality, or history, in other words, "imitates" language. Such peculiar inferences about "poetic" mimesis in the *Troilus*, however, warrant discussion in their own right.

POETICS AND ETHICS

The lyrical cores that constitute the exclamatory axis of the *Troilus* are icons of a traditional courtly poetic discourse. As we saw in chapter 4, this is a discourse where verbal signs are divorced from their ordinary functions of communicating in order to become objects of desire in their own right. The lyrical axis of the *Troilus*, where pleasure in signs tends to make them opaque, is functionally opposed to the narrative or constative axis of the poem, whose discourse is seemingly transparent—at least to the extent that it pretends to convey, from one mind to another, some extralinguistic truth or reality without calling attention to itself as a medium. To speak thus of the different axes of expression in the *Troilus* is to suggest that we are dealing with different modes of experiencing reality, thanks to the different operations of language as a medium of cognition.

However, one may also suggest that we are dealing with a poem whose axes of expression are based on complementary principles of semantics that Chaucer plays against each other in his lyrical-narrative poem. Although we shall return to this proposition shortly, let me suggest that the lyric and narrative axes of the *Troilus* correspond, respectively, to those complementary dimensions of verbal performance that linguists call the paradigmatic and the syntagmatic.[32] The paradigmatic axis of speech is disjunctive, and involves mental acts of association or substitution based on relationships of equivalence between terms, regardless of whether these relationships involve principles of identity or opposition. The syntagmatic is conjunctive, and embodies thought that is linear and dynamic because of the power of signification of

32. Ferdinand de Saussure, *Cours de linguistique générale* (Paris: Payot, 1969), 170–75; John Lyons, *Semantics* (Cambridge: Cambridge Univ. Press, 1977) 1: 240–42.

terms and propositions to determine each other in order to produce new significations. The narrative axis may be considered as that medium thanks to which arch-conventional, transpersonal lyric cores are amplified and translated into a linear sequence of human events that Chaucer alternately calls his "historie" or his "tragedye." A certain disparity between an instinctive pleasure in poetic signs and the semantics of a tragic narrative configuration underlies the deep ambiguity of the *Troilus* and invites the reader to ask, with Chaucer, what ethical principles ought to prevail in our own understanding of the motives, words, and actions of the fictive people whose lives are spelled out for us in the text of this poem.

The Christian Middle Ages inherited from Greek Pythagorism and from neoplatonism a metaphysics of harmony that attributed to the musical dimensions of lyric poetry (its metrics and its harmonic structure) a cosmic dimension. Like the Greeks, Augustine tended to consider prosody, especially metrics, as a branch of music, and in both the temporal and harmonic structures of music he saw expressions of the physical laws of the cosmos (itself a "tuning") as a whole. As we saw in chapter 2, metrics is based upon the mathematical relationship of the short to the long syllable, which is 1:2, and this proportion also pertains in the relationship between the oneness of the creator and the multitude of the creation. Augustine defines the "music" of poetic meter as the "art of proper measuring" (*Musica est scientia bene modulandi; De musica* I.ii). The term "measuring" implies either the regular movement of some body or the principle by which some body is moved. Poetry as proper movement is harmonious, which is to say that it expresses proportions that are cosmic and universally intelligible, and simply by enjoying harmony in music we may intuitively infer that our souls themselves consist in a sort of harmony.

From Boethius, Cassiodorus, and Isidore of Seville, as well, and later from the twelfth-century Platonists, came similar doctrines of music and poetry that encouraged poets to see the proportions and harmonies of *musica humana* and *musica instrumentalis* as reflections of cosmic order. Boethius held that "harmony united the differences and contrary powers of the four elements," and that without this harmony "all would perish." So too is the human soul a tuning of body and soul: "What human music is, anyone may understand by examining his own nature. For what is that which unites the incorporeal activity of the reason with the body, unless it be a mutual adaptation and as it were a tempering of low and high sounds into a single consonance?"[33] Isidore of Seville concludes his discussion of the arithmetic of musical harmony by saying, "Just as this ratio appears in the universe from the revolution of the spheres, so in the microcosm it is so inexpressibly potent that the man without its perfection and deprived of harmony does not exist."[34]

That Chaucer was heir to such myths of harmony is evident from a poem in book III of the *Troilus*, which is addressed to Venus and invokes the muse Calliope. Naively elated by Troilus's impending success in love, the narrator praises Venus as the source of harmony, both in human affairs and in the cosmos. Unlike Boethius, Chaucer's self-deluding narrator celebrates worldly human love, which is ephemeral, as a semanticization of the eternal harmony underlying the principle of being:

> In hevene and helle, in erthe and salte see
> Is felt thi myght, if that I wel descerne;
> As man, brid, best, fissh, herbe, and grene tree
> Thee fele in tymes with vapour eterne.
> God loveth, and to love wol nought werne;
> And in this world no lyves creature
> Withouten love is worth, or may endure.
> (III.8–14)

There is nothing new in proposing that the lyrical axis of the *Troilus*, in which the process of cognition is closely allied to the phonetic substance of speech, might be a motivating source of paradigmatic structures of signification; poets and linguists alike have been telling us for some time, each in his or her own way, that phonetic structures of meter and rhyme, or "figures of sound," tend to generate isomorphic structures at the level of meaning.[35]

Emphasizing that both meter and rhyme proffer structures of meaning that are independent of—and often functionally opposed to—the

---

33. Boethius, *De institutione musica* I.ii, ed. Gottfried Friedlein (Leipzig: Teubner, 1867); trans. Oliver Strunk, in *Source Readings in Music History: Antiquity and the Middle Ages* (New York: Norton, 1950), 79–86.

34. Isidore of Seville, *Etymologiarum* III.xv, ed. Lindsay (Oxford: Clarendon Press, 1911), trans. Oliver Strunk in *Source Readings* (see n. 33, above), 100.

35. Roman Jakobson, "Linguistics and Poetics," in *Essays on the Language of Literature*, ed. Seymour Chatman and Samuel R. Levin (Boston: Houghton Mifflin, 1967), 314.

linearity of syntax, Roman Jakobson finds in Gerard Manley Hopkins support for his claims for the relationship between the poetic and the paradigmatic semantic axis. Hopkins, Jakobson notes, insists that poetic artifice "reduces itself to the principle of parallelism," but parallelism that is "marked or abrupt," rather than "transitional or chromatic" (i.e., syntagmatic). What is important to this study of the *Troilus* is that Hopkins points to the rhetorical or *figural* character of such equivalences: "To the marked or abrupt kind of parallelism belong metaphor, simile, parable, and so on, where the effect is sought in likeness of things, and antithesis, contrast, and so on, where it is sought in unlikeness."[36]

To suggest that a medieval poet such as Dante or Chaucer also might have seen the intelligible surface of poetry, including narrative poetry, as a process of semanticization that begins as "figures of sound" at the level of *subsemantic structures of meter and rhyme should not seem problematical for descriptive critics who follow linguists such as Jakobson, Benveniste, and Greimas. But what is perhaps less easy for modern readers to understand is that because, for the medieval poet, the subsemantic strata of meter and rhyme are tied up not merely with the physiology of phonemic production but also with transcendental cosmic and metaphysical principles—of which language is only one intelligible surface among others—medieval poetics presupposes a notion of mimesis unfamiliar to us. It is, namely, one where the "reality" to be understood in a poem such as the *Troilus* is thought to lie neither primarily in the non-linguistic world of created things to which language seems to refer (for these are mere contingencies and accidents), nor in the individual consciousness, but more properly in those intangible laws of the cosmos that are embodied, if only faintly, in the transcendent "harmonic" resources of poetic language. Such attitudes explain at least in part why medieval lyric poets tended to strive not for originality but for perfection, not for individuality but for abstractness and universality. They explain, likewise, why, in the *Troilus*, the language of its central hero should derive from the most conventional resources of medieval courtly lyric, giving rise to the persistent but somewhat vague awareness among Chaucer's critics that he has effectively "medievalized" the legend of Troilus and Criseyde.

Chaucer was never uncritical about the conventional language of medieval courtly lyric, however. If the phonetic structures of lyric po-

36. Jakobson, 313.

etry are thought to express stable laws of cosmic harmony, the semantic structures of lyric poetry express a world of human turmoil. Meter and rhyme may very well seem to manifest proportions analogous to those subtending the cosmos, but when figures of sound are clothed with figures of thought drawn from a less pure world of mortal lovers, the "historie" that results is necessarily a tragic one. When we consider rhyme, or what medieval rhetoricians called *similiter desinens*, as one of the "musical" resources of poetic discourse, we may observe how instances of rhyme in the *Troilus* offer to the linearity of narrative syntax homophonies that form peculiar and often elliptical binarities, based on similarity, opposition, or contiguity. Random examples would include bridel/ydel, gladnesse/distresse, pleasaunce/governaunce, adventure/cure, strecche/wrecche, name/shame, fre/cruelté, godnesse/wikkednesse, welle/Helle, Allas/solace, nobleness/brotelnesse, daunce/desesperaunce, offende/amende, lepe/slepe, save/rave, ook/strook, rede/dede, quyken/stiken, deeth/breeth, Eleyne/peyne, Criseyde/deyde. For the most part, these nearly subliminal but troubling equivalences manifest themselves independently of the dramatic context of the story and of the consciousnesses of the speakers (including the narrator) who enact that story: the Trojans and the naive historian are people for whom courtly poetic language is "ordinary" language and for whom the semantic effects of rhyme remain only minimally significant. At times, though, it is possible for us to glimpse, at least, the extent to which "history" in this hyperpoetical habitat is determined by a kind of deadly verbal—rather, poetical—positivism. For instance, one of the most frequent rhyme pairs in the *Troilus* is "joye/Troye," so nearly alike in sound, so agreeable to tongue and ear, yet so grimly counterpoised in an antithesis whose sweep includes the very trajectory of human history of which Troy itself is the paradigm: there can be no "joy" in "Troy."

The more such troubling relationships of equivalence are projected into the syntactic and thematic surface of language, the more such relationships implicate the motives and desires of man as a concept-making and rhetorical animal. It is precisely at this threshold between cognition and expression that medieval theories of language were most rigorous, and within the discipline of rhetoric the categories of utterance called "tropes" and "figures of thought" drew special attention, not only as resources of style but also as deeds of discourse by which man may disclose or conceal the truth. Tropes are instances of speech in which, whether out of necessity or for ornamental purposes, a substitution occurs in which some signified (*signatum*) is represented by a signifier (*signans*) that is improper to it, thus breaking the conventional bond between signifier and signified. Augustine (*DDC* II.x.15) defines this substitution of figurative signs for proper ones as a *usurpatio*, a term whose political implications are clear. Such usurpation is warranted when it involves substituting higher meanings for lower ones, as in the metaphors of Scripture and of theologians that accommodate some otherwise unintelligible truth to the cognitive limitations of man's mind. Poetic metaphors, by contrast, *conceal* truth, and theologians did not fail to remind poets that their art was *infima inter omnes doctrinas*.[37]

While Christian thinkers had long been aware of the equivocal nature of all conventional verbal signs, Chaucer's age was one in which speculation about those cognitive procedures by which we invoke words to stand for things became especially precise. "Supposition theory" (*suppositio*) is the term used by the scholastics, after Peter of Spain, to designate such theories of referentiality. *Suppositio* is different from signification, since it involves the question as to how, in our utterances, we employ verbal signs, whose significations are multiple and equivocal, to name things. Supposition is logically posterior to signification: that is, words that signify acquire their *suppositiones* in the syntax of utterances.[38] William of Ockham distinguished several different modes of supposition. For instance, "personal supposition" occurs "when a term stands for what is signified, whether what is signified is a thing outside the soul . . . or a word or a concept, so that whenever the subject or predicate of a proposition stands for its significate, so that it is held significatively, it is always personal supposition."[39] "Discrete" or "distinct" supposition occurs when something singular is signified; "common" supposition when a common term stands as the subject of a proposition such as "Every man is an animal." As Gordon Leff writes of Ockham:

37. See Joseph Anthony Mazzeo, *Medieval Cultural Tradition in Dante's Comedy* (Ithaca, N.Y.: Cornell Univ. Press, 1960).

38. Claude Panaccio, "Guillaume d'Occam: Signification et supposition," *Archéologie du signe*, 265–86.

39. William of Ockham, *Summa logicae* I.lxiv, trans. Gordon Leff, *William of Ockham: The Metamorphosis of Scholastic Discourse* (Manchester: Manchester Univ. Press, 1975), 133.

It is important to distinguish inexact or loose supposition (*improprie*) from strict supposition. There can be a number of ways, whenever a term does not stand precisely for what is signified: for example, by the use of a proper name to describe what is represented (antonomastically), substituting the part for the whole (by synecdoche) or by metaphor, taking the term under which something is contained for the content, or the abstract form for the subject. They apply therefore only to conventional terms.[40]

For a logician such as Peter of Spain or Ockham, *suppositio* is strictly limited to problems of predication and argumentation, but for a poet such as Chaucer, who is not concerned with logical propositions, *ethical* questions of semiosis bearing on our motives and intentions in the way we exploit the equivocity of signs are uppermost in importance. Moreover, such ethical questions are wholly appropriate to a tragedy written in the "high" or "tragic" style, which was distinguished, according to medieval rhetoricians, not only by its themes (such as love and war) but by the abundance of tropes and figures, or by what rhetoricians called *ornatus difficilis*.[41] If "tragedy" is both a repertory of themes *and* a style of language, no serious poet who takes up, with the legend of Troy, the "tragedy" of human history can escape seeing the pattern of history as a consequence of the rhetorical functions of his discourse, including *figural* functions.

Indeed, the tragic plot itself, as it was commonly understood in the Middle Ages, is nothing other than the linear realization of an oxymoron: "Tragedy is to seyn," writes Chaucer in his translation of Boethius, "a dite of prosperite for a tyme, that endeth in wrecchidness" (*Boèce* II, *prosa* 2.1.70), and this of course is the story of Troilus: "In lovynge, how his aventures fellen / Fro wo to wele, and after out of joie" (I.3–4). Troping is a dislocation of the sign as a conventional bond of *signans* and *signatum*; if we consider that bond as a social *pact*, which is the very foundation of social order, then we can see the tragic configuration of history as the just fate of any society that lets itself be determined, as does the society of knights and ladies of Troy, by what we may call "Pandarus's law," since it is the verbal magic of Pandarus that catalyzes the events of this poem:

40. Leff, 157.
41. See The Parisiana Poetry of John of Garland, ed. and trans. Traugott Lawler (New Haven, Conn.: Yale Univ. Press, 1974).

> By his contrarie is euery thyng declared. . . .
> Eke whit by black, by shame ek worthinesse,
> Ech set by other, more for other semeth,
> As men may se, and so the wyse it demeth.
> (I.637–44)

As a basis for action, such laws are not only incompatible with virtue but are against nature: "For contrarious thynges ne ben nat wont to ben ifelawschiped togydre. Nature refuseth that contrarious thynges ben yjoined" (*Boèce* II, *prosa* 6.1.80). In Pandarus's verbal universe, "truth" can have no firm ground, since language proffers "meaning" that is always different from itself; nor, finally, can there be any enduring "troth" between lovers: desire is always the quest for someone or something *other*.

Pandarus himself is a strategist without telos, a man without center and without substance, a man of "wordes white" (III.1567) whose experience of life is vicarious—that is, made of substitutions, both in his sexual life and in his language: "To ese his frend was set al his desir" (III.486). Hence the self-defeating nature of his desire, which is only the desire to desire; hence too Pandarus's automatic assumption that Troilus, forsaken by Criseyde, will also seek some fast substitute in another woman. The game of desire is played by Pandarus above all in the *play* of language: that is, the equivocity of signs proffered "Bitwixen game and ernest, swich a meene / As maken wommen unto men to comen" (III.254–55). To the extent that love is a mere game, its manifestation in language is innocent: medieval speculations upon lying were careful to exonerate deception perpetrated in play and jokes, which, according to St. Augustine (*De mendacio* ii.2; iii.3), are clearly distinct from lying. But to the extent that Pandarus's white words are in fact "earnest," Pandarus does more than to deceive (*fallare*): he is both *mentiens et fallens*, to echo Augustine's distinctions.

As an artificer of words in a courteous and noble world, Pandarus is not constrained by the high style, but when opportunism dictates, he quickly falls back on the humbler and supposedly more practical "truths" of lower, less noble styles in order to expedite the coupling of women to men. Such departures from the noble style may be neutrally identified by modern linguists as "code-switching," but in the context of medieval poetics they identify Pandarus as a relativist of a socially subversive sort. He is an abuser of *sermocinacio*, a term sometimes translated as "dialogue" but one that applies more generally to the correspondence that must prevail between speech and rank of speakers; and he is a transgressor of *ydioma*, which is the art of making a person's speech appropriate to his character. Such incongruencies and improprieties of style are normally to be shunned by "good" poets, since "style," as medieval rhetoricians understood that term, was a notion that included not only the very body of a poem but the office of the poet and even the act of writing with pen and ink. As John of Garland put it (V.160):

> "Style" as a term is used metaphorically. For a style is the middle section of a column, on which rests the epistle, and whose lower section is called the base. "Style," then, in this sense, is the "poetic quality," or an "uprightness [*qualitas carminis uel rectitudo*] preserved throughout the body of the matter [*corpus materie*]. Sometimes style means the poem itself. Style means the office of a poet, as in the *Anticlaudianus. . . .* Finally, style means the pen we write with.

But Chaucer, through his narrator and characters, transgresses such constraints of discursive decorum precisely in order to instigate in his readers a moral consciousness of language that his narrator and characters themselves do not share. Indeed, a thesis by Reta Margaret Anderson (regrettably unpublished) shows to what extent the dramatic structure of the *Troilus* is subtended by a tension among three incompatible styles, all of which compete to define reality: Troilus himself is a too-willing prisoner of the high style, whose inflationary idealizations prevent him from acting *except* in language, and in language so conventional that it blinds him to history and to the flawed nature of people around him, including Criseyde.[42] The *Troilus* is more than a rhetorical poem, since Chaucer exploits the norms of rhetoric by transgressing them and makes of "rhetoricity" itself a primordial problem of his poetic world. Chaucer seems to have associated the archetypal disaster of Troy with the ethical problem of classical rhetoric as posed by Plato and as seen through the eyes of a post-Augustinian, medieval Christian. Chaucer obviously shared a prejudice against what John of Garland (V.160) called the "hunter of artifice by the Ciceronian tongue" in favor of the "embracer of Christian integrity" [*integritatis Christiane*], which is above all an integrity of the sign.

42. Reta Margaret Anderson, "Some Functions of Medieval Rhetoric in Chaucer's Verse Narrative," Ph.D. diss., Yale University, 1963.

TROY AND THE HISTORY OF DESIRE

Already in the basic dramatic setting of the Troilus we encounter strategical designs by which Chaucer underscores the vitiation of social
order that attends decadence in the use of language. Broadly speaking,
Chaucer's *Troilus* is the story of an erotic tragedy that unfolds within
the walls of Troy, a city of lovers besieged in war and a locus of love's
language. The individual experience of Troilus ("little Troy") is therefore but a synecdoche (*pars pro toto*), a fragment, of that larger historical violence occurring outside the city's walls. Seemingly, what happens inside belongs only to the sphere of love; what happens outside
belongs only to the sphere of war. As readers, with Chaucer, of an epic
tradition, however, we know that this war—which is really the war of
all history—has been initiated by an erotic transgression, by that
breaking of "trouthe" (troth + truth) which occurred when Paris, a
Trojan, absconded with Helen, a Greek; we also know (with our Boethian philosophical wisdom) that this war will be perpetrated yet again
and again through successive erotic transgressions in that "future"
which is our past and also (unless we use signs properly) the future of
England itself: the *Troilus* as an "English" poem is both tragic history
and potential prophecy.

In spatial terms, therefore, we have a dramatic setting in which any
occurrence in the speech of lovers of the conventional oxymorons of
violence (flames, wounds, dying, etc.) cannot fail to point outward to
an extramural violence that is *not* figurative but "real." Troy is a city
where people have forgotten how to use signs properly, and as a result
their erotic discourse of love is ornamented with figurative violence of
the most extravagant sort: arrow-wounds, hemorrhaging, chopping,
slashing, evisceration, starvation, drowning, chaining, madness, snar-
ing, convulsions, hanging, poisoning, imprisonment, dismemberment,
suicide, enslavement, etc. But all this merely figurative violence *is* ma-
terializing historically outside the city's walls. These characters speak
so "poetically" that they are voluntarily blind, as we must *not* be, to
the referential context of their figures, which is the war between the
Trojans and the Greeks. In creating a dramatic structure where a world
of speaking lovers is circumscribed by the hostilities of a military
siege, Chaucer is in effect placing language—more specifically, lyrical,
poetic language—on a stage whose context is historical; and it is precisely because the actors upon that stage do not know—or have forgotten—history that history "happens." Violence that is supposedly in-

existent because it is merely *figurative* violence becomes the real consequence of *figurativity as primal violence itself*—primal because it originates not in material things but rather in the signs by which we know (or refuse to know) those things. Thus, through the dislocation of the proper relationship between signifiers and their signifieds, men and women lose their capacity for knowing the truth unequivocally, for upholding a troth; they lose, finally, even their capacity for action—except, of course, in poetic language as false action. We are dealing here not merely with instances of "dramatic irony" but rather with deep-seated convictions of a late medieval poet about the danger that arises when words as conventional poetic signs are vitiated and cannot refer properly.

The narrator of the poem is of course the first who willingly abandons strict usage of verbal signs for more "poetic" substitutions of improper for proper terms, in accordance with the norms of the high style—hence his self-confessed pride in speaking of a sunset thus:

> The dayes honour, and the hevenes ye,
> The nyghtes foo—al this clepe I the sonne—
> Gan westren faste. . . .
> (II.904–06)

This infatuation with style is as morally debilitating as it is excessive, for the narrator has also been the first to ignore the theme of *salus*, or public safety, which is similarly proper to the high style; the narrator makes it clear that the war outside the city is important to him only insofar as its events pertain to the heart's war between Troilus and Criseyde. Though he mentions the erotic transgressions that have caused the war to break out in the first place, he declares in a conspicuous *occupatio* that for him to speak of the war itself now would only be a digression:

> But how this town com to destruccion
> Ne falleth naught to purpos me to telle
> For it were here a long digression
> Fro my matere, and yow to long to dwelle.
> But the Troian gestes, as they felle,
> In Omer, or in Dares, or in Dite
> Whoso that kan may rede hem as they write.
> (I.141–47)

This suppression of the epic story of Troy in favor of the romance of Troilus stems, of course, from the narrator's own frustration and despair in affairs of the heart. Like Pandarus, the narrator substitutes vicarious literary love, the love of letters, for the real thing, though in doing so he denatures the very heroic tradition which he names and in which his poem is situated. This patrimony of heroic texts constitutes nothing less than the collective memory of society, and must therefore be respected if society is to endure, as Chaucer himself implies in *The Legend of Good Women*:

> And if that olde bokes were aweye
> Yloren were of remembraunce the keye.
> (Text F, 25–26)

The fictive narrator of the *Troilus* is a bad reader and writer of *historia*, and the subversive imbalance in his ethical values is recapitulated more explicitly by the misuse of *litteratura* committed by other characters *within* the story. Indeed, the narration of the great wars of history is welcomed by the courtly ladies of Troy not as moral edification but as a mere pastime to amuse them while the men are away. Thus, when Pandarus, having become a procurer for Troilus, rushes to Criseyde's house in his friend's behalf, he finds the ladies gathered there ingenuously diverting themselves with the romance of Thebes—that is, the tragedy of another classical city destroyed by war. Pandarus excuses himself graciously for intruding upon the story. "Is it of love?" he asks, "O, som good ye me leere." But the harsher lessons of war in Thebes are of no interest to Pandarus, for when he finds out what they are reading he says:

> "Al this I knowe myselve,
> And al th'assege of Thebes the care;
> For herof ben ther maked bookes twelve.
> But lat be this, and telle me how ye fare.
> Do wey youre book, rys up and lat us daunce,
> And lat us don to May som observaunce.
> (II.106–12)

In this over-refined, "paved parlour" of poetry and laughter which makes so light of the burdens of history, the dead letter of war ignites the very spirit of love. We of the audience do not share, of course, such a dangerous finiteness of consciousness, for if the narrator can speak only metaphorically of love as an "encircling" of Troilus's heart, as a siege, we cannot escape seeing the heart's war as a synecdoche for the Trojan war, which is in turn a synecdoche for the macrocosmic violence of history as becoming. Moreover, the repressed moral significance of the story of Thebes will emerge to the surface with time, for it will be Cassandra who reveals to Troilus the tragedy of his destiny, and she uses the story of the fall of Thebes as a parallel (V.1458ff). Each horizon of reality in the universe of *Troilus and Criseyde* corresponds, at least potentially, to a distinct state of consciousness in the morally alert reader whose mind will not fail to move outward from the specific to the general, always by a process of analogy which can be stated as follows: Troilus: Criseyde:: Troy: Greece:: Being: Fortune. The last pair is of course Boethian: Fortune as "executrix of wyrdes." (*Wyrde* means "destiny" or "fate," being the equivalent of *fatum*, which is in turn derived from *for*, the verb "to speak"—fate as discourse.)

The extensively analogical structure of Chaucer's poetic world induces in his readers a moral perspective upon the limited nature and functions of courtly poetic discourse. For convenience, the analogies immanent in the universe of the *Troilus* may be expressed spatially as a series of concentric circles turning together upon the individual experience of Troilus himself.

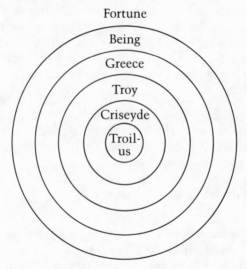

Fortune
Being
Greece
Troy
Criseyde
Troil- us

Though the narrator declines to explore what lies beyond the specific "cas" of Troilus and his "swete fo" Criseyde, the sheer abundance of

supposedly figural violence in the language of the poem points constantly to the "real" story outside, to a universal *historia* which, if we
too use poetic signs improperly, will presumably become our own
story as well. In short, through the dramatic organization of his tale,
Chaucer has brought to the oxymoron of erotic combat, which had
hitherto subtended courtly lyric in the world of romance, a new and
precise intellectual perspective: one that focuses our attention upon
the ethical problem posed by indulgence in oxymoron itself as a (dis)-
figuration of speech, as a dislocation of signs wrought by the tongues
of those blinded by passion.

If we may take for granted that Chaucer understood, whether intuitively or rationally, the ideological and metaphysical dimensions of
the dramatic setting that he created, then in my opinion much of the
fascination of the *Troilus* lies in those numerous poetic strategies by
which Chaucer manages to stage in our "dyrkyd memorie" those very
macrohistorical events of Troy's fall that the narrator himself tends to
repress, but with the consequence that these intrude with more and
more intensity upon our consciousness as the story moves toward its
conclusion. In other words, what interests me in this poem is the manner in which Chaucer makes *one* story "tell" *another* story that is
only latent or virtual, yet all-important because it is universal. It is
these strategies of totalization that will preoccupy us now.

LOVE AS WAR

The "fall" of Troilus begins when, in an excess of pride, the young soldier—instead of attacking the Greeks who have besieged Troy—ver-
bally assaults the god of Love as his mortal enemy. Cupid takes swift
revenge upon the words of the aggressor by firing his conventional arrow of desire. The historical violence of the battlefield is now denatured by poetic convention, and the *gesta* of epic are psychologized
as Cupid's arrow inflicts upon a hero its purely sexual wound: upon
seeing Criseyde, Troilus is "right with hire look through-shoten and
through-darted" (I.324). The young soldier retreats to his bedchamber
and indulges in extravagant heroics—not of the sword but of song. This
is the first lyrical core of the *Troilus*, and Chaucer's gesture of lifting
Troilus's song from Petrarch's *Canzoniere* ought not to be dismissed as
a mere "lyrical ornament," nor even as the graceful tribute of a young
English poet to a revered continental master, but as a more wily attempt to subvert the consecrated paradigms of the medieval erotic

lyric with the syntax of narrative, whose harsh trajectory links the latent violence of the "high" or "tragic style" to the full-blown historical events that are its consequence. Moreover, Petrarch's song itself may perhaps have been seen by Chaucer as an artful but dangerous reduction of a heroic narrative world, since it too resonates with classical metaphors that call to mind the wanderings of other amorous heroes— Odysseus, for example, or the less temperate Aeneas, buffeted by the storms of Juno's wrath:

> Al stereless withinne a boot am I
> Amydde the see, bitwixen wyndes two,
> That in contrarie stonden evere mo.
> (I.416–18)

The politically anarchic force of Troilus's very conventional sentiments of love is expressed by the Trojan prince himself, who, by becoming his lady's vassal, unintentionally prophesies Fortune's future sovereignty over Troy:

> For myn estat roial I here resigne
> Into hire hond, and with ful humble chere
> Bicome hir man, as to my lady dere.
> (I.432–34)

And later:

> Therto desir so brennyngly me assailleth,
> That to ben slayn it were a gretter joie
> To me than kyng of Grece ben and Troye.
> (I.606–09)

Just as it would be difficult for us not to see the flames of Dido's funeral pyre as the narrative fulfillment of all those instances of metaphorical "flames" of passion scattered throughout the previous books of the *Aeneid*, so too it is hard for us not to see a connection between the "hot fir of love" that burns Troilus and the flames that are destined to consume Troy. Moreover, Pandarus, as he counsels Criseyde to use her Venus-like element to "quenche al this," uses an image that would doubtless stir the hearts of the firemen of Troy as much as the hearts of its lovers:

> Nece, alle thyng hath tyme, I dar avowe,
> For whan a chambre afire is, or an halle,

> Wel more ned is, it sodeynly rescowe
> Than to dispute and axe amonges alle
> How this candele in the strawe is falle.
> (III.855–59)

Among the characters only Calkas, Criseyde's father, can foresee the flames of history that have been kindled by human passion, for he prophesies thus:

> That fire and flaumbe on al the town shal sprede,
> And thus shal Troie torne to asshen dede.
> (IV.118–19)

But Troilus will evade the tangible reality of war itself, in constant deference to the purely metaphorical violence of love:

> Alle other dredes weren from him fledde,
> Both of th'assege and his savacioun
> (I.463–64)

The more the narrator escalates the erotic psychomachia in which Troilus revels, the more he condenses Troilus's exploits in "real" battle to a few cursory hyperboles, to a kind of epic shorthand pertinent only so long as it relates to his progress in the tribulations of sexual desire. For Troilus fights not for *salus*, or civic well-being, but only as a lover:

> But for non hate he to the Grekes hadde,
> Ne also for the rescous of the town,
> Ne made hym thus in armes for to madde,
> But only, lo, for this conclusion:
> To liken hire the bete for his renoun.
> Fro day to day in armes so he spedde,
> That the Grekes as the deth him dredde.
> (I.477–83)

Moreover, each of Troilus's *gestes* in war is swiftly denatured as it is converted into some equivalent success in the more precious skirmish of love:

> But Troilus lay tho no lenger down,
> But up anon upon his stede bay,
> And in the feld he pleyde the leoun;
> Wo was that Grek that with hym mette a-day!
> And in the town his manere tho forth ay

289

> Soo goodly was, and gat hym so in grace,
> That ecch lym loved that loked on his face.
> (I.1072–78)

The narrator even has to remind *himself* that Troilus's "heigh servyse" of Mars (the God of war *and* the lover of Venus) is in arms, as opposed to deeds of love in his false epic world of the mattress and pillow:

> By day he was in Martes heigh servyse,
> *This is to seyn, in armes as a knyght;*
> And for the more part, the longe nyght
> He lay and thoughte how that he myghte serve
> His lady best, hire thonk for to deserve.
> (III.437–41; italics mine)

Pandarus constantly subordinates the horrors of the macrocosm to the frivolity of the microcosm, as in this moment when he greets Troilus at dawn after a night of languishing:

> This Pandarus com lepying in atones,
> And seyde thus, "Who hath ben wel ibete
> To-day with swerdes and with slynge-stones,
> But Troilus, that hath caught hym an hete?"
> And gan to jape, and seyde, "Lord so ye swete!"
> (II.939–43)

Pandarus both exploits and nullifies the terror of warfare by subjecting it to a comparison with the far keener pleasure of love when he brings to Criseyde the "good news" of the day: not that the war is ended but rather that Troilus is falling for her. Criseyde, who knows nothing of Troilus (much less of her other destiny, which is to fall in love with a Greek) answers Pandarus's good news with an unwitting pun on "die" (one of the many in the poem), a pun that is at her own expense because it is prophetic:

> "Now uncle deere," quod she, "telle it us
> For Goddes love; is than th'assege aweye?
> I am of Grekes so fered that I deye."
> "Nay, nay," quod he "as evere mote I thryve,
> It is a thing wel bet than swyche fyve."
> (II.122–26)

Now Pandarus himself becomes a narrator of the war, and in accordance with "Pandarus's law" (where everything is declared by its contrary), the topic of warfare becomes, in his discourse, a mere aphrodisiac. Both Hector and Troilus, he says, have only a "litel wownde" (Troilus's wound being, of course, Cupid's), and as Pandarus recounts the action, he does all he can to psychologize the epic soldier's conquering sword into a "sharpe kervying tolis" of a less epic sort:

> Now here, now ther, he hunted hem so faste,
> Ther nas but Grekes blood,—and Troilus.
> Now hym he hurte, and hym al down he caste,
> Ay wher he wente, it was arayed thus:
> He was hir deth, and sheld and lif for us;
> That, as that day there dorste non withstonde,
> Whil that he held his blody swerd in honde.
>
> Thereto he is the frendlieste man
> Of gret estat, that evere I saugh my lyve,
> And wher hym lest, best felawshipe kan
> To swich as hym thinketh able for to thryve.
> (II.197–206)

Pandarus's incendiary success in exciting Criseyde's curiosity (*curiositas* is generally a prelude to lust in medieval and Renaissance narrative) is only intensified by the interruptions, the digressions, the "diffisioun of speche" with which he delays the recounting of his "good news." Here Chaucer seems to be calling attention to the relationship between the rhetorical amplification of narrative as a *deferring* and the paradox (broadly understood by medieval poets) that improper desire is really only the desire to desire. In any case, just as Criseyde's curiosity flourishes on obstacles, so too her libido will feed itself on a rhetoric of violence and of negation in which both she and Pandarus freely indulge, without suspecting that by doing so they are promulgating the destructive forces of macrocosmic history. When Pandarus confesses (vicariously) Troilus's love for Criseyde, he draws his dagger and threatens to cut his own throat: if Troilus must die of love, he says, then the two friends must "die" (another sexual pun?) together. This gestural rhetoric is attended by a verbal game of negative suggestibility: for instance, Pandarus swears vehemently that Troilus desires "naught but youre frendly cheere" (is the figure "naught," or "O", yet another sexual pun?), and that without love this "upright" young man will soon be slayn:

> I se hym deye, ther he goth upright,
> And hasteth hym with al his fulle myght
> For to be slayn, if his fortune assente,
> Allas, that God yow swich a beaute sent!
> (II.333–36)

Criseyde instantly picks up the game: after a few lamentations and a curse of the god Mars (why not Venus?), she consents to save Pandarus's life by granting Troilus her "good chere" and asks a leading and tendentious question, "Ye seyn, ye nothyng elles me requere?" Now she concludes, with ambivalent haughtiness, "Ne shal I nevere of hym han other routhe" (II.489). It may be suggested that Chaucer is dramatizing through narrative and dialogue—and at the same time demystifying—a very basic tendency of conventional courtly love lyric discourse to function *negatively*: that is to generate itself, as we saw in chapter 4, by constantly negating the hope, or the possibility, of "joye" as sexual pleasure.

Just as Chaucer personifies in Pandarus a perversion of verbal signs in the *production* of meaning, so too he dramatizes a similar perversion in the process of its *reception*. A striking example of this occurs when Criseyde is first smitten with love for Troilus. Troilus, one will recall, is returning to Troy after a fine day of killing in the field. In the late Middle Ages, entries of kings and princes were always carefully staged public events of great political significance.[43] But our narrator disposes the setting of Troilus's triumphal return in such a way that we of the audience perceive, over and against the normal *social* significance of the occasion, the individuating responses of Criseyde's libidinal psyche, in which the trappings of the martial sphere become fiercely erotogenic. Hearing the sudden hue and cry of the townsfolk welcoming their victorious hero back into Troy, Criseyde goes to her window to observe the spectacle. So partisan is the narrator to the transforming power of her libido that he too all but forsakes the

---

43. Bernard Guenée and François Lehoux, *Les Entrées royales françaises de 1328–1515* (Paris: Editions du Centre National de recherche scientifique, 1968); Jacques Heers, *Fêtes, jeux et joûtes dans les sociétés d'occident à la fin du moyen-âge* (Montréal: Institut d'études médiévales; Paris, Vrin, 1971), 18ff; Lucie Brind'Amour, "Rhétorique et théâtralité: Étude de quatre entrées royales du xve s.," *Studi mediolatini e volgari* 23 (1976): 9–57, and 24 (1976): 73–133.

broader social dimension of the event and purveys to us only what Criseyde herself chooses to see: "to beholde it was a noble game." Before her creative glance, Troilus appears as a young, bareheaded—and quite phallic—young blade, astride a mount that spontaneously begins to bleed before her very glance, even though its master rides the lucky beast "ful softely."

Now fully given over to Criseyde's unbridled fantasies, the narrator tells us that Troilus looks better to Criseyde than Mars himself (the God she has just cursed), a comparison that implicitly identifies Criseyde herself with Venus—indeed, Venus herself is prevailing over this scene from her sphere in the heavens above. As viewed from Criseyde's window, the potency of the young knight in arms becomes suddenly very equivocal: what *can* the narrator mean when he speaks so blithely of Troilus's power "to don that thing?" *What* thing?

> So lik a man of armes and a knyght
> He was to seen, fulfilled of heigh prowesse;
> For bothe he hadde a body and a myght
> To don that thing, as well as hardynesse.
> (II.631–34)

As Criseyde stares at Troilus, she sees the young man "hym dresse" in his arms, which can mean either that she saw him "all equipped" or (as in modern French, *se dresser*) that she saw him "straighten up, become erect," and her response is to anticipate in her mind's eye the false erotic paradise that she and Troilus will indeed create for each other in the next book of the poem:

> And ek to seen hym in his gere hym dresse,
> So fressh, so yong, so weldy semed he,
> It was a heven upon hym for to see.
> (II.635–37)

This erotic "heaven" is all the more vivid for the traces of violence in Troilus's battered armor and for the many arrows stuck in his shield which (except for the one in his heart) he has victoriously withstood in his warlike service of love. Appropriately—again, to Criseyde's ears—the crowd now applauds, in the return of Troilus, the coming of their "joye": a keyword, of course, of the erotic lexicon of courtly art, one of whose semantic features in the Middle Ages was that of its modern French cognate, *jouïr*. Troilus responds to the "joy" of his admirers with a modesty that is nothing less than devastating, for it is precisely this sign of vulnerability in the young hero that overwhelms Criseyde like a fatal potion: "Who yaf me drinke?" she cries, and now an antiphony of blushes between Troilus and Criseyde removes any doubt about the potential reciprocity of their affections as lovers. In short, undertaken in love, the violence of combat has proved itself to be fiercely erotogenic—reversible though that proposition will be, since in the turn of events war too has been, and will continue to be, begotten by love.

Like painters of his age, Chaucer is now experimenting with multiple perspectives, where we of the audience observe, from our own perspective, a scene that is being also observed *within* the work of art by one of its figures: picturally speaking, our perspective on Troilus is at right angles with Criseyde's. So, in a sense, are our understandings.

Chaucer has disposed the public and the private spaces of Troy in such a way as to dramatize a courtly, aristocratic rhetoric of desire in which things come to signify whatever in "proper" speech they would ordinarily exclude, thereby challenging the moral obligation of man as a *social* creature to respect the proper relationship between signifiers and signifieds—that is, an ethics of *proprietas*. Boethius, as translated by Chaucer himself, put it thus: "Thow has lernyd by the sentence of Plato that nedes the wordis moot be cosynes to the thinges of whiche thei speken" (Boèce III, *prosa* 12, 205–07). Chaucer did not hesitate to assimilate such attitudes in his own moral framework:

> The wise Plato seith, as ye may rede,
> The word moot nedes accorden with the dede.
> If men shal telle properly a thynge,
> The word moot coseyn be to the werkyng.
> ("The Manciple's Tale," 207–10)

But the history of ideas does not suffice to show us how Chaucer exploited ideas pragmatically as a poet: that is, in a manner that sets the poet apart from the philosopher and schoolman. Analogy is a resource common to both poets and logicians, and by now it is obvious, I assume, that the erotic tragedy of Troilus and Criseyde is analogous to the larger process of universal history, and that the "fall" of Troy is prophesied and "staged" not just once but many times over in Chaucer's poem, from the moment when Troilus first collapses in his bed. However, there is a less "logical" yet very important dramatic progression in the *Troilus* with regard to the manner in which Troilus's (and ultimately Troy's) "falls" relate to "reality," and one may describe this peculiarly poetic progression in the following way. In books I and II, the "falls" of Troilus, which are only minimal physical acts, are purely figurative gestures that orchestrate, so to speak, a rhetorical *translatio* of the violence of the battlefield into the sphere of erotic desire; here, the primal events remain verbal, and the relationship of love to war is essentially parodic. However, in Books III and IV, as the lovers begin to act out their desire in concrete physical deeds, the sphere of love is no longer just a rhetorical *parody*, a mere shadow of war, but becomes invested with a specific course of events of its own which are now a comic *reduction* of the battlefield of history. In the last part of the *Troilus* there is a gradual convergence of the real actions of lovers with the real forces of the war as history: Troilus's "swete fo" will finally desert both Troy (as her father had done) and Troilus, and fall in love with a Greek; and now the fates of Troilus and Troy merge into a single *literal and historical* destiny. Thus, the progression in the plot of the *Troilus* (given *in* language) is doubled by a far more profound ethical "story" *about* language, especially poetic language itself, as a causal force in the violence of history.

Such a progression merits illustration. In Book II of the *Troilus*, the language of war is at least thrice removed from reality when the narrator narrates Pandarus's narration of Troilus's narration of love's (already figurative) wound. In this filtering of reality through multiple discourses, the epic heritage of Troy's siege is almost completely desemanticized by the rhetoric of courtly lyric and romance. Pandarus, though he could hardly be called a military leader, has held a strategical session with Troilus in a palace garden, beside a well, to "speken of an ordinaunce / How we the Grekes myghten disavaunce" (II.510–11): these are mere words about words about war. This garden, in Pandarus's skillful reporting, becomes a merger of the medieval *locus amoenus* of erotic love (here it is vicarious) and Edenic innocence. Though Chaucer's iconography is not always strictly programmatic, the well in the garden may symbolize both the element that is proper to Venus (water) and the paradisial Well of Life in Revelation 22:1. Pandarus and Troilus sport together in this garden like innocent Cupids, and here is the game of war at its most frivolous and absurd:

> Soon after that bigonne we to lege,
> And casten with oure dartes to and fro.
> (II.512–13)

Suddenly Troilus becomes tired and falls into a trance in which he dreams of love and utters a complaint to Cupid—this is one of the more prominent lyrical cores of the *Troilus*—and he bewails his erotic wound. The heroic young prince is reenacting not only Adam's loss of primal innocence but Mars's erotic downfall in a coma of heroic inactivity as well—this is a common theme of medieval and Renaissance painters. Interestingly, it is precisely at this moment of archpreciousness in speech and gesture that Troilus's "translations" of Fortune and death point outward to the nonfigural flames of Fortune and history that will finally engulf both the passionate prince and the city of lovers for which he is named:

> For certes, lord, so soore hath she me wounded,
> That stood in blak, with lokying of hire eyen,
> That to myn hertes botme it is ysounded,
> Thorugh which I woot that I moot nedes deyen.
> This is the werste, I dar me nat bywreyen;
> And well the hotter ben the gledes rede,
> That men hem wrien with asshen pale and dede.
> (II.533–39)

In Book III, with the consummation of their love, Troilus and Criseyde pass from the artifices of language to irrevocable deeds; consequently, the previously internal barriers to love are now superseded by the encounter with real obstacles and real events in the world of Troy: henceforth, the lovers' destinies as individuals will become more explicitly enmeshed with the larger forces of history. Book III itself seems at first to proffer a romantic oasis that is still perfectly autonomous from the tragedy of the war unfolding outside. Yet if there is a seeming autonomy in the bedroom comedies in which Pandarus, with his strategical "engines" of speech, "shapes the coming" of Troilus to Criseyde, there are also numerous indices that compel any diligent reader to sustain in his memory a narrative counterpoint between the stories of Troilus and Troy, even though the latter story remains almost subliminal. Chaucer's strategies of translation (*translatio, transsumptio*) are often subtle; they make special demands upon our readerly acuity if we are to catch the flashes of prophecy that cut so impersonally through the bedroom comedy and through the impassioned utterances of the lovers, orchestrating them with a terror that the lovers themselves do not detect. For instance, as Troilus anticipates his forthcoming rendezvous with Criseyde and vows to Pandarus that he will

love Criseyde faithfully, he simultaneously prophesies the death that
he himself is fated to experience as a consequence of his love, and the
subjugation of Troy after its defeat:

> But natheles by that God I the swere,
> That, as hym lyst, may al this world governe.—
> And, if I lye, Achilles with his spere
> Myn herte cleve, al were my lif eterne,
> As I am mortal, if I late or yerne
> Wolde it bewreye, or dorst, or sholde konne,
> For al the good that God made under sonne—
>
> That rather deye I wolde, and determyne,
> As thinketh me, now stokked in prisoun,
> In wrecchidnesse, in filthe, and in vermyne,
> Caytif to cruel kyng Agamenoun.
> (III.372–82)

Nor is Criseyde shielded from being identified by us with the larger
designs of Fortune, the strumpet-goddess of whom she is the unwitting agent. Accused—falsely—of loving Horaste, Criseyde bewails precisely the principle that she herself is destined to fulfill: "O brotel
wele of mannes joie unstable!" (III.820). Indeed, her subsequent oath of
innocence to Troilus is certainly equivocal: "untrewe / To Troilus was
never *yet* Criseyede" (III.1053–4, italics mine). Moreover, Criseyde,
who was hardly virgin in the first place, reveals in Book III that she has
no more espoused proper significations than she has the cause of mo-
nogamy; rather, she is as much a gamesperson of signs as Pandarus, as
we learn when Pandarus "dissuades" her from leaving his house (and
Troilus's bed) during a rainstorm: "I seyde but a-game, I wolde go"
(III.648). Even the high style (as Sanford Meech has observed)[44] is readily dispensed with by Criseyde once Cupid has given both her and
Troilus the pleasure "to maken of hire speche aright an ende," that is,
"hire speches to fulfelle" in bed (III.462, 510), for the next morning she
quips with Pandarus like an old barmaid:

> "Fox that ye ben! God yeve youre herte kare!
> God help me so, ye caused al this fare,
> Trowe I," quod she, "for al youre wordes white.

---

44. Sanford B. Meech, *Design in Chaucer's "Troilus"* (Syracuse, N.Y.: Syracuse
Univ. Press, 1959), 11.

O, whoso seeth yow, knoweth yow ful lite."
(III.1565–68)

There are of course many strategies by which Chaucer sustains a dim aura of epic history around his almost fabliau-like intrigue of nocturnal bedroom adventures, but it is from the sequence of actions themselves that we may view the bedroom as a comic reduction of the great battlefields of history—indeed, of a rather Virgilian history, at that. Just as a Venereal rainstorm in the *Aeneid* drives the two *venatores*, Dido and her Trojan prince (Troilus's brother), to seek refuge in a cave, where the royal pair commit their empire-wrecking fornication, so too a "huge rayn" and "a weder for to slepen inne" will unite Troilus and Criseyde in the same bedroom. And just as Sinon's lies allow the Greeks to sneak soldiers into Troy in the belly of the wooden horse, so too by the "engyn" of speech Pandarus will introduce Troilus, who has been concealed all evening in a closet ("stuwe"), into Criseyde's bedroom through a trapdoor; just as Troy falls, Troilus collapses in a less than heroic faint before his sweet foe:

The felyng of his sorwe, or of his fere,
Or of aught elles, fled was out of towne;
And down he fel al sodeynly a-swowne.
(III.1090–92)

Chaucer suggests, moreover, that if Pandarus is "author" of all these antiheroic farces, the vicarious thrills that he derives from this *mise-en-scène* of a high courtly poetics are subversive with regard to a nobler patrimony of heroic poetry whose purpose is to move men to action in fulfillment of duty. For while Troilus and Criseyde skirmish together in bed, Pandarus seeks out less exalted flames to warm him— those of the fireplace—and he feigns to distance himself from their sporting upstairs by pretending to read an "old romance" (III.979–80). Pandarus is not just sexually impotent: he is a "bad" poet and an enemy of the republic.

In Books IV and V, however, the vicissitudes of Fortune that the lovers have so extravagantly bewailed in the secret "stations" of love's progress begin to manifest themselves more distinctly as concrete political events, as public affairs unfolding in public places, thereby forcing us to situate the individual destinies of Troilus and Criseyde in a more precise historical—and poetical—determinism. We see them now as the social animals that they *must* be. Criseyde's father, Calkas, who has betrayed his native city to become counselor to the Greeks, now becomes anxious for his daughter's safety in Troy and convinces the Greeks to offer the Trojan prisoner Antenor in exchange for Criseyde. Thereafter, the seemingly autonomous events of love and war become sadly congruent, even though love itself will remain, throughout the *Troilus*, the prism through which the larger tragedy of the macrocosm—of Fortuna Major—will be refracted. Thus, in this poem, Troy itself will never fall, only Troilus; and Criseyde—for all the worldly joy that she has bestowed—will be the agent of his misfortune. But in the passions of individuals we still detect resonances of the larger, anarchic forces of history, such as when Troilus self-indulgently wishes that his personal catastrophe had befallen Priam, or his own brothers—anyone but *him*:

> Allas, Fortune! if that my lif in joie
> Displesed hadde unto thi foule envye,
> Why ne haddestow me fader, kyng of Troye,
> Byraft the lif, or don my bretheren dye?
> (IV.274–77)

As the moment draws near when Criseyde "moste out of the towne," all of the figurative language about love and death in the high courtly style becomes progressively invested with a stark reality that the characters themselves cannot fail to grasp, if only dimly.

The creation of physical distances in the last book brings to the narrator of the *Troilus* a perspective of finality that now *includes* history:[45]

> But Troilus, now far-wel al thi joie,
> For shaltow nevere sen hire eft in Troie!
> (V.27–28)

Nor can the characters of the poem remain blind to the macrocosmic turn of events:

> Now blisful lord, so cruel thow ne be
> Unto the blood of Troye, I praye the,
> As Juno was unto the blood Thebane,
> For which the folk of Thebes caughte hire bane.
> (V.599–602)

---

45. Patricia P. Kean, *Love Vision and Debate: Chaucer and the Making of English Poetry* (London, 1972), 1:147.

Troilus also becomes more abstract when he ponders his defeat by Cupid as a tragic example for future writers (and readers) of history ("storie"):

> Whan I the process have in my memorie
> How thow me hast wereyed on every syde,
> Men myght a book make of it, lik a storie.
> (V.583–85)

Troilus wanders reminiscing through the streets of Troy and onto the city walls, as if to retain, through the metonymy of place with experience, at least the memory of love. Chaucer is playing, here, with the traditional rhetorical technique of artificial memory by which orators used the images of physical spaces in order to remember their speeches: here, the places of Troy that call to mind Troilus's love (and the words to express that love) are not artificial but real. Moreover, these real spaces are doomed to destruction in real war. In short, by spatializing his love, Troilus underscores the tragic bond between his individual fortune and that of the city for which he is named. But Troy is now a mirror that will not reflect what Troilus desires. It is a city without love, which, in a universe of courtiers, is to say that it is without life. Criseyde's empty palace in Troy, Troilus says, might just as well fall:

> O paleys, whilom day, that now art nyght,
> Wel oughtestow to falle, and I to dye,
> Syn she is went that wont was us to gye!
> (V.544–46)

Troy's ghostly spaces are significant to Troilus only insofar as they are absences—empty signs—of his love for Criseyde:

> Fro thennesforth he rideth up and down
> And every thynge com hym to remembraunce
> As he rood forby places of the town
> In which he whilom hadde al his pleasaunce. . . .
>
> Upon the walles faste ek wolde he walke,
> And on the Grekis cost he wolde se
> And to hymself right thus he wolde talke:
> "Lo, yonder is myn owene lady free."
> (V.561–64; 666–69)

Criseyde too engages (though only briefly) in a sad metonymy of place with person from *her* side of the same landscape, as if a picture, being seen, were to see the seer seeing—though from a vanishing point. Well in advance of romantic lyric poets such as Wordsworth or Shelley, Chaucer is employing outer perspectives to illustrate a complex perspective intrinsic to the reminiscing soul. However, in this case, the lyric "I" does not seek presence-to-self; nor, for that matter, will Criseyde's search for Troilus as "other" last very long. Sincerity is no more Criseyde's trademark than it is Chaucer's:

> Ful rewfully she loked upon Troie,
> Bihelde the toures heigh and ek the halles.
> "Allas!" quod she, "the pleasaunce and the joie,
> The which now al torned into galle is,
> Have ich had ofte withinne tho yonder walles!
> O Troilus, what dostow now?"
> (V.729–34)

CONCLUSIONS: THE ENDS OF LOVE

Troilus and Troy will succumb by what is in reality a single violence whose twin visages are love and war, but right to the end of his poem, Chaucer staunchly abides by his principle of refracting the larger pattern of history through the prism of love—or, rather, through the dark mirror of love's language. In concluding his poem, Chaucer could perfectly well have fallen back on the straight narrative of Troy's destruction, and he still would have held our attention; yet it is precisely at this moment that he becomes most critical of poetic history as a *fictio rhetorica* (to use Dante's term), and critical, as well, of the reader who has indulged his desire in the love of letters. In the last book of the *Troilus*, not only is man's nature as a sign-making creature revealed in all its weaknesses and shortcomings, but in Diomedes we glimpse the potentiality of conventional signs to become vehicles of the most despicable intentions. Thus, while other poets of Troy's legend chose to glut us with the easy splendor of heroic swords and cut arteries, Chaucer remains centered upon language as a privileged field of aggression, starting with the silent calamity that begins in the dislocation of signs in the desiring psyche, where promises, meanings, values, and life itself are quite simply ignored or forgotten. Criseyde is Fortune's agent on earth, and because Criseyde is "slydinge of corage" (V.825), she will allow the wheel of history to turn without resistance: "Bothe Troilus and Troie town / Shal knotteles throughout hire herte slide" (V.768–69).

The opening assault in this war-become-words in which Troilus will be undone is made by Diomedes, a young, phallic Greek "of tonge large." The narrator hates Diomedes ("he that koude his good"); nor is Diomedes ashamed to divulge his self-seeking cynicism in his very first words: "He is a fool that wole foryete hymselve" (V.98). His initial public gesture is to lead off Criseyde's horse "by the bridel," the horse being an ageless symbol for the passionate or appetitive self, the rein being a symbol for the faculty of reason by which one governs passion. Diomedes himself will call attention to this gesture later (V.874), and Criseyde will give him her horse, which was originally Troilus's, just before "she yaf him hire herte." (V.1050). Diomedes welcomes Criseyde from the hands of Troilus with a speech "of this and that," and lest the conspicuous banality of his circumlocutions conceal from us the evil of his erotic aggression, Diomedes calls attention to his own bad faith in speaking: "I shall fynde a meene, / That she naught wite as yet shal what I mene" (V.104–05). Indeed, Diomedes is well schooled in the science of persuasion, for when he speaks of Calkas's possible "ambages," he proudly defines his terms: "That is to seyn, with double wordes slye, / Swiche as men clepen a word with two visages." (V.897–99). Diomedes is a perverter not only of loving hearts but of language:

> "Al sholde I dye, I wol hire herte seche!
> I shal namore lesen but my speche."
> (V.797–98)

Chaucer is compressing into this episode of deceitful gifts and eloquence the main points of Aeneas's narrative of the fall of Troy in Book IV of the *Aeneid*, when he tells how Sinon—a Greek who has supposedly escaped being unjustly sacrificed by his own people—convinces the Trojans that the Greeks truly wish to end the war and return home, thus preparing the Trojans to accept the wooden horse as a gift. Virgil himself hinted strongly at the penetration of the Trojan horse into the midst of the city as a grim seduction:

> "We cut through the walls and open the city's defenses.
> All gird themselves for work, lay down the rollers
> Beneath the horse's feet, throw ropes around its
> Neck. The fatal engine scales our walls,
> Pregnant with soldiers. Boys and unwed maidens
> Stand round, sing sacred songs, while each is eager

To touch the rope. Up, up, it goes and, baleful,
Slides down to rest in the middle of the city."[46]

In Chaucer's story, the tragic violence of history is gently trivialized
into gestures of false courtesy and speech, for Diomedes's lechery is
exerted strictly within the codes of courtly conduct. However, if
courtly discourse is an art of self-restraint, measure, and even ascesis,
Diomedes's discourse with Criseyde progresses like a house afire; for
in contrast with Troilus's shamefast inarticulateness (he who, even in
a pinch, "ne myghte o word for shame"; III.80), Diomedes offers
Criseyde first his "aid" (as a good knight should), then friendship, then
"service," then love—all this in less than seventy lines! Criseyde's defense in this logomachy of love is flawed from the start:

> she naught his tales herde
> But her and ther, now here a word or two.
> (V.178–79)

Chaucer now switches our attention to Troilus, who has collapsed
in his empty bed in Troy—yet another "fall"—and who begins a complaint in the mode of the traditional *ubi est* of medieval lyric. That
this collapse of Troilus in the "hertes werre" (V.234) is but a synecdoche for the larger workings of Fortune in the Trojan War is suggested
not only by Troilus's dream that "he sholde falle depe / From heighe o-
lofte" but also by his image of the "fir and flaumbe funeral / In which
my body brennen shal to glede" (V.303–04), which augurs the fate of
nothing less than a whole city of lovers about to be sacked and burned.
In hearing of Troilus's dream, Pandarus (like Pertelote in the "Nun's
Priest's Tale") dismisses these prophetic signs as unworthy of credence:

> Allas, allas, that so noble a creature
> As is man shal dreden swich ordure!
> (V.384–85)

Pandarus's counsel is that Troilus should forget these supernatural
signs—these "mervelous signals" as Chaucer calls them in *The Hous
of Fame* (459)—by rehearsing former adventures of lust:

46. Virgil, *Aeneid* II.234–240, trans. L. R. Lind (Bloomington: Indiana Univ.
Press, 1962), 29.

Ris, lat us speke of lusty lif in Troie
That we han led, and forth the tyme dryve.
(V.393–94)

Since medieval sign theory necessarily involves a problematics of memory (corporeal signs serve to recall—*recordare*—to us the incorporeal images residing in our memory), Pandarus's advice to Troilus that he "foryete or oppresse" the cause of this languor touches upon a notion that is implicit in the *Troilus*: namely, that the tragic violence of history originates in that most human flaw of forgetfulness. Dame Philosophy, by contrast, teaches—above all—remembrance, as we read in Chaucer's translation of Boethius:

> For certes the body, bryngyng the weighte of foryetynge, ne hath nat chased out of your thought all the cleernesse of your knowing. And if it be so that the muse and doctrine of Plato syngeth soth, al that every wight leerneth, he ne doth no thing elles than but recordeth, as men recorden thinges that ben foryeten. (*Boèce* II, *prosa* 12)

Boethius agrees with Lady Philosophy, adding that we forget knowledge a first time when our soul is joined to a body, and a second time whenever the soul is overwhelmed by passion. Fortune and Criseyde are both figures who promulgate the principle of forgetting: one at the level of empires, the other at the level of individuals. Moreover, since man is a creature who knows and communicates only through signs, it is through willful negation or misuse of signs that Criseyde "forgets" Troilus, as when she gives to Diomedes the very brooch that Troilus earlier had given her "for remembraunce of me" (V.1691). But it is especially in written signs, whose "grammatical" function in the Middle Ages was also held to be commemorative, that Criseyde transcribes (in her letter to Troilus) what is obviously a chronicle of amnesis. In *written* speech too is change:

> This Troilus this lettre thoughte al straunge,
> When he it saugh, and sorwfullich he sighte.
> Hym thoughte it lik a kalendes of chaunge.
> (V.1632–34)

But then, perhaps the "original" sin of forgetting lies with Troilus himself, not for "placing his faith in the wrong woman or in a bad woman," as Charles Muscatine has written, "but in the fact that he places his faith in a thing which can reflect back to him the image of that faith and yet be incapable of sustaining it."[47]

However one chooses to diagnose the human failures of Troilus and Criseyde, in my opinion the principal interest of the last book of the *Troilus*, if not of the poem as a whole, is the remarkable detail with which Chaucer reveals the "slydynge" of Criseyde's unrecording "corage" (V.825) beneath Diomedes's verbal onslaught, and it is clear that this drama of adultery may be considered the narrative surface of a deeper transgression of language itself, considered the living expression of the social order.

Diomedes is a practicing semiologist and a devil, and his cunning is never concealed from us, as he plots

> How he may best, with shortest taryinge,
> Into his net Criseydes herte bringe.
> To this entent he koude nevere fyne;
> To fisshen hire, he leyde out hook and lyne.
> (V.774–77)

Moreover, the bait that these lovers cast before each other is not always just verbal but includes body signs as well. Criseyde, for instance, lets her hair tumble "down by hire coler at hire bak behynde," and though the history of epic hair has yet to be written, it seems obvious to me that this is a symbol of potential dissoluteness—in contrast, for example, with Spenser's Alma, the lady of Temperance, whose "yellow golden heare / Was trimly wouen, and in tresses wrought" (*Faerie Queene* II.ix.19). Nor should we discount Criseyde's "browes joyneden yfere" as a sign of a lecherous disposition, if Curry's theories about the iconography of medieval portraiture are to be believed.[48] Such details are extravagant examples of what in rhetoric John of Garland (VI.369) calls *notacio*, "when inner nature is described by signs" (*Cum Natura Certis Describitur Signis*). Diomedes, on his side, has mastered all the *visibilia* of passion, even converting what are ordinarily infallible *natural* signs into *arbitrary* signs that are deceptive:

> And with that word he gan to waxen red,
> And in his speche a litel wight he quok,

47. Charles Muscatine, *Chaucer and the French Tradition* (Berkeley: Univ. of California Press, 1960), 164.

48. See Robinson's note on verse V.813, p. 834, of his edition of Chaucer's works (n. 22, above).

> And caste asyde a little wight his hed,
> And stynte a while; and afterward he wok,
> And sobreliche on hire he threw his lok.
> (V.925–29)

The principal assaults of Diomedes are verbal, though, and the principal capitulations of Criseyde are in kind. Thus, after their first meeting, Criseyde "graunted, on the morwe, at his requeste, / For to speken with hym at the leeste" (V.949–50). Though her motive is supposedly both to refute before Diomedes her father's predictions that Troy must fall and to defend the Troilus that she loves from comparison with any Greek, the fact is that she only praises her father's wisdom, and her refutation of pejorative comparisons of Troilus only turns into flattery of Diomedes: "That Grekis ben of heigh condicioun, / I, woot ek wel. . . . And that ye koude wel yowre lady serve, / I trowe ek wel, hire thank for to deserve" (V.967–68; 972–73). And now her flattery, which has perhaps been undeliberate, gives way to a very deliberate, whopping lie: though she admits to Diomedes that she loved her first husband, now conveniently dead, she denies having loved Troilus.

Or is it not conceivable that Criseyde's "lie" is a revelation of a truth that is only more shocking, that she never did love him?

> "But as to spek of love, ywis," she seyde,
> "I hadde a lord, to whom I wedded was,
> The whos myn herte, al was, til that he deyde;
> And other love, as help me now Pallas,
> Ther in my herte nys, ne nevere was."
> (V.974–78)

It is entirely in line with Chaucer's metalinguistic priorities that Criseyde's first overt act of infidelity—the act that makes possible all others—should be an act of speech rather than one of a more carnal sort. Chaucer has given us a vivid anatomy of deception and lying, both of its motives and its potential effects, and his fascination with such speech acts in the *Troilus* (as well in the *Canterbury Tales*) is quite simply a medieval poet's manner of exploring, within the poetic conventions given to him by the "authors" of the past, problems similar to those that had preoccupied churchmen ever since St. Augustine—among them, the problem of lying. When Chaucer's critics say that he "medievalizes" the story of Troy, they should also take cognizance of an archaic Platonic impulse in Chaucer—evident already in the *Book of the Duchess*—to explore (not logically, but through strategies of poetic composition) the danger that conventional poetic signs will denature, falsify, or subvert the truth of being.

It is precisely with regard to the relationship between discourse and "truth" that we shall consider Chaucer's rhetorical strategies at the very end of the *Troilus*. "Truth" is a problem pertinent not just to ethical dilemmas within the poem but also to the very problematical status of the poem itself as a *fictio rhetorica*. How can "truth" inhabit a poetic discourse that systematically veils truth? This is a question that Chaucer seems to have anticipated, as we shall see, but let us make a few remarks about the very word "truth" as a noun or substantive.

It is well known that grammatical theory in the Middle Ages always remained rooted in ontology: nouns *name* substances, but names do not tell us about the manner in which these substances exist: to do that is the role of the predicate.[49] The noun "truth" refers, then, to something timeless, to some God-given spiritual ideal; the way in which truth is manifested must be expressed by verbs forming the predicate. But how could a moral poet such as Chaucer take it upon himself to name, without compromising them, all of man's highest ideals in a narrative syntax that treats not of God's ways but of sinning man's? How can the syntax of historical narrative complete itself except at the expense of everything a priori that is spiritual, perfect, or universal—all the more since the very economy of narrative itself involves reversals, negations, or transformations of whatever material is subjected to structuration in narrative? In a suggestive article, the late Adrienne R. Lockhart shows, precisely, how ethical absolutes that are named in the *Troilus*—*honour, worthinesse, manhod, gentillesse,* and *trouthe*—do indeed become subject to a "pattern of semantic deterioration" and a "debasement of meaning" as Chaucer carries these universal moral values into the accidents of mortal affairs:

> On the aesthetic level, the artist who translates the ideal into the actual, who shows the working out of a set of abstract moral or theoretical ideals in a concrete realistic situation, must show the debasement of these ideals, since their achievement is not available to fallible human beings. The behaviour of characters in a work of medieval art is, from the point of

49. Bursill-Hall, 118–19.

view of the audience, under the judgment of an ideal Christian standard; the artist's creation is under the judgment of the ideal Creation by God.[50]

Lockhart quite justly sees "trouthe" as "the most central but the most difficult concept of all," and she concludes that the "pattern of semantic deterioration" she observes in the *Troilus* is "a metaphor for the artistic process itself; in that sense, the structural pattern of debasement of meaning parallels the central moral issue of *Troilus and Criseyde*, as it is explicitly stated in the epilogue."[51]

These profound insights are pertinent to Chaucer's strategies at the very end of the *Troilus*. In making "trouthe" the central issue of his poem, Chaucer invites us to judge not only his all-too-human characters but also the very language of poetry itself, thanks to which these fictive characters "exist." But is poetic discourse really competent to indict and judge itself, without promulgating new and perhaps even more serious errors?

In the light of this question we may understand why, instead of concluding his narrative of Troilus's ordeals in a world of speaking lovers where all signs carry the flaws of the mortals who employ them, Chaucer radically breaks with the story of Troy itself and depicts Troilus in the "holoughnesse of the eighthe spere" (V.1809), where he sees face to face (with "ful avysment"—that is, beyond the darkness and enigmas of mortal knowing—into the *primum mobile*. In the light of this same question we may also understand the sequence of speech acts by which Chaucer peels back the concentric layers of fiction that correspond to the different spheres making up the onionlike universe of his poem.

One will recall that from his sphere in heaven, Troilus laughs at the woe of mortals: "And dampned al oure werk that foloweth so / The blynde lust, the which that may nat laste, / And sholden al oure herte on heven caste" (V.1823–25). In damning *our* work, Troilus is in effect damning the "I-thou" of the fictive pact between narrator and reader, an unholy pact that has too long distracted us from less erroneous modes of apprehending truth. Suddenly the narrator exhorts "us," the unregenerate lovers of the "worldes brotelnesse," the "yonge fresshe folkes he or she," to renounce *our* vanity and to love the God in whose

50. Adrienne R. Lockhart, "Semantic, Moral, and Aesthetic Degeneration in *Troilus and Criseyde,*" *Chaucer Review* 8 (1973): 101.
51. Lockhart, 116–17.

image *we* are made. Then he condemns the "rascal" gods that the poets of antiquity worshipped and the "olde clerkis speche / In poetrie" (V.1894–95) that separates men from the truth.

Having dispersed, now, not only the fiction of his poem but also the fictions of narrator and audience, Chaucer addresses in their place the truly existing "moral Gower," another English moral poet who sought, as Gower himself put it, "the common vois which mai nought lie"[52] and who languished for an unrhetorical world of proper significations where, Gower says (vv.106–14):

> The citees knewen no debat
> The people stod in obeissance
> Under the reule of governance,
> And pes, which ryhtwisness keste,
> With charite tho stod in reste:
> Of mannes herte the corage
> Was schewed thanne in the visage;
> The word was lich to the conceite
> Withoute semblant of deceite.

Next, Chaucer addresses "philosophical Strode," an English logician—that is, a man whose intellectual goal was by definition to restore truth to the speech of man. Chaucer asks these two Englishmen

> To vouchen sauf, there nede is, to correcte,
> Of youre benignites and zeles goode.
> (V.1858–59)

Finally, Chaucer directly addresses the source of all true language, the *logos* itself in the person of Christ, who is a signifier consubstantial with the God he perfectly signifies, and whose triune mystery is an enigma that is not poetic (hence, apocryphal) but divine. *Trouthe*, then, lies less in worldly things to be spoken or learned than in a movement, a progress leading first from poetic fable to moral history, next to philosophy, and finally from prayer to illumination. While it is true that this stanza in the *Troilus* contains lines almost directly translated by Chaucer from Dante's *Paradiso* XIV.28–32, and while both poets are demarcating the border between rational and divine illumination, the difference between the circumstances of the two utterances is consid-

---

52. John Gower, *Confessio Amantis*, Prologue, v. 124, ed. G. C. Macaulay (Oxford: Clarendon Press, 1903).

erable: Dante's vision is still included in his poetic fiction, while that of Chaucer's narrator follows his rejection of poetry as a vehicle of grace. As in Augustine's *Confessions*, the conclusion of Chaucer's *Troilus* lies not in the completion of a fictive narrative sequence but rather in a sequence of distinct speech acts that break from narrative itself and coax the believing reader to find the unmediated presence of the "uncircumscript" illuminating word through prayer.

CHAPTER 10

Edmund Spenser, Troy,
and the Humanist Ideology
of Translation

 $\mathbf{F}$or *this reason I encourage all,
who have the capacity, to wrest from the now failing grasp of Greece
the renown won from this field of study and transfer it [transferant] to
this city, just as our ancestors by their indefatigable zeal transferred
here all the other really desirable avenues to renown. . . .*

*But once these studies are transferred to ourselves, we shall have
no need even of Greek libraries, in which there is an endless number
of books due to the crowd of writers, for the same things are said by
many since the day they crammed the world with books.* (Cicero,
Tusculan Disputations)

*For marke all aiges: looke upon the whole course of both the Greeke
and Latin tonge, and ye shal surely finde that, whan apte and goode
wordes began to be neglected, and properties of those two tonges to be
confounded, then also began ill deedes to spring, strange maners to
oppresse good orders, new and fond opinions to striue with olde and
trewe doctrine, first in Philosophie and after in Religion, right iudge-
ment of all things to be peruerted, and so vertue with learning is con-
temned, and studye left off: of ill thoughts cummeth peruerse iudge-
ment, of ill deedes springeth lewede taulke.* (Roger Ascham)

I shall end this book not with a summary of what has preceded, but by
exploring certain cultural thresholds that were crossed by the Humanists concerning theories of language and, more specifically, the ideology of translation. I shall hope that the sharp contrast of historical

attitudes and artistic reflexes that will emerge from this study of a Humanist text at its most optimistic moment will provide interesting hindsight upon medieval semiotics and poetics as we have studied them in the previous chapters, and I shall hope that this Janus-like chapter will serve as an appropriate conclusion to a book whose principal terrain is medieval culture.

I shall begin with some practical remarks about a broad shift in attitudes towards translation that occurred in England at the end of the Middle Ages, then I shall attempt to illustrate a remarkable enlargement in (or deepening of) the notion of translation that occurred in the Renaissance by discussing psychological and ethical questions raised by the rival versions of the "history" of Troy and Rome narrated by Paridell and Britomart in Book III of Spenser's *Faerie Queene.*

I shall suppose that, like Chaucer, Spenser was lucid about the ideological and ethical implications of renewing in his national vernacular—of "Englishing"—those legends drawn from classical antiquity that were paradigms of the historical process as well, and I shall assume that Spenser's awareness of the special poetic challenge posed by the tragic lesson of Troy shaped his basic strategies of composition. Spenser was the first English poet to explore seriously the psychic factors underlying the Humanist ethics of translation (in an enlarged sense), and I shall suggest that certain aspects of Stoic epistemology that had become current in the Humanist environment of the sixteenth century were incorporated by Spenser into a bold and positive statement about poetry as a responsible mode of translation.

TRANSLATIO, BEING AND BECOMING

If translation in the Middle Ages and the Renaissance may be said by us to have a history, writers of those periods saw history itself as a process of translation: hence, the twin doctrines of *translatio imperii* and *translatio studii* in medieval and Renaissance culture.

Although Chrétien de Troyes had asserted an unambiguous confidence in his culture as the heir of Greek and Roman *chevalerie* and *clergie,*[1] and although Chartrian platonism had exalted music and poetry as divine creative forces within the cosmos,[2] vernacular poets of

1. Michelle A. Freeman, *The Poetics of "Translatio Studii" and Conjointure: Chrétien de Troyes's "Cligès"* (Lexington, Ky.: French Forum, 1979).
2. Brian Stock, *Myth and Science in the Twelfth Century: A Study of Bernard Sylvester* (Princeton, N.J.: Princeton Univ. Press, 1972), 259, 264.

following generations were cautious about defending their *fabulae* and their *matière* against the hostility of the Church. Anxious about enduring charges (established by Augustine) that poets are liars and "theologians" of the city of man, or about the claims (solidified by Thomas Aquinas) that poetic discourse is at best inferior to that of philosophy,[3] medieval secular poets tended either to inscribe some kind of strategical, active self-doubt into their poetic ambitions or finally to retract their art, as Chaucer did (whether sincerely or not).

As we saw in the previous chapter, Chaucer's *Troilus* is laced with borrowings from works in foreign tongues, both ancient and contemporary, yet the diachronic and synchronic intertextualities are not clearly delineated, nor do they express a simple ideological grid. For, we learn at the poem's end, though classical culture had produced the wisdom and eloquence of Greece and Rome, these now fallen cultures had suffered the limits of being pagan. Inversely, though contemporary vernacular culture may have become debauched (and unworthy of the classical *auctores*), these newer cultures could nevertheless count upon, and invoke, the spiritual presence of Christ as redeeming *logos*. To the extent that it could be construed as an emulation in English culture of a pre-Christian, tragic legend of erotic love, the *Troilus* invited concern over the possibility that by its very success, such art might promulgate yet other cycles of pride and destruction, perhaps in England: hence, Chaucer's strategy of *conversio*, at the poem's end, to the *logos* and the economy of the Trinity.

However, the *Troilus* does not allow us to infer that the seed of cultural destruction is sowed (rather, transplanted) by infatuation with the sublime scandals of classical antiquity alone. On the contrary, the *Troilus* is a careful indictment of infatuation with *contemporary* courtly poetic conventions as well, especially those of France and Italy, whose poets were also emulating the triumphs—and the vanities—of classical eloquence. For instance, Chaucer surely expected his more astute readers to recognize that the *Canticus Troili* (I.400–420), in which Troilus consents to love Criseyde (hence, freely to will upon himself his tragic destiny), is a close translation of Petrarch's sonnet 88. The same readers would also see what is ominous in the narrator's boast that, "despite our tongues difference," his English song is perfectly adequate to the original avowal of love, which would have oc-

3. Joseph Anthony Mazzeo, *Medieval Cultural Tradition in Dante's "Comedy"* (Ithaca, N.Y.: Cornell Univ. Press, 1960), 67–69.

curred neither in Italian nor in Latin (the language of "my auctor called Lollius," Chaucer's fictive source), but in Greek: "I dar wel sey, in al that Troilus / Seyde in his song, loo! every word right thus / As I shal seyn." (I.396–98).[4] Clearly, if Chaucer's narrator claims to reproduce in *English* a *Greek* song derived from a *Latin* source by rewriting an *Italian* sonnet by Petrarch, the act of translating such "matter" involves far more than the neutral task of overcoming the gap of intelligibility between two (or four) distinct historical languages; it involves, rather, an underlying historical *ethics* of speech (*sermo*). To perceive this is to understand the process of historical differentiation in language (*lingua*) in the first place.

Similarly, we are surely to understand that the narrator's Ovidian infatuation, in the *Hous of Fame*, with Dido's cause, and the conspicuous disproportion in the resulting version of Virgil's *Aeneid* are misuses of poetic language and translations of improper fame—indeed, of infamy—into English culture.[5] In the *Legend of Good Women*, "Geoffrey," the translator/narrator, is rebuked by the God of Love for having "translated" (v. 255) the *Roman de la Rose*, which speaks disparagingly of women, and also for having "mad in English ek the bok / How that Crisseyde Troylus forsok" (v. 264–65). Though we as readers are not expected to endorse Alceste's defense of Geoffrey on the grounds that he simply took no heed of what he translated and "nyste what he seyde" (v. 345), this mock inquisition does nevertheless show that serious moral arguments could be brought to bear upon the wanton translator of alien texts: indeed, in this case, the narrator's "penance" is to translate from "bokes old *or* newe" (v. 274; my italics) yet more legends—this time legends of classical women who were virtuous and true.

In other words, Chaucer saw the justification for translation as a problem belonging to a "general" ethics of speech that emphasizes choices of both proper content and style in the process of translation. Moreover, as I suggested in the previous chapter, the style to which Chaucer addresses himself in the *Troilus* involves what rhetoricians of his age called the "high" or "noble" style, one marked not only by a propensity to deal with noble people and noble subjects (e.g., knights

4. Geoffrey Chaucer, *Troilus and Criseyde*, in *The Works of Geoffrey Chaucer*, ed. F. N. Robinson (Boston: Houghton Mifflin, 1957). All Chaucer references are to this edition and are included in my text.

5. Eugene Vance, "Chaucer's House of Fame and the Poetics of Inflation," *Boundary 2* 7 (1979): 17–39.

and love) but also by a propensity to exploit rhetorical tropes, or figures of thought, in its elocution. The generic term for figures of thought was, of course, *translatio* (or else *transsumptio*, which is semantically very close), the act of producing utterances in which an improper signified has been substituted for a proper one. While rhetoricians such as Geoffrey of Vinsauf could exalt the "translations" of *ornatus difficilis*, or figurative speech, as a source of esthetic delight,[6] in the *Troilus*, Chaucer emphasizes the subversive potential of *translatio* when it infiltrates the conventions of ordinary language, whether through the moral blindness of its speaking heroes or through the outright malice of its villains. The subsequent *translatio* of the "original" *Troilus* "out of Latyn in my tongue" by the narrator is merely an extension of its inaugural discursive profligacy. Because Troy is a city whose leaders have too wholly given themselves over to the metaphorical "hertes werre"—indeed, to metaphor itself—Troy is a body politic that must inevitably share the catastrophe of the loving and speaking hero who is its namesake.

Moreover, since the narrator of the *Troilus* is as much a fictive *persona* as any of the other characters in the tale he tells, the narrator undergoes a vicarious tragic experience of his own, one that leads to a change of heart with regard to his relationship, as an English poet, to his inherited material. Early in the poem, the narrator is confident of his understanding of the past, and almost patronizing when he speaks of classical eloquence; by the end of the poem he has become a far less proud translator, now disavowing emulation of the *auctores* of antiquity:

> Go, litel bok, go, litel my tragedye. . . .
> But litel book, no makyng thow n'envie,
> But subgit be to alle poesye;
> And kis the steppes, where as thow seest pace
> Virgile, Ovide, Omer, Lucan, and Stace.
> (V.1786–92)

He is equally concerned about the viability of his own poem in an English that is diverse in form and unstable, at least by comparison with the institution of classical *grammatica*:

6. Geoffrey of Vinsauf, *Poetria nova*, vv.765–1093, in *Les Arts poétiques du XIIe et du XIIIe siècle: Recherches et documents sur la technique littéraire du moyen âge*, ed. Edmond Faral (Paris: Champion, 1924); see also Julia Garcia Ebel, "Studies in Elizabethan Translation,, Ph.D. diss., Columbia University, 1964.

And for ther is so gret diversite
In Englissh and in writyng of oure tonge,
So preye I God that non myswrite the,
Ne the mysmetre for defaute of tonge,
And red wherso thow be, or elles songe,
That thow be understonde, God I biseche!
(V.1793–98)

However, just as Troilus must die to this "litel spot of erthe" (V.1815) in order to enjoy, with "ful avysement," the marvels of the eighth sphere (V.1811), so too the narrator must ultimately die to "old clerkis speche / In poetrie" (V.1854–55), and he enjoins his readers as well to cast their "heart's visage" to God and to espouse Christ as *logos*: that is, Christ as perfect translator of God's will to man.

TRANSLATION AND THE BODY POLITIC

Chaucer's attitudes about translation reflect a deeply entrenched medieval consciousness of two cultural legacies. On the one hand, there was the bitter lesson of Rome, which had succeeded Greece as the Troja Nova, appropriating as well the prestige of Greek culture and eloquence, only to fall in its turn—confronting medieval vernacular cultures with the painful prospect that history may be a cyclical process which cannot be arrested by human volition. On the other hand, there was the Judeo-Christian doctrine of history as a future-oriented, linear process of fall and redemption, whose linguistic equivalent was expressed in the opposition between the dispersion of meaning that occurred with the destruction of Babel and the reintegration of meaning through transcendence at Pentecost when the Holy Ghost appeared as a fiery tongue to all the different tribes of the Jews and imparted to them a common understanding of the resurrected Christ that transcended their separate historical languages.[7]

Given that true knowledge is a priori and is disclosed to us only from within, and given that the language of intellection is mental, not corporeal, it follows for St. Augustine (*De doctrina christiana* II.5–6) that such knowledge may be summoned from memory (though not communicated, strictly speaking) by signifiers of any conventional language (Hebrew, Greek, Latin). It follows, too, that the language of

7. George Steiner, *After Babel: Aspects of Language and Translation* (Oxford: Oxford Univ. Press, 1975), contains a useful bibliography.

the Bible may be translated into any historical language without destroying its original meaning, which is separate from any language: God will illuminate from within those who read with a properly directed will.

Despite the coherence of such reasoning, medieval writers (with the exception of French courtly writers of the twelfth century) were reluctant to proclaim their vernaculars as unequivocally legitimate languages, at least as compared with the sacred languages of Hebrew, Greek, and Latin. So long as political ideology in the Middle Ages was dominated by Augustinian neoplatonism, and specifically by the dichotomy between the city of man and the city of God, the claims of vernacular language on the intellect were no more worthy than those carnal (and poetic) desires that the vernacular was most wont to express. Just as the city of man is a place of false abundance, so too temporal signs are anything but the habitat of truth or beauty. Medieval Christian platonism was a religion stressing transcendence and resurrection, not immanence and incarnation. As we saw in chapter 2, Augustine says that if a line of poetry happens to be beautiful, such beauty is not in the actual sounds that we hear; these are evanescent, while the cause of their beauty is not. Nor do poets themselves create the beauty of their poetry. The beauty of poetry lies in the art of poetry itself, considered as a set of immutable, universal laws, and the immaterial beauty of these laws is at best only faintly apprehended in a material poetic utterance in this or that historical language.

Changes in the ideology of translation were closely linked to changes in political attitudes in the Middle Ages. With the assimilation of Aristotle's *Politics,* which was well underway by the time of the appearance of Aquinas's commentary upon that text, came new political attitudes emphasizing the necessity and validity of the art of politics. Man, St. Thomas says, following Aristotle, is by nature a political animal, and Aristotle and Thomas both insist on the primacy of the order of language in the political order. Other animals (e.g., bees and ants) may be social, too, but no other animals have speech. Speech is distinguished, moreover, from voice. Animals have voices—lions roar and dogs bark—with which to express their passions, but they have no speech to express their reason and therefore can express no virtues that are proper alone to man. Thomas writes:

> Since language is given to man by nature, therefore, and since language is ordered to this, that men communicate with one

another as regards the useful and the harmful, the just and the unjust, and other such things, it follows, from the fact that nature does nothing in vain, that men naturally communicate with one another in reference to these things. But communication in reference to these things is what makes a household and a city. Therefore, man is naturally a domestic and political animal.[8]

By the time of Chaucer's death, a new ideology of translation was well in the making on the Continent, and this is reflected in changes in terminology expressing the idea of translation. According to Gianfranco Folena, who has written a beautifully documented essay on this subject, the terms *interpretatio* and *translatio* had both been common during the Middle Ages, though the latter had become more prominent at the end.[9] *Interpretare* is the Latin translation of the Greek *hermeneuin*, and Folena believes that both the Greek and Latin terms apply above all to translation as an oral performance in which two interlocutors communicate through an interpreter. However, a more recent study of *hermeneuein* by Jean Pépin suggests that such a limitation does not really hold, and Jean-Luc Nancy has widened the philological debate even more by situating *hermeneuin* in a philosophical debate renewed by Martin Heidegger.[10] Moreover, one will recall that in Augustine's *De doctrina christiana*, it is clear that *interpretatio* applies both to the written *translatio* of the Scriptures and to the scientific reconstruction of its figurative meanings (*translationes*), both acts being, as Jerome had put it, *non verbum de verbo, sed sensum de sensu exprimere*.[11]

When *translatio* and its grammatical derivatives became current among the scholastics, it denoted the act of diligent translation from Greek or Arabic sources into Latin. Later, when it came to include, as

8. Thomas Aquinas, *In libros politicorum Aristotelis expositio*, ed. R. M. Spiazzi, O.P. (Turin: Marietti, 1951); bk. I, lesson 1, 11, trans. Ernest L. Fortin and Peter D. O'Neill, in *Medieval Political Philosophy: A Sourcebook*, ed. Ralph Lerner and Muhsin Mahdi (Glencoe, Ill.: Free Press, 1963), 310–11.

9. Gianfranco Folena, "'Volgarizzare' e 'tradurre,'" in *La traduzione: Saggi e studi*, ed. Centro per lo studio dell'insegnamento all'estero dell'italiano, Universita degli studi de Trieste (Trieste: Lint, 1973), 59–120, esp. 79.

10. Jean Pépin, "L'Herméneutique ancienne," *Poétique* 23 (1975); 291–300. See also Gabriel Nuchelmans, *Theories of the Proposition: Ancient and Medieval Conceptions of the Bearers of Truth and Falsity* (Amsterdam: North Holland, 1973), 98, 123, 136; and Jean-Luc Nancy, *Le Partage des voix* (Paris: Galilée, 1982).

11. Jerome, *Epistola* II.3.133, as cited by Folena, 63.

well, the act of translating from one vernacular to another, *translatio* still implied a labor of fidelity to the signified rather than emulation of the signifier, or what we would now call "artistic" translation.[12] Around the time of Chaucer's death, however, the Latin *translatare* began to give way to the neologism *traducere*, as well as to the vernacular Italian *tradurre*. According to Folena, this was because of the specific initiative of the Florentine Humanist Leonardo Bruni, who needed a term more energetic and dynamic than *transferre* and its derivatives, a term that would underscore notions of individuality and personal originality, in keeping with the new spirit of civic Humanism.[13]

Translation became a matter of doctrinal controversy in ecclesiastical politics as well, and Erasmus was at the center of the polemics:

> Indeed, I disagree very much with those who are unwilling that Holy Scripture, translated into the vulgar tongue, be read by the uneducated. I would that even the lowliest women read the Gospels and the Pauline Epistles. And I would that they were translated into all languages so that they could be read and understood not only by Scots and Irish, but also by Turks and Saracens. Would that, as a result, the farmer sing some portion of them at the plow, the weaver hum some parts of them to the movement of his shuttle, the traveller lighten the weariness of the journey with stories of this kind![14]

What is more, the new philological rigor of Humanists such as Erasmus often seemed to flaunt the medieval reverence (ill informed though it often was) for convention. A case in point is Erasmus's translation of the Greek *logos* in John 1 by *sermo* instead of *verbum*, a crux of translation that also happens to capture the very ideology of translation that motivated Erasmus to translate the gospel in the first place: following Augustine, Erasmus associated *verbum* with the inner activity of the

12. Folena, 68.

13. Folena, 102. For a historical discussion of Humanist ideology and translation, see Hans Baron, *Crisis of the Early Italian Renaissance*, 2nd ed. (Princeton, N.J.: Princeton Univ. Press, 1966), ch. 15: "Florentine Humanism and the Volgare in the Quatrocento," 332–53. See also Charles Trinkaus, *"In Our Image and Likeness": Humanity and Divinity in Italian Humanist Thought* (London: Constable, 1970), 596–601.

14. Desiderius Erasmus, *Paracelsis*, in *Christian Humanism and the Reformation: Selected Writings*, ed. and trans. John C. Olin (New York: Harper & Row, 1965), 96–97.

soul struggling to extricate itself from the world, while *sermo* signified for him a notion of divine oratory as colloquial fraternalism in Christ, expressed not only through the inner man but through the institutions of national grammars as well.[15]

"Openness" of the Scriptures became a new goal and could be pursued just as well in English as in Latin—all the more since, as John Purvey is believed to have put it (c. 1385–90) in the prologue to the second recension of the Wycliffite Bible, "The common Latin bibles have more need to be corrected, as many as I have seen in my life, than hath the English bible late translated."[16] It was supposed that translation would not only disseminate the treasures of both classical and Christian culture to the common man but would bring abundance to vernacular language itself and make it fecund. Quintilian's term *copia*, accordingly, displaced the medieval *amplificatio* as a rhetorical term, and as Erasmus wrote in his treatise on rhetorical *copia* (which was dedicated to John Colet for use in St. Paul's School in London), "There is nothing more admirable or more splendid than a speech with a rich *copia* of thoughts and words overflowing in a golden stream."[17] The goal of *copia* is especially enhanced, Erasmus believed, by the practice of translation:

> We will greatly increase the copia of our speech by translation from Greek authors, because the Greek language is especially rich in both word and thought. Moreover, it will occasionally be very useful to emulate (*certare*) them by paraphrasing. It will be of especial help to rewrite the verses of poets in prose and on the other hand, to bind prose in meter, and put the same theme into first one and then another type of verse. (*De copia* I.ix)

Translation was part of the Humanist cult of *verbal* opulence which coincided with the recognition that *material* bounteousness, "the art

15. For an excellent discussion of Erasmus's theories of language, including the notion of translation, see Marjorie O'Rourke Boyle, *Erasmus on Language and Method in Theology* (Toronto: Univ. of Toronto Press, 1977). The polemics that Erasmus stirred up by translating *logos* as *sermo*, discussed by Boyle in great detail, is essential to an understanding of the Humanist ideology of translation.

16. John Purvey (?), "On Translating the Bible," as published in *Fifteenth Century Prose and Verse*, ed. Alfred W. Pollard (Westminster, 1903), 195.

17. Desiderius Erasmus, *De duplici copia verborum ac rerum*, trans. Donald King and H. David Rix, *On copia of Words and Things* (Milwaukee: Marquette Univ. Press, 1963), 11; hereafter cited in my text as *De copia*.

of getting wealth," could be a natural and legitimate objective of the political arts.[18] As Nancy Struever writes concerning the material ideology of Coluccio Salutati:

> An essential characteristic of eloquence (*facundia*) is richness, and richness is not only a copiousness but a fluidity of form to correspond to the infinite variety of human nature to which one must appeal. Moreover, both Humanists and Sophists justify richness as a manifestation of high human potential rather than as necessarily immoral or voluptuous. . . . Richness is not meretricious ornament; nudity in discourse as well as dress is a false choice, unnecessary self-sacrifice.[19]

Moreover, richness of discourse was now thought to reside not merely in the signified, or the *sententia*, but in the very fabric of the signifier, in the *verbum* as a production of material sound: hence the value of poetry as a privileged resource of culture. Struever says of the early Humanists:

> Just as Gorgias emphasized the incantatory value of sound, and the affective pleasures of fictional imagery, of deception (*apate*), so all the major figures of Trecento Humanism engage in a defense of the sensual and imaginative pleasures of discourse as both functional and meaningful. The prototype here as in other aspects of Humanism is Petrarch. Since the chief sensual pleasure of language is sound, it is significant that this is precisely Petrarch's special injunction to readers: "*non modo corde concepte, sed etiam ore prolate*" (*Fam.* I.9–11).[20]

Such a reversal of attitudes made poets confident that poetic perfection was a legitimate goal. As Struever writes, "The unity of a language is its unique value; Bruni argues that each language has its own perfection because each has its own perspective. And the unity first plotted

18. Aristotle, *Politics* I.7. On the notion of verbal *copia*, see the following by Terence C. Cave: "Mythes de l'abondance et de la privation chez Ronsard," *Cahiers de l'association internationale des études françaises* 25 (1973): 247–60; "Copia and cornucopia," *French Renaissance Studies, 1540–1570: Humanism and the Encyclopedia*, ed. Peter Sharratt (Edinburgh: Edinburgh Univ. Press, 1976), 52–69; *The Cornucopian Text* (Oxford: Oxford Univ. Press, 1979).

19. Nancy S. Struever, *The Language of History in the Renaissance: Rhetoric and Historical Consciousness in Florentine Humanism* (Princeton, N.J.: Princeton Univ. Press, 1970), 57.

20. Struever, 47–48.

through rhetorical analysis becomes a unified culture; Poggio Bracciolini fits literary remains and physical ruins into one symbolic whole; the total symbolic heritage of forms, designs, words becomes historical evidence."[21]

Emulation of the signifier (as well as of the signified) began to alter the nature and purpose of translation, especially in the disciplines of poetry, rhetoric, and history, as opposed to philosophy and theology. This new priority corresponded to a new attitude among the architects of Humanist vernacular culture, who no longer considered the cyclical pattern of *translatio imperii* and the natural flux of the creation as ontological conditions necessarily to be bewailed or transcended, but rather as *positive* dimensions of man's potential for individual and social fulfillment. A new and very unmedieval affirmation of the historical here and now of the individual translator's own language—"la propriete et le naïf de la Langue an laquele il translate," to use a phrase of Jacques Peletier's cited by Terence Cave[22]—entailed, as well, a dialectical sense of the "there" and "then" specific to the original text, which had been lacking in Chaucer, as we saw in chapter 9.

This dialectical sense of cultural alterity summoned, in the translator, far more than knowledge of another language and a grasp of the *sententia*: it summoned an artistic performance in its own right. As Terence Cave writes of the French Humanists, "The translation theory of Dolet and the rest, which rejected literalness as inconsistent with the *propriété* of the vernacular, is here given a new direction: paraphrase-translation (directed toward *sententiae* rather than *verba*) has been relegated to a kind of propaedeutic function, and *elocutio* begins to be explored as the domain of positive difference, within which imitation will deploy itself centrifugally."[23]

In England one finds a perfect contrast between late medieval and Humanist perspectives on translation in the separate efforts of William Caxton and Gavin Douglas to translate the *Aeneid*. Caxton's "translation" is not of the Latin text but of a footloose French paraphrase that is already heavily medievalized in its way of describing sentiments and events. Moreover, Caxton's perspective upon English as a host language is scarcely more definite than his sense of the "original." Caxton writes as follows concerning the gap of understanding, first, between

21. Struever, 70.
22. Cave, *Cornucopian Text*, 58.
23. Cave, *Cornucopian Text*, 62.

Old English and the English "now used," and second, between the English "now used" and the English he spoke as a child:

> And certainly it was wreton in suche wyse it was more lyke to dutche than englysshe; I coude not reduce ne brynge it to be understonden / And certaynly our language now used varyeth ferre from that whiche was used and spoken whan I was borne / For we englysshe men / ben borne under the domynacyon of the mone, whiche is never stedfaste / but euer wavereth / wexyng one season / and waneth & discreaseth another season / And that comyn englysshe that is spoken in one shyre uarieth from another.[24]

Caxton's writing need not be disparaged because of this posture of humility, for his *Eneydos* has strengths in its own right. Yet the difference between his presuppositions as a translator and those of Douglas illustrates that with Douglas, a cultural threshold has been passed. Virgil's text is now perceived as a specific entity possessing its own truth, and Douglas struggles, he says, "as the wyt micht atteyn, / Virgillis versys to follow and no thing feyn."[25] Douglas chides Caxton (I, Prologue, vv. 142–45) for even naming his work after the *Aeneid* and for "perverting" the story of the original: "I hafs na thing ado tharwith, God wait, / Ne na mair lyke than the devill and Sanct Austyne. / Have he ne thank tharfor, bot loyfs hys pyne, / So schamefully that story dyd pervert." Douglas respects the philological rigor of his Italian Humanist predecessors, in particular Lorenzo Valla, even though such rigor could not dispel the intrinsic difficulty of the original *Aeneid*: "The worthy clerk hecht Lawrens of the Vaill, / Among Latyns a gret patron sans faill, / Grantis quhen twelf heris he had beyn diligent / To study Virgill, skant knew quhat he ment" (I, Prologue, vv. 127–30). Douglas also has a clear sense of his host language, "the language of Scottis natioun," as distinct from English, and Douglas is aware, finally, that to translate is necessarily also to interpret.

For the English Humanists as on the Continent, translation became an exercise in emulation through imitation.[26] Roger Ascham, writing

24. William Caxton, *Caxton's Eneydos, Englisht from the French Liure des Eneydes, 1483*, ed. W. T. Cully and F. J. Furnivall, Early English Text Society (London: N. Trubner, 1890), 2.
25. Gavin Douglas, *The XIII Bukes of Eneados of the Famous Poete Virgill* (London, 1553), Bk. I, Prologue, vv. 265–66.
26. Cave, *Cornucopian Text*, 57–62.

in 1570, formalized a process called "double translating," which was a pedagogical exercise of translating passages not just from Latin to English, but from English back into Latin again. Like Du Bellay in France, Ascham considered his double translation a preliminary step in that larger process of learning through imitation by which all cultures come to maturity: "Poetrie was neuer perfited in *Latin*, until by trew *Imitation* of the Grecians it was at length brought to perfection."[27] On the other hand, Ascham also indicted certain acts of translation as culturally subversive—for instance, presuming to translate romances from Italian into English. Translation must be undertaken with as much respect for the integrity of the host culture as for the original, and what is translated must be fit for the moral well-being of the English nation:

> Ten *Morte Arthures* do not the tenth part so much harme as one of these books made in *Italie* and translated in England. . . . And bicause our English men made *Italians* can not hurt but certaine persones, and in certaine places, therefore these *Italian* bookes are made English, to bryng mischief enough openly and boldly to al states, great and meane, young and old, euery where.[28]

Theories of translation became implicated not only in rivalries between national cultures but in bitter professional rivalries between individuals as well. In 1582, Richard Stanyhurst published his bold and vigorous translation of the first four books of the *Aeneid*, and he took great pains to dissociate his work from the previous translation by Thomas Phaer. First, with regard to Phaer's lexical material, Stanyhurst scorns "borrowing his termes in so copious and fluent a language, as our English tongue is." Upon comparing the translations, Stanyhurst says, "I was forced to weede out from my verses such choise words, as were forestald by him: unlesse they were so feeling, as others could not countreuale theyre signification." Stanyhurst exonerates such inevitable lexical convergences by reminding us that Phaer himself had not been "thee first founder" of such felicities in English, "so hee may not bee accoumpted thee only owner of such termes." Second, on the level of translation as interpretation, Stanyhurst claims to be more authentic than Phaer:

27. Roger Ascham, *The Scholemaster*, in *English Works*, ed. William Aldis Wright (Cambridge: Cambridge Univ. Press, 1904), 293.
28. Ascham, 231.

Moore ouer in soom poinctes of greatest price, where thee matter, as yt were, dooth bleed, I was mooued to shun M. Phaer his interpretation, and clinge more neere to thee meaning of myne authoure, in slising thee husk and cracking the shel, too bestow the kernell vpon the wittye and enquistiue reader.

Third, Stanyhurst takes pride on another, most un-Virgilian, score: the speed with which he has concocted his translation of Book IV: "M. Phaer took too the making of that book fifteen days. I hudled up mine in ten."[29]

Needless to say, translations as manifestations of driving personal ambition nourished English culture with lively critical debate at a formative period of literary taste, and Thomas Nash would not agree that Stanyhurst had lived up to the eloquence of Virgil, who, in Stanyhurst's words, had expressed "the secrets of Nature, with woordes so fitlye coucht, with verses so smoothly slyckte, with sentences so featlye ordred, with orations so neatlie burnisht, with similitudes so aptly applyed, with each *decorums* duely observed." In 1589, Nash came in for the kill:

> But fortune, the Mistres of change, with a pitying compassion respecting master *Stanihursts* praise, would that *Phaer* shoulde fall that hee might rise, whose heroicall Poetrie, infired, I should say inspired, with an hexameter fury, recalled to life whateuer hissed barabarisme hath bin buried this hundred yeare, and reuiued by his ragged quill such carterlie variety as no hodge plowman in a countrie but could haue held as the extremetie of clownerie; a patterne whereof I will propounde to your iudgements, as neere as I can, being parte of one of his descriptions of a tempest, which is thus: *Then did he make heauens vault to rebounde, with rounce robble hobble / Of ruffe raffe roaring, with thwick thwack thurley bouncing.*[30]

---

29. Richard Stanyhurst, *The First Fovre bookes of Virgil his Aeneis translated in too English heroical verse* (Leyden, 1582); reprinted in *English Scholar's Library of Old and Modern Works*, ed. Edward Arber (London, 1880–84; rpt., New York: Franklin, n.d.), 10:5–6.

30. Thomas Nash, "To the Gentlemen Students of Both Universities," *Elizabethan Critical Essays*, ed. George Gregory Smith (Oxford: Clarendon Press, 1904), 1:315.

SPENSER AND THE MOTIVES OF TRANSLATION

One may infer, from the preceding, that during the sixteenth century the notion of translation attained the same maximal range as that of *hermeneuin* in classical Greece. Thus, translation implied (1) the act of conveying a document into a language other than its original; (2) the interpretation of what the original document meant; (3) the emulation of the original document as a rhetorical performance; (4) the perpetration of some historical action within a national culture. The latter three dimensions of translation are linked, respectively, with Renaissance principles of allegory and *allegoresis*,[31] with the Humanist cult of individualism, and with the Humanist poet's sense of prophetic voice.

Interesting though the external history of both the art and the ideology of translation in the Renaissance may be, when Spenser brought his artistic intelligence to bear on such questions, he raised for his readers and critics a challenge of a different sort. The Paridell-Hellenore episode deals with the legend of Troy, hence with a legend depicting the mythic dawn of English history, which we are invited to consider as a "translation" in the material sense of the term. We shall see that Spenser dealt resourcefully with the problem of translation, not only as a question of external culture but also as a matter of deep psychology and of ethical choices involving the individual's interpretation of the past as a determinant of the future. In the remainder of this chapter, I shall examine this episode as a special metapoetic moment that expresses Spenser's ideals as a poet, and I shall suggest that new recourse, surely indirect, to certain Stoic theories freed Spenser from the constraints of the more recent medieval poetic tradition exemplified by Chaucer.

One will recall that the setting for this *mise-en-scène* of poetic translation is Malbecco's castle, where two errant knights, Britomart and Paridell, are Malbecco's unwelcome guests. Hellenore is Malbecco's lecherous wife. Since the quests of Britomart and Paridell are motivated by opposite drives—she personifies chastity; he, lechery—the versions of the Troy legend that they narrate will be substantively at odds. It is precisely the relationship between inner motive and the

---

31. Maureen Quilligan, "Allegory, Allegoresis, and the De-allegorization of Language: The *Roman de la Rose,* the *De planctu naturae,* and the *Parlement of Foules,*" in *Allegory, Myth and Symbol,* ed. Morton W. Bloomfield (Cambridge, Mass.: Harvard University Press, 1981), 163–66.

translation of the past into the living present that Spenser asks us to ponder in this episode. We must therefore pay special attention to what it is that Britomart and Paridell each *have in mind* while they narrate their versions of the legend of Troy.

Britomart personifies chastity, yet her quest as a knight is hardly to eradicate sexuality—*voluptas*—from herself or from others. On the contrary, Britomart is on a quest to find Artegall, her destined spouse; thus, as readers have long recognized, her quest is really for a chastity that consists in realizing the proper end of human sexuality, which is procreation in marriage.[32] We also see in this episode that Britomart's quest for the proper end of love—of a love from which a new British culture will arise—also includes a hermeneutical quest for the proper translation of antique legend into the living language which is to be the medium of that new culture.

Since Spenser is concerned with the inner motives of responsible translation, let us recall what events have led to Britomart's setting forth on her quest. One day as a child, Britomart chances upon a magic mirror hidden in her father's closet that has been fashioned by the prophet Merlin. This mirror holds the power to reveal to her father prophetic images of future enemies of his kingdom. The first potential "enemy" that Britomart sees, ironically, is herself—though only for a moment, because the image of an unknown knight soon appears before the virgin's gaze: "Eftsoones there was presented to her eye / A comely knight" (III.ii.24).[33] That Britomart's future spouse Artegall should appear at first as her enemy is more than a conventional Ovidian oxymoron; it expresses implicitly a doctrine of love as a positive transgression of the soul. Ficino said that love is a kind of death that is voluntary, therefore sweet, and only partial because the lover survives his death-to-self when he finds himself reflected (and therefore resurrected) in the other.[34] The person who loves no one but himself commits homicide, theft, and sacrilege. Love, then, is itself a process of double translation: of self into otherness and of otherness into self.

32. C. S. Lewis, *The Allegory of Love* (Oxford: Clarendon Press, 1936), 297–360.
33. Edmund Spenser, *The Faerie Queene*, in *The Works of Edmund Spenser: A Variorum Edition*, 8 vols. (Baltimore: Johns Hopkins University Press, 1932–38), vol. 3.
34. Marcilio Ficino, *Commentaire sur le Banquet de Platon*, ed. and French trans. Raymond Marcel (Paris: Belles-Lettres, 1956), *Oratio secunda*, 156. See also Edgar Wind, *Pagan Mysteries in the Renaissance* (New Haven, Conn.: Yale Univ. Press, 1958), ch. 10: "Amor as a God of Death," 129–41.

Artegall's image is cast as a vivid emblem whose blazon identifies the knight as the successor of Achilles: "Achilles armes, which Arthegall did win" (III.ii.25). By his person, then, Artegall is a historical translation of the person of Achilles, though the translation is at this point incomplete and therefore equivocal. It lacks *enargeia*: will English Artegall inherit (as did Roman Aeneas) the destructive legacy of Greek Achilles's wrath? Will Artegall be smitten with love for an English Polyxena (for instance, Britomart herself) and slain by an underhanded Paris?

Will England burn like Troy?

The emblem of Artegall that Britomart ponders in Merlin's prophetic mirror posits a notion of translation that engages the individual's power both to incorporate past history and to renew or redefine its course by his own future energies.

Artegall's emblem engenders affections in Britomart's will, not abstractions in her intellect. By his voluntarism, Spenser is aligned with the central priorities of English Humanism, as opposed to those of Ficino. Discussing the exchange between Ficino and John Colet, Sears Jayne writes:

> The fact that the intellect-will conflict is the central issue between Ficino and Colet is significant for several reasons. For one thing it shows that the conflict between intellect and will, or contemplation and action, is one of the major problems of Renaissance theology, as it is in the fields of metaphysics and politics. . . . On the surface most later Renaissance statements of the intellect-will problem seem to follow the direction pointed out by Colet, toward emphasis on the will, but the ultimate outcome of the conflict is identification of the two faculties as reflected in *Paradise Lost* in Milton's observation that "Reason is also choice," and in Bacon's *Advancement of Learning*, where Bacon hopes that contemplation and action may be more nearly and straightly conjoined and united together than they have been.[35]

The cult of emblems in Humanist spirituality was part of a broader quest for a new semiotics centered in the incarnate Christ and entailing a change of attitude toward the bond between *verbum* and *res*, be-

35. Sears Jayne, *John Colet and Marsilio Ficino* (Oxford: Oxford Univ. Press, 1963), 75–76.

tween signifier and signified. Augustinian semiotics had stressed the radical duality of the sign *(signans* and *signatum)* as a negative dissimilitude: the signifier is corporeal, transitory and arbitrary, while the signified that it evinces is mental and potentially spiritual and eternal. In the Humanist movement, the thrust of cognition is as resolutely outward and downward as it is inward and upward, oriented as much toward the shared discovery of Jesus as an exoteric, colloquial presence in the world as transcendence in the "negative way." While Augustinians stress a movement of transcendence from the carnal letter to the spirit, Erasmus stresses the immanence of the incarnate Christ in the very letter of Scripture. As Boyle writes:

> Thus, the humanist persuasion that an eloquent text orates reality expands in Erasmus to a lively faith in the real presence of Christ as text. . . . This text is the divine *sermo,* who is Christ, preserved for the eyeful reading of Everyman. Scripture is the phantasm. If the theologian is to effect in his listeners that sense of vivid presence which propels human emotion towards act, then he must focus on the picture alphabetized: Christ the text. Eyeing that image will loosen his tongue. . . . By perceiving the text and by assimilating it into his heart's eye, the theologian will be possessed by that phantasm which guarantees true eloquence, because it is the true image of the mind of him who authors all things.[36]

Embodied in the emblem, this new semiotic doctrine valorizing the immixture of signifier and signified, of word and image, found historical legitimacy (at least in the eyes of Humanist philosophers) in myths of the Egyptian hieroglyph that came into vogue with the discovery of the hieroglyphics of Horapollo.[37] Before the flood, Adam or Seth was supposed to have inscribed all knowledge on two indestructible pillars, which were known to the Egyptians. As Christophoro Giarda wrote in 1626, "For from these the Egyptians borrowed the excellent doctrine of the hieroglyphs which we admire so much. The Greeks followed in their footsteps and left no Art or Science unadorned by Symbolic Images. What kind of stone or metal is there in which they did not ex-

36. Boyle, 83.
37. G. Boas, *The Hieroglyphics of Horapollo,* Bollingen Series 23 (New York: Pantheon Books, 1953); Ernst Gombrich, "Icones symbolicae," *Journal of the Warburg and Courtauld Institutes* 11 (1948): 163–92; reprinted in *Symbolic Images* (London: Phaidon, 1972).

press the forms of the sciences?"[38] Hieroglyphs intrigued Humanists such as Ficino and Erasmus because their images, it was supposed, pleasurably both offered and withheld access to the secrets and mysteries of nature. As a Humanist semiotic practice, the emblem inspired by a hieroglyph was imagined to produce an iconic signification where word and image were indissoluble. As Claude-Françoise Brunon has recently written, "Du même coup l'image s' impose, dans le procès de signification, comme signifiant majeur, à égalité avec le verbe, dans un rapport de complémentarité si étroite que les théoriciens de l'emblème ne surent mieux l'exprimer que par la métaphore de l'étroite et indissociable liaison de l'Ame et du Corps.[39]

As a class of sign, the secular emblem was imagined to assume semiotic functions previously reserved, by the scholastics, to the sacramental sign. Like the hieroglyphic emblem, the sacrament (Greek, *mystérion*) communicates something hidden or secret.[40] Though external and corporeal, the sacrament imprints a seal (*signaculum*), a signature (*signatio*) upon the soul. This mark, according to Thomas Aquinas, is the *character* of grace, just as the piece of money is marked with the *character* of the minter's die. The sacraments are founded upon the *passion* of Christ, but they evoke more than mere passions in us because these are transient, while the character of the sacraments is indelible.[41] The character imprinted in the soul is of the kind that determines figuration, an *ornatus animae*[42] very similar in function to the positive rhetorical functions ascribed to fantasms by the Humanists. In order better to understand the historical context of Spenser's positive valorization of fantasy as the motor of heroic action in Britomart, let us now briefly explore a shift in doctrines of fantasy that occurred with the rise of Humanism, in particular, and the resurgence of certain elements of Stoic psychology.

38. Christophoro Giarda, as translated and quoted by Gombrich, 150.

39. Claude-Françoise Brunon, "Signe figure, langage: Les *Hieroglyphica* d'Horappolon," in *L'emblème à la Renaissance: Actes de la journée d'études du 10 mai 1980*, ed. Yves Giraud (Paris: Société d'édition d'enseignement supérieur, 1982), 47.

40. Pierre de Ghellinck, *Pour l'histoire du mot "sacramentum"* (Paris: H. Champion, 1924).

41. Thomas Aquinas, *Summa theologica, 3a, quaestio 63*: "De effectu sacramentorum, qui est character."

42. For an interesting discussion of this term in relationship to "character," see St. Thomas Aquinas, *Somme théologique: Les sacrements*, French trans. A.-M. Roguet, O.P. (Paris: Desclée, 1951), 2, p. 354.

"SO FULL OF SHAPES IS FANCY /
THAT IT ALONE IS HIGH FANTASTICAL."

Thus exclaims the lovesick Orsino at the beginning of *Twelfth Night*, pursued, he complains, by desires like "fell and cruel hounds." But these are hounds that Orsino still loves to feed, and he knows that words are their favorite food.

But for poets, fantasms also feed words; and for Spenser, in particular, the most pressing concern about fantasms expressed in Books III and IV of the *Faerie Queene* is ethical and pragmatic: what kind of fantasms engender proper discourse, and what kind of discourse engenders, in turn, proper historical action?

These problems originated, of course, with Plato, and their natural habitat remained the Western dialectical tradition.[43] Plato's recognition of the anarchic potential of fantasms in the psychic and political life of man leads straight to his convictions about what constitutes the proper discursive life of the soul. If man experiences beauty and desire, he necessarily does so through images—icons or simulacres. Though these are scarcely to be considered as having in their own right either truth or being, they do have the capacity to perturb the life of the soul and hence to degrade it. The rhetorician is one who is content to live for and by such appearances, without any concern for their pertinence to truth. And unless he is a rhapsode whose gift of speech comes from God, the poet too is to be repudiated as a mere imitator of appearances, as a liar—or, at the very best, to be disdained as a mere locust singing in the tree while we philosophers teach each other through dialogue how properly to love the truth. The philosopher, then, is the only true "philologist," the true lover of discourse. Only language, instituted by the first legislator and now duly mastered in public debate, will bring order and rectitude to fantasms that besiege the soul, whether from without or from within; and only through philosophy may we be free of mere opinion and appearance, and become impassioned rather by spiritual beauty that is both true and good.

The Platonic bias against passions instigated by fantasms is strongly maintained by Ficino: "Then again, reason within us is called Her-

43. Monique Canto, "Le faux-semblant et ses oeuvres: De l'icône dans la pensée platonicienne" (forthcoming); I have greatly benefited from discussions with Monique Canto about the points discussed here. See also Janine Chanteur, *Platon, le désir et la cité* (Paris: Editions Sirey, 1979), 230–44.

cules: he destroys Antaeus, that is, the monstrous images of fantasy, when he lifts Antaeus up from the earth, that is, when he removes himself from the senses and physical images. He also subdues the lion, meaning that he curbs passion."[44]

In the tradition of Aristotelian psychology, which came to prevail (with some inflections) among the Scholastics, the faculty of *phantasia* was axiologically somewhat more neutral, indicating above all the capacity of the soul to translate into itself images of what has been perceived outwardly by the senses, and to do so even when such things are absent. However, fantasms can also be produced from within the mind itself (as in dreams), and fantasms can be deceptive when they do not correspond to something real.[45] Fantasms provide to the soul a kind of mental language that leads, through dialectical reasoning, from confused to distinct knowledge, and therefore to abstract understanding that is universally true and communicable. Thomas Aquinas fully acknowledges the primacy of fantasms to intellection, yet looks forward to a mode of understanding after death that will transcend fantasms:

> Therefore, when at its creation the soul is infused in the body, the only intellectual knowledge that is given it is ordained to the powers of the body. Thus, through the agent intellect it can make potentially intelligible phantasms actually intelligible, and through the possible intellect it can receive the intelligible species thus abstracted. Hence it is, too, that, as long as it has been united to the body in the state of this life, it does not know even those things whose species are preserved in it except by insight into phantasms. And for this reason, also, God does not make any revelations to it except under the species of phantasms, nor is it able to understand separated substances, inasmuch as these cannot be sufficiently known through the species of sensible things. But, when it will have its being free of the body, then it will receive the influx of intellectual knowledge in the way in which angels receive it, without any ordination to the body. Thus, it will receive species of things

44. Marcilio Ficino, *The Letters of Marcilio Ficino*, trans. members of Language Department of the School of Economic Sciences (London: Shepheard Walwyn, 1981), Letter 27, 3:61.

45. Aristotle, *Aristotle's "De anima" in the Version of William of Moerbeke and the Commentary of St. Thomas Aquinas*, III.iii,Lectio 5, trans. K. Foster and S. Humphries (New Haven, Conn.: Yale Univ. Press, 1951), 390–91.

from God himself, in order not to have to turn to any phantasms actually to know through these species or through those which it acquired previously.[46]

Clearly, neither tradition will explain the positive linking of fantasy, will, eloquence, and heroic action that set Spenser's age so distinctly apart from that of Chaucer—who showed us, for example, a Troilus whose downfall and debilitating eloquence began when, after sighting Criseyde, he withdrew unheroically from the world into his bedroom "to make a mirrour of his mynde / In which he saugh al holly hire figure" (I.365–66). However, one may suggest that certain Stoic theories of representation, as refracted through such classical sources of Humanism as Cicero, Pseudo-Longinus, and Quintilian, brought to Spenser useful doctrines validating the primacy of the fantasm as both the source and the proper end of effective eloquence.

For the Stoics, the production of a fantasm in the mind is a physical event, since the mind itself is physical. Here is how F. H. Sandbach summarizes the Stoic notion of *phantasia*:

> *Phantasia* is a word that belongs to philosophical language, in which it functions as the noun of the verb *phainesthai*, "appear," with a wide range of meaning. "Presentation" is more technical, but it seems to indicate what the Stoics meant by the word.
>
> A *phantasia* is, according to them, an impression (*typosis*) or alteration (*heteriosis*) in the psyche, and in that part of it they called the *hegemonikon*, or command-centre. It occurs when something "becomes apparent," *phantazetai*. We should call it a mental event, and associate it with changes in the brain. For the Stoics the two things are one and the same: the psyche is material, and any mental event *is* a physical event. So presentation is a physical change in the psyche. The word was first used to give a name to what happens when sense-organs are turned to the outer world. Objects in that world make an impression on the percipient.[47]

---

46. St. Thomas Aquinas, *Truth*, Question 9, art. 3, trans. Robert W. Mulligan, S.J. (Chicago: Henry Regnery, 1952), 1:420.

47. F. H. Sandbach, *"Phantasia Kataleptike,"* in *Problems of Stoicism*, ed. A. A. Long (London: Athlone Press, 1971), 10. See also Joseph Moreau, *Stoicisme, Epicurisme, tradition hellénique* (Paris: Vrin, 1979), 80–84.

As in the emblem, where image and word are completely and materially enmeshed, so too, for the Stoic, the perception and the perceived participate in a single material order of being, though the subsequent act of acknowledging what we grasp (*katalepsis, comprehensio*) as a *phantasia* includes an act of assent by the will. Truth in cognition has the quality of *enargeia*, a term the Stoics borrowed, according to Sandbach, from the Epicureans.[48] However, a presentation may arise not only from exterior objects but from within the soul, and in this case it may be called a *phantasma* or a *phantastikon* or "imaginative product." Sandbach specifies, though, that the word *phantasia* itself could also be applied to dreams and to the hallucinations of madmen.[49]

There have been several attempts in recent years to assess the influence, both direct and indirect, of Stoicism on Renaissance thought. William J. Bouwsma, for example, has gone so far as to suggest that Stoicism and Augustinianism are the two main ideological poles of Humanist culture.[50] While one may question the distinctness of these two poles—especially in a culture that was eclectic in the extreme—and while I believe that Augustine himself clearly illustrates, at times, characteristics that are supposed to belong to the "other" Stoic pole, few would dispute that Stoic influence became important in the sixteenth century, though piecemeal and not as an integral doctrine.[51]

Rhetoric, moreover, was one of the main channels of Stoic ideas to the Renaissance, however much the orators' own purposes differed from those of the apathetic Stoic sage. Recent studies by Claude Imbert and P. H. Schryvers have brought new precision to our understanding of the historical bond between rhetoric and Stoicism in classical Humanist sources.[52] Both Imbert and Schryvers stress the impor-

48. F. H. Sandbach, "*Ennoia* and *Prolepsis* in the Stoic Theory of Knowledge," in *Problems of Stoicism* (see n. 47), 32.

49. Sandbach, "*Phantasia Kataleptike*," 11.

50. William J. Bouwsma, "The Two Faces of Humanism: Stoicism and Augustinianism in Renaissance Thought," in *Itinerarium Italicum: The Profile of The Italian Renaissance in the Mirror of Its European Transformations*, ed. Heiko A. Oberman and Thomas A. Brady, Jr. (Leiden: Brill, 1975), 3–60.

51. Since Stoic doctrine was never dominant, integral, or pure, the question of Stoic "influence" on Humanism is a perilous one. Charles Trinkaus's treatment of Stoic thought in the Renaissance wisely stresses the fusion of Stoic thought with Christian platonism rather than its viability as a distinct "face" or "pole" of Humanist thought. See "Stoicism" in the index of his *"In Our Image and Likeness,"* 982, for his scattered remarks upon Stoicism.

52. Claude Imbert, "Stoic Logic and Alexandrian Poetics," in *Doubt and Dogmatism: Studies in Hellenistic Epistemology*, ed. Malcom Schofield, Myles Burn-

tance of Stoic theories to Pseudo-Longinus and Quintilian, who held *phantasia* to be a genetic force in eloquence. Imbert makes a crucial point about the somatic dimension of *phantasia*. Speaking of pseudo-Longinus, she writes:

> In Chapter XV of the treatise *On the Sublime*, pseudo-Longinus takes two sources of sublimity which the previous chapters have identified (*eidos* and *pathos*), and summarizes them under the single concept of *phantasia* or presentation. He thus unites a Platonic notion which sees the sublime as the effect of a transcendent vision of the Forms (*Symposium*), with a theory of deriving from the Sophists (or even from Homer), according to which a divine inspiration possesses the poet's body and determines his words (*Ion*). Longinus relies on a general thesis about the nature of language: "the term *phantasia*," he explains, "is used generally for anything which in any way suggests a thought productive of speech (*gennétikon logou*)." Without pausing over a definition which he takes to be thoroughly familiar, he adds that in rhetoric and aesthetic theory the term has a more specialized sense: it designates that state of emotion or enthusiasm by virtue of which a speaker can *see*, and make his audience *see*, whatever he is talking about.
>
> A *phantasia* is thus a vision which can be communicated in its entirety by language: language makes the *phantasiai* explicit, and *phantasiai* bring language into existence.[53]

Imbert underscores another point in Stoic epistemology important for Alexandrine and, later, for Humanist theories of representation: if fantasms derive not only from external, empirical realities but from within the soul as well, it is precisely the capacity of the artist to *produce* nonexistent things, as well as to derive them from what exists, that carries to perfection images of what has been sensed naturally. Such artistic fantasms "translate," in a way, the hidden secrets of nature.

---

yeat, and Jonathan Barnes (Oxford: Clarendon Press, 1980), 182–216; P. H. Schryvers, "Invention, imagination, et théorie des émotions chez Cicéron et Quintilien," in *Rhetoric Revalued*, ed. Brian Vickers, Medieval and Renaissance Texts and Studies (Binghamton, N.Y.: Center for Medieval and Early Renaissance Studies, 1981), 47–57.
53. Imbert, 182.

P. H. Schryvers has studied in detail the link between the Stoic *phantasia, inventio,* and *enargeia* in Cicero and especially Quintilian. Eloquence, for Quintilian, depends first of all on the state of the orator's soul: it must itself be both moved as it conceives images, and transformed in accordance with their nature (*Hunc adfici, hunc concipere imagines rerum et transformari quodammodo ad naturam eorum*).[54] In a sense, then, fantasms translate the soul even to itself. Once moved by a *phantasia* (or, in Latin, *imago, visio*), the soul elaborates upon it, inventing details that are "true" to the extent that they are probable, and thereby making the original image both more intense and more clear; the result is *enargeia.* Quintilian gives an example: the report that a town has been sacked (VIII.iii.68–70). In itself, a mere report is not moving:

> But if we expand all that the one word "stormed" (*expugnatio*) includes, we shall see the flames pouring from house and temple, and hear the crash of falling roofs and one confused clamour blent of many cries: we shall behold some in doubt whether to fly, others clinging to their nearest and dearest in one last embrace, while the wailing of women and children and the laments of the old men that the cruelty of fate should have spared them to see that day will strike upon our ears. . . . And we shall secure the vividness we seek, if only our descriptions give the impression of truth, nay, we may even add fictitious incidents of the type which commonly occur.

The process of elaborating or embellishing our discourse (*ornatus*) produces *enargeia* or *evidentia,* "which others call representation" (*representatio;* III.iii.61). Moreover, among the rhetorical resources for *ornatus orationis,* metaphor (*translatio*) is by far the most beautiful (*pulchrissima*), and "shines in our discourse with its own light" (VIII.vi.5).[55]

Like the Stoics, Quintilian insists upon the corporeality of verbal expression and of understanding. The speaker "excites us by his very breath or spirit" and he inflames the soul not with roundabout images of things, but with things *themselves* (*"nec imagine et ambitu rerum sed rebus incendit";* X.i.16). The effect is one of begetting somatic

54. Quintilian, *Institutio oratoria,* I.ii.30, ed. and trans. H. E. Butler, Loeb Classical Library (Cambridge, Mass.: Harvard Univ. Press; London: Heinemann, 1921).

55. Brian Vickers, *Classical Rhetoric in English Poetry* (London: Macmillan, 1970), 100–103, discusses the affective potential of figures.

understanding in the soul as if it were a newborn child: "Then all is life and movement, and we receive the new-born offspring of his imagination with enthusiastic approval" (VIII.i.16).

The pertinence of Quintilian's rhetoric of presence and his materialism to Humanist theories has been emphasized by Terence Cave, though Cave rightly stresses that the "*Institutiones* was not systematically imitated by humanist theorists (perhaps precisely because it was well known)."[56] I would suggest, for instance, that one of the distinct achievements of Humanist theory was to situate such theories of "translation" in a broad Ovidian cosmological process of becoming (*fieri*). A visual dramatization of this dynamism may be found in Botticelli's famous *Primavera*, whose iconographical program begins on the right with Zephyr's amorous pursuit of Chlora. As Chlora looks intently into Zephyr's face, she is physically "inspired" during the transgression, and out of her mouth flows an eloquence not of words but of flowers. Chlora is simultaneously transformed by Zephyr's *pneuma* into Flora, whose dress is now *ornamented* with the living flowers of Chlora's breath, and whose swollen lap is filled with even more real flowers. Flowers also bloom copiously in the grass at Flora's feet. The closely identified processes of translation and ornament give forth abundance, *copia*, not of words but of living things. Moreover, the horizontal translation of people and substances into one another entails somatic violence and life-giving transgressions; these produce *variety*, as opposed to the stagnation of *sameness*. Here is how Edgar Wind summarizes the scene I have just evoked:

> In the guise of an Ovidian fable, the progression Zephyr-Chloris-Flora spells out the familiar dialectic of love: Pulchritudo arises from a discordia concors between Castitas and Amor; the fleeting nymph and the amorous Zephyr unite in the beauty of Flora. But this episode, *dinotando la primavera*, is only the initial phase in the Metamorphoses of Love that unfolds in the garden of Venus.[57]

Without pausing to speculate upon what precise historical links, whether accurate or distorted, direct or indirect, may exist between Stoic doctrine and Spenser, one may easily see that Humanist theories of fantasy, translation, and *enargeia* provide a basis for the complex economy of erotic wounds culminating in marriage that winds through

56. Cave, *Cornucopian Text*, 134.
57. Wind, 103.

books III and IV of the *Faerie Queene*, as well as for a subjacent "sexual textuality" that Terence Cave and Robert Cottrell have recently described in writers such as Rabelais and Montaigne.[58] Indeed, Spenser invites us to believe, as a good orator should, that the discourse of the poem itself originates in Spenser's own nearly ineffable fantasms of his sovereign Elizabeth—more precisely, in fantasms inspired by her virtue of chastity. In his proem to Book III, Spenser insists that no "liuing art," whether that of painters or of poets, may adequately represent the "pourtraict of her hart." Since even the "choicest wit" could not presume to convey Elizabeth's "glorious pourtraict" *directly* ("plain"; III.pr.iii)—that is, without ornament—the poet asks that he "in colored showes may shadow it," so that the "liuing colours" of his fictive characters will become true mirrors in which Elizabeth may contemplate her own virtues. In other words, "antique praises unto present persons fit" will overcome the poet's "want of words," and through this poetic *translatio* from the past, abundance (*copia*) in the present will be achieved—including, Spenser must have hoped, the abundance of Elizabeth's patronage of England's new but penurious epic poet.

Having viewed the emblem of Artegall, Britomart responds at first more in body than in mind, and the somatic effect begins, as usual, with the wound of Cupid's figurative arrow:

> But the false Archer, which that arrow shot
> So slyly, that she did not feele the wound,
> Did smyle full smoothly at her weetlesse wofull stound.
> (III.ii.26)

The potentially true and prophetic fantasm engendered by Artegall's image from without is soon rivaled, however, by false images begotten from within, and Britomart's soul becomes a battleground between what exists and what does not:

> And if that any drop of slombring rest
> Did chaunce to still into her wearie spright,
> When feeble nature felt her selfe opprest,
> Streight way with dreames, and with fantasticke sight
> Of dreadfull things the same was put to flight,
> That oft out of her bed she did astart,
> As one with vew of ghastly feends affright:

---

58. Cave, *Cornucopian Text*, 183–222, 271–321; Robert Cottrell, *Sexuality / Textuality* (Columbus: Ohio State Univ. Press, 1983).

> Tho gan she to renew her former smart,
> And thinke of that faire visage, written in her hart.
> (III.ii.29)

Britomart insists as much upon the somatic as upon the psychic devastation caused by her fantasm of Artegall:

> Sithens it hath infixed faster hold
>   Within my bleeding bowels, and so sore
>   Now ranckleth in this same fraile fleshly mould,
>   That all mine entrailes flow with poysnous gore,
>   And th'vlcer groweth daily more and more;
>   Ne can my running sore find remedie,
>   Other then my hard fortune to deplore,
>   And languish as the leafe falne from the tree,
> Till death make one end of my dayes and miserie.
>   (III.ii.39)

In order for Britomart's fantasms to become generative and productive in the microcosm, they must now be edified by the proper discourse. Britomart is brought before the prophet Merlin, who indoctrinates her not dialectically but with a metaphorical prophecy of the unfolding tree of history reaching from its roots in Troy upward to Britain, its final, triumphant "translation." That such a notion of history as translation should now be linked to the metaphorical discourse of positive prophecy, instead of to the philosopher's rational discourse about tragic history, clearly separates Spenser's Humanism from Chaucer's medieval Boethianism:

>   enrooted deepe must be that Tree,
>   Whose big embodied braunches shall not lin,
>   Till they to heauens hight forth stretched bee.
>   For from thy wombe a famous Progenie
>   Shall spring, out of the auncient *Troian* blood,
>   Which shall reuiue the sleeping memorie
>   Of those same antique Peres, the heauens brood,
>   Which *Greeke* and *Asian* riuers stained with their blood.
>
>   Renowmed kings, and sacred Emperours,
>   Thy fruitfull Ofspring, shall from thee descend,
>   Braue Captaines, and most mighty warriours,
>   That shall their conquests through all lands extend,
>   And their decayed kingdomes shall amend:

339

> The feeble Britons, broken with long warre,
> They shall vpreare, and mightily defend
> Against their forrein foe, that comes from farre,
> Till vniuersall peace compound all ciuill iarre.
> (III.iii.22–23)

Britomart is assured that the apparent randomness of her glance in Merlin's mirror, followed by the wound inflicted by a blind Cupid, was in fact part of this divine program, and that her will must submit to the will of God.[59] Voluntarism is now the terrain of heroic ethics, and duty consists in making the individual will conform to a divinely ordained system of nature. In Britomart's case this essentially Stoic imperative to conform[60] is sweet:

> It was not, Britomart, thy wandring eye,
> Glauncing vnwares in charmed looking glas,
> But the streight course of heauenly destiny,
> Led with eternall prouidence, that has
> Guided thy glaunce, to bring his will to pas:
> Ne is thy fate, ne is thy fortune ill,
> To loue the prowest knight, that euer was.
> Therefore submit thy wayes vnto his will,
> And do by all dew meanes thy destiny fulfill.
> (III.iii.24)

Properly indoctrinated, Britomart is now able to elaborate without guilt upon her fantasm in a manner that includes *voluptas* among the legitimate motives of her quest to translate the Trojan past into a Brit-

59. Trinkaus, 83, makes statements about Salutati's voluntarism that pertain to Spenser: "He rejects and turns away from the medieval natural philosophers who sought to consider the soul as essentially an object of nature and thus dissectable into its various parts which act or are acted upon in a calculable way. To Salutati the essence of the soul is its will, as we have seen, and the essence of will is its freedom, its subjectivity. Yet he does not wish to detach the will altogether from the world of examinable regularity that is called nature, but wishes rather to give subjectivity an equal or parallel status with objective cause and effect as part of the totality of a divinely guided universe—the doctrine of 'coefficiency.'"

60. The Stoic position underlying Spenser's ethics of *conciliatio* and *convenentia*, whether conscious or not, is not difficult to perceive. Indeed, the idea that Britomart's conforming to nature includes conforming to her *own* nature is an important one in Stoic philosophy and ethics, expressed by the term *oikoiosis*, and its implications for Renaissance psychology need more exploration. See the highly in-

ish future. A remark that Nancy Struever makes about Lorenzo Valla applies to Spenser: "In the discussion of the predicaments 'action' and 'passion' in the *Dialecticae disputationes*, Valla suggests a significant enlargement of the domain of human activity, of transivity, in his reduction of passion to action: to feel a passion is no different from knowing a danger, he claims."[61] When she meets the Redcross Knight in Faery Land, Britomart wastes no time "of diuerse things discourses to dilate, / But most of Arthegall, and his estate" (III.iii.62). After they part, Britomart continues her *amplificatio* as a purely mental language, and such a mental language is augmented as much by "feigning" as by proper intellection, in the scholastic sense of the term.

> But *Britomart* kept on her former course,
> Ne euer dofte her armes, but all the way
> Grew pensiue through that amorous discourse,
> By which the *Redcrosse* knight did earst display
> Her louers shape, and cheualrous aray;
> A thousand thoughts she fashioned in her mind,
> And in her feigning fancie did pourtray
> Him such, as fittest she for loue could find,
> Wise, warlike, personable, curteous, and kind.
> (III.iv.5)

That Britomart should "feign" Artegall's portrait to herself is hardly a novel conception of historical truth. Already for Quintilian, the language of history was essentially poetical. As opposed to forensic or political eloquence, which persuades, the language of history is only a narrative; in order to hold the interest of the reader, it tends to rely on "remoter language" and on greater license of figures to avoid tedium (*verbis remotioribus et liberioribus figuris narrandi taedium evitat*; X.i.31.). Like Quintilian, Erasmus too allowed for fabrications that translate reality to the soul if they at least resemble what is real: "If

---

teresting article by S. G. Pembroke, "*Oikeiosis*," in *Problems in Stoicism*, 114–149. See also Victor Goldschmidt, *Le Système stoicien et l'idée de temps* (Paris: Vrin, 1969), 103f,f 129.

61. Nancy S. Struever, "Lorenzo Valla: Humanist Rhetoric and the Critique of the Classical Languages of Morality," in *Renaissance Eloquence: Studies in the Theory and Practice of Renaissance Rhetoric*, ed. James J. Murphy (Berkeley: Univ. of California Press, 1983), 194. On *voluptas* and ethics, see Wind, ch. 5, "Virtue Reconciled with Pleasure," 78–88; see also Trinkaus, ch. 3: "Lorenzo Valla: *Voluptas* et *Fruitio, Verba* et *Res*," 103–70.

entirely fictitious narratives are introduced as if they are true because they will help us get our point across, we must make them as much like the real things as possible."[62]

For Spenser, fantasms are as necessary to the life of the soul as living forms are to nature. The main question raised by the experience of a fantasm is not its strict ontological pertinence but rather its ethical consequences in the pragmatic realms of heroic speech and action. Just as, for the scholastics, valid logical propositions were invoked to mediate between the individual contemplative soul and what exists outside and beyond it, so now, for the Humanists, fantasms are inculcated in the psyche with the goal of motivating the heroic will to speak *and* act responsibly in the world. Chaucer exhorts us, at the end of the *Troilus*, to repudiate and transcend, along with the "false worldes brotelnesse" (V.1832) and "payens corsed olde rites" (V.1849), "the forme of olde clerkis speche / In poetrie" (V.1854–55); Spenser asks us, rather, to seek out what is right and virtuous in the past and to translate its substance, through productive fantasms that engender actions, into new corporeal forms—including epic poems.

History, then, may be properly "translated," whether in word or deed, only when the souls of its agents are enflamed by proper fantasms. Although Britomart's psyche will later be besieged by erotic fantasms of a most anarchic sort when she witnesses "with greedy eyes" the tapestries and the mask of Cupid in the House of Busyrane, at the moment when she enters Malbecco's castle, she is still inculcated with fantasms that will properly subtend her orthodox narration of the Trojan legacy that she is destined to fulfill.

The episode in Malbecco's castle orchestrates very clearly the ethical and historical consequences of both proper *and* subversive fantasms. If Spenser, with his inner gaze fixed on Elizabeth, and Britomart, with her inner gaze fixed on Artegall, are oriented toward true virtue and glory, such is not the case with Paridell. On the contrary, he is a student of the lascivious, and when Hellenore enters the hall to dine and sits down beside him, he eyes her with adulterous intentions. Fortunately for Paridell, Sir Satyrane is seated in such a way that his blind eye prevents him from observing the flurry of "speaking" glances between the two:

62. Desiderius Erasmus, *De duplici copia verborum ac rerum comentarii duo*, trans. Betty I. Knott, *Copia: Foundations of the Abundant Style* (Toronto: Univ. of Toronto Press, 1978), 634.

But his blinde eie, that syded *Paridell*
All his demeasnure from his sight did hyde:
On her faire face so did he feede his fill,
And sent close messages of loue to her at will.
And euer and anone, when none was ware,

With speaking lookes, that close embassage bore,
He rou'd at her, and told his secret care:
For all that are he learned had of yore.

Ne was she ignorant of that lewd lore,
But in his eye his meaning wisely red,
And with the like him answerd euermore.
(III.ix.27–28)

Paridell now internalizes Hellenore's image, a "firie dart, whose hed / Empoisoned was with priuy lust."

He from that deadly throw made no defence,
But to the wound his weake hart opened wyde;
The wicked engine through false influence,
Past through his eyes and secretly did glyde
Into his hart, which it did sorely gryde.
But nothing new to him was that same paine.
(III.ix.20)

The lubricious fantasm of Hellenore will henceforth guide Paridell's false eloquence in the narrative that he is shortly to perform:

Then *Paridell*, in whom a kindly pryde
Of gracious speach and skill his words to frame
Abounded, being glad of so fit tyde
Him to commend to her, thus spake.
(III.ix.32)

The story that Hellenore inspires, moreover, is a masterpiece of deviant history. Paridell begins by boasting of Paris as the origin of his lineage and by praising Helen's beauty, and he considers the scandal by which Paris and Helen brought Troy to ashes not as infamy but as "noble fame." He credits Paris with preserving the Trojan relics and with founding a new kingdom on the Isle of Paros, which Paridell claims as the seat of his ancestry. True to his lineage, Paridell now wanders through the world "for faire ladies loue and glories gaine"

(III.ix.37). Britomart, however, who has been indoctrinated quite otherwise, interprets the fall of Troy as a tragedy rectified only with the founding of Britain:

> Whenas the noble *Britomart* heard tell
>   Of *Troian* warres and *Priams* Citie sackt,
>   The ruefull story of Sir *Paridell*,
> She was empassioned at that piteous act,
> With zelous envy of Greekes cruell fact,
> Against that nation, from whose race of old
> She heard that she was lineally extract:
> For noble *Britons* sprong from *Troians* bold,
> And *Troynouant* was built of old *Troyes* ashes cold.
>   (III.ix.38)

Britomart is dismayed by Paridell's outrageous translation of Troy's legend and politely requests that he go back in his tale to speak of Aeneas, "sith that men sayne / He was not in the Cities wofull fyre / Consum'd, but did him selfe to safetie retyre" (III.ix.40).

Paridell obliges her but presents his audience with a tendentious *Aeneid* whose hero is anything but exemplary. After wandering "through fatall errour long," Aeneas was forced, he says, into wedlock with Latinus's daughter, though with bloody rather than amorous consequences, and then fled the scene after slaying Turnus. When war broke out once again between the Trojans and the Latins, Aeneas's son also abandoned his clan with "all the warlike youth of Troians bloud" and established his own throne in Long Alba, until Romulus finally removed it to Rome.

While it may be said that Paridell has given us a story that *does* have a basis in the *Aeneid*, he has culled from that poem only the details that make the heroic fame of Aeneas equivocal: Aeneas and his successors are depicted by Paridell alternately as bunglers and opportunists.

Once again, however, Britomart interrupts Paridell, and once again she reorients his deviant story with a more orthodox line:

> There, there (said Britomart) afresh appeard
> The glory of the later world to spring,
> And Troy againe out of her dust was reard,
> To sit in second seat of soueraigne king,
> Of all the world vnder her gouerning.
> But a third kingdome is yet to arise

Out of the Troians scattered of-spring,
That, in all glory and great enterprise,
Both first and second *Troy* shall dare to equalise.
(III.ix.44)

Paridell glibly exclaims that he has forgotten all of this, an amnesis of the past obviously caused by his scandalous infatuation with the present:

Ah Fairest lady knight, (said *Paridell*)
Pardon, I pray, my heedlesse ouersight,
Who had forgot, that whilome I heard tell
From aged *Mnemon*; for my wits been light.
(III.ix.47)

For Hellenore is hanging on his every word and savoring the erotic fantasms that his language instills in her mind:

But all the while, that he these speaches spent,
Vpon his lips hong faire Dame *Hellenore*,
With vigilant regard and dew attent,
Fashioning worldes of fancies euermore.
(III.ix.52)

Paridell's eloquence is nourished, in turn, by the spectacle of Hellenore's lascivious rapture:

The whiles vnwares away her wondring eye,
And greedy eares her weake hart from her bore:
Which he perceiuing, ever priuily,
In speaking, many false belgardes at her let fly.
(III.ix.52)

Paridell is the very paradigm of the subversive historian, and Spenser is dramatizing the psychology of his performance in the light of Humanist theories of eloquence. Thus, the debate between Paridell and Britomart is marked by spontaneity, both in delivery and in response. Spenser takes great care to make the encounter between the two knights one where the cyclical violence of wars that occurred in the historical past translates itself now into a *hermeneutical* clash whose conflicting forces will generate yet another historical event of import. Spenser is giving renewed dramatic life, here, to the rhetorical notion exalted by Quintilian as the supreme achievement of the orator: "extempore" eloquence (*ex tempore dicendi facultas*; X.vi.7). An orator's fantasms are what motivate his impromptu eloquence:

> Consequently those vivid conceptions of which I spoke and which, as I remarked, are called φαητασιασ, together with everything that we intend to say, the persons and questions involved, and the hopes and fears to which they give rise, must be kept clearly before our eyes and admitted to our hearts: for it is feeling (*pectus*) and force of imagination (*vis mentis*) that make us eloquent. It is for this reason that even the uneducated have no difficulty in finding words to express their meaning, if only they are stirred by some emotion. (X.vii.15)

In his discussion of the fortune of Quintilian's notion of extempore eloquence in continental Humanism, Terence Cave says that it is

> the paradigm of performance, the moment when discourse asserts its freedom to exercise intrinsic powers. Not only does this moment appear in Quintilian's theory as the goal or fruition of all conscious preparation (X.vii.1); it also presupposes (as does the distinction between true and false imitation) the authenticity of a hidden nature. All this theory depends, indeed, on the art-nature antithesis as an opposition between reflection and intuition, or between the rational and the irrational; impromptu speech is a transgression. . . . Likewise, Erasmus's Folly, from the beginning of her demonstrative exercise, repeatedly rejects rhetorical planning in favour of extempore speech; immediacy, in her view, is a sign of nature and consequently a guarantee of authenticity.[63]

Cave also emphasizes the link between improvised or extempore eloquence and *copia*, and, by extension, the ethical opposition between avarice and productive expenditure, or between productive expenditure and profligacy. Given that the setting for this encounter between a chaste and a lecherous knight is the castle of a jealous miser, Malbecco, Cave's remarks go straight to the heart of the issues in this episode in the *Faerie Queene*:

> This concept is the topic of *Institutiones* X, and is thus inseparably linked with *copia*: the amassing of a treasure (reading, imitation, lexical accumulation, and the modes of figurative

63. Cave, *Cornucopian Text*, 127.

transformation) is considered throughout in the perspective of its eventual expenditure, that is to say, of mastery, the exercise of rhetorical power. The notion of "having ready for production" "having at one's fingertips" (*in promptu habere*) is present from the outset in the negative image of the miser hoarding his treasure.[64]

Noting that Erasmus, in *De copia*, associates impromptu eloquence with Proteus, Cave adds that "the figures of expenditure relate improvisation to the ambivalent theme of prodigality or 'improvidence.'"[65] One may easily see how the ethical issues raised as a rhetorical event in the Malbecco episode radiate into much of the narrative substance of Books III and IV, beginning with the immediate consequence of the episode: having eloped with Paris, stolen her jealous husband's treasure, and burned his castle, Hellenore is abandoned by Paris and reduced to fornicating with satyrs in the forest: culture has once again reverted to wild nature. Britomart, by contrast, will become the married mother of New Troy.

The story of Britomart, with its multiple meanderings, subtypes, and subplots, embodies a Humanist understanding of translation as a process of cosmic change whose chief hero is man and whose god is Proteus. Proteus contains Pan, for it is only through variety that natural fulness is achieved. As Edgar Wind writes of Pico's Orphism:

> In Pico's oration *On the Dignity of Man*, man's glory is derived from his mutability. The fact that his orbit of action is not fixed like that of angels or of animals, gives him the power to transform himself into whatever he chooses and become a mirror of the universe. He can vegetate like a plant, rage like a brute, dance like a star, reason like an angel, and surpass them all by withdrawing into the hidden centre of his own spirit where he may encounter the solitary darkness of God. "Who would not admire this chameleon?"
>
> In his adventurous pursuit of self-transformation, man explores the universe as if he were exploring himself. And the further he carries these metamorphoses, the more he discovers that all the varied phases of his experience are translatable into each other: for they all reflect the ultimate one, of which they

64. Cave, *Cornucopian Text*, 126.
65. Cave, *Cornucopian Text*, 126.

unfold particular aspects. If man did not sense the transcendent unity of the world, its inherent diversity would also escape him.[66]

Since the language of man is a mirror of reality, it follows that man's discourse must *also* abound in variety. As Erasmus puts it in his *De copia*:

> Variety is so powerful in every sphere that there is absolutely nothing, however brilliant, which is not dimmed if it is not commended by variety. Nature above all delights in variety; in all this huge concourse of things, she has left nothing anywhere unpainted by her wonderful techniques of variety. Just as the eyes fasten themselves on some new spectacles, so the mind is always looking round for some fresh object of interest. If it is offered a monotonous succession of similarities, it very soon wearies and turns its attention elsewhere, and so everything gained by the speaker is lost all at once.[67]

Since Spenser shared with other Humanists of his age the conviction that the practice of eloquence determines the course of history in the body politic here and now, he also dramatizes in this episode a current political problem which he saw as crucial to the state of England. Thus, the forthcoming seduction of Hellenore by Paridell and the destruction of Malbecco's castle are not only Spenser's rereading of events that led to the downfall of Troy in the past, but a warning to his audience as well that England too could possibly be destroyed by such conduct in the historical present.

Though the historical allegory in the Paridell story is not entirely clear, it is difficult not to see the person of Mary Queen of Scots behind the figure of Hellenore; for just as Malbecco's castle will be consumed in flames (as was Troy), so too was Mary suspected of conspiring with the Earl of Bothwell, whom she later married, in the murder of the Earl of Darnley, her first husband, and in the blowing up of his castle. From Spenser's Elizabethan perspective, Mary, as a Catholic, could have inspired only error in history: hence the preposterous claim on the part of Paridell that Brutus founded not only Troynovant but "Faire Lincolne" as well, which is supposedly the equal of Troynovant, the Faery name for London. Though it is true that Lincoln and Lincolnshire had

66. Wind, 158.
67. Knott, *Copia*, 302.

once enjoyed great economic prosperity and had been a center of English Catholic theology and learning, by Spenser's time the fate of Lincoln could have been envied by none. Not only had Lincolnshire been spoliated under Henry VIII and Edward VI, but it had been the seat of the Catholic uprising of 1536. It had remained, moreover, a stronghold of Catholic recusancy well into Elizabeth's reign: for example, on August 2, 1587, William Wickham, Dean of Lincoln, pronounced a funeral sermon in Mary's honor.[68] Paridell's praise of Lincoln may have been music to Hellenore's treacherous ears, but it could only have seemed ridiculous to those who had Elizabeth's cause at heart. In any case, if the consequence of Paridell's deviant eloquence is that Hellenore, "this second Hellen," reenacts in Malbecco's castle the events of Troy, her deeds are clearly as much a "translation" of the legend of Troy as are Paridell's words:

> When chaunst *Malbecco* busie be elsewhere,
> She to his closet went, where all his wealth
> Lay hid: thereof she countlesse summes did reare,
> The which she meant away with her to beare;
> The rest she fyr'd for sport, or for despight;
> As *Hellene*, when she saw aloft appeare
> The Troigne flames, and reach to heauens hight,
> Did clap her hands, and joyed at that dolefull sight.
> (III.x.12)

To summarize, the Malbecco episode may be considered as a poetic essay exposing the inner motives and the outer historical consequences of improper translation, as opposed to those of proper translation. By stressing the rhetorical basis of the relationship between fantasms, invention, and proper action in the light of political responsibility, Spenser endows the idea of translation with an amplitude that makes it akin to his own epic ambitions. Unlike Chaucer, Spenser no longer needed to censure poetry itself as a rhetorical act but only poetry deleterious to the body politic. With the innumerable defenses of poetry that had been written both in England and on the continent since Chaucer's time, Spenser's ideological position as translator and emulator of the past was secure in Books III and IV (though his confi-

68. *Victoria History of the County of Lincoln*, ed. William Page (London: A. Constable, 1906); vol. 2 is devoted to the ecclesiastical, economic, and political history of the county.

dence did become strained in Book V when he grappled with the more painful and immediate history of British government in Ireland). In contrast with Chaucer, who had felt compelled to renounce the poetic heritage of the *auctores* in the *Troilus* in favor of contemplation, philosophy, and prayer, Spenser reflects those Humanistic priorities that promulgated an ethics of action within the temporal world.

Spenser diverges even further from his medieval forebears in his reluctance to privilege problems of verbal translation over translations that must occur in *non*verbal systems as well: nations, persons, and even things—like languages—must all flow into each other if the creation is to fulfill its destiny. Spenser reflects, in this manner, a massive reaction among Humanists against what had come to be seen as a scholastic complacency to speculate about the world through an all-encompassing, yet denaturing, mirror of language. Thus, for Spenser, the notion of translation leads outside or beyond the rarifying space of language and straight into the mysteries of material forms, including humankind. Meaning resides in matter itself, in the material words that express that matter, and in the very bodies of men and women who utter those words. Poetry and history unfold together as twin visages of a single temporal process that hangs at every moment upon the willingness of individuals to recognize and to serve the goals proper to their natural being. Translation is a process of unbinding and unfolding that leads to fruition, abundance, variety, and plenitude; inversely, mistranslation leads to sterility, destitution, redundance, and annihilation.

In the Renaissance, Proteus was the god of translation, not of translation as servile mimesis but translation as positive difference. Just as the Greeks once had to be translated into Latin, so now the Latins must be rendered in English if our affections are to be fully released in meaningful historical action. Translation that is servile, literal, and overconstrained will deny those affections; translation that is truly eloquent will move its readers to release the forces that are within them. Just as the question of verbal translation is polarized by a distinction between the good and the evil, the true and the false, so too Spenser's Proteus is a nexus of conflicting principles. On the one hand, he is "that old leachour" who assaults the virtue of Florimell "with flattering words" and with progressively degrading transformations of his form—first into a Faery knight, thereafter a king, a giant, a devil, a centaur, and finally a storm; on the other hand, it is in Proteus's own hall that the Thames and Medway are wedded, and where the gods of the sea gather to celebrate this fusion of forms into unity and abundance:

> O what an endlesse worke haue I in hand,
>   To count the seas abundant progeny,
>   Whose fruitfull seede farre passeth those in land,
>   And also those which wonne in th'azure sky! . . .
>   So fertile be the flouds in generation,
> So huge their numbers, and so numberlesse their nation.
>   (IV.xii.1)

Within this hall, affections abound, yet order prevails: "Yet were they all in order, as befell, / According their degrees disposed well" (IV.xii.3). Moreover, even lusty old Proteus himself is resigned to obeying Neptune's command to release Florimell so that she can be wedded to Marinell, thereby healing forever the young knight's otherwise incurable erotic wound. Proteus symbolizes the transforming power of desire, and, like Proteus, this desire must be kept within limits and properly focused in order to be a unifying power and a source of renewal and abundance; otherwise, it leads to dissolution, to fragmentation, and finally to the inchoate mass of warring atoms from which it was first summoned into existence (and thenceforth sustained) by the Word.

INDEX